T0330341

the WorldatWork

handbook of total rewards

the WorldatWork

handbook of total rewards

A COMPREHENSIVE GUIDE TO COMPENSATION, BENEFITS, HR & EMPLOYEE ENGAGEMENT

Second Edition

Compiled and Edited by Dan Cafaro

WILEY

For general information on our other products and services or for technical support, please contact our Customer Care Department within the United States at (800) 762-2974, outside the United States at (317) 572-3993, or fax (317) 572-4002.

Wiley publishes in a variety of print and electronic formats and by print-on-demand. Some material in-cluded with standard print versions of this book may not be included in ebooks or in print-on-demand. If this book refers to media such as a CD or DVD that is not included in the version you purchased, you may download this material at http://booksupport.wiley.com. For more information about Wiley products, visit www.wiley.com.

Library of Congress Cataloging-in-Publication Data

Names: WorldatWork (Organization), author. | Cafaro, Dan, editor.
Title: The WorldatWork handbook of total rewards : a comprehensive guide to compensation, benefits, HR & employee engagement/WorldatWork, Total Reward Association ; compiled & edited by Dan Cafaro.
Description: Second edition. | Hoboken, New Jersey : Wiley, [2021] | Includes index.
Identifiers: LCCN 2020043564 (print) | LCCN 2020043565 (ebook) | ISBN 9781119682448 (cloth) | ISBN 9781119682462 (adobe pdf) | ISBN 9781119682493 (epub)
Subjects: LCSH: Compensation management—Handbooks, manuals, etc.
Classification: LCC HF5549.5.C67 W675 2021 (print) | LCC HF5549.5.C67 (ebook) | DDC 658.3/2—dc23
LC record available at https://lccn.loc.gov/2020043564
LC ebook record available at https://lccn.loc.gov/2020043565

Cover Design: Wiley
Cover Image: © GaudiLab/Shutterstock

10 9 8 7 6 5 4 3 2 1

Contents

Acknowledgments

WorldatWork would like to thank the following individuals who were instrumental in helping review, revise, and update this latest edition of the *Handbook of Total Rewards*.

CONTRIBUTORS

Randall K. Abbott, Willis Towers Watson
Pleasure Allen, ITA Group
Steve Balsam, PhD, Temple University
Victor S Barocas, Strategic Management Group LLC
Morag Barrett, SkyeTeam
Jamie Barrette, Facebook
G Michael Barton
George S. Benson, PhD, the University of Texas at Arlington
Alden J Bianchi, Esq., Mintz Levin
Steve Brink, Associates for International Research, Inc.
Lori Block, Buck Global
John M. Bremen, Willis Towers Watson
Ted Briggs, Better Sales Comp Consultants
Leslie Chacko, Marsh & McLennan
Brett Christie, WorldatWork
Jerry Colletti, CSCP, Colletti-Fill LLC
Jim Fickess
Mary Fiss, CSCP, Colletti-Fill LLC
Jeff Foster, PhD, Passkeys International
Karen Frost, Alight
Lewis Garrad, Mercer
Linda Ginac, Human Capital Software
Thomas Hackett, CBP, CCP, GRP, SPHR, DG, McDermott Associates LLC
Janice Hand, Aon
Richard Harvey
Brie Harvey, Achievers
Wolfram Hedrich, Oliver Wyman
Derek Irvine, Globoforce
Asumi Ishibashi, Willis Towers Watson
I.M. Jawahar, PhD, Illinois State University
Gary Johnsen, Deloitte Consulting LLP
Carol Kardas, CCP, SPHR, SHRM-SCP, KardasLarson LLC
Linda Larson, WorldatWork
Edward E. Lawler III, PhD, the Center for Effective Organizations (CEO) at the University of Southern California's Marshall School of Business

Gerald E. Ledford Jr., PhD, the Center for Effective Organizations (CEO) at the University of Southern California's Marshall School of Business
Lynne Levy, Workhuman
Joseph L Lineberry Jr.
Brent Longnecker, Longnecker & Associates
Rich Luss, Willis Towers Watson
Scot Marcotte, Buck Global
M. Michael Markowich, DPA, Markowich Consulting Group
Robert McCaffery, Human Resources Management Consultant
Linda McKee, CCP, Honeywell International Inc.
James McMahon, QualSight LASIK
Neta Meidav, Vault
Kathryn Neel, CPA, Semler Brossy
Barbara Parus
Viet Hoang Phan, Marsh & McLennan
Daniel Purushotham, CCP, CBP, MBA, PhD, Central Connecticut State University
Nancy Romanyshyn, Willis Towers Watson
Karol M Rose, FlexPaths LLC
S. Scott Sands
Richard Sanes, EY
Kathryn Scherich, Semler Brossy
Brittany Smith, WorldatWork
Thomas H. Stone, PhD, Oklahoma State University
Jamie True, LifeWorks by Morneau Shepell
Elaine Walker, CCP, Bentley University
Jon Werner, PhD, University of Wisconsin–Whitewater
Valerie Williams
Stephanie Wilson
Lori Wisper, Willis Towers Watson
Christina Zurek, SHRM-CP, ITA Group

REVIEWERS

Bilal Ahsan, GRP, TE Connectivity
Katie Benedict, CCP, CBP, GRP, Cooper's Hawk Winery and Restaurants
Reina Castro, CCP, PHR, New Oasis Human Resources
Lana Chaim, CCP, GRP, HR Compensation
Sherry Fultz, CCP, CBP, Houston Endowment Inc.
Kevin Gunnell, CBP, MBA, SPHR, The Church of Jesus Christ of Latter-day Saints
Dean Holt, CCP, CBP, GRP, LifeNet Health
Kim Huerta, CCP, Huerta Consulting Group, LLC
Dr. Fran Luis Knight, CCP, SPHR, Becton Dickinson
Jennifer Mackin, CCP, CBP, Mackin Compensation Consulting

Anjana Menon, JPMorgan Chase & Co.
Nicole Nienaber, CCP, GRP, WLCP, Paycor
Donna Page, CCP, USAA
LoriAnn Penman, CCP, SPHR, SHRM-SCP, TTC Inc.
Priyanka Ponnappa, GRP, HR Program Manager/Business Partner
Dave Rocheleau, CCP, Royal Bank of Canada
Dave Tuck, CCP, Hoskin & Harcourt LLP
Marjorie Williamson, CCP, SPHR, SVP, Sensus

Foreword: Finding Our Way Forward

By Scott Cawood, WorldatWork

The Fourth Industrial Revolution (4IR) is blurring the lines between people and technology and it is affecting the way people work and the way businesses produce value. We also have more competitors and threats to our organizations than ever before, including the ease of market entry by new startups, advancing speed and technology, and global pandemics like coronavirus that have the potential to wipe out value seemingly overnight.

We are also in the midst of massive work changes. The impact that 4IR will have on the workplace will be the most profound of any previous industrial revolution. While IRs 1 through 3 had direct ramifications on our manufacturing ability to mass produce and improve quality, 4IR will have a much more direct impact on how we work and will likely dismantle much of the traditional workplace as we know it. Leaders need to ready both their people and their workplaces for an on-demand world that favors purpose over profit and speed over structure.

Businesses and governments must learn to lead and adapt to these changes and support the workforce transition. If managed well, the future of work may be one where many more people are able to fulfill their full potential and deliver higher value to their organizations.

These changes mean that total rewards and HR professionals will have their biggest opportunity to influence a much better experience for their people while at the same time contribute to the growth of the organization. To do this, it will require an HR transformation from a focus on employment and compliance to the magic that happens when we truly put people first. Focusing more on work and people and less on rules and policies helps to unleash the productivity and elevate the experiences of workers to produce outcomes that better the world.

Organizations are increasingly transforming their business model to invest more in the experiences of their people. Thus, the Workplace Revolution continues, as more research and data support the idea that an elevated employee experience improves the customer experience, supports attraction and retention, builds commitment, and drives productivity.

HR has gotten caught up in too much focus on the employment side of the worker experience, which doesn't add enough value and takes up valuable time cultivating your most critical asset. With unique skills at a premium, an organization's ability to grow its own talent in meaningful ways and provide them with an optimal employee experience will increase its and your chances of success.

THE WORKPLACE REVOLUTION

People are at their absolute best – happiest, most engaged, and most productive – when they are truly able to make an impact, and that outcome has a great deal to do with the workplace you are creating.

Workplace sustainability is about reimagining the people experience in your organization to deliver the highest economic, social, and environmental value. This shift must be more than a lagging response to a changed and forever changing world. Creating strategically designed workplaces for how people need and want to work is a required capability as we enter this new work environment. Are you ready for the challenge?

Sustainability and disruption are two words we tend to hear a lot in business interactions. In fact, hardly a day passes without someone dropping one of these terms to contextualize how we now need to think, act, and work. On the surface, it might seem that these concepts don't fit together, but in reality, they are critical to your future. Sustainability is the ability to exist constantly. Disruption is when an innovation displaces an existing constant. To sustain, you will need to disrupt. To disrupt, you will have to out-innovate an existing product, service, or business.

Today we have a unique opportunity to bring the work of advancing sustainability from the periphery of business into its core functioning to fully leverage your workplace and your people. Workplaces can be the best enabler to almost everything you want to do – likely more than even leadership.

The next decade of workplaces will operate in a juxtaposition to what we currently know – they will be more chaotic, inconsistent, less rule-based, fluid, and elastic – all to keep pace with the extreme market volatility taking place on a global level. The speed, change, and turbulence ahead will require different solutions and more connectivity than at any other time in history.

The answer is not to "batten down the hatches" and ride out the storm, but to reimagine how people want and need to work within these new parameters. The Workplace Revolution will undoubtedly be one of the largest opportunities for human resources and total rewards professionals to make an impact on the business. There will no doubt be winners and losers, and all indications point to technology and speed as the continued culprits – which means that most of our traditional people processes are not dynamic enough to keep up. If our workplaces do not do their part to accelerate innovation, agility, and the insight to know when to pivot, they will have failed us.

A FORMULA FOR SUSTAINABILITY

Workplace sustainability will require you to disrupt many of your existing people programs such as hiring, job descriptions, job titles, performance feedback, and onboarding. This internal disruption is needed to attract and keep the very best people. The changes may seem daunting but they are coming, and our goal should not be to deflect, but, rather, to align so we can offer our people the best experience possible. A significant driver of this is that the traditional employer and employee contract no longer exists and has been replaced with an on-demand, highly digital, and likely a much shorter-term relationship that absorbs more of the full person into the work situation than ever before.

In addition to your efforts to find great new hires, you also must work diligently to keep them focused on your ever-evolving supply chain. This is trickier than it sounds. New hires are an at-risk group often with the highest turnover and now, with easier and more choices of where and how and when to work, the competition for talent will continue to affect each of our ability to deliver. New workers' decisions to join, stay, or leave are heavily influenced by the interview and onboarding process, which sets the tone for their anticipated experience ahead.

Employee referrals are terrific programs that can yield better overall performance than no referral. However, the reason new hires may be more successful than other hires is that those who referred them do a great job of ensuring their success by taking responsibility for the onboarding themselves. This means extra attention and support for the new hire.

Research by Emilio J. Castilla, a professor at MIT Sloan School of Management, found that if the referrer leaves before the new hire starts, then performance is not any better than other hires. This is important to note because it shows we are not paying enough attention to many disconnected parts of the hiring process, and even if we were, the escalating pace of internal changes will require additional support if we want sustained performance and tenure.

If you need a place to start, go directly to the basics. Examine whether your hiring process is really serving your needs in a way that allows you to build sustainability. Also, ensure that you are currently providing fair and equitable pay, giving your people a sense of purpose in your organization's mission. Do you provide a broad offering of flexible rewards that support the most important moments in your employees' lives? Do you provide opportunities for continuous development, professional growth, recognition, and an assurance that they are encouraged to be themselves?

If sustainability is, in part, nurturing those talented people in your organization, how do you best develop them so that they are prepared for the work that will come? Are they prepared to evolve with changes in the marketplace, changes in technology, changes in the in the types of jobs that are and will be available? Even when a particular job is going away, you don't have to lose a creative, intelligent person if you have a plan in place to reskill.

Sustaining and growing your own talent pool will play a very prominent role in long-term success, especially as more routine skills become less valuable and needed in workplaces. When you unite these factors, you have a formula for your organization's sustainability, and the stronger you get, the more disruptive you can be!

WHO YOU ARE AND WHO YOUR ORGANIZATION REALLY IS

I'm thrilled to be part of an organization doing work that adds a lot of value to both organizations and the individuals within those organizations. I think you'd agree that you never find, hire, keep, and grow your people without the use of total rewards. They are, without a doubt, my absolute favorite part of the employee experience. They, too, are the most critical part of the employee experience to get right.

You never have a life moment without having a total rewards response. You get married: There's a total rewards response. You have a baby, take a transfer: There's a total rewards component. You get a promotion, get a raise, get a new job – all of these things are more successful when you have a total rewards component in place.

We have the ability in the total rewards space to impact all of life's biggest moments. When you take a moment and think of the impact you can have on so many people, it really does become an honor to serve in this profession.

We do need to change the one-size-fits-all approach that we tend to use to design our pay, benefits, wellness, performance, and recognition plans. I like programs that are designed to be legally compliant and fair, but that also reach each individual where they are and deliver to them what they need to be at their absolute best. We all have different life experiences and are motivated by different things, and our reward programs can be more attuned to these nuances while also serving large groups of people.

Rewards programs, when optimally designed and delivered, signal to employees that you care about them. You care about what they're doing, the way they are doing it, the ideas they have, and what they get for delivering outstanding work. Rewards reinforce that you deeply value who they are and what they do.

All leaders must be skilled in how to deliver rewards programs. It isn't just a TR or HR function. Everybody has somebody they report or align into – even if you're a gig worker, you connect with someone inside the organization. Those conversations – from feedback to recognition – are part of the opportunity to reward and recognize in ways that are meaningful to your workers.

TOTAL REWARDS: A PANACEA FOR CHAOS

When you're out driving and you pause for a moment and let someone pull in front of you – the minute you do that, what are you looking to have happen? You're looking to see if they wave, and when they do, you feel amazing. You're like, "Oh, I'm awesome!" and you go about your day feeling you made a difference.

That is a rewards moment. That's how total rewards work. It's an elevated moment in time where something meaningful happens and it compels you to be a little bit better, make a different choice, take a higher road, or give a little bit more for the organization. Rewards moments tell you a lot about who you are and who your organization really is and are the most critical aspect of the employee experience.

The world of work is changing, and for the better. We are learning how to engage a diverse group of individuals on common themes and are working to find meaning at a time when we have seemingly unlimited amounts of information that must be vetted to cull out what is important. Remember that a well-designed rewards program is a panacea for the chaotic pace of the world. So, next time you're out driving and you let somebody pull in front of you, look for the wave and see how good you feel. From there, take that moment and turn it back onto your employees, co-workers, and organization. Together, we can make a difference for millions of workers around the world – and that, my friends, is the greatest reward of all.

Scott Cawood, EdD, CCP, CBP, GRP, CSCP, WLCP
is the CEO of WorldatWork.

Introduction: 4IR: It's the End of Work as We Know It (and the Rewards Are Fine)

By Lori Block and Michael Davidson

The evolution of the social contract between workers and management through the twentieth century was tempestuous. A social contract, usually tacit rather than spelled out, is an agreement between individuals and authorities that exchanges individual freedoms for the protection of rights and maintenance of order:

> [The social contract] purports to define the terms on which that society is to be governed: the people have made a contract with their ruler which determines their relations with him. They promise him obedience, while he promises his protection and good government. While he keeps his part of the bargain, they must keep theirs, but if he misgoverns the contract is broken and allegiance is at an end. (Gough 1936)

That social contract has continually been broken, mended, and altered by degrees since then. The hurricane of change that blew through life at the end of the 19th century affected how, where, when, and even if people earned their daily bread. When Roethlisberger and Dickson (1937) described organizations as "social systems," their concern was balancing the needs of workers and employers. Writing of the Hawthorne experiments in the 1920s, they noted, "Mechanical processes, the type and quality of materials used, were based upon carefully contrived experiment and knowledge; the human policies of the Company, upon executive conceptions and traditional practices. In determining human policies, the Company had no satisfactory criterion of the actual value of its methods of dealing with people."

THE FORCES OF CHANGE

The Workforce

Before industrialization really took hold, workers were not unlike the current free agents of today – less specialized, more mobile, and hired pretty much on a project basis. Either they were peasant farmers, producing what they needed, or urban workers, members of craft guilds working with their own tools and in their own specialties.

But as capital became concentrated in manufacturing, families migrated to cities to work in factories, which arose in response to the need to better organize work. Within these factories, structured hierarchies developed, and labor became more functional. The factory offered a more efficient method of production than individual, self-employed craftsmen and labor workers. Yet the defining feature of the factory wasn't necessarily large-scale production, but the "predominance of authority among the coordinating devices used within the given organizational form" (Kapas 2008). By planning production, managing the workforce through open-ended employment contracts, and issuing orders instead of working in partnership with labor providers, companies could allocate resources more efficiently (Coase 1937). Finally, growth in the size of the organization meant these orders needed to be issued and monitored through a hierarchy of supervisors and managers.

Inequities in the social contract between the two parties were inevitable at this stage. There were few if any benefits available to workers at the beginning of the century. The average workweek in factories was 53 hours (Fisk 2001). Employers had the upper hand in any dispute, because they could hold out longer economically than any worker who, as Adam Smith (1776) wrote in *An Inquiry into the Nature and Causes of the Wealth of Nations,* "could not subsist a week, few could subsist a month, and scarce any a year without employment." In Britain, this eventually led to the rise of trade unions and, in the early years of the twentieth century, welfare reforms, including old-age pensions and unemployment insurance. In the United States, the federal Fair Labor Standards Act of 1938 set standards for a reasonable workweek, established minimum wages, prohibited child labor, and protected collective bargaining. The adoption of the US Social Security Act in 1935 established a permanent old-age (and later disability) pension system.

Over the past century, the demographics of the workplace have changed enormously. Technology – from electrically powered machines to telecommunications – improved safety in the workplace, and those same advances in the home freed women from housework to pursue paid jobs. Improved medical treatment and new drugs meant that illnesses were not as deadly, and returning to work from an injury happened faster. A rising population, immigration and improved education all contributed to the expansion of the workforce (Fisk 2001).

The beginning of the 21st century saw a new form of work: the technologically enabled gig economy and portfolio work (people who work on a number of different projects for different organizations). Today this form of work accounts for nearly 16 percent of the US workforce (Katz and Krueger 2016). According to a 2014 survey examining agile working, about half of these gig employees don't receive training, and only one-third receive performance appraisals. Fewer than half of employers surveyed "bothered to include them in internal communications or consider them for recognition awards" (CIPD 2014). As this method of hiring continues to evolve, governments are issuing various regulations, which go beyond minimum wage and other basic requirements, in an attempt to maintain some level of balance within the construct of the social contract. These regulations range from mandating that employers provide such basics as paid sick leave to requirements that employers develop policy statements outlining how they protect against slavery in their supply chains.

(At the time of publication, California's legislature passed – and its governor signed – AB5, which would impede organizations from classifying certain workers as contractors. This ground-breaking law is scheduled to take effect in 2020, although last-minute changes could be enacted. Meanwhile, some commercial sectors, including ride-hailing and trucking companies, are voicing their opposition.)

It seems in this regard, what's past is prologue, at least in some respects. But before drawing any premature conclusions, let's examine other forces that have affected the world of work.

Management

With the rise of railroads, telegraph communications and steam power, businesses became efficient only at very large scales. Business owners realized they needed new techniques to manage their resources, build and maintain raw material supply chains and increase productivity. Shareholders needed to see better control of the organization to enhance profits. Education was on the rise, and a new professional class of engineers, accountants, and supervisors began to work toward realizing this new paradigm.

The argument was expressed most clearly by Alfred D. Chandler Jr.: "No matter how efficient a plant might be, it would be hugely wasteful if raw materials did not arrive on time or if the output couldn't be quickly distributed and sold. Managers were essential; so were statistical controls. Coordination and organization mattered. Companies that surmounted these problems succeeded. . . . The rise of big business involved more than tycoons. Its central feature was actually the creation of professional managers" (Samuelson 2006).

The beginning of what Kiechel (2012) called the "Management Century" saw experiments in applying scientific theory to the management of people. Frederick Taylor's time and motion studies sought to break tasks down to their most basic units, making people part of the machinery. Elton Mayo's studies at the Western Electric Hawthorne plant found that, regardless of the type of intervention to improve the working environment, workers responded to being consulted, to having the changes explained to them first, and to the resulting group dynamic, by becoming more productive. Other insights included Douglas McGregor's "Theory Y," which stresses the importance of job satisfaction and autonomy in motivating workers, and Peter Drucker's vision of the workplace as a social network where skill and talent were to be respected rather than simply harnessed to a time clock. Their goal was to balance the push for economic results with the human needs of the workers who produced those results.

Yet the stopwatch mentality – the professional manager's microscopic analysis of every aspect of the business – soon led to more aggressive corporate strategies. Eventually, the forces of deregulation in the United States and United Kingdom, global trade and computer technology showed managers and shareholders that industry consolidation, corporate mergers and hostile takeovers were the path to increased profits and/or greater shareholder value, at least in the short term. No longer were the needs of those at the heart of the business – employees, customers, stockholders – prioritized in the rush for control over every aspect of the value chain, including the human element. As Kiechel (2016) noted, "Most famously at General Electric under Jack Welch, the old employer-employee contract, with its implicit assurance of something like lifetime employment, was ripped up."

Today's management challenges focus on work–life balance issues, flexible work and formal evaluations. In a report published by the European Foundation for Management Development, the majority of those surveyed believed that their organization relied too much on compensation as a key engagement strategy, rather than recognizing the need to provide challenging and interesting work (Dent, Holton, and Rabbetts 2010). The report concludes, "It is easy to lose sight of the importance of the relational and people aspect of motivation especially when people around you are losing their jobs and you are working in overload model . . . In addition, many organizations have less scope to employ the traditional means of reward and recognition."

Today, we are in the early stages of the Fourth Industrial Revolution: Often referred to as digital transformation or DX, it encompasses a wide range of technologies – such as artificial intelligence, quantum computing, the internet of things (IOT) and 3D printing – and it was a key topic at the 2019 World Economic Forum (WEF) conclave in Davos, Switzerland. The WEF posits that this revolution will bring with it a "fundamental change in the way we live, work and relate to one another. It is a new chapter in human development, enabled by extraordinary technology advances commensurate with those of the first, second and third industrial revolutions. These advances are merging the physical, digital and biological worlds in ways that create both huge promise and potential peril" (WEF 2019).

Many of the workplace challenges employers and employees alike face today are rooted in this revolution, as the WEF's use of the word "peril" would suggest. Similarly, this revolution will continue to bring forth a wealth of new opportunities for greater productivity, enhanced work–life balance, and increased levels of engagement as a result of greatly improved employee experiences and, more broadly, the opening up of new types of jobs, many of which are likely unimaginable today.

Human Resources

Before World War II, there was nothing that really compared with the modern HR function in an organization. The job of recruiting and training employees fell to line managers and the occasional specialist, such as the recruiting officer or corporate trainer (Rotich 2015). Their responsibilities were largely recordkeeping with little involvement in employee relations. The function was separate from the rest of the organization and it shared very little in the development of the organization's business strategies. Conversely, the organization's business strategies at times seemed irrelevant to the business of HR. With the rise of motivation practices occasioned by the Hawthorne studies, various attempts at employee satisfaction began to be implemented, such as better wages and working conditions.

It wasn't until the postwar period that management started paying more attention to properly managing people in the workplace. This was as a result of the new human relations movement, based on scientific management theories developed in the 1930s. The personnel function widened to include motivation techniques, employee welfare issues, formal job descriptions, compensation strategies, and performance evaluation and rewards systems (Whatishumanresource.com n.d.).

One of the biggest impacts of this new personnel function on employees was in the area of the performance appraisal. The process was opaque to the employee, held little in the way of development possibilities and was linked to material outcomes: Poor performance often meant a cut in pay while good performance could mean a raise or bonus, reflecting the belief that money was the most powerful tool to motivate employee productivity (Bhuiyan, Chowdhury, and Ferdous 2014). The process was largely unfair, often biased, and demoralizing to the employee.

After the Korean War, a new class of college-educated managers emerged with a greater sense of social responsibility than their predecessors. Beginning in the 1960s, the personnel function started to become known as human resources. Increased regulatory compliance requirements and a recognition that HR could contribute to the organization's profitability resulted in the growth of the HR department. HR functions became more integrated and focused on organizational effectiveness.

The 1980s saw an increase in companies focusing on employee motivation and engagement, with efforts to improve communication, team building, worker health and financial fitness, employee career development and succession planning, and more equal working environments. (Or, as we sum it all up, focusing on the total well-being of the individual.) The technological changes wrought by the development of computers further enhanced both communication and employee engagement efforts, with a deepening focus on organizational culture.

In its August 2018 annual workplace survey, Gallup found that worker engagement was higher than previous years, and satisfaction with benefits such as time off, flexible working hours, performance and pay plans, a general improvement in the level of job autonomy, as well as relationships with co-workers and supervisors, had increased slightly over prior years (Harter 2018). The report concludes that "the 21st century workforce expects to have a manager who coaches them based on their strengths – this growing awareness and action of many workplaces likely explain the gradual shift upward in the percentage of engaged workers."

With this evolution comes new labels for the HR function and its leaders: the CHRO function is now led by the chief people officer (CPO), to highlight just one popular label set.

EMPLOYEE BENEFITS AND THE BIRTH OF RETIREMENT

Health Care

A key influence over the changing state of the employer-employee relationship was the development of single-payer (government) health-care insurance in England, Germany, and eventually across most European countries. The United States is virtually alone in not following this path, largely due to vehement resistance (and effective lobbying) from various health-care interest groups in the early twentieth century. Therefore, we'll focus on the American experience in this section.

The need to protect income from loss due to workplace injury, disability, or death saw the development of mutual-aid societies. By the turn of the century, employers began introducing modest "sickness insurance" programs as a practical response to workplace injuries and as a way to strengthen the ties between workers and their employer (Field and Shapiro 1993). The development of insurance products based on standard actuarial principles began in England in 1850 but didn't take off in the United States until after World War II.

In the US in the 1930s, the Blue Cross–type plan emerged, covering hospital costs; Blue Shield plans eventually covered physician services. During and following the war, more and more employers offered health-care benefits as a way around national wage controls. Between 1950 and 1965, employer outlays for health care rose from 0.5–1.5 percent of total compensation costs (Field and Shapiro 1993). Slowly, some key principles came into being: premiums based on actual risk, cost sharing through deductibles and co-insurance, the introduction of major medical benefits, control of payments to health-care providers and monitoring of utilization.

Since then, there have been exponential advances in health-care diagnostics, treatments and, perhaps greatest of all, pharmaceuticals. The result has been that health-care costs have risen dramatically during the past three-plus decades, presenting significant challenges for employers seeking to maintain competitive benefits, and in more recent years, for employees who despite employer-sponsored health-care coverage often struggle with increased premium contributions and high out-of-pocket costs.

At the same time, evidence over the years has demonstrated a strong correlation between healthy employees and workplace performance. *The Journal of Occupational and Environmental Medicine* conducted one of the most extensive studies (Fabius et al. 2016). In this study, researchers found that the "portfolio" performance (as measured by stock value) comprised of 20 winners of the Corporate Health Achievement Award – bestowed by the

American College of Occupational and Environmental Medicine – outpaced the performance of the S&P 500 during a 14-year period (1999–2012) by about 80 percent. Subsequent updates of this study show similar results.

Retirement

Successful savings and investing require foresight, discipline and skill. In the beginning of the industrialization process, when retirement was an emerging stage of life, workers had no role models to copy. Retirement saving did not seem necessary. The coming of industrialization saw the locus of work move from households to large enterprises. Employment of those older than 65 declined as their productivity weakened, but most people had no assets in old age. As medical and public policies in the workplace improved, people started living longer but with smaller families they had fewer resources to bolster their needs in "retirement."

American Civil War veterans were paid pensions for disabilities incurred during the hostilities, but those benefits ran their course. At last, corporate pensions were introduced by large employers, giving them the opportunity to remove older workers without damaging relations with the rest of the workforce.

From 1949 to 1979, retirement programs expanded. Wage controls and the TaftHartley Act of 1947 ceiling on direct wages led employers and unions to offer better health care, retirement and other "fringe benefits." The closure of Studebaker auto plants led to the establishment of the Employment Retirement Income Security Act of 1974 (ERISA) and Social Security enhancements.

In the final 20 years of the twentieth century, defined benefit pension plans flourished, though they were not perfect. In addition, Social Security was able to replace about 40 percent of pre-retirement pay. The introduction of Medicare in 1966 covered most health-care spending. Since 2000, there has been a shift from defined benefit to defined contribution plans and a withdrawal from retiree health insurance. Social Security continues to face economic challenges, workers are living longer and there is a reduction in lifelong careers.

A NEW WIND IS BLOWING: TOTAL REWARDS MEETS TOTAL WELL-BEING

While employer-sponsored health-care programs are geared to defray the cost of medical care, and retirement programs aim to help employees provide financially for their retirement, many employers realize that prevention – of ill health and of financial stress – is critical to defraying costs and boosting productivity. The RAND Corp. found that 69 percent of employers surveyed in 2013 had purchased screening services and intervention services (Mattke et al. 2013).

The WorldatWork Total Rewards Model demonstrates the dynamic relationship between employers and employees. This concept was originally introduced around the start of the new century – in part, we would suggest in blunt honesty, as a way to articulate to employees the fact that rising healthcare costs were impacting employers' ability to provide meaningful salary increases. However, it has evolved to depict the strategic elements of the employer-employee exchange as well as to reflect how external influences and an increasingly global business environment affect attraction, motivation, retention, and engagement. (See Total Rewards Model on page XX.)

Total rewards programs, particularly those designed to support an individual's professional, physical, financial, and social/community (i.e., total) well-being, are used as a strategic tool for achieving business results by being able to more effectively retain, attract, and support more productive employees. Programs typically encompass compensation, benefits, work–life effectiveness, recognition, performance management and talent development (IBISWorld 2019). These programs are continuing to evolve to meet today's challenges. For example, paternity leave is being given equal weight as maternity leave, and "family leave" is increasingly being expanded to encompass other needs, such as caring for an elderly parent.

Similarly, company-sponsored volunteer and community involvement programs are becoming a vital element of employers' total well-being strategy (Buck 2018). Not only do these programs help attract and retain the younger generations of the workforce they also strengthen the commitment and well-being of the entire employee population.

DIGITAL TRANSFORMATION OF HR

Much is being written – and will be written – on the topic of digital transformation (DX), so we won't delve deeply into this topic here. But ignoring it completely would make this section incomplete.

DX is often referred to as the Fourth Industrial Revolution, comparing it to prior transformative revolutions such as steam, electricity, and computers. If the level of investment is any indicator, DX certainly qualifies, with IDC estimating that global spending on DX exceeded $1.1 trillion in 2018 and is expected to reach almost $2 trillion by 2021 (Fitzgerald and Simpson 2018). With 97.2 percent of companies materially investing in DX technologies (Deloitte 2017), there is little doubt that this transformation will impact the social contract moving forward.

Much of the focus in DX revolves around productivity and quality increases, but we know from the previous revolutions that there will be a tremendous disruption to the workforce in these times of change. During the computer revolution in the 1980s, there was a definite increase in the efficiency for production workers. However, it was more than offset by the dramatic impact to the rest of the organization. Jobs expanded in the information workers category and their productivity decreased by almost

7 percent in that same period (Economist 2000). Entirely new IT organizations were created to manage the new technologies, and there was fierce demand, from all market sectors, for incredibly scarce IT talent. According to the US Bureau of Labor Statistics (BLS) (2019), it took almost 10 years before the entire US market showed a net increase in productivity from the computer revolution.

This next evolution in the social contract involves not only deploying the new DX technologies, but also ensuring that employers are effectively aligned, and that employees clearly understand the impact to them, are engaged, supportive and appropriately trained to support the transformation in the coming decade.

To underscore the importance of this, a 2018 survey showed that most executives (64.7 percent) said they were experiencing significant challenges in business adoption of DX technologies and when asked what factors were impeding their ability to deploy and capitalize on the latest DX technologies, only 5 percent felt the problem was technology, the other 95 percent could all be considered cultural barriers (New Vantage 2018). It is clear when you look across all the challenges in the Digital Revolution that you cannot achieve your DX goals through technology alone; the human aspect is critical to success.

GEOPOLITICAL FORCES

On August 19, 2019, the following headline appeared in the *New York Times*: "Shareholder Value Is No Longer Everything, Top C.E.O.s Say" (Gelles and Yaffe-Bellany 2019). The article was reporting on a statement signed by 181 CEOs and released by the Business Roundtable (2019), in which these leaders committed to leading their companies "for the benefit of all stakeholders – customers, employees, suppliers, communities and shareholders." In other words, reaffirming their commitment to the social contract between organizations and individuals, and other stakeholders.

"The American dream is alive, but fraying," Jamie Dimon, chairman and CEO of JP Morgan Chase & Co. and chairman of the Business Roundtable, wrote. "Major employers are investing in their workers and communities because they know it is the only way to be successful over the long term. These modernized principles reflect the business community's unwavering commitment to continue to push for an economy that serves all Americans" (Business Roundtable 2019).

The statement articulates the "fundamental commitment" all of the signing companies share with all of their stakeholders. These commitments are: delivering value to customers, investing in employees, dealing fairly and ethically with suppliers, supporting the communities in which they work, and, listed last, generating long-term value for shareholders.

Of the investment in employees, the statement reads: "This starts with compensating them fairly and providing important benefits. It also includes supporting them through training and education that help develop new skills for a rapidly changing world. We foster diversity and inclusion, dignity and respect."

Nobel economist Milton Friedman (1970) declared, "There is one and only one social responsibility of business: to use its resources and engage in activities designed to increase its profits so long as it stays in the rules of the game, which is to say, engages in open and free competition, without deception or fraud." Yet these leading global employers issued their powerful statement in the face of the Friedman Doctrine: They not only put forth that organizations have responsibilities to several other stakeholders but that they placed customers and employers at the top of their list of responsibilities.

Other employers have, for years, made this argument and aspired to operate in this fashion. There is even a classification for these types of organizations: B Corporations, whose mission is "driving a global movement of people using business as a force for good" (Certified B 2019).

With the geopolitical forces currently underway, will corporations serve as an effective bulwark against societal regression and, in fact, accelerate advances in individual well-being around the world? They certainly have the resources and voice to do so.

1   The Power of Total Rewards

Sixty-five years ago, when a group of visionary professionals formed what was to become WorldatWork, the world of work and the world of pay were much simpler than they are today. Compensation was the primary "reward" and benefits, still in their infancy, were a separate and seemingly low-cost supplement for employees. The concept of combining these things – let alone using them with still other "rewards" to influence employee behavior on the job – was decades away.

Today we are only partially through an evolution from a largely industrialized business environment to a far more virtual, knowledge- and service-based environment, at least in North America and Europe. Among some major shifts:

- Business increasingly operates as a global village, with work moving to different parts of the world to take advantage of lower-cost labor and address skill gaps.
- Technology continues to revolutionize work, not only in terms of automating more jobs, but also in enabling the virtual workplace as professionals increasingly conduct business in home offices or remote locations.
- Women are equally represented in the overall workforce, if not yet fully in the ranks of senior management.
- Traditional hierarchical distinctions have eroded in the name of faster decision-making and speed to market. Teamwork is one of the most common behaviors rated in performance reviews.
- More businesses and business units in the United States are owned by European or Asian parents, which expect their practices and norms to be followed and respected in the workplace.

- Job mobility is taken for granted. According to the Bureau of Labor Statistics, the average worker in 2020 currently holds 10 different jobs before age 40, and this number is projected to grow. Forrester Research predicts that today's youngest workers will hold 12–15 jobs in their lifetime.
- Gender, race, and religious differences are a common part of most work environments. Diversity has become a respected value, demonstrated through a range of specific programs.
- Business leaders increasingly regard employees as drivers of productivity, rather than as relatively interchangeable cogs in a larger wheel.

Along with these changes have come dramatically different views about the nature of rewards. In the shift toward a more knowledge- and service-based economy, the relationship, or deal, between employer and employee began to evolve as well. Viewing employees as performance drivers meant thinking differently about what it would take to attract, keep, and engage them in giving discretionary effort on the job. And so *total rewards* entered the lexicon to address these needs.

BROADENING THE DEFINITION OF TOTAL REWARDS

The definition of total rewards always sparks debate. For example, Figure 1.1 includes a comprehensive list of items that have shown up at one time or another in one organization's definition of total rewards. From this, it is easy to see how people can use the term in conversation only to find that they are referring to very different notions.

Generally speaking, there are two prevailing camps of definitions:

- *Narrow definitions.* These virtually always comprise compensation and benefits, and sometimes they include other tangible elements (e.g., development). This sometimes is referred to as *total compensation* or *total remuneration.*
- *Broad definitions.* These can expand to encompass everything that is "rewarding" about working for a particular employer or everything employees get as a result of their employment. Sometimes terms such as *value proposition total value* are used interchangeably with *total rewards.*

While the narrower definitions have been around for a long time, it is the broader notion that is generating buzz. Indeed, much of the current activity in total rewards involves organizations moving to a broader definition. There are several reasons for this:

- *Erosion of the "core" elements of the package.* The traditional elements of rewards – pay, benefits, and stock awards – are no longer differentiating factors for organizations. The competitive position for pay is trending toward median or mean. Benefits costs continue to rise. Stock programs, such as the distribution of options, do not offer the appeal they once did.

FIGURE 1.1 Total rewards: different things to different employers.

Direct Financial
Base Salary
Bonus
Cash Profit Sharing
Employee Referral Program (Cash)
Stock Programs
Suggestions Programs (Cash for Ideas)

Indirect Financial
Adoption Assistance
College Savings Plan
College Tuition and Fees
Commuter Reimbursement (Pretax)
Company Cafeteria
Company Store
Dependent Care
Dependent Scholarships
Discount Tickets
Educational Assistance
Fitness Facilities Discounts
Health and Welfare Benefits
Incremental Dependent Care (Travel)
Insurance (Auto/Home) via Payroll Deduction
Long-Term Care Insurance
Matching Gifts
Relocation Program
Retirement Plan(s)
Saving Bonds via Payroll Deductions
Scholarships
Stock Purchase Program
Student Loans
Tuition Reimbursement

Work
Autonomy
Casual Dress Policy
Challenging Work
Constructive Feedback
Covered Parking
Ergonomics/Comfortable Workstations
Flexible Work Schedules
Free Parking
Interesting Work
Job Skills Training
Modern, Well-Maintained Workspace
Open Communication
Performance Management
Promotion Opportunities
Safe Work Environment
Suggestion Program (No Cash)
Telecommuting Opportunities
Uniforms/Uniform Allowance
Workshops

Career
360° Skills Assessment
Career Advancement
Coaching
Lunch and Learn Series
Management Development
Mentoring Program
Open Job Posting
Preretirement Counseling
Service Awards
Training and Development

Affiliation
Athletic Leagues
Community Involvement
Diversity Programs
Employee Celebrations
Employee Clubs
Professional Associations
Seminars
Spring and Holiday Parties
Support Groups
Volunteer Connection

Other/Convenience
ATMs Onsite
Carpooling/Van Pooling/Shuttles
Car Seat Vouchers (for Newborns)
Child Care Resources
Credit Union
Employee Assistance Program
Employee Card and Gift Shop
Expectant Parent Program
Legal Services
Medical Center
Military Deployment Support
Online Services
Onsite Dry-Cleaning Pickup
Onsite Flu Shots
Onsite Food Services
Onsite Post Office
Personal Travel Agency
Wellness Program
Worldwide Travel Assistance

Given all of this, a logical response is to broaden what organizations provide for the overall employment package.

- *Pressure for operational efficiency and effectiveness.* Total rewards can represent a major cost element. As organizations seek to manage costs tightly, there is more emphasis on ensuring that all costs are counted and managed. By redefining rewards more broadly and focusing on those elements that achieve the biggest payoff, organizations can drive toward efficiency.
- *Catering to diverse needs.* Organizations today are managing a much more heterogeneous population. For the diverse workforce, no single component becomes a value driver. Employees have choices to make and a need for greater flexibility. A broad definition of total rewards helps employers show how their slate of rewards responds to the broad needs of today's global workforce.
- *Need to more strongly reinforce business strategy.* Organizations are concerned about sending clear business messages to employees. A properly structured total rewards package sends a key message. By aligning all the components of total rewards with the overall business vision, a company ensures its workforce is on the same page.

Given these factors, it is not surprising that a broader definition is gaining favor in the marketplace. Organizations still need to decide how broadly they want to define total rewards, based on what they can adequately measure and manage.

What Is Total Rewards?

Total rewards encompasses the elements – compensation, well-being, benefits, development, and recognition – that, in concert, lead to optimal organizational performance. When designed strategically and executed in alignment with business goals, total rewards programs fuel motivated and productive workforces that feel appreciated and rewarded for their contributions, driving the organization to ever greater success.

The Total Rewards Model

Initially introduced in 2000, the WorldatWork Total Rewards Model continually evolves to reflect changes in organizations' needs, workforce expectations, workforce demographics, and the total rewards profession.

The practice of total rewards requires in-depth knowledge, specialized skills, and up-to-the-minute insight into the most critical issues facing today's workforce. The model captures the broad influence that total rewards practices and its practitioners have on organizational strategy and workforce outcomes.

The 2020 Total Rewards Model encompasses five components, each of which includes programs, practices, and nuanced dimensions that collectively define an organization's strategy to build a productive, inspired, and committed workforce.

Compensation

Pay provided by an employer to workers in exchange for services such as time, effort, and talent. This includes both fixed and variable pay tied to overall contributions.

Well-Being

The state of a workforce that is productive, comfortable, happy, and healthy, considering physical, emotional/mental, financial, and environmental factors. Total rewards professionals influence this state through organizational strategic influence and building programs that support workforce success inside and outside of work.

Benefits

Programs focused on health and welfare, income protection, financial preparedness, retirement and time off, including leaves of absence, aimed to provide holistic well-being and security for the workforce and their families.

Development

Encompasses the rewards and opportunities that employers offer their workers to advance their skills, competencies, responsibilities, and contributions – in both their short- and long-term careers.

Recognition

Formal or informal programs that thank, validate, recognize, and celebrate workforce contributions while aligning and strengthening organizational culture.

Internal Influences

A TR program must also align with overall business strategy, be championed by leaders and fit within the organizational culture. Other workforce elements, such as the business implications of inclusiveness, are crucial for program success.

In these challenging and hyper-accelerated times, diversity and inclusion (D&I) is a strategy area that requires TR practitioner competency. No longer in a support function alone, TR pros are now expected to be the strongest advocates of cultural intelligence and behavioral change. Organizations are relying on them to understand, influence, and reflect D&I principles in the design and delivery of their TR programs.

The internal influences that inform the design and implementation of total rewards initiatives and programs include business strategy, culture, workforce, inclusion, and leadership.

Strategy

Total rewards strategies are a mechanism to make a strong business strategy come to life. Whether the goal is operational excellence, product/service leadership, or customer engagement – rewards programs help communicate expectations, align efforts, and motivate the behaviors required to deliver results.

Culture

Simply stated, organizational culture refers to a set of shared values and beliefs that form over time as people interact and work together. It encompasses an organization's vision, values, norms, and ultimately influences workforce experiences and outcomes. Total rewards offerings can help transform and re-enforce desired cultural norms, and significantly influence how work is performed and recognized in the organization.

The Workforce

Rewards must be tailored to meet the needs of an increasingly diverse pool of employees that is defined by geopolitical trends, tech advances, and talent demographics, including today's up-to-five-generation workforce. Savvy total rewards pros see this as an opportunity to attract the highest performers and "best" the competition.

Inclusion

In these hyper-accelerated times, diversity and inclusion strategies provide organizations with a competitive advantage in talent attraction and work-force productivity. Total rewards leaders can help organizations achieve greater diversity while building an inclusive culture by developing clear approaches for pay equity and transparency, career development, inclusive benefits, and more.

Leadership

Total rewards programs are only effective when leaders play an active role to promote understanding and appreciation of the rewards programs. Total rewards practitioners must work with organizational leaders to ensure that total rewards initiatives align with business goals and that they are well-understood, used, and appreciated by workers for maximum impact.

External Influences

The fundamentals of designing an optimal TR design strategy have remained relatively steady for 20 years. Organizations must be cognizant of several external factors, such as the competitive (product and labor) markets, the regulatory environment and the social and cultural norms affecting each area. A deep understanding of these factors will provide TR pros the context needed to build effective TR programs that drive performance outcomes.

Outcomes

While total rewards plays a leading role in the employee experience, it does not exist in a vacuum. Initiatives must be completely woven into the enterprise's HR strategy, considering the human capital and societal influences that affect program design and strategy. Upskilling, the gig economy, regulatory changes, AI's impact, data analytics, pay equity, and other HR factors all influence the total rewards strategy.

Alignment of strategy, culture, and TR elements result in a differentiated value proposition for workers and the organization: an inclusive environment where engagement is enhanced and performance (individual/team/business) is elevated. Key performance indicators in this area may include pay equity, perception of fairness, strength of employment brand, financial performance, overall productivity, employee engagement, and satisfaction.

WHY THE TOTAL REWARDS APPROACH WORKS

Throughout the decades, there has been compelling evidence showing that the best way to attract, engage, and retain employees is to focus on total rewards, not just pay and benefits.

In the 1950s, Frederick Hertzberg conducted his famous study of factors affecting job attitudes. He identified 16 factors and categorized them into 10 "hygiene factors" and 6 motivators (growth, advancement, responsibility, work itself, recognition, and achievement). Note that the motivators do not include pay and benefits – these are hygiene factors. To motivate, a total rewards approach must be taken.

Since the 1960s, psychologists (including Abraham Maslow) have stressed how fewer tangible needs, such as growth and self-actualization, were equally important to individuals' sense of worth. Figure 1.2 illustrates how total rewards maps to Maslow's famous hierarchy. This message has been reinforced over the years by other leading thinkers and management gurus, including Maslow, Ed Lawler, Peter Drucker, and Edward Demming.

Most data show that work and career opportunities, leadership, and recognition are leading drivers in employee engagement and retention – not pay.

FIGURE 1.2 Transactional rewards and Maslow's hierarchy.

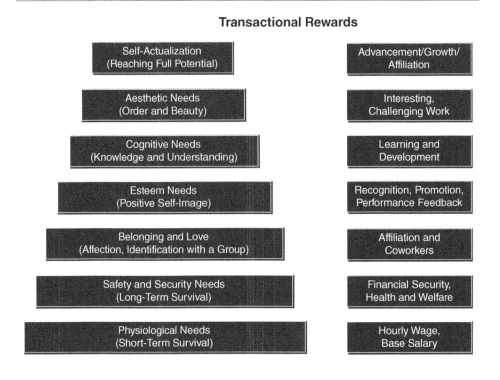

Transactional Rewards

Self-Actualization (Reaching Full Potential)	Advancement/Growth/ Affiliation
Aesthetic Needs (Order and Beauty)	Interesting, Challenging Work
Cognitive Needs (Knowledge and Understanding)	Learning and Development
Esteem Needs (Positive Self-Image)	Recognition, Promotion, Performance Feedback
Belonging and Love (Affection, Identification with a Group)	Affiliation and Coworkers
Safety and Security Needs (Long-Term Survival)	Financial Security, Health and Welfare
Physiological Needs (Short-Term Survival)	Hourly Wage, Base Salary

What do you do when you get a job offer? Take a sheet of paper, draw a vertical line down the middle, label one column "stay" and the other "take the offer." Then fill in the columns with a list of the total rewards associated with each opportunity. If a total rewards mindset is used to make this individual decision, shouldn't the same mindset be applied when thinking about how to attract, retain, and motivate the broader workforce?

In today's environment, the case for a total rewards approach is stronger than ever:

- *Total rewards addresses today's business needs for managing costs and growth.* Research suggests that a more limited view of rewards can be more costly because organizations tend to respond to every situation with cash. Total rewards supports moving away from ineffective programs toward those that help drive the business forward.
- *Total rewards meets the evolving needs of today's employees.* As the workforce continues to diversify, employees' expectations change. For example, there is stronger emphasis on job enrichment, flexible work schedules, and the overall work environment. A total rewards approach better addresses many of these varying employee needs.

- *Total rewards fits with a movement away from cash and stock.* As the role of stock becomes deemphasized in most companies, the hunt is on for other items that help redefine a compelling and differentiated offer in the market for talent. Total rewards can help do this.

THE TOP FIVE ADVANTAGES OF A TOTAL REWARDS APPROACH

1. Increased Flexibility

With the one-size-fits-all approach essentially gone, the twenty-first century is well on its way to becoming the "rewards your way" era. Just as companies create niche products and services to cater to small consumer segments (micromarketing), employers need to start creating different blends of rewards packages for different workforce segments. This is particularly true in a global labor market where workforce diversity is the rule, not the exception, and when specific skills are in short supply.

A total rewards approach – which combines transactional and relational awards – offers tremendous flexibility because it allows awards to be mixed and remixed to meet the different emotional and motivational needs of employees. Indeed, flexibility is a two-way street. Both employers and employees want more of it.

As the importance of flexibility has become more understood, more companies are allowing employees to determine when they work, where they work, and how they work. Total rewards recognizes that employees want, and in many instances demand, the ability to integrate their lifestyle and their work.

2. Improved Recruitment and Retention

Organizations are facing key shortages of best-in-class workers (top performers), information technology (IT) workers with hot skills, and workers for entry-level, unskilled jobs. The classic initial solution to a recruitment and retention dilemma is to throw money at the problem. But because this solution is so overused, it does not offer a competitive advantage. Furthermore, it immediately raises costs.

A total rewards strategy is critical to addressing the issues created by recruitment and retention. It can help create a work experience that meets the needs of employees and encourages them to contribute extra effort – developing a deal that addresses a broad range of issues and spending rewards dollars where they will be most effective in addressing workers' shifting values.

Indeed, today's workers are looking beyond the "big picture" in deciding where they want to work. Work and personal life should be seen as complementary priorities, not competing ones. When a company helps its employees effectively run both their personal and work lives, the employees feel a stronger commitment to the organization. In addition, numerous studies show that employees look at the total rewards package when deciding whether to join or stay with an organization.

An actual summary statement can be prepared for potential employees, enabling them to see the whole value of being employed by a company. As such, as highly desirable job candidates explore their options with various companies, companies with total rewards have a competitive advantage because they are able to show the "total value" of their employment packages.

3. Reduced Labor Costs/Cost of Turnover

The cost of turnover – often the driver of recruitment and retention – is sometimes invisible and far from cheap. According to Work Institute, the estimated costs of employee turnover ranges from 33 percent to 200 percent of the departing employee's salary. Willis Towers Watson research shows that the cost of salesforce labor, for example, during the notice, vacancy, and transition periods is significant. To replace a direct channel industrial salesperson, soft-dollar costs can range from 25 percent to 100 percent of the actual out-of-pocket costs.

In addition, the cost of turnover includes indirect costs such as losses from customers and sales, as well as decreased efficiencies as productive employees leave, and the remaining workers are distracted.

4. Heightened Visibility in a Tight Labor Market

Talent shortages have become a chronic condition of business life, and experts agree that the tight labor market is going to get tighter. As a result, employers can no longer afford to simply view their employees as interchangeable parts. Organizations quickly are realizing that every employee matters even more when there are not enough employees to fill the available jobs.

In addition, demographic shifts (e.g., the increasing number of women in the workforce) coupled with new economic forces (e.g., global competition) have changed the employment landscape, creating an unprecedented need for committed employees at a time when loyalty is low. If people can find an environment that's more in sync with their needs, they will make changes for that. Likewise, they will stay put when they feel their needs are being met.

By gaining a clear understanding of what employees value, and mixing and matching rewards within a comprehensive framework, companies can reallocate their investment dollars to match what employees say they value most, and can communicate the total package versus a patchwork of individual components.

5. Enhanced Profitability

Aside from the high costs of technology, HR professionals also are saddled with escalating benefits costs and changes in health care coverage and medical protocols. Employees want a "new deal" at the same time that companies – struggling to deliver their financial targets – are readily cutting programs to trim costs. How to balance these two realities? Change the mix.

A big misconception about total rewards packages is that they are more expensive. That's because a number of companies equate the notion of rewards with "more" – more pay, more benefits, and more combinations of rewards. What companies need to realize is that by remixing their rewards in a more cost-effective way, they can strengthen their programs and improve employees' perception of value without necessarily increasing their overall investment. It's largely a matter of reallocating dollars rather than finding more dollars.

Indeed, as companies discover the power of targeted reallocation of rewards and begin promoting the total value of their programs, they are abandoning the practice of setting pay, benefits, and other budgets in isolation, without reference to broad strategic and cost objectives. As they begin understanding their true aggregate costs – often for the first time – they are positioned to measure the extent to which their expenditures are in line with, over, or under competitive practice. And they can then measure whether they're getting a reasonable return on their overall investment.

In addition, today's workforce includes several distinct generations, each with a different perspective of the employer–employee relationship. Most employee research indicates that younger employees place a far higher priority on work environment and learning and development than on the traditional rewards components. In contrast, older workers put more emphasis on pay and benefits. All employees are concerned with health care, wealth accumulation, career development, and time off. It simply is no longer possible to create a set of rewards that is universally appealing to all employees or to address a series of complex business issues through a single set of solutions.

The challenge is to develop and implement a flexible program that capitalizes on this diverse workforce (Figure 1.3). Valuing each employee includes understanding that everyone does not want to work the same way or be rewarded the same way. To achieve excellence, employers need a portfolio of total rewards plans.

DEVELOPING A TOTAL REWARDS STRATEGY

While many organizations agree with the *idea* of total rewards, they often don't actually put a total rewards strategy into practice. The compensation department may design a sales compensation program separately from the benefits department that revises the 401(k) program. This piecemeal approach is common, but it's akin to building a state-of-the-art skyscraper on

FIGURE 1.3 Total rewards strategy.

top of the foundation of a 30-year-old, mid-rise office building. That skyscraper isn't going to be structurally sound using a base that wasn't designed to support it. The same thing can happen when new or revised benefits are built without regard to the overall compensation and benefits structure.

The Total Rewards Blueprint

Starting a total rewards program on the right foot is a matter of taking a complete inventory of the programs already in place, ranking each program's effectiveness, and finding the linkages between the rewards and the business strategy.

- *Inventory.* Find out what's already in the mix – every program, plan, and perk, even those not currently in use.
- *Rank.* Determine the effectiveness of each program and how close it is to being a best practice in the industry. Effectiveness can be defined several ways. For instance, low participation can mean low interest, or possibly low understanding of a particular program. Ask line managers to list the top five and bottom five programs in the current package.
- *Link.* This is a difficult but important step. Look at the company business strategy and map where rewards complement or help to drive the specifics of the strategy.

For example, consider an organization that developed a business strategy that focused on providing an integrated customer service experience to its clients. If the company tried to blend 10 separate products and 3 different sales groups into one seamless offering, the structure of the company's sales force and the compensation programs likely would *not* support this collaborative approach. In fact, the pay structure for the sales force, customer service reps, and sales support team could be inconsistent and actually motivate people *not* to work together. Good compensation programs are important, but linking total rewards to business strategy is essential.

Five Common Ways a Total Rewards Strategy Can Go Astray

1. *Trying to reengineer programs in pieces.* When moving to a total rewards approach, review and reengineer the *entire* program. Don't reengineer the short-term variable pay programs this year and take on base salary programs next year. This defeats the purpose of making sure all the programs are working together to deliver the business results necessary for success.

2. *Trying to implement changes all at once.* Yes, reengineering the entire program is essential; however, implementing the changes all at once can have a detrimental effect. It's much better to phase in new rules and new programs over time. There's only so much change that employees can absorb and adapt to at once. In addition, it is necessary to build in time for managers and employees alike to move through the learning curve. When planning to implement radical changes to a total rewards program, it's advisable to allow a two- to five-year timeline.

3. *Limiting the number of people involved.* A broad coalition of people should be involved in a total rewards effort. All stakeholders need a place at the table – human resources, executives, finance, employees, board of directors, customers. While it may be easier to exclude some groups for the sake of simplicity, it's far too easy to overlook key elements without input of every group that will be impacted by the programs.

4. *Not doing a thorough impact analysis.* Before implementing any piece of the total rewards program, do a thorough analysis of the financial, organizational, employee, and customer impact of the plans. View these impacts both today and into the future. Don't forget to look at the full range of outcomes. What happens to the total rewards program if company profits drop by 50 percent, or sales and revenues increase threefold? It's a huge disservice not to know how the program elements will behave at different points in the company's life cycle.

5. *Not communicating effectively.* Many times when companies make these kinds of large-scale changes to their compensation and benefits programs, they communicate too much, too early, to employees, creating a workforce that gets full on hype and expectations. The flipside, communicating too little, too late, also is a problem because employees don't understand the business reasons for the changes or how these changes will impact their individual situations. Proper communication of total rewards changes is essential to success. Determine the right amount of information, the right time to deliver it, and the right format to use for delivery.

CRYSTALLIZING THE SPIRIT OF YOUR TOTAL REWARDS PLAN

When carefully evaluated, developed, and woven into a comprehensive total rewards strategy, the elements of the total rewards puzzle work together to produce an impact on employee attraction and retention that is greater than any of the elements considered individually. It is truly a strategy whose whole is greater than the sum of its parts.

In addition, a total rewards strategy maximizes the organization's return on compensation, benefits, and other rewards dollars invested; provides managers with multiple tools for encouraging employee development and rewarding performance; and creates a rewards package that meets or exceeds the value of a competitor's total rewards offerings. As with any effective, competitive HR program or initiative, a total rewards strategy should not be created in a vacuum. It should provide specific, motivating direction when choosing what to focus on (and choosing what *not* to focus on). Rewards strategies should follow two primary aims:

1. Articulate a distinctive value proposition for current and prospective employees that attracts and retains employees who have the capabilities and values the employer needs.
2. Provide a framework from which the employer designs, administers, and communicates rewards programs with the maximum motivational impact to drive desired behaviors.

The total rewards strategy should ensure that the rewards framework matches the strategic needs of the business, and that the mechanics of the total rewards structure reinforce the desired corporate culture and management style. Also, it should help structure the components of the rewards system to influence and motivate employee behavior in the right direction.

Issues That a Total Rewards Strategy Should Address

A well-conceived TR strategy should address several elements:

- *Strategic perspective.* A total rewards strategy begins with an articulation of the company's values and business strategies. The link to business needs and aims should be spelled out right up front. The total rewards strategy is the place to be clear about where, when, and how the links between business goals and rewards should and should not be made.
- *Statement of overall objectives.* The strategy should include statements that describe how the rewards system will support the needs of the business and the company's customers, employees, shareholders, and other key stakeholders. This typically includes a delineation of the role of each reward element. If you cannot clearly define a role for any given element of total rewards, then you should question why it is being offered at all.
- *Prominence.* The strategy should describe the overall importance of rewards relative to other tools that can focus and affect actions and decisions (e.g., shared values, cool products, inspiring leadership, etc.). One way to think about prominence is to imagine an employee talking to a friend about working for the company. As the employee relates what is great about the company, prominence involves two key questions:

1. At what stage in the conversation would you like the employee to mention the rewards package (as opposed to things such as the culture, quality of leadership, focus on customers, etc.)? This helps define the importance of total rewards in the context of the total employee experience. Do you lead with total rewards, or is it a supporting component?
2. Which elements of the package would you like to hear mentioned first, and which should be mentioned last – or not at all? What does your company want to be famous for? What is the signature program? These questions are aimed at culling the handful of reward elements that deserve 80 percent or 90 percent of your attention in design, administration, and communication.

- *Performance measures.* The strategy should clearly identify the performance criteria to be rewarded, the appropriate level of measurement for each (e.g., corporate, business unit, region, work group, individual, etc.) and which reward elements will be linked to which measures. Also, the strategy should describe the degree to which rewards are expected to drive employee actions and decisions through variability, influence over outcomes (controllability), and the explicitness of the pay-performance link.
- *Competitive market reference points.* The total rewards strategy should describe the types of companies, industries, or other reference points that will be used as the basis for determining the competitiveness of the rewards package. What are the comparators? Do they differ among business units? Why?

A common response to the question about comparators is that they should be composed of companies against which we compete for talent. It's a sound approach, usually resulting in a list dominated by companies in the same industry or geography. Another angle to consider is what you want the company to be famous for. Perhaps benchmark the company's signature program against companies that already are famous in that area, even if it means looking beyond the industry or geography.

- *Competitive positioning.* The strategy should clearly describe the desired competitive position relative to the competitive reference points in the labor market. Ideally, it should define how the competitive positioning is expected to vary with performance or other criteria.

It is worth noting that many companies define the median as the desired competitive benchmark for all components of rewards with increasing frequency. This raises a question: If you position all elements at the median, how will you differentiate? Defining a "signature" program is one way to avoid the creation of a plain set of rewards that looks like what every other company offers:

- *Degree of internal equity and consistency.* The statement should address the extent to which the total rewards strategy will be applied uniformly throughout the company, both horizontally and vertically. To take the view that both internal and external relativities are important is fine, but defining a strategy is about making choices. A good strategy clearly defines which is more important when the two are in conflict.

- *Communication and involvement.* The strategy should define how much information about the rewards programs will be disclosed and explained to employees. It also should outline the degree of participation that employees will have in the design and ongoing administration of the rewards programs. This includes a clear delineation of where HR's responsibility for designing and managing rewards ends and management's accountability begins. It also should include the company's policy toward employee unions, works councils, and other representative or collective bargaining units.
- *Governance.* While core principles governing the rewards program should remain fairly constant, the underlying programs need to be revised and refreshed periodically to ensure that they are competitive and compelling. The rewards strategy should delineate how frequently such reviews will occur, and who plays which roles in carrying out the review and redesign.
- *Data and information management.* The rewards strategy should specify guidelines for data management, information sources, collection and reporting methodologies, and processes for using data for decision support. The strategy also should include an overall process for measuring the efficacy of the total rewards program, and the supporting data.

The Bottom Line

Effectively executing an appropriate total rewards strategy can increase a company's market premium. Unfortunately, weak execution means many companies are leaving at least some of this money on the table.

Problems with execution are understandable. Many rewards and benefits programs evolved in a fragmented way, without consideration for how the parts fit together or whether they reinforce business goals. Even in organizations with truly integrated designs, effective delivery depends on successful implementation of performance management, change management, communication, and the use of technology.

Every organization can develop and execute a superior total rewards solution. By taking a step back and analyzing the design and delivery of each component of their total rewards strategy, companies can identify the steps they need to take to maximize its effectiveness (see Sidebar 1.1).

WFA: REEVALUATING THE TOTAL REWARDS EQUATION

Total rewards has typically focused on compensation, well-being, benefits and, more recently, career development and recognition. With the recent demonstrated success of remote work, organizations are realizing that work

---

Sidebar 1.1: Reevaluating Total Rewards Strategies for the Growing Remote Workforce

By Steve Brink

Before the 2020 global pandemic, a 2018 study by GlobalWork-placeAnalytics.com highlighted that just 3.6 percent of the United States labor force worked remotely 50 percent or more of the time.

The same report tells us that 56 percent of employees have jobs that could be accomplished remotely. As quarantine/social distancing was implemented, most of the workforce performed their tasks from home, with the exception of certain sectors (e.g., service, manufacturing, etc.).

The remote work experiment forced by COVID-19 has been viewed by most as a success. But this has raised HR policy questions about WFH (Work from Home) and, taking a step further, working where you want to live versus living close to the work office. The value of on-premise/co-location working has come into question, and this experience brought those questions to the forefront.

If proximity and ease of commute are no longer issues, what factors drive our preferred work/live location? Is it being close to family members, or a location that aligns with your hobbies and passions? Whatever the answer, what we're really discussing here is the role of location in the total rewards matrix.

---

location is also an important consideration, possibly on par with these other elements of the total rewards matrix. Work from Anywhere (WFA) is an important evolution, as it means companies have another powerful new lever to use in driving their talent strategy. Companies that recognize this and thoughtfully invoke work location in their employee value proposition could significantly benefit by:

- *Attracting talent.* Many times, the available talent we need/want cannot be sourced in the location in which we operate. Consequently, we either settle for candidates in our current market or we employ mobility to move talent to the job location. Both are costly solutions. As organizations are able to facilitate effective remote work, they will be able to attract new types of talent that prefer their current location or prefer a remote work environment. In other words, that key software developer who didn't want to leave Austin, Texas, is now in reach.
- *Retaining talent.* Every organization has lost talent due to personal needs. Maybe a key employee's spouse gets a new job across the country or needs to move to take care of an aging relative. The amount of institutional knowledge these employees take with them is staggering, and companies spend significant time and monies replacing that staff

and training new workers. By investing in distributed work, companies may save that talent and organizational knowledge, thus minimizing disruptions and saving on costs and time. One would also think that if employees are able to live where they want, they will be happier and want to stay with an organization that facilitates that lifestyle.

- *Enhancing talent.* By now, we all know the benefit of diverse and inclusive teams. Diversity means a lot of things, and one definition could include work location. People who live in San Antonio see the world quite differently than people in San Francisco – and that's a good thing. Diversity provides a unique blend of ideas and different perspectives that fuel creativity and performance in our business. By no means does location replace other diversity – and inclusion-related efforts, but it can play a role in enhancing an organization's D&I strategy.

Companies that hit the mark here will provide additional benefits to their employees, including:

- Less time spent commuting
- Reduced transportation expenses
- Lower day-to-day costs (such as wardrobe costs and restaurant meals)
- Increased productivity
- Improved quality of life
- Ease of family care arrangements
- Enhanced flexibility to work in their preferred style/hours/etc.

Work from Anywhere

There are many, many resources discussing the tools and technology needed to facilitate remote work, but thus far, there has been little conversation around the compensation-related aspects of this WFA strategy.

COVID-19 skyrocketed WFA to a top-of-mind priority for leaders in the mobility industry. Facebook made a big announcement in May 2020 that it expected 50 percent of its workforce of 18,000 to work remotely in 5–10 years. Facebook saw remote working as a way to retain talent that wanted to leave the Bay Area and to attract talent that might already be remote and prefer not to move. This was a major shift of philosophy for Facebook, which once provided a $10,000 bonus if you lived within 10 miles of the office. While not as public, many other companies (both within and outside of the tech industry) announced similar plans on increasing their remote worker mix.

There's an important caveat to this strategy. Facebook agreed to this WFA approach but indicated that salaries would be adjusted based on the cost of living in the location in which the employee resides. There are myriad ways to accomplish this salary localization, and this section will provide a view on different strategies to employ to set pay for those working from anywhere.

Understanding Cost of Living and Cost of Labor

First, as a reminder, there is a difference between cost of labor and cost of living.

Cost of living is the cost to live in a specific location and is based on the price of goods and services, housing, and tax rates. *Cost of labor* is typically the predominant pay for a particular role in a specific location given criteria such as industry, years of experience, and/or seniority/responsibility. It's a supply/demand-based approach, which has been used to set pay for years.

FIGURE 1.4 Work where you live.

With the choice of working from home on the rise, what is the value of salary in different cities across the world? This inforgraphic helps understand the equivalent value of USD 100,000 salary across major city centers, desirable towns, and countries. Salaries have been adjusted for cost of living and income tax differences.

Source: "Reevaluating Total Rewards Strategies for the Growing Remote Workforce" by Steve Brink, President & CEO of AIRINC. AIRSHARE, Aug 4, 2020. © 2020, AIRINC U.S.A., https://www.air-inc.com/ Reprinted with permission from AIRINC.

But with the rise of WFA, that supply-demand equation is being turned on its head. From a cost-of-labor perspective, the supply and demand of labor has been historically contained within a particular market. But now that we are able to acquire and employ talent across the world, our labor market is now global, which makes for a very different supply–demand equation.

In a perfect world, we would create a new mechanism to determine cost of labor (i.e., international pay scales based on global supply/demand or skills-based pay). But those capabilities do not exist (yet).

In the mid-term, some companies are looking to cost of living as a way to take their current compensation approach and weave it into this WFA world.

In the cost-of-living example, we consider a position in Atlanta that earns $100,000. The graphic illustrates an equivalent salary for a sample of locations across the United States, given differences in cost of goods and services, housing, and tax rates. At these pay levels, a person would have similar purchasing power to that which they enjoyed in Atlanta. You can see that variations in the cost of living may warrant a significant difference in the required salary to maintain this purchasing power.

Setting the Pay Level

Your total rewards philosophy will determine the best way to pay remote workers. As mentioned, in the past, salaries were typically based on office location. As employees increasingly WFA, there is no office location by which to set salaries.

In this new environment, work follows the employee, not the other way around. Therefore, a strategically aligned rewards philosophy is important so that your pay methodology is clear for in-office and WFA workers. It is imperative to establish a process for setting pay, as it will assist in ensuring pay equity and fairness relative to others.

Below are the four major ways to set compensation levels for WFA workers. Again, the appropriate approach should be dictated by your total rewards philosophy and organizational approach to WFA.

1. Align All Compensation with Company HQ

In this approach, pay, no matter if in-office or distributed, is based on the HQ location and each employee's role.

A remote worker in a low-cost-of-living location might receive a "windfall," or an increased purchasing power, due to the difference in cost of labor at the HQ location and cost of living in the worker's location. Conversely, a remote employee who lives in a high cost-of-living location might experience lower purchasing power.

The fundamental philosophy is that a given role has a certain value to the organization, and it does not matter where the role is located.

Companies that employ this strategy might pay a national rate for a position, as opposed to a location-specific market rate. This could be helpful if you have multiple offices or no major office.

2. Current Market-Level Pay for Their Location

This approach assesses the market-pay rate for the position in the location of the remote worker. This means organizations would pay for the position based upon how other organizations in the remote worker's location pay for a similar position (i.e., market competitive pay for that role at that location).

It takes significant time and survey vendor fees to understand what the market pay rate is in a particular location. Companies will need to subscribe to a compensation survey database so they can get the best market information possible. Unfortunately, there may be some locations where market pay data does not exist or is insufficient.

Discussions around pay (including a reduction in pay for WFA employees because a role might have a lower cost of labor in one location versus another) can be challenging. This approach is not always transparent, and there may be questions about the criteria used when evaluating market pay.

The philosophy here is that you are maintaining a competitive pay offering in a location for every remote worker. This focus on each labor market makes sense if your philosophy is to pay the going rate in each geographic location.

As stated previously, it should be noted that market pay is misaligned with WFA. The idea of market pay is a supply/demand argument specific to a location (because in the past, the supply could only come from that location). Since WFA supply/demand is nationwide/global, it doesn't really "fit" to base pay on a particular market because that doesn't match the true "supply" for the remote position. For this reason, companies should think carefully about the application of this approach in a WFA compensation strategy.

3. Develop Geographic Differentials Structure

The prior two approaches provide two extremes; the first is a one-size-fits-all approach while the second applies differentiated, individualized salaries for each remote worker. This third option is a middle approach to provide some differences in pay but not by every individual/location. For larger companies with diverse work locations, this is already a popular approach.

In this approach, organizations define a salary structure that is for HQ or a specified base location. Based on estimated competitive pay, you establish a geographically differentiated salary structure. You can have as many as you want. In the above example, we have as many geographic differences as there are remote workers, but usually a company will have 3–10 different structures, depending on how many work locations there are.

For example, you might have five different structures (A through E). Structure A is for high wage locations, while Structure E is for low wage ones. Structure C could be the structure that is the base level (100 percent). Structure A and B would be set higher (110 percent and 105 percent, respectively). Levels D and E would have their structures at 95 percent and 90 percent. These figures are for illustrative purposes only.

Each remote worker location would be slotted into one of these five sample salary structures. The philosophy in this approach is market-based but simplifies to a few salary structures versus each remote worker having their own salary structure. This third approach is easier than approach No. 2, as it is more manageable over time and recognizes that there are pay differences across locations versus approach No. 1.

A corollary to this approach is to use cost of living information to set geographical differences instead of assessing competitive pay based on each marketplace. The geographic differentiated salary structures would be set in a similar way but using cost of living data to create the various salary structures (A through E in our example).

The cost-of-living data are usually easy to find. Having access to this information significantly reduces the complexity of the pay approach (i.e., we don't need to consider role, experience, or other market pay criteria). Transparency to workers is also improved, because remote workers "feel" the difference in paying for goods and services, housing, etc. When basing salaries on market pay, transparency is diminished because there are a variety of factors considered that aren't typically communicated to employees, such as peer group, selected roles, or sample size.

Many companies use this cost-based approach, as it is defensible, easy to communicate, and easily understood by employees.

4. Pay Based on Cost of Living

This next approach is a newer concept and might be best aligned with an increasingly distributed workforce. In this approach, companies set competitive pay based on the HQ location, and then use a cost of living approach to adjust the compensation up or down based on where the employee lives/works.

This approach is similar to the cost-of-living option in approach No. 3, but more specific to an individual situation (as we see in approach No. 2). However, unlike approach No. 2, cost-of-living data is much easier to obtain than competitive pay data in each location, and it's simpler and more straightforward for employees to understand. Consequently, this is much easier to maintain, and also optimizes the compensation for each person based on the location that they have chosen to live. By assessing competitive compensation at HQ and translating it to remote workers using cost of living, companies ensure that everyone across the organization – no matter where you work – enjoys similar purchasing power. This is an excellent way to preserve internal equity across an organization.

There is a variation of this approach, which might be beneficial to both the employee and the company, as some organizations explore a type of *gainsharing*. In this scenario, companies split any gains between the difference in HQ salary and the cost of living-based salary in the remote worker's location. For example, if the HQ salary is set at $100,000 and the remote worker's cost of living adjusted salary is $90,000, the gainsharing salary would be $95,000 (splitting the difference of $100,000 and $90,000). The company receives an ongoing savings on pay given the $5,000 reduction, and the remote worker benefits by having more purchasing power than they would under a different approach. Win–win.

Personalizing Rewards

In closing, there is a continued trend toward WFA/remote work. Distributed work and location as a total rewards component continues the well-established HR trend of personalization of rewards. Personalization grows through cafeteria-style benefit plans and multiple career paths. WFA is just another step in aligning individual personal preference and perceived value to create happier, more productive employees.

Work location has always been a key element of the compensation pillar. Now, WFA will allow employees to choose their own work location, which will further drive perceived value and allow for trade-offs in other areas of the total rewards matrix.

Companies should recognize this trend and develop a clear rewards philosophy and an approach to setting pay for remote workers that is consistent with their talent strategy and goals.

2 Everything You Want to Know about Compensation (but Were Afraid to Ask)

Compensation systems have moved from backroom systems largely run by HR into complex management systems that serve as the foundation for organizational alignment and employee motivation, as well as providing important support for job families and career pathing.

Compensation systems are important tools for managers, HR business partners, and senior management. In large organizations with shared-services models or centralized compensation functions, HR business partners often broker compensation services on behalf of their business unit or division. Some organizations now allow line managers direct access to salary structures, market pricing, and incentive payout predictors in order to recommend initial hiring salaries, merit increases or incentive payout. Senior management is typically actively involved in both setting objectives for compensation and reward systems and monitoring/evaluating results.

In smaller organizations, HR business partners or one-person HR departments take on overall responsibility for everything from developing pay strategy to overseeing pay administration for the local employee workforce.

The following discussion focuses on the fundamentals of compensation systems within larger organizations. However, the concepts outlined are applicable to organizations of all types and sizes. New approaches and ideas are constantly being tested; the key, as always, is to ensure that the final system meets the organization's needs.

THE FOUNDATION: THE COMPENSATION PHILOSOPHY

Successful compensation programs are the result of well-defined and closely managed systems. A compensation philosophy provides the foundation to ensure that each of the different programs and systems is working in harmony with the others. A compensation philosophy should explain:

- Who the organization defines as labor competitors.
- How the organization prefers to set pay levels for its various job titles compared to the market (at the market, ahead of the market, below the market, on a total compensation basis, etc.).
- What the balance is between internal and external equity.
- The roles of managers, compensation, and HR in managing pay.
- What technology or systems will be used to manage pay.
- Frequency and timing of key events, such as merit increases (annual or semi-annual, etc.).
- The type of incentives in use, as well as eligibility.
- The type of organizational culture and/or business results desired by the company, and how the compensation systems will support each.
- ROI (return-on-investment) requirements for different types of programs.
- Sunset dates for any key programs, if applicable.
- The scope and type of programs used (e.g., the extent of variable pay).
- The role of quasi-compensation systems, such as rewards and recognition.

These collective areas provide insight and direction to senior management and the compensation function, as well as the entire HR organization. In some cases, a compensation philosophy is a written document, often summarized in employee handbooks. In other cases, the philosophy is less documented and instead is a recognized set of practices.

Compensation philosophies provide an important foundation for the development of all compensation programs. The most important part of the process is the discussion behind each element. Does your organization plan to emphasize incentives? If so, do you wish to provide incentives at a level that matches your competitors, or do you wish to exceed competitors' program designs in order to capture the best talent? These important conversations are typically created by a cross-functional group of compensation specialists, line managers, and HRBP. An edited compensation philosophy statement is outlined in Figure 2.1. See Figure 2.2 for sample questions to use to guide a compensation philosophy planning meeting.

ALIGNING COMPENSATION WITH BUSINESS STRATEGY

The following "ideal" characteristics are necessary for every compensation program in order to attract, motivate, and retain qualified employees that support business strategy. (*Note:* These characteristics are primarily for all positions

FIGURE 2.1 Sample compensation philosophy.

ABC believes in creating a high-performance culture for our employees. In our belief, a motivated and engaged workforce will provide job satisfaction for our employees, above-average shareholder returns, and sustain our high-performing culture. We offer a wide variety of programs to motivate employees, depending on the location and business unit. Please check with your manager or ABCHR (our online reference tool) for information for plans in your location.

As a global organization, we provide flexibility to all regions to create specific compensation programs for approval by corporate compensation.

The corporate compensation group develops an overall strategy in alignment with the company's total rewards strategy, created in 2015. Business-unit compensation develops local strategies based on approval from corporate compensation. Line managers are responsible for setting individual pay levels.

In general, our programs have the following components on a worldwide basis:

- Base salary is based on local market conditions and targeted to be competitive with those companies that we directly recruit from. Line managers have the authority to recommend higher than competitor pay levels, based on consultation with their HRBP and the Corporate Compensation Department.

- Incentives are offered to roughly 25 percent of our workforce and are generally focused on mission-critical roles, directors and above or those positions where our competitors have implemented incentive plans.

- We believe in transparency. Therefore, all employees can view their own salary range and the range of any positions that they are around two candidates. All managers can view salary ranges for all subordinate positions, plus the ranges up to two levels beyond their current position. This information is available in ABCHR.

- Incentives are funded by several metrics, which are set each year by our senior leaders. They include factors such as profitability, market penetration and customer satisfaction. In addition, we use a balanced scorecard approach that measures employee retention and operational excellence.

- We use salary ranges as a tool to manage employee salaries. All employees below the maximum of their salary range are eligible for annual merit increases, which are designed to be competitive with other employers of our size. Merit budgets are set using external, country, and regionally specific data. Merit budgets are communicated to all line managers, who are responsible for communicating the budget to all employees. Employees over the maximum of their range are eligible for lump-sum payouts that do not add to base pay.

- We offer a competitive benefits package, which is designed to be generally comparable to our market competitors for labor.

FIGURE 2.2 Guiding a compensation philosophy development meeting.

1. What is the organization's compensation philosophy? What do we believe is important, and why? Should we pay more or less than competitors? Why or why not? How do we, as an organization, define pay-for-performance?
2. How will we determine incentive eligibility? Which positions will be eligible for incentives, and why? Will we grant incentives to those positions that do not receive incentives at our competitors for labor?
3. How transparent will we be? Will we share market data, salary ranges, merit budgets, etc., with all employees or just with managers?
4. Will the organization provide incentives based on specific job market data, or by salary grade?
5. How important is internal equity in our organization? To what extent do we wish to encourage transfers?
6. How does the Corporate Compensation Department work with other groups? What information will be shared, and at what levels?
7. What current compensation programs are working effectively, and which may need to be altered? Why?
8. Philosophically, how long should it take for a fully qualified individual with at-target performance to reach the midpoint or targeted pay?
9. What cycle will we use for various compensation programs? The calendar year or fiscal year?
10. What measures of corporate performance should be used throughout the organization to fund and guide compensation programs? Balanced scorecard? Corporate measures or divisional measures, or a blend of both?
11. To what extent will our compensation philosophy exceed federal or state laws?
12. How often will we review our philosophy, and who is responsible and accountable for beginning the review?

except single incumbent senior management positions.) These characteristics are the foundation for an ideal pay structure that ties to business strategy:

- *Meets the organization's unique needs.* To some degree, each company is unique within its own industry or geographical area. Unique characteristics need to be recognized and addressed when designing compensation programs, and particularly, pay structures. Compensation systems must reward business strategy goals and objectives.
- *Internal equity.* A measure of how an organization values each of its jobs in relation to one another. Although formal job evaluation systems have become less prevalent in recent years, state-level programs that emphasize comparable pay, plus the constant need to maintain internal equity as a motivation tool places the importance of formal understanding of how to assess internal equity.

- *External competitiveness.* A measure of an organization's pay structure compared to that of its competitors. This critical element is often dependent on job family and salary structure.
- *Affordability.* A measure of how costly a compensation program is to a company. If pay structures are not developed responsibly, an organization could incur labor costs that exceed what it can afford to pay. Base pay, for example, is earned once and paid forever. Thus, merit increases and base pay are fixed costs.
- *Legal defensibility.* Compensation programs must adhere to specific federal and state laws designed to provide fairness in how employees are paid. These laws are discussed at the end of this chapter.
- *Understandable/saleable.* To be accepted and understood, compensation programs must be well communicated at all levels of the organization. In most organizations, line managers and HR business partners are responsible for explaining the impact of compensation systems on individual employees and groups.
- *Efficient to administer.* With increased pressure to improve productivity and reduce costs, it is important that an organization's compensation program be as simple and straightforward as possible to maintain and administer. A balance needs to be struck between what appears to be the "best" program and what is efficient, effective, and easiest to administer. Complex measurements for incentive systems, for example, reduce employee light of sight, and employee motivation to work to meet the needs of the program.
- *Support sustainability and organizational ethics.* The compensation program should reward performance fairly without encouraging inappropriate behaviors. Rewards should reflect both individual employee and company performance.
- *Flexible design and administration.* Flexible pay programs are necessary tools to compete for labor in the marketplace. As such, they must be flexible and capable of changing as needed without requiring a redesign every time a new need arises.

Most compensation programs will balance each of these objectives as sometimes these characteristics may be in conflict. For example, it may not always be possible to maintain internal equity when a company is trying to be externally competitive. Therefore, it is important to recognize the possibility of such conflict and review the business strategy and/or how mission-critical the positions are to determine the appropriate balance of all features of the compensation program. Pressures for pay transparency can complicate balancing each of these objectives (see Sidebar 2.1).

Although compensation is the largest component of the total rewards system and a major cost factor for organizations, many employers have not had a formal discussion in place to ensure that compensation dollars are used wisely. Additionally, the broader concept of directing employees' behaviors to desired outcomes through rewards is not always integrated into an organization's overall strategic planning process, although it typically arises in the strategic planning implementation process as illustrated in Figure 2.3.

Sidebar 2.1 Pay Transparency

Pay transparency has emerged as a major issue due to various factors. Sources such as Glassdoor and Indeed.com release pay information that has been gathered directly from individuals. Employees who feel that they are underpaid are known to create spreadsheets that crowd-source pay data directly from co-workers. Various states have created pay equity or pay transparency laws that restrict companies from asking individuals for pay data, which makes the process of quickly obtaining competitive market data more problematic. In addition, these practices create pressure on organizations to be more transparent about pay data.

Despite these pressures, individual pay information remains largely confidential within organizations, unless an individual decides to share actual pay information. Privacy concerns, concerns about disrupting motivation levels, and concerns related to internal equity continue to drive tight control over information related to individual salaries. From time to time, small startup organizations experiment with full transparency, but such approaches are extremely rare.

FIGURE 2.3 Stragetic planning implementation process.

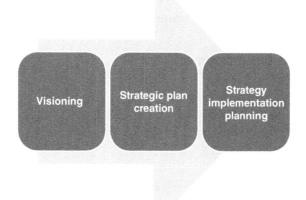

COMPENSATION PROGRAMS – ELEMENTS OF COMPENSATION

Compensation systems are usually divided into base pay and variable pay systems as shown in Figure 2.4.

FIGURE 2.4 Base pay versus variable pay.

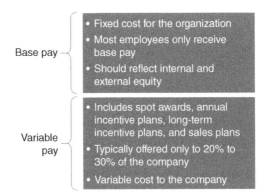

Much of the innovation in compensation is occurring in the variable-pay element. Companies are making greater use of variable-pay programs by expanding them to a significantly broader portion of the workforce than they have in the past. However, market pressures and stabilizing merit increase budgets are creating new solutions toward managing base pay. A detailed summary of the various programs within each of these areas is summarized in Figures 2.5 and 2.6.

UNDERSTANDING BASE PAY

Every organization must decide how much to pay each of its employees, however, HR business partners, compensation specialists, and line managers

FIGURE 2.5 Base pay programs.

- Salary, hourly, or piece rates
- Knowledge- or skill-based pay
- Competency-based pay
- Differentials
- Shift pay
- Weekend/holiday pay
- Expatriate remuneration
- Market adjustments
- Merit increases
- Lump-sum increases
- Step-rate increases
- General increases
- Cost-of-living increases
- Promotional increases
- Red- or green-circle pay

FIGURE 2.6 Variable pay programs.

- Based on organizational, group/team or individual performance
- Profit-sharing plans
- Performance-sharing plans
- Group/team incentives
- Individual incentives
- Short-term incentive plans
- Sales incentive plans/commissions
- Executive incentive plans
- Discretionary bonuses (annual or spot)
- Equity-based compensation
- Stock options
- Stock grants
- Restricted stock
- Performance unit plans

often have different viewpoints about how to manage this process. HRBP and line managers tend to think first about the requirements of the person, while specialists tend to think first about the requirements of the job.

Edward E. Lawler III, PhD, director of the Center for Effective Organizations at the University of Southern California's Graduate School of Business Administration, wrote in his book, *Strategic Pay*, "Organizations hire individuals, but once individuals join most organizations, the amount they are paid is determined primarily by the type of job they do." Therefore, it is important for HRBPs and line managers to understand the steps required in job-level pay determination, as well as individual-level pay determination. Job-level pay determination includes job analysis, job evaluation or job worth determination, salary structure placement, incentive pay determination, and performance management. Understanding such programs will allow HR business partners and line managers to more effectively work with their compensation specialists.

Job Analysis

Job analysis is considered the first step in determining basc pay under any pay system as job analysis allows us to understand the specific steps undertaken by an individual or group of individuals. This process is formally called *job analysis,* which is sometimes accompanied by a job description or job summary.

The depth of the job analysis is dictated by time, economics, and whether the analysis will be used for purposes other than compensation. At one time, job analysis was conducted for all positions; some organizations analyzed jobs on a regular cycle, such as every two to three years. Entry-level compensation specialists and/or HRBPs completed this work by interviewing incumbents or managers or reviewing completed structured questionnaires. In recent years, this practice has fallen by the wayside as organizations have looked for ways to streamline their processes and reduce headcount. In addition, many organizations now rely on line managers to create job descriptions or to describe job content. Some organizations use sources such as Indeed or LinkedIn to identify job descriptions from competitors to use as the foundation for defining jobs.

Currently, most compensation departments have streamlined methods of analyzing jobs, including matching to position surveys, using prewritten job descriptions, requesting thumbnail descriptions of job duties and accountabilities or analyzing job content only when the position is being evaluated or reviewed for compensation purposes. As job analysis has become more abbreviated, job description preparation has declined. Many organizations have eliminated job descriptions, or only prepare them if required or requested to do so. Others have moved to high-level job summaries, which outline key accountabilities with little specificity. However, companies with internal-worth job evaluation systems, described later in this chapter, typically will use a proscribed format for job descriptions to ensure that all meaningful data are compiled.

Despite its decline, there is a role for job analysis, which provides meaningful information for staffing and recruiting and performance management, as well as compensation decisions. Job analysis can be gathered through interviews and structured questionnaires.

In any of its guises, job analysis is typically performed when a position is first created, or when job content changes in a substantial way. Streamlined job analyses are most common when an organization reorganizes, downsizes, or changes its overall scope and direction. Some jobs are so stable that the analysis remains stable over time, or only minimal revisions are required.

As corporate human resources departments downsize, many organizations have begun to shift the responsibility for job analysis from compensation to HR generalists to line management. This can create challenges when the compensation department requests specific information required for determining job worth, which line management or line HR has not gathered. Therefore, it is important to understand the depth of job analysis required for your organization under different circumstances.

Job Evaluation – Internal Equity

In many organizations, the job analysis phase is either very short or in some cases, nonexistent. Therefore, the first visible step for many HRBPs or line managers is job evaluation. There are two major schools of job evaluation: market-driven systems and job-worth systems. Market-driven systems are the most prevalent.

Market-Driven Systems

In a market-driven compensation system, the "going rate" for the position is the primary determinant of pay. See Chapter 8 for further discussion on the subject. Compensation specialists then attempt to resolve any potential inequities that are created by one of several methods:

- Paying one position above the market in order to obtain internal equity
- Paying each position slightly different than market pay, in order to obtain internal equity
- Targeted each position at the market and using incentive systems as a way to address inequities
- Targeting pay for each position at market

Each of these approaches has advantages and disadvantages. The most current trend is to target pay for each position in the market. This creates the need for constant communication and has also driven line manager desires to have more transparency in terms of viewing market data.

Market-driven systems should be monitored closely to track changes in pay. The move from one set of external comparisons to another can result in substantial changes in recommended pay levels. For example, not-for-profit organizations typically pay less than general industry for director-level positions. Changing the market reference point from services to manufacturing could imply that the whole compensation system is out of whack when it is not. With enough time and attention, inequities that arise from a market-driven pay system can be corrected. However, line managers are often frustrated by inequities with the market, especially when a hot candidate for a hard-to-fill job is being recruited or when there are numerous long-service employees in low market value positions.

Job-Worth Systems

In a job-worth system, the primary determinant of pay is the value of the job to the organization. In some cases, a job-worth system can result in pay differences from the external marketplace. Again, managers may struggle with implementation as they attempt to find a way to reflect the market without violating the spirit of the internal job-worth system. At one time, companies were attempting to find neutral ground between internally and externally driven systems, using complex multiple regression models. Over time, such systems have fallen into disfavor because of their administrative complexity. In addition, such systems mitigate the problems associated with either a purely market-driven or purely internally driven system; they do not eliminate them.

Job-worth systems typically grant points for the presence of various factors such as the skills required to perform the job, the effort required to achieve results, the number of employees supervised, and the size of the assets managed. Figure 2.7 illustrates the Hay system, one of the largest and most prevalent point factor systems in use. At one time, many US organizations used the same or largely identical factors to determine job worth. In Canada, pay-equity laws require the use of four generic factors: skill, effort, responsibility, and working conditions. In the most formal systems, a maximum number of points are available for each factor, leading to the name *point-factor system*. As the needs of organizations have become more complex, most

FIGURE 2.7 Point-factor categories.

Hay point-factor system	Job-worth factors
	  – Skills
	  – Responsibility
	  – Effort
	  – Working conditions

organizations have moved away from job-worth systems towards market-driven systems. Some organizations, such as manufacturing and the government sector, continue to use point-factor systems.

Pay equity and comparable worth laws in various states have resurfaced interest in job-worth approaches as methods to explain and support pay decisions.

Market-Driven versus Job-Worth Systems

Market-driven and job-worth systems yield different results. In the case of a discrepancy, internally driven job-worth systems will err on the side of maintaining internal equity, and external, market-driven systems will err on the side of reflecting how the outside world pays the position.

The debate regarding the appropriateness of either system has gone on for some time. Internal-equity proponents speak about the scarcity of appropriate market data reference points and the need to address employees' ongoing efforts to compare worth internally. Market proponents point to the differences between internal job evaluation systems and the marketplace, with differences of 5 percent to 20 percent not uncommon. In the end, a market-based approach has proven to be the most popular; WorldatWork reported in 2015 that 88 percent of organizations had an established method for evaluating jobs, most of which used market-driven systems (see Figure 2.8).

Which Approach Is Best?

Because of the differing results between market-driven and job-worth systems, the majority of organizations have moved to a market-driven pay system. This has placed enormous emphasis on the need for accurate and timely external market comparison data. In addition, many organizations have begun to shift the responsibility for determining job worth to the line. In major organizations, including those with limited corporate or shared-services compensation staff, local HR is required to determine the worth of the position by matching directly to databases of surveys or internal reference points. Organizations with managerial self-service models accompanied by extensive technological support often require managers to identify job worth through the selection of a salary grade with only minimal oversight from HR.

Regardless of which kind of system is used, the results of a job evaluation will indicate the salary grade in which a job will be placed.

FIGURE 2.8 Market-driven systems.

	Ranking	Classi-fication	Point-factor	Job component	Market pricing
Senior management (n = 616)	3%	6%	16%	2%	74%
Middle management (n = 625)	3%	7%	19%	2%	70%
Professional (n = 625)	2%	7%	20%	2%	69%
Sales (n = 552)	2%	7%	17%	2%	72%
Administrative (n = 623)	2%	8%	20%	2%	68%
Production (n = 543)	3%	10%	17%	2%	69%

Market Analysis

Whether an organization uses an internally or externally driven pay system, it is important to compare pay practices to the external market. Most organizations participate in regular surveys that gather data from a specific set of competitors and release overall averages on an annual basis. Typically, however, every position is not included. Those positions that are included (often called benchmarks) typically exist in most organizations with fairly similar responsibilities.

Salary surveys with national and geographic data may be purchased from numerous organizations, including all of the major consulting firms such as Mercer, PayScale, or Willis Towers Watson. Most of the major survey providers have set up web-enabled access allowing for instantaneous access to data. Salary survey data provides real-time information on various jobs and job families, as seen below.

Variable Pay

- Based on organizational, group/team or individual performance
- Profit-sharing plans
- Performance-sharing plans
- Group/team incentives
- Individual incentives
- Short-term incentive plans
- Sales incentive plans/commissions
- Executive incentive plans

- Discretionary bonuses (annual or spot)
- Equity-based compensation
- Stock options
- Stock grants
- Restricted stock
- Performance unit plans

Some companies find that it is impossible to match all of their positions, and thus need to conduct custom surveys to gather specific information (see Sidebar 2.2).

Sidebar 2.2 Conducting Surveys

Sometimes it is important to gather survey data on what local competitors are doing. Before beginning a custom survey, check to see if a survey already is conducted in the area; WorldatWork or local compensation and benefits groups can help identify existing surveys, saving organizations the time, effort and expense of conducting their own. If a custom survey is necessary, the following steps can prove useful:

- Decide on the depth of the information that needs to be gathered and what jobs should be included. Asking about base salaries when total compensation data are needed will only provide part of the answer. Prepare job descriptions or summaries for each position to be surveyed.
- Contact the competitors with whom the organization would like to work. Selecting the wrong competitors in a market-driven system can be a major mistake, yielding results that are unusable. Volunteer to analyze data fully, in the format the survey participants would like to see and promise a quick response in providing results. Often, an external consultant, who can guarantee confidentiality, can perform data analysis effectively. The use of a third party to gather and analyze data is essential in some industries where the exchange of salary data can give the appearance of collusion and raise antitrust issues.
- Ask for a wide range of data such as salary range minimums, midpoints, and maximums as well as current average pay levels and typical starting salaries. The more data that are collected, the better the chance of making a true comparison. If an organization has an average pay level that significantly exceeds the midpoint because of high tenure in a particular job, data on the typical starting salary for that job can help prevent a misleading comparison. It also is useful to ask about incentive targets, typical payouts, and descriptions of what incentive plans reward. If an

organization pays for skills or knowledge, it should ask about the number of steps used by other organizations and the requirements to progress through each step. If an organization uses salary bands, it should ask about the range widths of each band used by other organizations.

* Share the survey results quickly, including data from the organization conducting the research. Everyone appreciates a prompt reply, and responsiveness can help ensure that these organizations participate in future surveys.

Compensation departments at large organizations usually participate in a number of surveys each year and are requested to participate in custom surveys on an ad-hoc basis throughout the year. Typically, organizations participate in annual market studies that often are tied to the end of the fiscal or calendar year. Published surveys have their own timelines that are set by the firm that compiles and analyzes the data. HRBPs and line managers can help the compensation department identify benchmark jobs and which surveys to participate in.

SALARY RANGES OR MARKET VALUE RANGES

Salary ranges and market value ranges are one of the most important determinants of pay on a daily basis. Understanding the fundamentals of ranges is critical.

Every salary or market value range has a minimum, midpoint, and maximum. These factors define the lowest possible level that someone should be paid, a *targeted pay level* or market-based pay level and a maximum pay level. Some companies divide their ranges into thirds; others use quartiles. Most organizations use the same terms in relation to managing pay within a range, as specified in Sidebar 2.3.

Sidebar 2.3 Terms Used in Managing Pay

Spread: The difference between the minimum and the maximum is often referred to as the "spread."

Starting pay point: The minimum or lower portion of the structure viewed as the lowest pay level a company would offer.

Midpoint/middle of the range: Defined as the place where fully qualified individuals are paid. Most compensation systems gear merit increases to move employees closest to, or within 10 percent of, the midpoint of the salary or market range. The maximum is the highest rate paid for a position in that grade.

Red/green circle: Employees above the maximum of the range will likely have their pay frozen until salary range adjustments bring them back within the range. This is referred to as *red-circling*. Employees whose starting pay falls below the minimum are referred to as *green-circling* and typically have their pay levels increased to the range minimum at the next review cycle.

Annual adjustments: Typically, ranges are reviewed and updated annually. Most often, the entire range is moved upward by a selected percentage, although in some cases organizations may elect to increase different salary grades by different levels to fine-tune their relationship to the market or to fix existing problems.

Forced distribution: Forced distribution of merit increases to remain within a specific budget is prevalent. In such systems, managers are required to only spend a specific amount, forcing them to distribute merit increases in such a way as not to exceed the budget.

Typically, the midpoint is geared to the marketplace as much as possible. The focus on midpoints can often cause problems for line managers and employees, who rightfully look at the entire salary range as their pay potential. Many employees question why they are unable to move up in their ranges, or always are compensated at approximately the same place in the range. It is important to remember that in a market-driven system, an employee who is at the maximum of a 50 percent wide range is being compensated 25 percent more than the going rate for that job. In a market-driven system, jobs are placed into grades based on the market. The position is slotted into the grade with the midpoint closest to the market value of the position. In an internally driven system, jobs are placed into grades based on point values.

Bands versus Ranges

Salary bands and salary ranges share many characteristics. Salary bands are typically wider than ranges and may include smaller market-based ranges within each band. This approach allows for more focus on individual market compensation levels. Such systems meet the goal of being flexible and responsive. In some organizations, all pay grades have been collapsed into as few as five pay bands. In many systems, each position has its own "band within the band," reflecting its competitive market, often referred to as the competitive zone.

Employees and line managers must be educated to understand that their salary band encompasses numerous positions and that the most relevant comparison for the employee is the comparison to market, or their competitive zone. In some organizations, the competitive or market zone is defined as plus or minus 10 percent of the market; other organizations elect to target competitive pay with plus or minus 20 percent. For many line managers and employees, the relatively tight difference between beginning and ending of market reference points implies that pay opportunities have been decreased, in comparison to more traditional salary ranges. Careful communication is key, as is ensuring that the ultimate design meets the organizational strategy.

STYLES OF RANGES

Attraction to salary bands has ebbed and flowed. Organizations using career bands also utilize hybrid approaches such as career banding (banding together several jobs in a family within a band), broad banding (creating ranges within each band that are tied to market data) or using wide ranges (to attempt to reduce the number of grades). Overall, many organizations design their salary ranges and use the decided format for a significant time. Changing between ranges and bands, or between market ranges within bands to regular ranges is infrequent. Thus, the selection of the style of range must be implemented carefully and after much consultation.

Organizations continue to use different ranges that reflect different marketplaces and/or to divide specific job families such as manufacturing, call center, or other specific roles.

RANGES AND THEIR CONNECTION PAY INCREASES

Ranges also are used to determine the size and frequency of merit increases. The most typical tool is a compa-ratio, which represents the individual's salary divided into the salary range midpoint. Many companies strive to have their consistently high-performing employees paid between 90 percent and 110 percent, or 95 percent to 105 percent, of the midpoint. To accomplish this, high-performing employees with low compa-ratios receive larger pay increases than high-performing employees with higher compa-ratios. This will move the high-performing employee's pay relatively quickly to the middle zone of the range. However, in organizations with very wide ranges and modest merit budgets of 2.5 percent, it is not uncommon for even a high-performing employee to take five years or more to reach the middle zone of the salary range. A sample compa-ratio-based merit structure based on a 3 percent average is shown in Figure 2.9. In this approach, a high-performing person who happens to be at the bottom of the range, perhaps because they were recently promoted, can expect a pay increase of up to 8 percent while a high-performing individual at the top of the range may only see a 1 percent increase.

FIGURE 2.9 Salary increase matrix using the compa-ratio approach.

Salary Increase Matrix using the Compa-ratio Approach				
Performance	**Compa-ratio**			
	0.80–0.89	0.90–0.99	1.00–1.09	1.10–1.20
Outstanding	7.0–8.0%	6.0–7.0%	5.0–6.0%	4.0–5.0%
Above Average	5.0–6.0%	4.0–5.0%	3.5–4.5%	3.0–4.0%
Average	3.0–4.0%	2.5–3.5%	2.0–3.0%	1.5–2.5%
Below Average	1.0–2.0%	0.8–1.8%	0.6–1.6%	0.4–1.4%
Unsatisfactory	0%	0%	0%	0%

In this approach, merit dollars are targeted toward both high performers and all employees whose pay falls at the bottom part of the range. However, it has become increasingly difficult to meet these common goals effectively with merit budgets of 2–3 percent. Automated tools ease the administrative burden, yet still leave the most onerous task untouched – determining how to allocate a limited budget. HRBPs play a critical role in helping line managers to make sound merit decisions, rather than succumbing to the pressure to simply offer everyone the same amount. Forced distribution of merit increases to remain within a specific budget are prevalent, testing the pay for performance philosophy used by many organizations. WorldatWork provides important and specific detail on merit increase practices on an annual basis.

Larger companies are implementing a variety of new administrative methods tied to salary range management in order to control the costs associated with base pay. Lump-sum increases for individuals who have reached target pay or the middle portion of the salary range are more common. Other hybrid approaches include partial lump-sum and partial base-pay increases for individuals approaching the midpoint, or the upper portion of a range. Such systems work well to control fixed costs but often lead to turnover as employees look for increases to their base pay.

COMPETENCIES/SKILL-BASED

In the 2000s, organizations began to examine competency and skill-based pay. Competencies can be created to reflect overall organization needs or the specific technical skills required for a position or job family. The majority of organizations have moved away from competency-based pay because of the complexities inherent in such systems (see Sidebar 2.4), and are instead focusing on using competencies as a key element in their selection systems, performance management systems, and employee development systems.

Sidebar 2.4 Factors in Assessing Appropriate Total Compensation

Helping people move along in their careers is one of the most important – and rewarding – roles played by HRBPs. One component of this role is to ensure that an employee's total compensation remains appropriate when the employee changes positions. To make an appropriate analysis, consider the following questions:

- Is either position eligible for the incentive plan? If so, what is the amount of the potential payouts? Does eligibility or payout timing change?
- Are there any perquisites tied to either position that could change, such as the use of a company car? How much do these perquisites add to the total compensation package?
- Does the new position require a move? What are the provisions of the organization's relocation policy? Are there different tax implications in the new location? Employees who are transferred between divisions sometimes find that their Social Security withholding starts again if the divisions are different legal entities. Some locations are subject to state or local income tax; others are not.
- Are there any special pay practices tied to either position that could change?
- What will the employee's new position in the range be? Will this make the employee eligible for a merit increase sooner?
- Does this change affect eligibility for benefits? Eligibility for the pension plan or 401(k) plan?

VARIABLE PAY

Variable pay plans represent the best, most consistent methods to pay for performance, enabling an organization to deliver targeted results while rewarding employees who are responsible for those results.

Designing Annual or Long-Term Incentives

A variable pay plan design is complex and requires a number of steps. Many large organizations have multiple variable pay programs in use at any time, and each program must work with all other programs.

- *Target Payout* Each plan sets a target payout level that often is expressed as a percentage of pay or midpoint, although it also can be expressed in terms of dollars. Sometimes there is a minimum or maximum amount that will be paid. Occasionally, plans will specify that minimum payouts

FIGURE 2.10 Types of variable pay.

1. Spot awards	Spot awards are given as quickly as possible based on superior performance or contribution. Such plans can range from $25 gift cards through formal programs offering 10 percent of base pay. Spot award programs are typically designed by HR and funded by the department.
2. Annual incentives	Annual incentives include the use of formal criteria in order to receive a payout. Typically, goals are cascaded down through the organization.
3. Long-term incentives	Long-term incentives are given only to the highest levels of management. Three- to five-year goals are set out. Payout occurs at the end of the three to five years.

will occur even if the plan's performance requirements are not met. Such a design is extremely rare but is sometimes considered in organizations that are substituting incentive pay for merit increases or other increases in base pay. In such cases, employees quickly begin to view minimum guaranteed payments as deferred base pay. A more effective approach is to fund the plan based on actual performance, and to set the funding at a level that requires stretch, but not impossible, performance levels. Maximum payouts are typically designed to control costs and prevent windfalls.

- *Performance Criteria* The best incentive plans measure and reward behaviors that are specific, measurable and within the participants' control. Designing plans that are within the participants' control often is the most troublesome part of developing or managing an incentive plan. In many cases, the behavior that managers want to encourage is beyond the employees' control. The design should create and encourage the line of sight between employees' day-to-day actions and the plan characteristics. In other words, a job family that cannot influence stock price should not be placed in an incentive plan that pays out based on increases in stock prices.

  Financial and operational incentive metrics are common. Balanced scorecard plans reward multiple areas and allow for tighter connection to business strategy as shown in Figure 2.11.

- *Duration* Each plan sets a time for measurement of performance and payment of bonuses. Typically, incentive plans are most effective when rewards are given soon after the results are measured, although longer time frames tend to be used for higher-level jobs. Management incentive plans generally are paid out annually, with ties to the organization's fiscal-year results. Lower-level employees, such as hourly workers, may have

FIGURE 2.11 Balanced scorecard.

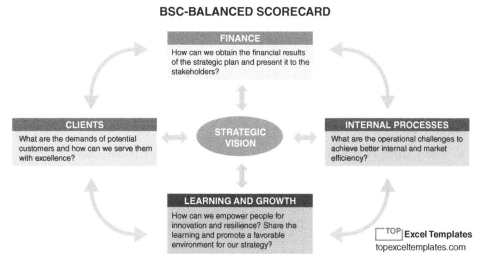

SOURCE: Balanced Scorecard (BSC) + Strategy Map – example template Excel spreadsheet. Retrieved from: https://topexceltemplates.com/free-templates/balanced-scorecard-strategy-map -example-template-excel-spreadsheet/

quarterly incentives. Typically, incentive plans are most effective when rewards are paid out as soon as possible after the results are measured. Many companies pay out incentives in separate checks to highlight the reward.

Reasons for Failure

Incentive plans typically fail when employees are not motivated or cannot influence results. Lack of motivation may be owing to a number of reasons.

- *Award Size* Awards that are too small will serve as irritants, not motivators. In general, 10 percent of pay is considered the smallest possible amount that can lead to changes in behavior. As merit budgets decline to the 2- to 3-percent range, this belief is being challenged and a 5-percent payout level is becoming more acceptable.
- *Plan Complexity* Any plan should be simple and easy to understand. Plans that measure three, four, or more things often fail, either because employees cannot understand what is expected or because employees perceive that their efforts in any one given area will not lead to a significant reward.
- *Control over Results* Incentives that are based on the wrong things can lead to an atmosphere of entitlement (i.e., rewards are "automatic") or windfalls (i.e., rewards are "unpredictable"), not motivation.
- *Senior-Level Support* Senior managers may change their minds about what behaviors they want to motivate, or they may eventually come to

believe that the amount they are paying to motivate performance is too much. In some cases, managers will not want to oversee a plan that creates a total compensation package that is higher than their own. Each of these factors can lead to a plan that is not supported by senior management, and, thus, does not succeed.

Other Considerations with Incentive Plans

Equally, there are many reasons why employees may not feel that they can influence the results, including:

- The plan uses funding measures (such as *economic value added*) that are complex and difficult to measure.
- The company sets performance targets too high.
- A high-performing group or division reports into an underperforming business unit with the business unit-wide performance incentive plan funding.

Incentive plans can be highly effective, but there are as many plans that underperform as plans that perform on target. Working closely with line managers and testing the plan to see how it fits the overall compensation program can minimize the risk of creating a plan that does not perform. Finally, incentive programs are more difficult to take out than to put in, therefore it is important that HRBPs and line managers spend time to think through the ramifications of implementing a plan.

Merit Budget and Pay for Performance

Merit budgets play an important role in organizations, as most employees will only see changes to their pay through merit, or a promotional increase. Compensation departments are responsible for creating merit budgets, determining annual changes or updates to ranges and creating supplemental budgets for promotions and market adjustments.

Merit matrix design is typically based on several factors:

- The degree of market movement for key benchmark positions from the prior year
- Company philosophy related to the market
- The company's ability to pay

Limited changes in market movement will often result in salary ranges that are not increased. Matrix development has been facilitated by Excel templates that develop the framework and allow for analysis of projected costs against the proposed budget.

Salary ranges are reviewed annually and are updated based on market data, comparisons to other organizations, and current position in the range. If the market has not changed substantially salary ranges may not change.

Organizations often use various methods, including merit budgets, promotional budget, and market adjustment budget. These budgets are often managed separately. Some organizations integrate merit and market adjustments, and others separate the two, depending on the type of ranges in use and the overall company philosophy.

In all cases, HR and the finance department work together closely to develop merit, market, and/or promotional budgets and to analyze potential costs. Senior management approves the budget prior to implementation.

Overseeing Salary Management

Along with ensuring that salary increases are given on time and that performance appraisals are accurate and timely, it is important to ensure that overall salary levels are appropriate. Therefore, it is important once a year to review the equity of the organization, division, or group to determine if there are any pay problems that need resolution. Many companies complete this step concurrent with the preparation of the merit matrix. The following steps may be taken:

Analyze the pay for all employees, sorted by salary level and job title. Request the average salary, average compa-ratio and the number of people in each portion of the salary ranges. The report also should detail each person's salary, time of service, last performance rating, date placed in current position, position in the range, last increase amount and next increase date.

Analyze the data. Review the data, using VLOOKUP up and pivot tables to identify potential problems. An employee who has long-term service in the job and solid performance history but is paid at the minimum of the range or at the bottom of his or her competitive zone should be considered for a special increase. In addition, look to see if individuals performing the same job are paid equitably. A report that can help identify problems lists position in the range, sorted by sex and equal employment opportunity (EEO) code. Finally, look to see if there are any "compression" problems (i.e., too little difference between an individual's pay and that of his or her supervisor). Although the days of maintaining higher salaries simply because of supervisory responsibilities are over, compression problems must be reviewed and explained.

Prepare an initial analysis of what kind of special pay adjustments are necessary to fix any inequities, including the amount of the increase and timing. Revise as necessary. Decide whether to request special pay increases all at one time, or whether they should be phased in at the time of service anniversaries or salary reviews.

This analysis is often combined with a diversity program analysis, which reviews actual or perceived inequities between various groups and/or individuals.

Proving the ROI

Compensation systems remain high-priority areas of focus for organizations. Efforts to better tie pay with performance, to target pay toward high performers and mission-critical positions and to prove return on investment

(ROI) are all key areas for the future. External scrutiny has become more common, as have requests for pay transparency. In addition, the ongoing pressures between costs and motivation are never-ending. Training in rewards management is a key element for success, as is remaining up to date on market trends through conferences.

THE REGULATORY ENVIRONMENT: THE FLSA AND OTHER LAWS THAT AFFECT COMPENSATION PRACTICES

One of the most important aspects of a compensation system is that it complies with existing laws and regulations, and that it be legally defensible in this era of litigation. It is critical for compensation experts and HR professionals to work closely to ensure that the organization's pay system is defensible and that everyone who works with compensation understands the relevant regulations. Figure 2.12 summarizes some of the existing laws that affect compensation practices, the most prominent (for pay program design purposes) being the Fair Labor Standards Act of 1938 (FLSA).

The remainder of this chapter addresses the laws regulating compensation practices.

FIGURE 2.12 Compensation regulation.

Rule	Details	Governing Body
Railway Labor Act	Grants the right of non-managerial and airline employees in the private sector to bargain collectively with their employers on questions of wages, hours, and work conditions	National Mediation Board
Davis-Bacon Act	Establishes wage and fringe-benefit standards for laborers and mechanics for federal public construction projects that exceed $2,000	US Department of Labor
Walsh-Healey Public Contracts Act	Establishes wage, hour, overtime pay, child-labor and safety standards for employees of manufacturers or suppliers of goods for federal contracts in excess of $10,000	US Department of Labor

Fair Labor Standards Act (FLSA)	Deals with minimum wages, overtime pay, equal pay for both sexes, child labor, and recordkeeping for employees engaged in interstate commerce or in production of goods for interstate commerce, or employed by an enterprise engaged in interstate commerce or production of goods for interstate commerce	US Department of Labor
Equal Pay Act (EPA)	Prohibits wage differentials based on sex for employees engaged in commerce or in production of goods for commerce, or who are employed by an enterprise engaged in commerce or production of goods for commerce	Equal Employment Opportunity Commission (EEOC)
Title VII of the Civil Rights Act (Equal Employment Opportunity Act)	Prohibits discrimination based on race, color, religion, sex, pregnancy, or national origin for employers with 15 or more employees and whose business affects commerce; employment agencies; labor organizations engaged in an industry affecting commerce; the federal government; and the government of the District of Columbia	Equal Employment Opportunity Commission (EEOC)
Service Contract Act (SCA)	Establishes wage and fringe-benefit standards for employees of suppliers of services to the federal government in excess of $2,500	US Department of Labor

(continued)

FIGURE 2.12 *(Continued)*

National Foundation Arts and Humanities Act	Establishes wage and working-condition standards for professionals, laborers, and mechanics directly engaged in working on projects receiving funding from the foundation	US Department of Labor
Age Discrimination in Employment Act (ADEA)	Prohibits job discrimination in hiring, firing, or conditions of employment against individuals aged 40 or older for employers of 20 or more individuals, employment agencies, and labor organizations	Equal Employment Opportunity Commission (EEOC)
Americans with Disabilities Act (ADA)	Prohibits discrimination against individuals with disabilities in employment, public services, public accommodations, and telecommunications for employers with 15 or more workers	US Department of Labor (DOL) Equal Employment Opportunity Commission (EEOC) Federal Communications Commission (FCC)
Civil Rights Act of 1991	Establishes two standards of discrimination under Title VII: disparate treatment and disparate impact	Equal Employment Opportunity Commission (EEOC)
Internal Revenue Code	Defines deductibility and tax treatment of compensation for all employees and all employers	Internal Revenue Service (IRS)
Securities and Exchange Commission (SEC) regulations	Regulate plans that provide employer stock to participants for all publicly held companies	Securities and Exchange Commission (SEC)
State laws	Affect minimum wage, hours, overtime pay, discrimination, and taxes for various employers	Vary by state

FAIR LABOR STANDARDS ACT OF 1938

The Fair Labor Standards Act of 1938 (FLSA) was born of the Great Depression and Franklin D. Roosevelt's "New Deal" administration. Roosevelt sent the bill to Congress in 1937 with a message that the United States should be able to give "all our able-bodied working men and women a fair day's pay for a fair day's work."

After a long, hard-fought battle, the FLSA was signed into law on June 25, 1938, and took effect on October 24, 1938. Its primary objective was workers' rights, and it was intended to eliminate detrimental working conditions, establish a minimum wage rate, and protect the educational opportunities of youth.

During his fireside chat right before the implementation of the act in October, Roosevelt commented that, with the exception of only the Social Security Act, the FLSA was the most far-reaching, far-sighted program for the benefit of the workers that had ever been adopted. He went on to say that, without question, this act started the United States toward a better standard of living and increased purchasing power to buy the products of farm and factory. Roosevelt then admonished some business leaders by saying that the American people should not let any "calamity-howling executive" with an income of $1,000 a day, who has been turning his employees over to the government relief rolls in order to preserve his company's undistributed reserves, tell you that a wage of $10 a week is going to have a disastrous effect on all American industry. Roosevelt closed his comments about the FLSA by declaring that this type of executive is a rarity with which most business executives most heartily disagree.

Hence, the FLSA became the principal federal statute that affects the design of direct compensation programs. In the beginning, only about one-fifth of the working population was affected by the act, which established a minimum wage of 25 cents per hour and a maximum workweek of 40 hours, or $11 per week. In its current state, after several amendments over the years, the act now covers more than 143 million workers in the United States and the current minimum wage is $7.25, but the maximum workweek is still 40 hours.

Effective January 1, 2020, the act was updated for the first time in more than 15 years, with the following changes:

- Raised the standard salary level to $684 ($35,568 annually) per week
- Raised the total annual compensation threshold for "highly compensated employees" to $107,432 per year
- Allowed the use of nondiscretionary bonuses and incentive payments (including commissions), paid at least annually, to satisfy up to 10 percent of the standard salary level
- Revised the special salary levels for workers in the US territories and the motion picture industry.

What Is the FLSA?

Congress enacted the Fair Labor Standards Act (FLSA) of 1938 to establish a floor for minimum wage (see Figure 2.13), overtime, recordkeeping, and child labor for employers nationwide.

Since it was enacted, a preponderance of case law provided a better understanding of the concept of the FLSA. However, recent amendments and interpretations by the courts have made it extremely important to understand the language of the FLSA. Moreover, because today's workforce and workplace are very different from what they were in 1938, it has become a challenge to comply with the FLSA while still meeting business needs.

Who Does the FLSA Affect?

The FLSA covers employers who are involved in interstate or foreign commerce, state and local government employees, federal employees employed by the Library of Congress, the US Postal Service, the Postal Rate Commission, and the Tennessee Valley Authority. Coverage is broadly interpreted and includes nearly all employers of all sizes. The 2020 amendment expanded coverage to include making an additional 1.3 million workers eligible for overtime pay. Certain employees, however, are considered exempt from some of the provisions of the FLSA, including minimum wage, overtime pay, and certain recordkeeping provisions. All other employees – designated as nonexempt – are subject to all of the provisions of the act.

FIGURE 2.13 History of the federal minimum wage.

1938	$0.25 per hour
1078	$2.65 per hour
1979	$2.90 per hour
1980	$3.10 per hour
1981	$3.35 per hour
1990	$3.80 per hour
1991	$4.25 per hour
1996	$4.75 per hour
1997	$5.15 per hour
2007	$5.85 per hour
2008 (July)	$6.55 per hour
2009 (July)	$7.25 per hour

The major provisions of the FLSA cover rules for:

- The determination of a minimum wage and a regular rate of pay to be used in the calculation of overtime
- The determination of which activities shall constitute hours worked
- Which positions can be classified as exempt
- Child labor restrictions
- Recordkeeping requirements

What Is Covered?

Minimum Wage

Minimum wage for covered, nonexempt workers is $7.25 per hour (as of July 24, 2009). Certain full-time students, student learners, apprentices, and workers with disabilities may be paid less than the minimum wage under special certifications issued by the US Department of Labor.

Tipped Employees

Tipped employees must be paid a cash wage of at least $2.13 per hour. This rule applies to employees who receive at least $30 per month in tips. However, if an employee's tips combined with the employer's contribution of $2.13 per hour does not equal the applicable minimum hourly wage, the employer must make up the difference to meet minimum wage.

Hours Worked

Hours worked are defined as the time when an employee begins, or is required to be available to begin, his or her principal activities of work until the conclusion of the employee's workday (when he or she ceases to perform the principal activities of work). The workday does not necessarily equate to the "scheduled workday" for the employee and can be much longer or shorter.

Workweek

A workweek is defined as seven consecutive, 24-hour periods totaling 168 hours. This is the unit of measurement used to determine compliance with minimum wage and overtime provisions. As defined in FLSA, the following applies to a workweek:

- It can begin on any day of the week and at any hour.
- It does not have to coincide with the duty cycle or pay period, or with a particular day of the week or hour of the day.
- Each workweek stands alone and cannot be averaged over two or more workweeks.
- Once the beginning and ending time of the work period is established, it remains fixed regardless of how many hours are worked within the period.

- The beginning and end of the work period may be changed, provided that the change is intended to be permanent and is not designed to evade the overtime requirements of the Act.

Rates of Pay and Overtime Calculations

The FLSA requires overtime pay, at a rate of time and one-half the regular rate of pay, for hours worked in excess of 40 in a workweek. Computing an employee's regular rate of pay can be complex. In general, the regular rate is the employee's average hourly earnings for a given workweek.

The regular rate of pay consists of all remuneration for employment, including:

- Base rate
- Shift premium
- Piece rate
- Nondiscretionary bonus
- Other regular pay allowances

Types of compensation that may be excluded from the "regular rate" include:

- Discretionary bonuses and gifts
- Reimbursement for expenses
- Payments for time not worked
- Benefit plan contribution
- Overtime premiums
- Third-party payments for insurance, pensions, etc.

The FLSA also explains how to calculate hourly rates of pay for multiple specific payment contexts (e.g., piecework rates and commissions). While the general rule for overtime pay requires employers to pay at least one-and-one-half times the regular rate of all hours worked over 40 in each week, the Act provides specifics for varying cases.

Child Labor Restrictions

The FLSA was created in part to protect the educational opportunities, health, and well-being of the youth under the age of 18 in the United States. There are restrictions on hours of work for minors under the age of 16 as well as a hazardous occupation restriction for all minors under the age of 18. Youths who are over 18 years of age may perform any job for unlimited hours. Provisions for nonagricultural jobs and farm jobs identify permissible jobs and hours, by age.

Nonagricultural jobs: Youth (minors under the age of 18) employment in non-agricultural jobs is subject to the following provisions:

- Minors between the ages of 16 and 17 years may work for unlimited hours in any nonhazardous job
- Minors between the ages of 14 and 15 years may
  - Work in nonmanufacturing, nonmining and nonhazardous jobs
  - Work no more than 3 hours on a school day, 18 hours in a school week, 8 hours on a nonschool day or 40 hours in a nonschool week

- Not begin work before 7:00 a.m. or end after 7:00 p.m., except for the period June 1 through Labor Day, when evening hours are extended to 9:00 p.m.
- May work up to 23 hours in a school week and 3 hours on a school day (including during school hours), if enrolled in an approved Work Experience and Career Exploration Program (WECEP)
- At any age, minors may deliver newspapers, perform in radio, television, movie or theatrical productions; work for parents in their solely owned nonfarm business or gather evergreens and make evergreen wreaths

Farm Jobs: Youth (minors under the age of 18) employment in farm jobs is subject to the following provisions:

- Minors over the age of 16 years may work for unlimited hours in any job, whether hazardous or not.
- Minors between the ages of 14 and 15 years may work in any nonhazardous farm job outside of school hours.
- Minors between the ages of 12 and 13 years may work outside of school hours in nonhazardous jobs, with a parent's written consent or on the same farm as the parent.
- Minors under the age of 12 years may work on farms owned or operated by the parent, or with a parent's written consent, outside of school hours in nonhazardous jobs on farms not covered by minimum wage requirements.
- Minors at any age may be employed by their parents in any work on a farm owned or operated by their parents.

The FLSA identifies restrictions for youth covered by the Child Labor Law. Generally, youth under the age of 18 are prohibited from working in occupations that are identified as hazardous. There are some exceptions that apply to work in agriculture. The following includes hazardous occupations banned for minors under the age of 18:

- Occupations in or about plants or establishments that manufacture or store explosives or articles containing explosive components
- Coal mining and mining other than coal
- Forest fire fighting and prevention, timber tract, forestry service, and occupations in logging and sawmilling
- Logging occupations and occupations in the operation of any sawmill, lath mill, shingle mill, or cooperage stock mill
- Exposure to radioactive substances and ionizing radiations
- Work involving power-driven hoisting apparatus
- Work involving power-driven metal forming, punching, and shearing machines
- Work involving the operation of power-driven meat processing machines, slaughtering, meat and poultry packing, processing, or rendering
- Occupations involved in the operation of bakery machines
- Occupations involved in the manufacture of brick, tile, and similar products
- Occupations in roofing operations

- Work involved with balers, compactors, and power-driven paper products machines
- Work involved with power tools, including saws, shears, woodchippers, and cutting discs
- Work involved in wrecking, demolition, and ship breaking
- Driving a motorized vehicle
- Trenching or excavating

Nursing Mothers

The Patient Protection and Affordable Care Act (PPACA), Section 7, of the FLSA, provides a break time requirement for nursing mothers.

Employers must provide reasonable break times for an employee to express breast milk for one year after the child's birth. The employer must provide a private location (not a bathroom), for the employee to express breast milk. State law may provide a greater employee benefit.

Only employees who are not exempt from FLSA's overtime pay requirements are entitled to breaks to express milk. State law may be different.

Employers with less than 50 employees are not subject to the break time requirement if it would impose an undue hardship.

Employers are not required to compensate nursing mothers for breaks taken for the purpose of expressing milk, if the employee is completely relieved from duty. If employers provide compensated breaks, an employee may use that break time to express milk and must be compensated the same as other employees for that break time.

Recordkeeping Requirements

Employers are required to keep records on wages, hours, and other information for all employees. These records must be saved for at least three years. No particular form is required nor are time clocks required.

Records required for nonexempt employees include:

- Name, home address, occupation, sex, and birth date if the employee is younger than 19 years
- Hour and day when the workweek begins for the employee
- Regular hourly pay rate for any week when overtime is worked
- Hours worked each workday and each workweek
- Total daily or weekly straight time earnings
- Total overtime pay for the workweek
- Deductions or additions to wages
- Total wages paid each pay period
- Date of payment and pay period covered

What Is Not Covered?

The FLSA does require payment for time not worked, such as:

- Vacation pay
- Holiday pay

- Severance pay
- Sick pay
- Meal periods of 30 consecutive minutes or more, duty-free
- Rest periods (breaks) of more than 20 consecutive minutes if the employee is completely relieved of duties

The FLSA does not mandate the following:

- Time clocks to record hours worked.
- Any kind of special pay or premiums for Saturday, Sunday, holiday, or sixth- or seventh-day work.
- That employees be paid at premium rates for hours worked in excess of eight hours per day, unless the employer chooses and is eligible for the 8/80 option.
- That an employer differentiates between exempt and nonexempt employees in any way other than minimum wage payments, overtime premiums, and records.
- The beginning and ending of a workweek in terms of starting and stopping on a specific calendar day or time.
- Meal period and rest period requirements (*Note:* The FLSA does mandate the ability to exclude such time in the calculation of regular rate).
- The frequency in which employees receive compensation (*Note:* Though the FLSA does not set specific intervals for pay periods, most states have regulations regarding the timing and payment of wages).
- Limitations on the number of hours worked in a day or in a workweek (*Note:* The FLSA does state that any work in excess of 40 hours in the workweek will be treated as overtime and compensated at one-and-one-half times the regular rate of pay).
- Pay for travel time outside of normal work/business hours when travel is overnight.
- That employers compensate employees on an hourly rate (*Note:* earnings may be determined on a piece-rate, salary, commission or other basis, but the FLSA does require that overtime calculations be based on the regular hourly rate of pay).
- Pay stubs or W-2s.
- A notice or reason for discharge or immediate payment of final wages to terminated employees.

Did You Know?

- Tipped employees can be paid a minimum wage of $2.13 per hour if they receive at least $30 per month in tips.
- Some states have higher minimum wage standards than those required by the FLSA. If a company employs workers in those states, it must comply with state regulations.
- The workday does not necessarily equate to the "scheduled" workday for the employee and can be much longer or shorter.

- The FLSA does not require employers to compensate nonexempt employees on an hourly basis.
- "Waiting to be engaged" and "engaged to wait" have different meanings under the FLSA.
- Employees must be paid for all hours worked, even if a supervisor did not approve the time worked.
- Employees must be paid for the time they take to seek medical attention for on-the-job injuries.
- Youth between 14 and 15 years of age cannot start work before 7:00 a.m. and must end work by 7:00 p.m. on any given workday (the time is extended to 9:00 p.m. from June 1 through Labor Day).
- The FLSA requires employers to keep pay records for at least three years.
- Meal and rest periods are not required under the FLSA.
- The FLSA does not mandate overtime pay for more than eight hours worked in one day. State and local regulations or union contracts may require payment of daily overtime.

SHERMAN ANTITRUST ACT OF 1890

The Sherman Antitrust Act of 1890, as amended, prohibits every contract, combination or conspiracy in restraint of trade and allows for the imposition of substantial penalties for violations thereof. Named after Sen. John Sherman, the act was proposed to address growing concern over the rapidly increasing prominence of large corporations, corporate trusts, and business combinations in the US economic landscape toward the end of the nineteenth century. Set forth as Title 15, §§ 1–7 of the US Code, the Sherman Act is based on Congress' constitutional power to regulate interstate commerce and was enacted at a time when the only similar laws were state statutes governing intrastate business.

Though the Sherman Act had immediate potential to aid the federal government in addressing concerns over increasing corporate power, its potential was not realized for several years. Initially, Supreme Court decisions effectively prevented its use by the federal government. Thereafter, Congress gradually put in place the supporting legislation and agencies necessary to successfully challenge anticompetitive activities. This building process began in 1904 when President Theodore Roosevelt launched his "trust-busting" campaigns and the Supreme Court found in favor of the federal government, dissolving the Northern Securities Company.

The Sherman Act's reach increased during the Taft and Wilson administrations with the enactment of the Clayton Antitrust Act and the establishment of the Federal Trade Commission in 1914. Further, the addition of supplementary legislation, such as the Robinson-Patman Act during President Franklin Roosevelt's administration, continued to improve the federal government's ability to challenge corporate actions on antitrust grounds. Finally, as federal antitrust agencies began broadening their interpretations of the antitrust statutes in the 1980s and 1990s, antitrust enforcement reached new heights, beginning with the 1982 breakup of the AT&T monopoly and culminating with the widely publicized Microsoft case, which ended in 2002.

Virtually since its inception, antitrust has been controversial. Proponents have seen it as a preserver of competition and a protector of consumers, while critics have viewed it as being based on flawed economic assumptions and as a destroyer of free markets and property rights.

Although the law prohibits contracts or conspiracies that result in trade restraint, the specific practices that are illegal are not spelled out in the law. Instead, they are left to the courts to decide, based on the facts and circumstances of each case. For example, the Supreme Court decided long ago that contracts or agreements that restrain trade "unreasonably" are prohibited, with the definition of "unreasonable."

Enforcing Antitrust

Antitrust enforcement primarily is handled by two government agencies: the Antitrust Division of the Department of Justice (DOJ) and the Federal Trade Commission (FTC). The DOJ concerns itself primarily with "conspiracies," "monopolies," and the like, while the FTC directs its attention to "unfair trading practices" in pricing, sales practices, etc. For issues related to the workforce, the Department of Labor is the enforcer.

These two antitrust organizations operate in a somewhat different fashion. The DOJ by itself cannot issue an order to impose a penalty. It must initiate a suit through the courts. The defendant may demand a jury trial. The FTC, however, is an autonomous administrative agency: It is complainant, judge, jury, and prosecutor all in one, and it can issue its own cease-and-desist orders. At no time is there a jury trial in an FTC procedure.

In either type of antitrust action, the defendant may appeal the verdict to higher courts. However, in a case that may involve thousands of pieces of evidence in the form of vouchers, receipts, purchase orders, etc., the courts tend increasingly to rely on "expert" government testimony as to what is "unfair" or "monopolistic." The Supreme Court, in particular, usually upholds the government's case.

DAVIS–BACON ACT OF 1931

Under the provisions of this act, passed in 1931, federal contractors and their subcontractors are to pay workers employed directly on the site of the work no less than the locally prevailing wages and fringe benefits paid on similar projects. The Department of Labor maintains a very helpful website with more detailed information related to this act, which is located at https://www.dol.gov/whd/govcontracts/dbra-guidance.htm.

NATIONAL LABOR RELATIONS ACT

The National Labor Relations Act (NLRA) of 1935 was enacted with the intention of creating a better environment for collective bargaining. The NLRA was created to provide a more equitable environment for labor and management dispute resolution, and covers all employers involved in interstate commerce (with the exceptions of airlines, railroads, agriculture and the government). The NLRA guarantees the right of employees to select or reject third-party representation, as well as the rules for bargaining in good faith and controlling against unfair labor practices. The enforcing agency of the NLRA is the National Labor Relations Board (NLRB). It is interesting to note that neither the federal courts nor the US Department of Labor have jurisdiction in matters concerning the NLRB.

WALSH–HEALEY PUBLIC CONTRACTS ACT (PCA)

The Walsh–Healey Act, as amended, provides general employment regulations and establishes minimum wage and maximum hours for work on contracts for employers holding manufacturing or supply contracts with the federal government in excess of $15,000. Although the law requires employees to be paid the minimum prevailing manufacturing wage established by the Secretary of Labor, the secretary has, as a result of litigation, issued the minimum wage as the "prevailing" wage since the 1960s. The law also established certain child labor and safety standards. The US Department of Labor (DOL) is the enforcing agency for the Walsh–Healey Act.

SERVICE CONTRACT ACT (SCA)

Passed in 1965, the Service Contract Act applies to federal contracts for services in excess of $2,500 and requires service contractors to pay minimum wages and fringe benefits as established to be prevailing by the Secretary of Labor. As with the Davis–Bacon Act, pay scales are based on "prevailing" wages, which is typically interpreted by the government as union-equivalent wages and benefits in the local labor market. The act also includes certain safety standards. The US Department of Labor is the enforcing agency of the Service Contract Act.

Recordkeeping and posting requirements, government investigations and hearings, court actions, and blacklisting of violators have been established as enforcement mechanisms for the Davis–Bacon, Walsh–Healey, and Service Contract Acts.

THE TAX CUTS AND JOBS ACT OF 2017 (TCJA)

TCJA includes several changes to how executive compensation is treated under the Internal Revenue Code.

The legislation reduces the corporate tax rate from 35 percent to 20 percent and, in doing so, amends or eliminates many current provisions including executive compensation requirements of the current tax code.

Notable changes include:

- Elimination of nonqualified deferred compensation arrangements
- Elimination of nonqualified stock options as a long-term incentive vehicle
- Elimination of performance-based exceptions to 162(m) or the $1 million cap on compensation deduction expense

Tax-exempt organizations being subject to a new 20 percent excise tax on compensation over $1 million paid to current or former five highest-paid employees, effective for tax years after Dec. 31, 2017.

ANTI-DISCRIMINATION LAWS

The federal government enacted several statutes in the 1960s that were designed to ensure the fair treatment of specific segments of the population regarding their rights as individuals and employees. The most important of these are the Equal Pay Act of 1963 and Title VII of the Civil Rights Act of 1964.

Equal Pay Act (EPA) of 1963

As early as World War II, the National War Labor Board was created as the arbiter of salary disputes between labor and management. In 1942, it issued an order for salary adjustments to "equalize the wage or salary rates paid to females with rates paid to males for comparable quality and quantity of work on the same or similar operations." A bill requiring "equal pay for comparable work" performed by males and females was introduced in Congress in 1945 and rejected, as were several similar bills for the next 18 years.

The EPA, which prohibits gender-based compensation discrimination, was successfully enacted in 1963. Specifically, the act prohibits an employer from discriminating "between employees on the basis of sex by paying wages to employees . . . at a rate less than the rate at which he pays wage to employees of the opposite sex . . . for equal work on jobs that require equal skill, effort, and responsibility, and are performed under similar working conditions." There are, however, four exceptions (affirmative defenses). Unequal payments can be based on (1) a seniority system, (2) a merit system, (3) a system that measures quantity or quality of production, or (4) any other factor aside from sex.

The act, an amendment to the Fair Labor Standards Act, was originally enforced by the Wage and Hour Division of the Department of Labor, and employers subject to the FLSA were subject to the provisions of the Equal

Pay Act as well. In 1979, the Equal Employment Opportunity Commission (EEOC) became the enforcing agency.

Plaintiffs who file lawsuits under the Equal Pay Act must show that they are paid less than a person of the opposite sex for doing substantially equal work (in the same job family) that requires substantially equal skill, effort, and responsibility and is performed under similar working conditions. Once the prima facie case has been established, the burden shifts to the employer to prove that the pay difference is based on a seniority system, a merit system, a system that measures earnings by quantity or quality of production or some other factor aside from gender.

The bottom line of the Equal Pay Act for pay program design and administration is that if, on the average, men and women are paid different rates when they perform work that is substantially the same, these differences must be shown to be attributable to one of the "allowable differences."

The effects of the Equal Pay Act have been far-reaching and include the revision of employee benefit programs to eliminate gender-based differentials, greater emphasis on written job descriptions, greater emphasis on job-content-oriented procedures for assignment of pay grades and ranges to specific jobs, and greater emphasis on written policies and procedures.

Title VII of the Civil Rights Act of 1964

The most comprehensive of the civil rights statutes, this legislation was created to prohibit discrimination by employers on the basis of race, color, religion, sex or national origin, in the hiring, firing, training, compensation or promotion of employees. On the last day of debate, sex was added as a prohibited basis of discrimination, creating overlap with the Equal Pay Act.

For cases subject to this overlap on sex-discrimination in pay, the Senate added the Bennett Amendment that (ambiguously) states, "It shall not be an unlawful employment practice under Title VII for any employer to differentiate upon the basis of sex in determining the amount of the wages or compensation paid to employees of such employer if such differentiation is authorized by the provisions of the Equal Pay Act." Regardless of how the amendment is interpreted, differences in pay may be defended if attributable to work that is not substantially equal, or is based on seniority, merit, or quantity and quality of work.

The Civil Rights Act is enforced by the EEOC, which was created by the act. Virtually all employers with 15 or more employees are covered.

Employees who file lawsuits under the act must demonstrate either "disparate treatment" or "disparate impact." Under "disparate treatment," the plaintiff must prove that the employer deliberately discriminated, based on the employee's race, color, religion, national origin, or sex. If this is done, the employer must demonstrate a legitimate nondiscriminatory basis to justify the practice; then, in order to prevail, the employee must prove that any such "justification" is just a pretext for discrimination.

Under "disparate impact," the employee must establish a prima facie case showing adverse impact on a protected class. Then the employer must validate the challenged practice by demonstrating a business necessity for the practice and proving that no alternative exists that would produce a less adverse impact.

The bottom line of Title VII for pay program design and administration is that pay programs should produce pay rates that treat all classes of employees similarly, and any differences should be attributable to job-related, defensible causes (seniority, performance, and the like). Case law resulting from litigation under Title VII created the concept of "bona fide occupational qualifications" (BFOQ). This concept specifies that job qualifications imposed by employers must be defensible and necessary for an employee to perform the job.

The Pregnancy Discrimination Act of 1978

This Act amends Title VII of the Civil Rights Act of 1964 and prohibits sex discrimination based on pregnancy. Women affected by pregnancy, childbirth, or medical conditions related to pregnancy or childbirth shall be treated the same in all employment-related purposes, including receipt of benefits, as others not affected by pregnancy.

Title VII of the Civil Rights Act of 1991

This amendment to the Civil Rights Act of 1964 addresses several Supreme Court decisions that did not follow established precedents. Some key cases that shaped this Act were *Price Waterhouse v. Hopkins* (1989) and *Wards Cove Packing Co v. Antonio* (1989). Decisions made in these cases made it more difficult for plaintiffs to prevail in a dispute.

The 1991 Act clarified each party's obligations in a disparate impact case (*Wards Cove Packing*), shifting the burden of proof to the employer. The employer must prove that a challenged practice is job-related and consistent with business necessity.

The update addressed mixed motive cases. In a mixed-motive case (*Price Waterhouse*) the employer will be found guilty of discrimination if an illegal factor motivated the employment decision.

The Act also provides for a jury trial as well as compensatory and punitive damages in Title VII and ADA claims of intentional discrimination. Caps are placed on the maximum amount of damages awarded based on employer size.

The Act expands the right to challenge discriminatory seniority systems. If an illegal employment practice occurs within a seniority system, the seniority system may be challenged at several points in time: (1) when the seniority system is adopted; (2) when the individual is subjected to the system; or (3) when the individual is negatively impacted by the system.

Age Discrimination in Employment Act (ADEA) of 1967

The Age Discrimination in Employment Act, passed in 1967 and amended several times, protects workers aged 40 and older from employment discrimination. The ADEA applies to private employers with at least 20 employees, state and local governments, employment agencies, labor organizations, and the federal government. While it prohibits discrimination in all terms and conditions of employment, it has been applied mainly in cases involving retirement, promotions, and layoff policies.

The purpose of the act is to "promote employment of older persons based on their ability rather than age, to prohibit arbitrary age discrimination in employment, and to help employers and workers find ways of solving problems arising from the impact of age on employment."

The law prohibits mandatory retirement (with some exceptions, generally involving public safety), limiting or classifying employees in any way related to their age (such as with maturity curves), reducing any employee's wage in order to comply with the act, and indicating any preference based on age in employment advertising. Individual state laws sometimes are more restrictive than the federal law.

There are several statutory exceptions to the ADEA:

- Bona fide executives who are entitled to $44,000 per year or more in retirement benefits from employer contributions. Mandatory retirement at age 65 is allowed.
- Elected (or high-level appointed) officials in the government are not covered.
- Bona fide occupational qualifications (BFOQ), defined as an occupational qualification that is reasonably necessary to the normal operation of the employer's business. Employers may discriminate on the basis of age if it is reasonably necessary to the normal operation of the business
- Bona fide seniority system
- Firefighters and law-enforcement officials
- Bona fide benefit plan
- Reasonable factors other than age

The EEOC has been charged with the enforcement of the act since July 1979. The plaintiff must prove that he or she is a member of a protected group and that he or she has been adversely affected by a personnel policy or action (prima facie case). Once this is established, the burden shifts to the employer, who may argue that the adverse treatment occurred based on considerations other than age or that the decision or policy was rightly based on age (e.g., if age is a BFOQ for the job).

Executive Order 11246

This presidential order, signed by President Johnson in 1965 and amended since that time, requires companies holding federal contracts or subcontracts in excess of $15,000 not to discriminate in their employment practices (which include pay practices) on the basis of race, color, religion, sex, sexual orientation, gender identity, or national origin. Additionally, there is a requirement to take affirmative action to ensure that employment decisions are made in a nondiscriminatory manner. Executive Order 11246 also prohibits employers from taking adverse employment actions when applicants and employees discuss information about pay.

For service and supply contracts in excess of $50,000, contractors must also develop and implement written affirmative action plans that include goals and objectives of increasing minority and female participation in their workforce.

This executive order is enforced by the Office of Federal Contract Compliance Programs (OFCCP) in the US Department of Labor. The OFCCP also investigates complaints of discrimination and conducts on-site compliance reviews to determine federal contractors' compliance with the mandates.

Rehabilitation Act of 1973

The act covers persons employed by, or seeking employment from, federal departments and agencies or businesses performing federal contract work in excess of $2,500. Recipients of federal assistance are also protected from discrimination based on any mental or physical disability that substantially limits one or more major life activities. Section 503 of the Act applies to private industry and Section 504 applies to institutions receiving federal grants. Discrimination in employment is prohibited in all terms and conditions of employment, which certainly includes compensation. The standards for determining employment discrimination under the Rehabilitation Act are the same as those used in title I of the Americans with Disabilities Act.

The act is enforced by the OFCCP, which requires covered employers to utilize affirmative action to employ and advance qualified disabled individuals. The act also requires employers "to make reasonable accommodation to the known physical or mental limitations of an otherwise qualified, handicapped applicant, employee or participant." Further, the act requires the elimination of physical barriers, to ensure that the "facility is readily accessible to and usable by qualified handicapped individuals."

Charges under the Act proceed in the same way as for Title VII. If, for example, a human resource policy or action has an adverse effect on a disabled person, the employer must then show that the adverse treatment was based on considerations other than the disability (e.g., seniority or performance) or that the disability was a legitimate basis for such policy or action. This last defense is rare in compensation cases.

Vietnam Era Veterans Readjustment Act (VEVRAA)

The Vietnam Era Veterans Readjustment Act, as amended, requires companies doing business with the federal government to take affirmative action to recruit, hire, and promote veterans, including disabled veterans and recently separated veterans. Employers may not discriminate in the employment and advancement in employment of protected veterans.

The act is enforced by the OFCCP, which investigates complaints and checks for compliance with the act during on-site investigations.

Americans with Disabilities Act (ADA) of 1990

The Americans with Disabilities Act (ADA) of 1990 was enacted to include any company involved in interstate commerce with 15 or more employees. A charge of discrimination must be filed within 180 days of the alleged discriminatory act. The Act is enforced by the EEOC.

A disability is defined as an impairment that substantially limits or restricts a major life activity such as hearing, seeing, speaking, breathing, performing manual tasks, walking, caring for oneself, learning, or working. Any employee or job applicant who meets the following criteria may be covered under the ADA:

- Has a physical or mental impairment that substantially limits one or more of the major life activities
- Has a record of any such impairments
- Is regarded as having such impairments
- Is associated with anyone having such impairments

This provision is designed to protect any qualified individual, whether or not they are disabled, from disability-related discrimination. The individual must be qualified for the job and must be able to perform the essential functions of the job. A definition of essential functions should include the following criteria:

- Reason the position exists is to perform the function
- Limited number of other employees available to perform the function
- Degree of expertise or skill required to perform the function

Under the ADA, if an employer can reasonably accommodate a request by a disabled employee (or applicant), the person is required to accept it. A reasonable accommodation is any change or adjustment to a job or work environment that permits a qualified applicant or employee with a disability to participate in the job application process, to perform the essential functions of a job, or to have the benefits and privileges of employment equal to employees without disabilities. Failure to provide reasonable accommodation to a qualified individual with a disability is a violation of the ADA, unless to do so would impose an undue hardship on the operation of the business. The Act identifies three criteria to measure reasonableness of accommodations:

1. The size of the business
2. Number (or type) of facilities
   - Budgetary constraints
   - Type of operation

- The composition
- The makeup of the workplace

3. Nature and cost of accommodations

Americans with Disabilities Act Amendments Act (ADA Amendments Act) of 2008

The ADA Amendments Act was enacted to restore the intent and protections of the 1990 American with Disabilities Act. Supreme Court decisions (*Sutton v. United Air Lines and Toyota Motor Manufacturing, Kentucky, Inc., v Williams*) made under the ADA narrowed the scope of protection intended by the ADA.

The ADA Amendments Act made several significant changes to the definition of "disability" to ensure the definition would be broadly interpreted and applied without extensive analysis by an employer. The amendment expands the definition of "major life activities" by providing a nonexhaustive list of major life activities that specifically includes the operation of major bodily functions. The Act makes it easier for employees to show that their disability influences one of their "major life activities."

Uniformed Services Employment and Reemployment Rights Act (USERRA) of 1994

USERRA prohibits employment discrimination against a person based on past military service, current military obligations or intent to serve. USERRA applies to those who perform duty, voluntarily or involuntarily, in the "uniformed services," as well as the reserves. Employers cannot deny employment, reemployment, retention in employment, promotion, or any benefit of employment to a person based on a past, present, or future service obligation, regardless of the size of the organization.

The Act establishes a five-year cumulative total of military service with a single employer, with some exceptions. The purpose of the law is to minimize disruption to people in uniformed services as well as employers by providing for prompt reemployment on completion of service. The law is also aimed at minimizing disadvantages to civilian careers resulting from uniformed service.

Employee rights under this Act include:

- Continuation of position, seniority, status, and pay rate as if there had not been a break in employment, with the same seniority, status, and pay.
- Reasonable efforts (training or retraining) must be made to enable returning service members to qualify for reemployment.
- While the individual is performing military service, the individual is entitled to the same rights and benefits afforded to other individuals on nonmilitary leaves of absence.

- If performing military duty longer than 30 days, the individual may elect continuation of employer sponsored health care for up to 24 months and may be responsible for up to 102 percent of the full premium.
- If performing military duty less than 31 days, health care coverage is provided as if the individual remained employed.
- Pension plans are protected, with individuals treated as if they had continuous service with the employer.

USERRA covers nearly all employees, including part-time and probationary employees. The Act applies to virtually all US employers, regardless of size. The US Department of Labor's Veterans' Employment and Training Service (VETS) administers USERRA.

Genetic Information Nondiscrimination Act (GINA) of 2008

The Act protects employees or applicants against discrimination based on genetic information in any aspect of employment, including hiring, firing, pay, job assignments, promotions, layoffs, training, fringe benefits, or any other term or condition of employment. Genetic information should not be used in an employment decision because it is not relevant to an individual's current ability to do the job.

The Act prohibits discrimination against employees or applicants based on an individual's genetic tests, tests of an individual's family members, and information relating to an individual's family medical history.

Genetic information about applicants, employees, or family members must be kept confidential and in a separate medical file apart from the personnel file.

The EEOC enforces Title II of GINA, which focuses on genetic discrimination in employment.

Lilly Ledbetter Fair Pay Act of 2009

The law extends the time frame for filing pay discrimination claims brought under Title VII, ADEA, ADA, and the Rehabilitation Act. The law creates a rolling time frame for filing wage discrimination claims taking the position that each paycheck containing discriminatory compensation is a separate violation regardless of when the discrimination began.

This law overturned the Supreme Court's decision in *Ledbetter v. Goodyear Tire & Rubber Company*, which restricted the time period for filing complaints of employment discrimination regarding compensation.

This Act covers employer decisions about base pay or wages, job classifications, career ladder or other noncompetitive promotion denials, and failure to respond to requests for raises.

The EEOC enforces this Act.

3 Market Pricing and the Battle for Prize-Winning Talent

Being aware of prevailing wage rates in the external marketplace is critical to an organization's success. Employers need to keep a watchful eye on fluctuating pay rates and market price their jobs to maintain competitiveness. Market pricing is defined as the process of analyzing external salary survey data to establish the worth of jobs, as represented by the data, based on the "scope" of the job (company size, industry type, geography, etc.). Market pricing continues to outpace all other methods as the dominant form of job evaluation, particularly for executive jobs. More than one-third of organizations market price at least 80 percent of their jobs, according to a 2020 study conducted by WorldatWork and gradar, Inc. When jobs are market priced, the external market is the key determinant of job value that influences pay philosophy.

In this method, job rates are set based on the organization's best estimate of the typical wage rates in the external marketplace for that job. Job descriptions are used to match appropriate jobs. Market data are analyzed and benchmark jobs are arranged into a job-worth hierarchy. Jobs with no market data are slotted using relative worth.

With so many salary surveys available, where does one begin sorting through the maze of data to arrive at competitive market rates? Where can employers find sound, unbiased data that correspond to the jobs they need to market price? How should an organization communicate its pay program to employees? These seemingly never-ending questions can make a compensation analyst's head spin.

The successful execution of pay programs calls for a delicate balance between often-competing objectives; for example, the desire to attract and retain the best-qualified employees versus competitive constraints on labor costs. Organizations need to weigh the cost of the compensation program against other factors, such as being less competitive in the labor market to improve operating margins.

WHERE DO YOU BEGIN?

To maintain a competitive edge, organizations should make pay adjustments according to job market fluctuations. So, where should the compensation professional begin? First, the organization's pay structure should be examined. Salary structures are the foundation of most employee compensation programs. They represent job hierarchies and pay ranges within an organization. The salary structure may be expressed in terms of job grades, job points, pay lines, or any combination of these. These structures reflect the internal job value hierarchies and external job value relativity.

It is understood that the greater the relative worth of the job – as determined by job content and labor market analysis – the higher its pay grade and range. Pay grades and ranges are determined by market rates for comparable jobs (external competitiveness), in conjunction with management's judgment about the relative worth of the job's content (internal equity).

The process of developing a pay structure involves the following steps:

- Job analysis.
- Job documentation.
- Job evaluation.
- Collecting and analyzing labor market data.
- Establishing pay rates or ranges.

JOB ANALYSIS

Job analysis is a systematic process for obtaining important and relevant information about the duties and responsibilities that make up the job content. For compensation purposes, this includes clarifying the nature of the job, including tasks and responsibilities, as well as the level of work being performed. This also may include specific skill or knowledge levels required to perform all aspects of the job at a competent level. The first step is to determine what information needs to be collected. Data should include the extent and types of knowledge, skill, mental and physical effort, and responsibility required for the work to be performed.

JOB DOCUMENTATIONS AND JOB DESCRIPTIONS

Job descriptions are narrative statements of the nature and level of work being performed by persons occupying a job, along with specific duties, responsibilities, and specifications necessary to perform the job. Increasing legislation and employee litigation have made job documentation a must. Most formalized pay programs use written job descriptions to document job content. A job description should describe and focus on the job itself and not on any specific individual who might fill the job.

From a market-pricing standpoint, job documentation is needed to evaluate the content of a job in relation to other jobs in the marketplace. Job documentation also is needed for the following HR administration purposes:

- Ensure that employees are assigned to appropriate jobs.
- Facilitate job-content evaluation.
- Facilitate salary-survey exchanges (if job matching).
- Explain, and, when necessary, defend certain pay-program decisions to employees and others.
- Assist in attraction and selection efforts.
- Establish performance standards.
- Facilitate organizational design.
- Assist in establishing career paths.

JOB EVALUATION

Job evaluation is a formal, systematic process for determining the relative worth of a company's jobs. It is used to ensure that a company's compensation system is equitable. The job, not the employee, is evaluated and rated.

Two basic methodologies have been used in developing a job-worth hierarchy: one starting with and emphasizing market data; the other starting with and emphasizing job content. In both cases, job content is important – the difference is in the starting point. Each employer must determine which approach suits the organization's needs. To a great extent, this will be determined by the number of distinct jobs in the organization, and the necessary resources for the pay program's design, installation, and maintenance. The nature of the labor market also is critical.

BENCHMARK JOBS

Market pricing begins with the selection of benchmark jobs, which serve as market anchor points. Although most pay programs recognize the market's role in ranking jobs, some existing formal systems use market rates as the primary basis for establishing job worth. Benchmark jobs are chosen, priced from survey data, and assigned relative values based on market levels. All other jobs then are positioned in relation to these benchmarks.

Benchmark jobs closely resemble other jobs performed in other organizations and/or across industries. Benchmark jobs should:

- Be well-represented positions in the marketplace.
- Be important in the organization's internal hierarchy.

- Represent many organizational levels or grades in the salary structure(s) utilized by the company.
- Be matched to 70 percent or more of the duties found in the survey jobs.
- Generally have multiple incumbents with the exception of managerial and executive-level positions within an organization.

Benchmark jobs also serve as internal anchor points for non-benchmark jobs. For example, a bookkeeper and an administrative assistant assigned the same pay grade and salary range now become the anchor points for assigning other positions without market data matches. Assignments of non-benchmarked jobs is called slotting because it involves comparing or evaluating the value of the job, not based on market factors or points, but on the job's relative worth compared to other jobs that were evaluated.

COLLECTING THE RIGHT DATA

Now that you've identified, analyzed, documented, and evaluated the jobs that need to be market priced in your organization, it's time to collect market data for your selected benchmark jobs. The process of collecting this data is part of market pricing. Many employers establish their job-worth hierarchy primarily on the basis of external market data, such as salary levels paid by other employers for jobs similar to their own. To use market data properly to establish the job-worth hierarchy, employers must identify the relevant markets and be able to collect external pay data on at least 50 percent of their organization's jobs. All remaining jobs will then be slotted into the pay structure as appropriate.

The overall purpose for collecting market data is to make informed decisions about the organization's compensation program. These decisions involve pricing jobs, analyzing pay trends, identifying pay practices, and establishing a job-worth hierarchy. A variety of data collection methods and factors is available to help determine the method that should be used.

Caution. In gathering and analyzing salary survey data, a determination should be made as to whether jobs described in the survey are comparable to jobs in the organization. If so, it is valid to use the survey data. If job documentation is inaccurate, incomplete, or outdated, invalid comparisons and decisions may result.

DECISION FACTORS IN COLLECTING MARKET DATA

Organizations should take the following factors into consideration when deciding which data collection source to use:

- *Cost.* Is the cost of the survey reasonable for the number of positions for which you will be able to market price and the number of employees represented in the data? Do you have the budget for the survey?

- *Time.* If you are considering conducting your own survey or having a customized survey completed for you, how much lead time do you need? How old are the data reported in the survey?
- *Reliability/accuracy.* Is the source of the data credible? Have the data been verified for accuracy? Is the sample size significant enough to accurately represent the marketplace?
- *Availability.* How easy are the data to access? How open was the survey for participation? Can you purchase the survey even if you didn't participate?
- *Confidentiality.* Is the information collected in the survey kept confidential?

Exxon, nursing groups in Utah and Connecticut, along with the Federal Reserve Bank of Boston, were accused of price fixing salaries based on surveys they devised. Both the DOJ and the FTC established some basic steps to follow to ensure you are not impeding the free market for labor through survey design. These following steps are called the antitrust safety zone:

- An independent third party (consultant, academic institution, government agency, or trade association) should manage the survey. The DOJ and the FTC allow some exchange of information without a third party, depending on the use and the anticompetitive effect. When conducting your own survey, seek legal counsel.
- Data provided by survey participants must be more than three months old.
- Use at least five survey participants, with no individual participant's data representing more than 25 percent weighted basis of a given statistic.
- The results must be reported so recipients cannot determine specific participant data.

KNOW THE MARKET: HALF THE BATTLE

Knowing the organization's relevant labor market is key in selecting and participating in the right surveys. The relevant labor market can be defined in terms of "employee sources and destinations," which could be described as the markets from which the organization draws employees and the markets to which it loses employees. These markets can be defined in terms of industry, organization size, and/or geographic location. Figure 3.1 lists types of labor markets that might be identified for three job groups in a pharmaceutical firm with annual sales of $2 billion.

There are numerous valid and reliable methods of market pay data collection and analysis. Before collecting pay data, an organization should define its relevant labor market, which may consist of:

- Similar organizations in the local labor market (i.e., similar size or comparable industry).
- All employers in the local market.

FIGURE 3.1 Sample labor market – large pharmaceutical firm.

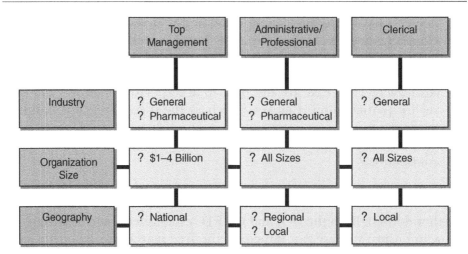

- Similar organizations in the regional or national market (i.e., similar size or comparable industry).
- All employers in the regional or national market.

Employers will want to use surveys that include data from competing organizations in the labor market. Therefore, this survey sample may vary widely between different groups of jobs. Typically, considerations include the geographic area, size of the organization (number of employees), revenue, industry, and other factors deemed pertinent to the group being surveyed.

GATHERING VALID DATA

There is no exact market rate for any job. Compensation professionals must rely on market data to determine going market rates for jobs, but a plethora of available surveys can be mind-boggling. It's also a double-edged sword. On a positive note, there is an abundance of information from which to choose. On the flip side, wide-scale availability can lead to careless survey selection and inappropriate data.

Factors, such as sample size, participant base, statistical analyses, survey methodology, and job-matching procedures, impact the accuracy of the final market rate composite for a benchmark job. As a rule of thumb, salary information is expected to be reflective of the marketplace within plus or minus 10 percent. Consequently, a market index of 95 percent to 105 percent can be viewed as fully meeting competitive market pay levels.

In addition, availability of pay data on the internet is growing. Employees with a roving eye are swayed easily by the extensive salary information that's available on websites devoted to listing salaries by job title and location.

However, not all posted data are reliable or validated. Before using this data, organizations need to ask:

- What is the targeted audience for the website?
- What is the data source?
- Are the data from employer-based surveys or from individuals who enter the site?
- How is the website maintained?

To ensure collection of the relevant data, organizations first should determine:

- What compensation data need to be collected?
- For what jobs are salary data needed?
- From which labor markets are survey data needed?
- Does the data focus exclusively on base pay or does it include target incentive pay?

An organization should conduct a needs assessment to reveal the type of surveys required for its job market pricing effort. This appraisal shows what data need to be in the surveys, which jobs need to be reported, and what industry and regional breakdowns are needed. Multiple surveys, when available, help to cull all of the pertinent data and ensure a more accurate picture of the relevant labor market.

DATA SOURCES

Purchase Published Surveys

There are thousands of published surveys available for purchase. The purchase price varies by survey source, survey scope, type of analysis, and overall sophistication of the final product. Also, most survey providers give a substantial discount to survey participants. Employers will want to use surveys that include data from competing organizations in the labor market. Therefore, this survey sample may vary widely between different groups of jobs. Typically, considerations include the geographic area, size of organization, revenue, industry type, and other factors deemed pertinent to the job group being surveyed.

Caution: When using the same survey source from year to year, ensure that changes in the survey participant group do not unduly influence changes in market rates.

Be aware that incumbent numbers may have a dramatic impact on the survey averages. A large employer who is hiring many people may report a lower average per job compared to last year because of new hires who are brought in at a lower rate than more senior incumbents. Conversely, a company downsizing may show higher pay rates year-over-year if layoffs tend to cull the less senior and lower-paid workers.

By carefully identifying the organization's needs and researching a wide variety of available surveys, you can accurately select the ones that will deliver

---

Survey Content Checklist

Before purchasing a survey, ask the following questions:

- What information was collected? Is it consistent with your needs?
- What companies were surveyed? Do they match your needs?
- How much data are available for each job or role?
- Are the appropriate statistics reported? (For example: average, weighted average, median, percentiles, bonus/incentive, total compensation/total cash)
- What is the effective date of the data in the survey? Is it current enough for your needs? Can the data be aged easily?
- How expensive is the survey? Is there a price advantage for survey participants? Can nonparticipants purchase the survey?
- Has the survey been conducted by a reputable third-party survey provider? Does the survey have a history of providing credible information?
- Can the survey organization provide additional data analyses? Can you do additional analyses?

---

the most relevant data to your company. The following information will be useful in your survey search.

Conduct Your Own Survey through a Third Party

After thorough investigation of the data collection alternatives, an organization may decide to conduct its own survey, ranging from formal and comprehensive to a quick, informal phone or fax survey for limited data. Conducting your own survey allows you to gather data that meet your specific needs. The company will have more control over the data collection and analysis if it conducts the survey itself, although it may be the time-consuming choice.

Compensation surveys can range from quick phone surveys covering readily available information to highly complex studies involving sensitive information and requiring sophisticated mathematical analysis. A survey can be conducted by the following methods:

- Telephone interviews
- Online questionnaires
- Email interviews
- Any combination of the above

Regardless of the method used to collect data, be specific and consistent about the information you are gathering. Make sure you're getting the same type of information from all participants: range, starting rate, number of incumbents in the job, etc.

The cost of gathering data is important and must be taken into consideration. Parameters should outline time constraints, reliability of the data, the need to control the quality of the data collected, and the necessity to keep the data confidential. Data access is another consideration. Many companies choose to only provide survey data through a third party (versus another employer) for a number of valid business reasons.

The third party can be a professional association, graduate students from a local university, or a consultant – anyone who is knowledgeable about survey methodology and research. In many cases, participants in a survey sponsored by an individual company pay nothing to receive a copy of the survey results. The advantage of using a third party is that the company can target its competitors and may receive a higher participation rate because of third-party confidentiality.

Use Free Sources

Many consulting organizations have websites containing sample survey data. Before using such data, you should be sure the information is current and includes adequate descriptions on the benchmark jobs. The Bureau of Labor Statistics (BLS) offers free downloadable information on salaries and wages. The home page address is http://www.bls.gov.

Collecting public information (e.g., proxy statements) is another reliable source of free information.

CAPTURING COMPETITIVE MARKET DATA FOR HIGH-DEMAND JOBS

In light of the shortcomings of traditional surveys, how do you measure the market for high-demand, hot-skills jobs? Remember, hot skills are needed in the market, but are in short supply and in high demand; for example: nurses, engineers, IT, telemarketers, etc. Some techniques include:

- Shift the focus from the more broadly defined job role to individual employees with specific skills (e.g., SAP application developer) needed to do the work.
- Create high-technology skill and skill-level definitions.
- Define base skills and capture compensation data on them to serve as a reference point for determining the premium for high-technology skills.
- Capture a richer array of survey data by blending data to get a "feel" for the job.
- Conduct the survey more frequently than once a year. Some skills are in high demand and the market will adjust rapidly.

In the case of IT pay, companies are finding market data useful in determining appropriate pay ranges for their employees, and also for valuing worker's knowledge and skills acquisition. Like base pay, the market value for skill-based pay is driven by supply-and-demand economics. However, unlike salaries, skill-based pay tends to fluctuate more dramatically from quarter to quarter in reaction to the market.

CRUNCHING NUMBERS

Now that the survey data have been selected, it is time for data analysis. Interpreting published survey data is complicated by the fact that survey administrators can choose different approaches to collecting and displaying survey results. The challenges are in making sound decisions about the data that need to be extracted from a particular source and interpreting these data appropriately when they are analyzed across several sources. Although numbers and formulas can seem intimidating, "easy does it" is the rule of thumb with this simplified process.

Survey data analysis is not a science; it's more of an art. The key to interpreting data successfully is to understand how statistics are computed in any given survey and blend that information into your own organization's compensation philosophy. If this information is not documented in the survey report, contact the survey publisher to verify computations.

Several issues should be considered when analyzing survey data:

- Options for measuring central tendency
- Percentiles
- Aging data
- Weighting market data across survey sources

Options for Measuring Central Tendency

What's the best measure of a job's going market rate? Most surveys provide multiple measures of central tendency, or the measure of the "center" of all data collected for the data set. The common measures of central tendency are median (exact middle point in the data), mean (average), and mode (the most frequently occurring single data point in the data set). In most surveys, the common measures of central tendency are reported as the unweighted average, the weighted average, and the median. The best one to use depends on the information being sought. Unweighted average gives equal weight to every organization represented in the data. It answers the question: "On average, what are companies paying for this job?" (See Figure 3.2.)

- *Weighted average* gives equal weight to every salary represented in the data. It answers the question: "On average, what are incumbents in this job paid?" You can weight by number of companies ($n = 136$), or number of employees ($n=150$).
- *Median* identifies the middle rate in the data set. It answers the question: "What is the exact middle salary in a set of ranked salaries?" For example, if the data set contains the ranked salaries of 51 accountants, the middle salary would be the 26th ranked salary because there are exactly

FIGURE 3.2 Unweighted average by number of surveys.

Survey	Number of Companies Represented	Number of Employees Represented	Base Salaries Reported
1	56	60	$47,500
2	47	55	$53,100
3	33	35	$55,400
	136	150	Total: $156,000
			Average: $52,000 ($156,000/3)

FIGURE 3.3 Weighting by number of employees.

Survey	Number of Companies Represented	Number of Employees Represented	Base Salaries Reported	Weighted Average of Base Salaries Reported
1	56	60	$47,500	$2,850,000
2	47	55	$53,100	$2,920,500
3	33	35	$55,400	$1,939,000
	Totals	150	$156,000	$7,709,500
			Weighted Average:	$51,397 ($7,709,500/150)

25 salaries ranked below it and 25 salaries ranked above it. A large difference between mean and median statistics can be the result of a sample that is skewed high or low by a few unusual cases. Means, or averages, can be affected dramatically by such skewing; medians are less susceptible to data extremes. Which statistics to use is still a matter of choice. However, unless you have a high degree of confidence in the sampling representation and the data analyses, the median is likely the best estimate of the "typical" pay for the job. In Figure 3.3, the median salary is $53,100.

Percentiles

Surveys also may provide information in the form of a percentile, which defines the value below which a given percentage of data fall. For example, if a salary survey shows $60,000 or the 90th percentile for the data, then 90 percent of survey respondents pay below $60,000 and 10 percent of survey respondents pay above $60,000. The 10th, 25th, 75th, and 90th percentiles are the most often reported. The data point at the 50th percentile also is the median of the data set. Percentiles may be important to an organization whose philosophy is to pay above market or track market leaders.

Aging Data to a Common Point in Time

It is important to age published survey data to one common point in time so that accurate and consistent market comparisons can be made between the market and internal average pay. You can combine data from multiple surveys to reflect a common point in time by determining the annual aging factor.

Important considerations in selecting an annual aging factor and the date to which you want to age the data include:

- Compensation levels increase at different rates in the marketplace. For example, the rate of increase in executive pay generally exceeds the rate of increase in non-exempt pay on an average annual basis. Consequently, you should research market movement based on such considerations as:
  - Industry type: health care, finance, manufacturing, service, etc.
  - Job level: nonexempt, exempt, or executive
  - Geographic location: Southern, Eastern, Western, Central
  - Type of compensation: base salary or total compensation
- To select an appropriate annual aging factor (e.g., increase nonexempt data by 4 percent and executive data by 5 percent), you can review surveys that present data on annual-increase budgets, such as the annual WorldatWork Salary Budget Survey. This approach assumes that actual pay in the labor market increases by the budgeted increase amount.
- The year-over-year increase in mean/median market rates within a single survey source often is reported in the survey's introduction or executive summary. This change in mean/median market rates is potentially one of the more accurate measures of market movements. However, the increases are historical rather than projected.
- To age data across two calendar years, you should develop a separate aging figure for each year, and then combine the two percentages.
- The lead, lag, or lead-lag structure policy will determine to what point in time you should trend your survey data for purposes of establishing competitive pay structure midpoints. For example, if your fiscal year is January through December and your policy is lead-lag, you will trend all data to July 1.

Weighting Market Data Across Survey Sources

A decision regarding weighting survey data will be a function of a number of criteria, including:

- *Compensation strategy.* You will weight surveys in your industry more heavily if you have established a strategy that defines your competitive labor market as industry-specific.

- *Quality of surveys.* The statistical analyses provided – participant base and number of cases per job, among other factors – contribute to the perceived quality of a survey. Based on judgments about this quality, some surveys will receive more weight than others. For example, if one of your sources is an in-house survey, you may choose to weight this source more heavily than sources obtained externally.
- *Quality of job match.* Certain job matches are more appropriate than others based on job content, and market data can be weighted accordingly. This job-specific weighting factor can supplement or override previously established survey source weights. To generate an objective weighting factor at the job level, the number of cases (employees or companies) can be used to weight the raw data. Surveys that most accurately capture your labor market and best reflect your jobs' contents – and provide accurate and appropriate statistical analysis – are those to which you will give the most weight.

DEVELOPING MARKET INDEX OF COMPETITIVENESS

The market index will reflect market-pricing decisions already made in selecting appropriate surveys and survey statistics and in matching your jobs to survey jobs. How do you develop an analysis of your organization's overall pay competitiveness?

Use the following formula to calculate the market index of competitiveness:

Market index = Company average salary ÷ Market average salary.

For example, according to Figure 3.4, Job D is the least competitively paid relative to the market. What else do you notice about company salary versus market salary? What is the overall market index?

FIGURE 3.4 Company salary versus market salary.

Job	Market Average Salary	Company Average Salary	Market Index
A	1,300	1,400	1.08
B	1,430	1,450	1.01
C	1,570	1,500	0.96
D	1,730	1,600	0.93
	6,030	5,950	0.99

How do you know if jobs and incumbents are paid competitively? Answering these questions correctly requires thoughtful review and interpretation of the data in relation to these issues:

- *Nature of the job.* Some jobs serve as entry-level positions through which employees pass quickly. Thus, job tenure is low and turnover is high. If employees typically are hired at grade minimum or low in the range, the job will have a low market index – a situation that is both expected and acceptable, assuming you can attract adequate numbers of qualified candidates.
- *Type of job evaluation plan.* If the company uses a "market pricing and slotting" evaluation plan, a job with a high or low market index can be re-slotted into a different grade based on market pricing results. If, however, the company uses a quantitative evaluation system, such as job content or point factor method, a job with a very low or very high market index may have to be "green-circled" or "red-circled" to ensure the continued internal equity of all jobs. (See Sidebar 3.1.) Number of incumbents in the job. It is more typical for a heavily populated job to have a normal distribution of pay, and, therefore, to be paid closer to the market rate composite. Consequently, in a bank, a market index of 83 percent for the teller job will be of greater concern than the same index for the single-incumbent accounting manager job.
- *Individual incumbent characteristics.* Employee factors such as education, skill, ability, seniority, and individual performance must be considered when interpreting the comparison of market rate composites with internal pay levels. It is acceptable and desirable to pay incumbents above or below market on the basis of individual characteristics.

Sidebar 3.1

Green-Circle Rate

A green-circle rate is below the minimum of the range rate and usually occurs when the wage structure is changed upward and the employee was at the bottom of the salary range. To rectify this situation, the employer can raise the pay immediately or in a couple of steps. All green-circle rates should be examined for discrimination.

Red-Circle Rate

A person paid above the maximum of the range for his or her job receives a red-circle rate. A red-circle rate is above the established range maximum assigned to the job grade. This situation is more difficult to deal with than a green-circle rate. Solutions vary from doing nothing to reducing the pay to the top of the range. Per company policy, an employee may not be eligible for further base pay increases until the range maximum surpasses the individual pay rate.

Market Adjustments

If you completed a market study for a position that already exists, you may recommend the position to be assigned to a different salary grade and/or recommend pay adjustments for current employees in the job. This action is called a market adjustment.

If a pay grade change is not recommended, you may suggest pay increases to employees who are not being paid close to or over the midpoint, or market rate, for the job. In this instance, the decision to provide pay increases will be based, in large part, on how difficult it is to fill the position, how important the position is to your business, and your company's compensation philosophy.

Below New Range

When an employee's salary is below the new range, the organization may select from a variety of methods to bring the salary within the new range. However, the amount of the increase will be affected by the amount by which the employee is below the minimum and the number and the size of increases it would take to get to the minimum.

For example, if your organization has a policy limiting the amount of any one increase or the total annual increase in pay, it will be necessary to determine if one increase will close a large percent gap, or if two or more increases will be required.

Caution: Although there is no federal law pertaining to the payment of employees below salary ranges, one must be cognizant of the employees below the range. Some organizations might have a policy stating that it is acceptable to have employees below the range; however, it is the organization's responsibility to ensure the policy is administered consistently and does not adversely affect any one employee or groups of employees.

MARKET BLIPS – A WORD OF CAUTION

Typically, "blips," or unusual swings of the market, are associated with a "hot-skills" job or a tight labor market in a specific location. They usually occur when the demand for a specific job increases because of an external event, or, on a smaller scale, when an organization is new to the area and it pays above market to initially attract critical talent.

For example, getting compensation right for technology professionals is an especially nagging problem. For decades compensation and benefits teams have experienced constant market price volatility for tech jobs, driven by the swinging pendulum of hot skills and tech labor supply and demand. No less of a challenge has been the multidimensionality of hard-to-fill tech positions with their countless combinations of skills, knowledge, and experience in jobs that no salary survey can possibly capture.

And it's not just the tech skills that make it difficult: Try calculating pay and balancing internal equity when there's also hybridism in how these jobs fit along a tech-business continuum. Layered throughout the enterprise, tech jobs often require knowledge and experience in specific company products or services, business processes and solutions, and even industries and customer niches.

In this scenario, an organization that adjusted all of its salary grades upward to accommodate this "hot skill" for some specialized positions (e.g., coder) had to reassign some employees into a lower grade. In some instances, the organization red-circled employees who were paid over the new range maximum.

Before seeing a "blip" in the market for jobs that you have priced:

- Consider delaying a change in salary grade for the position and communicate to the hiring manager the ability to hire-in at midpoint of the range or above.
- Consider removing the range maximum for these "hot-skills" positions that are difficult to recruit but whose wages are temporarily inflated.
- If you are beginning to see a trend in market data over time for a position that is not classified as "hot-skilled," review data over a three-year period to see if a grade movement is appropriate.

Get creative! If you're keeping a close watch on your total rewards budget, you can add to the compensation of "hot-skills" individuals without adding to their base salary with lump-sum merit increases, recruitment bonuses, retention bonuses, and a plethora of rich benefits and well-being offerings.

APPROACHES TO PROGRAM COSTS

Compensation professionals need to understand how pay program design and administration methods affect program costs or budgets. The design of successful compensation and benefits programs calls for a delicate balance between often-competing objectives: Employers want to attract, motivate, and retain the most qualified employees, while facing competitive constraints on labor costs. To accomplish these objectives successfully, employers need to weigh the cost of the compensation program against other factors, such as being less competitive in the labor market to improve operating margins.

Whether market pricing individual jobs based on a job evaluation process or conducting a market analysis of benchmark positions to determine salary structure and pay competitiveness, determining the compensation program's cost is an important part of the planning process.

Costing of compensation programs can be as simple or as sophisticated as you choose to make it. It is important, however, to identify both first-year costs and any ongoing costs associated with the program. In many industries, labor costs account for 50 percent of all operating costs. With typical merit and salary programs, costs are compounded because the base salary of the employee is not fixed but keeps growing over time with each new merit increase awarded. To determine the costs of compensation decisions, you will need specific information regarding three key elements:

- Size of the average increase if looking at structure adjustments and amounts of actual increases if looking at market adjustments.
- Number of employees receiving increases (participation), including the length of time between increases (frequency).
- Timing of when the increases become effective (effective period).

There are three primary approaches.

All-at-Once Approach

The simplest option is to increase pay to eligible employees who are paid below market by giving those employees a salary increase in an amount that will move them up to market rate. In doing so, the initial cost of the increase will be higher than other options, but each employee will immediately be paid at market rate. However, it will be important to work with your finance department to ensure that by doing this, you will not impact your company's profit margins significantly.

Phase-In Approach

Although giving all employees a salary increase at one time is fairly straightforward and easy to administer, not all organizations have the available funding to support this type of increase in the first year. A way to administer the same increase, but lower the first-year cost, is to phase in the increase throughout the first year. This is accomplished by staggering the increases over a longer period of several months (or longer) to lower the first-year costs.

Wait-and-See Approach

The wait-and-see approach is another way to address a group of employees paid below market rate. Occasionally, the demand for a job or group of jobs may increase. This increase could lead to a temporary higher market wage for this group of employees.

With the wait-and-see approach, the compensation professional will "wait and see" what the market does before any increases are given. By waiting a set period of time, the market wage may either stay at the new higher level or decrease to a previous level. If the market wage decreases to a previous level, then the wage increase witnessed was a temporary increase based on external or unusual market conditions. If the wage increases continue, then the compensation professional will follow one of the two previous methods (all at once or phased-in) to implement a salary increase. If you notice that the market wages for a particular position have remained relatively flat for an extended period of time and then appear to spike, you may want to take a wait-and-see approach. However, be aware that the wait-and-see approach may cost you more than wages if the market is paying a premium for skills and you are not. Some of your employees may be lured away to the highest bidder, which could cause higher turnover in those hard-to-fill positions.

HOW TO KEEP EMPLOYEES IN THE LOOP

Pay delivers a strong message. Research indicates that the most financially successful companies are more likely to communicate pay information to their employees, as well as provide training to first-line supervisors on pay communications.

Employees have a desire to know what methods are used to define and determine the value of jobs within their organization. In the context of this chapter and as stated previously, pay is calculated through market pricing according to the organization's compensation philosophy. Openly communicating pay policy – in addition to your total rewards strategy – helps build trust in the employer-employee relationship and breaks down any misconceptions about their overall remuneration that may have arisen.

Who Should Communicate the Message?

The person who communicates the pay information to employees should not be a fellow employee in the same department. The communicator should be chosen based on the specific pay action and audience and could be any of the following individuals:

- Supervisor
- Department manager
- HR manager

To relay pay messages to employees in a lasting manner, the supervisor is the most effective channel and should be at the center of the communications effort. Employees' perceptions about the organization's pay system are shaped through dialogue with their managers and via formal and informal communications programs.

As ongoing communication with employees enhances the effectiveness and acceptance of the pay program and helps reduce misperceptions, it is critical that the communicator is equipped with the right information. "Train the trainer" sessions will help supervisors communicate the most accurate and up-to-date pay information to employees.

Managers can't afford to guess about competitive compensation in the marketplace. A ballpark answer is not good enough. They need to communicate precise answers to head off any employee concerns. If the compensation program is to contribute effectively to the overall employee relations program, employees in the organization must perceive that their level of total pay is fair and competitive. Although employees may argue for pay adjustments based on comparisons with only the highest-paying employers, they usually recognize that an employer responds to labor market averages. They will not become seriously dissatisfied unless they perceive their total compensation level as lower than that of a significant majority of employees performing similar jobs through the relevant labor market.

What Information Should Be Communicated?

The supervisor or manager should communicate pay adjustments simply and concisely from the employee perspective, while focusing on the main elements of the pay action, including:

- What is the reason for the pay action?
- How will the pay action be processed?
- When will the pay action become effective?
- Is the pay action a one-time adjustment?
- Will the pay action be in a lump sum or a periodic action?

OPENING THE PAY DIALOGUE

A major part of every manager's or supervisor's job is answering questions about the compensation program. In today's competitive business environment, many companies have abandoned secrecy about their pay program in favor of openly conveying information to their employees. Increasingly, organizations are making public information about pay ranges and merit budgets.

For example: After performing a market pricing analysis for an accounting clerk position, it is decided there will be a pay adjustment. When communicating this information to employees who will be granted the increase, the manager or supervisor should be prepared to answer a variety of employee questions and observations, including:

- "Why can't I receive the full increase now?"
- "Why didn't I receive an increase when my coworker, who has not been here as long I as have, received an adjustment?"
- "What do I need to do to get the increase?"

Being aware of potential questions and appropriate answers is key to effective communication. It is a good idea to brainstorm possible questions and answers with coworkers. In doing so, you will be able to anticipate problem areas and be prepared to address employees' questions and concerns. An open exchange of dialogue will enhance communication, understanding, and reinforce employees' trust in the organization.

4 Linking Pay to Performance via Merit Pay

The purpose of merit pay is to reward individual contributions from employees and to encourage their best performance possible. It is often included within the broader concept of "pay for performance." In the past 20 years, much has changed concerning organizational performance management practices, and their handling of various forms of incentive pay. While some have called for the end of merit pay plans, according to a 2019 survey by Mercer, they remain one of the more widely used means by which US organizations determine employee pay increases. To paraphrase Mark Twain, the "death" of merit pay plans has been greatly exaggerated. The purpose of this chapter is to address how merit pay can serve to reward employee contributions and encourage individual performance. In theory, if all employees operate at peak efficiency relative to their capabilities, the organization will thrive.

The logic behind merit pay is straightforward: If pay is more contingent on performance, then employee motivation to achieve high performance is increased (see Figure 4.1). Three motivational theories are relevant here:

1. Reinforcement theory states that merit pay should motivate improved performance because the monetary consequences of good performance are made known – the better one's performance, the greater the pay increase will be.
2. Expectancy theory states that merit pay should motivate improved performance because performance is instrumental to the attainment of a pay increase – improved effort to perform leads to increased pay.
3. Equity theory states that merit pay should lead to improved performance because a pay raise is seen as a fair outcome for one's performance input – the more one contributes to the organization, the greater the pay increase.

FIGURE 4.1 Linking pay to performance.

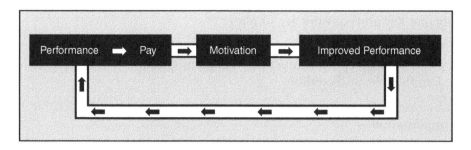

A successful merit pay program will do the following:

- Reward employees for achieving performance results and exhibiting behaviors aligned with the objectives of the organization, which ideally are linked directly to the strategic business plan and mission of the organization.
- Provide rewards commensurate with contributions, i.e., bigger pay increases for stronger performers.
- Be communicated easily to employees.
- Be understood readily by employees.
- Recognize "bottom-line" considerations and the organization's ability to deliver pay increases.
- Be rational, structured, and administered in a logical manner.
- Conform to legal requirements.
- Use a well-founded, credible means of evaluating performance.
- Conform with and support management philosophy.

All organizational incentives – including merit pay plans – should be planned carefully to achieve these goals. If an organization takes the time to design its merit pay plan carefully, it can establish a linkage between pay and performance.

DETERMINING WHAT TO REWARD

Before a merit pay plan can be designed, the first steps are to determine:

- What the organization values.
- Which types of individual employee contributions should be rewarded.
- The organization's ability to pay.
- The organization's ability and willingness to communicate the plan.
- The organization's ability to administer the plan.

Some organizations make these determinations through the planning efforts of senior management, who refer to the overall business strategy and mission. Other organizations use a structured human resource planning

FIGURE 4.2 Getting started on a merit plan.

Verify that key prerequisites are in place:

- Top management support
- An established performance-management system that is reliable, valid, fair, flexible, and credible

Conduct research to verify that merit pay is appropriate and workable for the organization:

- Review of prior merit pay theory and research
- Collection of information on other employers' experiences with merit pay, focusing on those that are regarded as highly successful and highly unsuccessful as well as those that are similar in management style and organization
- Evaluation of the effectiveness of the merit pay program by establishing a baseline of employee attitudes and perceptions about pay

Form an employee task force to oversee the development of the plan and ensure workforce buy-in, with the following functions represented:

- Line management
- HR professionals
- Employees representing different "levels" in the organization
- Nonexempt employees, if appropriate for the organization's culture

---

effort, which relies on formal performance-planning and goal-setting activities. Other organizations make informal determinations. Steps to start a merit pay plan are listed in Figure 4.2.

Without a clear understanding of the organization's values and expectations, it is possible that employee contributions that are contrary to the organizational objectives will be rewarded. A successful plan requires that individual goals be aligned with the organization in terms of:

- *Identity,* which relates to whom the organization serves and what products and services are provided.
- *Strategic plan,* which relates to how the mission of the organization is accomplished.
- *Objectives,* which relate to what corporate goals have been established.

Once the link between individual and organizational objectives has been defined, merit pay can be used to align individual goals with those of the organization. When used properly, merit pay will reinforce the accomplishment of individual contributions that are in line with the identity, strategic plan, and objectives of the organization.

Merit pay also must be consistent with regard to the business environment of the organization. Business environment characteristics that support or detract from merit pay are shown in Figure 4.3.

FIGURE 4.3 How business environment characteristics relate to merit pay.

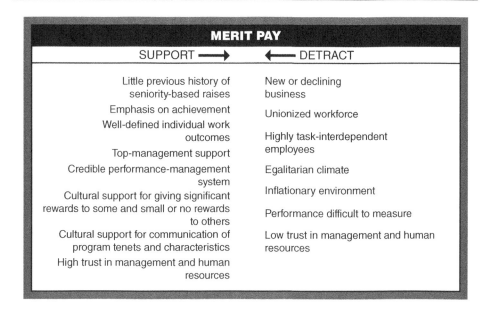

MERIT PAY	
SUPPORT ⟶	⟵ DETRACT
Little previous history of seniority-based raises	New or declining business
Emphasis on achievement	Unionized workforce
Well-defined individual work outcomes	Highly task-interdependent employees
Top-management support	
Credible performance-management system	Egalitarian climate
Cultural support for giving significant rewards to some and small or no rewards to others	Inflationary environment
	Performance difficult to measure
Cultural support for communication of program tenets and characteristics	Low trust in management and human resources
High trust in management and human resources	

DOCUMENTING PERFORMANCE STANDARDS

The second step in developing a merit pay plan is to devise a system that establishes and evaluates performance against individual objectives. Performance standards, also known as performance goals or objectives, are written statements that help determine the extent to which employees have contributed to the mission of the organization. These standards establish the basis on which employee contributions are evaluated, and they define the expected level of performance. A variety of rating systems are used to describe how successful an employee has been in attaining objectives. Some examples of common performance standards are shown in Figure 4.4. The past two decades saw an increase in organizational use of forced rankings, and then a rather abrupt decline. While this is a story for another setting, what has not changed is the need for clear performance standards to be set, and then for managers and others to make use of those standards to differentiate between levels of individual employee performance.

While establishing performance standards, it is critical to determine which standards best meet an organization's needs. Objective standards – such as quality and quantity of work performed – should be assessed as well as more intangible, subjective aspects of the job such as teamwork, cooperation, and customer service.

Documentation of work standards is an essential part of the performance evaluation process. This is most often done as an annual event in which supervisors and subordinates discuss goals and objectives for the coming

FIGURE 4.4 Examples of common performance standards.

Quality
Demonstrates work quality by producing goods or services that meet or exceed preset, measurable standards (e.g., less than one defect per thousand items).

Quantity
Meets or exceeds specific production quotas within a given period of time.

Communications
Effectively expresses thoughts verbally, in writing and nonverbally. Listens attentively and makes productive use of acquired information. Gains agreement and acceptance of plans, ideas, or activities being discussed while incorporating others' good suggestions.

Creativity and Innovations
Conceives, encourages, develops, and applies imaginative concepts that improve operating procedures and efficiencies, or that make better use of company assets.

Interpersonal Teamwork
Works well with others toward the accomplishment of goals. Earns respect and trust. Makes a contribution to the team's achievements. Shows consideration for the feelings and needs of others.

Planning and Organizing
Defines and prioritizes objectives. Installs a thorough, appropriate plan of action. Establishes procedures to monitor progress toward task completion. Can manage multiple projects, priorities, or deadlines to accomplish long- and short-term goals.

Problem Analysis
Identifies problems, secures relevant information and relates data from different sources to determine possible causes of problems.

year while evaluating the prior year's performance. In some organizations, determining and documenting work standards is a cooperative effort between managers and employees. Other options include the following:

- Have managers determine objectives and then communicate them to the employee.
- Have employees present goals to their managers for discussion.

However work standards are established, obtaining employee buy-in is essential. If employees cannot comprehend the standards or accept their reasonableness, they are unlikely to perform in a manner that is consistent with the mission of the organization. To help ensure that employees accept and act on performance standards, three actions should be taken:

1. *Emphasize results and behaviors rather than traits.* Performance standards should reflect what the person produces (results) or what the person does (behaviors) rather than personality characteristics (traits). For example, it is better to measure the quality of performance by using a result such as "number of customer complaints" or a behavior such as "is always courteous to customers" than it is to use a trait such as "is nice to people."

2. *Employees should participate in setting standards.* For employees to act on performance standards, they must be committed to them, which means that they need to have a sense of ownership in the process. When employees are given an opportunity to help establish performance

goals and objectives, they are more likely to feel as if they "own" the process and to protect their ownership interests by meeting the standards.

3. *The standards should be flexible.* It is the nature of work and organizations to be in a constant state of flux. Consequently, performance objectives and standards that are viable now may – because of influences outside the control of the employee – become obsolete. An organization should be willing to modify standards as shifting demands dictate.

ESTABLISHING A MERIT BUDGET

A fundamental feature of any merit pay plan is an established budget that has been endorsed by management. Every year that a merit pay plan is in effect, the budget process should consist of two key activities:

- Determine the size of the budget.
- Allocate funds to business units within the organization.

Determining Budget Size

Salary-increase budgets are typically established each year based on many factors, including:

- Actual or anticipated organization financial results
- Cost-of-living and/or inflation
- Industry trends
- Competitive factors such as retention rates and recruiting successes
- Cost of labor and the competitive position of the organization's pay in the marketplace
- Group (e.g., division or department) performance and needs

In most organizations, it is common to obtain or develop salary budget surveys each year that show expected increase rates for similar employers. WorldatWork and many of the major compensation consulting groups conduct annual salary budget surveys and publicize their findings widely.

On the basis of survey information, and after taking into account the organization's financial situation, senior management ordinarily will approve a not-to-be-exceeded "bottom-line" increase budget computed as a percentage of current payroll. Recently, merit-increase budgets have averaged approximately 3 percent annually.

Determining Budget Allocation

The next step in the budget process is to determine how funds are to be distributed to business units within the organization. A common method of allocating merit pay dollars is to use a uniform budget. Under this procedure,

FIGURE 4.5 Example of a uniform-budget allocation.

Department	Total Payroll Dollars	Merit Budget Percentage	Merit Budget Dollars
Finance	$2,450,500	4.0%	$98,020
Human Resources	$1,750,900	4.0%	$70,036
Marketing	$4,375,055	4.0%	$175,002
Production	$7,980,250	4.0%	$319,210
Totals	$16,556,705	4.0%	$662,268

merit pay budgets are distributed to divisions or departments as a percentage of "eligible payroll," which is defined as the aggregate base salaries of all employees who are eligible to participate in the merit pay plan.

Eligibility may be driven by a calendar date. Some organizations include only those employees who have exceeded a minimum service requirement such as six months at the time of their expected date of increase. Other organizations will include all employees on payroll, but will prorate increases for those employees with a partial year of service.

Using the uniform-budget approach, every business unit in the organization shares proportionally in the amount of money available for salary increases. Figure 4.5 is an example of a uniform-budget allocation.

Use of uniform budgets fails to take into account that some business groups are more or less successful than are others. Furthermore, in organizations with geographically dispersed business activities – some of which may be located in areas with different cost-of-living, inflationary, or competitive pressures with respect to the workforce – a uniform budget may be inappropriate.

To respond to differing achievement levels of the various business units or the need to pay different wages in certain locations, some organizations use a flexible-budget approach. The flexible-budget method introduces a level of complexity into the budget process that is not present in uniform merit budgets. Unlike uniform budgets, flexible budgets require sound measures of business-unit performance and geographic pay differences to distribute budget dollars. Many organizations are ill-prepared to track or calculate these differences accurately. Figure 4.6 is an example of a flexible-budget allocation (budget percentages have been rounded). In this example, Marketing and Production were viewed as contributing more significantly to company performance in the prior year than other departments, and were allocated higher merit budget percentages. Additionally, Finance and Human Resources are located at headquarters, which has a lower cost of living, and were allocated smaller merit budgets.

FIGURE 4.6 Example of a flexible-budget allocation.

DEPARTMENT	TOTAL PAYROLL DOLLARS	MERIT BUDGET PERCENTAGE		MERIT BUDGET DOLLARS	
Finance	$2,450,500	3.1%		$75,966	
Human resources	$1,750,900	3.6%		$63,032	
Marketing	$4,375,055	4.3%		$188,099	
Production	$7,980,250	4.2%		$335,171	
Totals	$16,556,705	4.0%		$662,268	

SETTING MERIT PAY POLICY

The essential goal of a merit pay plan is to link pay to performance in a way that is consistent with the mission of the organization. To cement this link, pay increases must vary according to the level of an employee's contributions and efforts. There are two required conditions:

- Variations in employee performance must be measurable and measured.
- Managers must be provided with the necessary "tools" to determine the appropriate rewards.

These tools are to be found in the established guidelines or policies that govern pay increases as well as in the process for implementing these guidelines.

POLICY DECISIONS

Key factors in creating a merit pay policy are the size, timing, and delivery of merit increases.

Size: Absolute vs. Relative

The size of pay increases is a critical component in merit pay programs. Two conditions are necessary to motivate employees most effectively to meet and exceed performance standards for their positions:

- The absolute size of the merit increase must be significant enough to make a noticeable difference to employees (e.g., the increase must not be so trivial as to be deemed inconsequential). The failure to provide noticeable differences in pay is a common complaint made against many merit pay plans in action.
- The relative size of the increase must be significant enough that real differences in performance are recognized by meaningful differences in rewards.

A successful merit pay program will ensure that increases awarded to the "best" contributors will be substantially greater than increases awarded to average or below-average performers. If differences among pay increases are deemed by recipients to be trivial, the merit pay program will be undermined because employees will not be motivated to improve their performance. For example, a merit pay program that provides 1 percent increases for "exceptional" performers is likely to be perceived by employees as not providing significantly different rewards. However, a merit pay program that offers an additional 4–5 percent increase for exceptional performance is more likely to alter employee behavior and be motivational.

Timing: Anniversary vs. Common Review

Another issue that must be addressed is the date merit-increase decisions are made. Survey data suggest that common review dates are used by almost two-thirds of organizations, while one-third stagger increases, mostly by providing them on anniversary dates.

Using an anniversary-date approach spreads the administrative burden (tasks such as completing performance reviews, making increase decisions, and processing pay increases) throughout the year for managers and human resources staff. Payroll increases also are staggered, reducing the financial impact that accompanies a single jump in salaries. Also, the anniversary-date approach focuses the performance evaluation and increase on an individual employee, ideally leading the employee to believe the process is focused specifically on him or her.

A disadvantage of an anniversary-date approach is that relative performance (e.g., comparative evaluations), may be hard to judge, particularly if performance is evaluated at different times for all employees. Another disadvantage becomes evident when conservative budget management accentuates the natural tendency of many managers to "save" money until year-end. When this occurs, employee increases at the beginning of the year may be smaller than increases at the end of the year, and the result may be to penalize some employees unfairly.

A common (i.e., annual) review date consolidates the administrative burden for management and human resources, and increases can become part of the yearly budgeting process. Further, because increases for all employees are determined at the same time, appraisal ratings for all employees can be collected and relative performance can be factored into the decision more easily. If the merit budget is based on business-unit performance, the linkage among business-unit performance, individual performance, and merit increases can be clearer with a common date.

Disadvantages of common review dates are that the workload may be onerous if the timing of the salary-increase program coincides with other major efforts (such as year-end financial closings, open enrollment for benefits, and departmental budgeting), and cash-flow implications for the organization may be extreme when all increases occur simultaneously.

The decision concerning whether to use an anniversary-date versus a common-review-date approach to administer merit increases should be determined by the availability of performance data for employees and organizational units, and the availability of management and human resources. In organizations where budgets for salary increases are allocated based on organizational performance during a fixed period of time, employee and departmental performance also may be evaluated during the same time period. In such cases, a common review date might make sense. Anniversary-date increases might be more appropriate in organizations that stagger appraisals of performance or that permit little or no increase-budget variability among departments and in organizations that want to emphasize the individual's performance against absolute standards instead of emphasizing relative performance.

Another issue is whether to permit variability in time between increases in the pay program. In some organizations, the time between increases is not uniform for all employees; rather, performance differences are reflected not only in the size of increase but also in frequency. Excellent performance may be rewarded with larger and more frequent rewards. For example, top contributors might receive relatively large pay raises every 6 to 9 months, while average performers might wait 12 to 15 months for a lesser increase.

Delivery: Base vs. Lump Sum

Under traditional merit pay plans, merit increases are built into employees' salaries for as long as they remain with the organization. Hence, the increases are permanent, and their values are compounded over time as additional increases are granted.

An alternative to base-salary increases is the use of lump-sum increases. Lump-sum increases are one-time payments made in lieu of a traditional base-pay increase, and they typically are delivered annually via the merit pay program. Similar to a "bonus" payment, a lump sum must be re-earned each year based on performance – it is not built into base salary. Often, lump-sum payments are provided to employees who are near, at, or over the maximum of their salary range (often called "red circle" employees).

The advantages of lump sum increases for the organization are clear: While retaining a pay-for-performance relationship, payroll costs over time are lessened because of the lack of a compounding effect. Also, the "sanctity" of pay ranges is protected because the number of red-circle employees can be controlled. In organizations where employees are at or over the maximum of their grade, but are not permitted to receive increases, lump sums provide a mechanism to continue to reward and motivate strong but highly paid contributors.

There are fewer advantages of lump sums for the employee, though receiving the annual increase at once rather than having it paid out over 12 months – as is the case with a base-pay increase – may appeal to some. For long-term and highly paid employees, who may be near the top of their salary range with no room to grow, lump sums provide a means to continue to receive rewards.

Frequently, lump sums issued in lieu of merit increases are a concern for employees because their base pay will be less over time. Longer-term employees approaching retirement typically exhibit the most concern. Many employers allay this concern by counting lump sum awards toward final average-earnings pension calculations. Similarly, such payments often are tied to benefits. For example, benefits such as life insurance, which are linked to salary, will reflect lump sum payments in addition to base salary. This solution addresses a number of issues:

- The motivational link between performance and reward can be maintained.
- The organization reaps the benefit that lump sum payments provide in controlling total compensation costs.
- Employee benefits entitlements are not seriously reduced.

However, caution should be used with this approach because employees may react negatively when their base salaries do not change or grow relatively slowly over time.

POLICY IMPLEMENTATION

A merit pay policy answers the following questions about salary increases: How much? When? How? How frequently? These decisions can be summarized in a simple compensation tool called a merit pay matrix. A merit pay matrix details the amount and timing of increases for various levels of performance at various locations in the pay grade. A merit pay matrix may be interpreted as an operational statement of an organization's pay-for-performance theory or policy. It spells out the contingency between pay and performance in specific terms.

Merit pay matrices range from simple to complex, depending on the number of variables on which pay is made contingent. Generally, there are three alternatives for issuing merit increases:

- Based only on performance
- Based on performance and position in range
- Based on performance and position in range using variable timing

Performance

This method, which uses the simplest form of merit matrix (Figure 4.7), is most common in organizations without well-defined salary grade structures. Pay increases are granted based solely on performance, resulting in top performers receiving bigger increases than lower performers. Typically, salary increases are calculated as a percentage increase in base pay.

FIGURE 4.7 Linking merit increases to base pay.

Performance Rating	Fixed Increase Amount	Discretionary Increase Amount
Outstanding	8%	6–10%
Consistently Exceeds Standards	5%	4–6%
Meets Standards	3%	2–4%
Does Not Fully Meet Standards	0%	0–2%

Note: The matrices displayed in Figures 4.7, 4.9, and 4.10 use ranges of increases, rather than single percentages. This provides for more managerial discretion in awarding increases, and it more closely links pay and performance. In some companies, however, each cell of the matrix is occupied by only a single number.

Basing merit increases on performance alone ignores internal pay comparisons. Within a performance class, higher-paid employees receive greater absolute increases, even though the merit percentage reward is the same. This has the effect of perpetuating pay inequities that might exist, and it may reward long-tenured and/or highly paid employees disproportionately.

An alternative is to calculate merit increases as a percentage of the employee's salary-grade midpoint rather than their base pay. This approach provides larger relative dollar increases to employees within a performance class who are paid lower in their salary range than it does for employees who are high in their range (see Figure 4.8). Over time, inequities in salaries of employees in the same salary grade will be reduced as lower-paid employees are accelerated toward midpoint and higher-paid employees are "slowed down." This method reduces some of the bias toward long-term/highly paid employees that may be inherent in a performance-only merit matrix.

The advantage of either approach to calculating merit increases based only on performance is that the method is:

- Simple to budget
- Easy to administer
- Straightforward to communicate

Performance and Position in Range

Larger organizations may have more complicated grading structures that base increases on both performance and position in range, which is commonly defined by quartiles, or, if greater precision is required, by compa-ratios. This practice is based on the concept that the midpoint repre-

FIGURE 4.8 Linking merit increases to salary-grade midpoints.

Increase as a Percentage of Base Pay

Employee	Current Pay Rate	Increase Percentage	Increase Dollars
A	$25,000	4.0%	$1,000
B	$35,000	4.0%	$1,400
C	$45,000	4.0%	$1,800

Increase as a Percentage of $35,000 Midpoint

Employee	Current Pay Rate	Increase Percentage of Midpoint	Increase Dollars	Effective Increase Percentage
A	$25,000	4.0%	$1,400	5.6%
B	$35,000	4.0%	$1,400	4%
C	$45,000	4.0%	$1,400	3.1%

FIGURE 4.9 Linking merit increases to performance and position in range.

Performance Rating	Position in Range Before Increase			
	1st Quartile or Below	2nd Quartile	3rd Quartile	4th Quartile
Outstanding	8–9%	6–7%	4–5%	3–4%
Consistently Exceeds Standards	6–7%	4–5%	3–4%	2–3%
Meets Standards	4–5%	3–4%	2–3%	X
Does Not Fully Meet Standards	0–2%	X	X	X

sents a "competitive" or "fair" wage for a particular set of skills in the marketplace, and that, over time, employees with a similar level of sustained performance should be paid an equivalent amount. Thus, a merit-increase guide chart similar to Figure 4.9 will cause employees with the same performance to converge, over time, on a target point (typically the midpoint) by awarding bigger increases to employees lower in their range and smaller increases to employees higher in the range.

A merit-matrix approach has several advantages:

- The tendency is reduced to perpetuate tenure-based pay inequities and to continue to "overpay" (relative to market) highly paid employees.
- The approach is more likely to be deemed "fair" by the workforce because, over time, employees with similar performance in the same salary grade will tend to be paid comparably.

Basing merit increases on both performance and position in range introduces a level of complexity into the process not found in the simpler performance-only model. Of course, it is also more difficult to administer and communicate.

Performance and Position in Range Using Variable Timing

A more complex model for administering merit increases involves the concept of variable timing. The guide chart shown in Figure 4.10 demonstrates how the size and frequency of increase can be varied based on performance and position in range. In this model, top performers receive bigger and more frequent increases, while average and below-average contributors wait longer for smaller increases.

There are several advantages to this approach:

- Top performers will receive bigger rewards with greater frequency, yielding significant increases because of the compounding effect.
- During times of tight budgets, rather than issuing "below market" increases at regular intervals, "normal" increases can be granted at moderately delayed intervals. For example, rather than granting a 3.5 percent increase at 12 months, an organization may prefer to grant a 4.7 percent increase at 16 months.

FIGURE 4.10 Linking merit pay to position in range using variable timing.

Performance Rating	1st Quartile or Below	2nd Quartile	3rd Quartile	4th Quartile
Outstanding	8–9% 6–9 months	6–7% 9–12 months	4–5% 10–12 months	3–4% 12–15 months
Consistently Exceeds Standards	6–7% 8–10 months	4–5% 10–12 months	3–4% 12–15 months	2–3% 15–18 months
Meets Standards	4–5% 9–12 months	3–4% 12–15 months	2–3% 15–18 months	X
Does Not Fully Meet Standards	0–2% 12–15 months	X	X	X

The disadvantages of variable timing are:

- It is much more complicated to administer.
- It is difficult to track and maintain budgets.
- It is difficult to monitor the consistency of application throughout the year.
- It is more complex to communicate.

A successful merit pay plan requires more than well-developed policy statements and a conceptually sound design. It also requires administrative processes and procedures that are logical and easily understood. Some of the administrative issues that should be given consideration to ensure that a policy is implemented as intended are communication, training, and perceived fairness.

MANAGING A MERIT PAY PLAN

The merit pay "equation" is simple: Significant performance efforts yield significant rewards, which in turn motivate significant performance efforts. However, this equation relies on trust to enforce the contract between employees and the organization. Employees must trust the organization to fulfill its commitment that today's efforts will be compensated fairly tomorrow, and the organization must trust that employees will be motivated by performance-based rewards.

As in any relationship, trust can be promoted through openness and candor, or thwarted through secrecy and obfuscation. Honest, open communication between management, human resources, and employees serves as the means by which the messages of merit pay can be conveyed and reinforced.

Traditionally, many organizations have been unwilling to share much of their compensation-related data. Usually, these organizations have the mistaken belief that employees neither want nor need to know about such matters, and that providing "too much" information to employees somehow reduces management's ability to exercise flexibility and discretion.

Today, more organizational leaders understand that no matter how carefully designed a compensation program might be, success requires adequate communication. Thorough communication permits employees to test the validity of the organization's promises while conveying to them that the organization has nothing to hide. It also establishes opportunities for dialogue on issues of critical importance, enhances credibility by obtaining employee buy-in, and promotes overall trust.

A successful communication program requires a careful balance between an insufficient amount of information and too much information. Management should release enough information about the plan to demonstrate its faith in the process, but not so much information that its ability to exercise managerial discretion is impeded. Employees should be provided enough information about the merit pay plan that it serves as a performance motivator without breaching their right to privacy.

How much to communicate to employees will be influenced by many factors, including the organization's culture, management's willingness to share information that traditionally may have been confidential, and the readiness and ability of human resources to support the communications effort. Some of the key elements often introduced in a comprehensive communications program are:

- General information about the performance-appraisal program and process.
- General information about the organization's compensation program (e.g., how pay is determined, how jobs are evaluated, and what the salary ranges are).
- More specific information about the merit pay program (e.g., salary-increase budgets, performance-rating distributions, and merit matrices).
- Size of an individual's increase, minimum, and maximum raises granted and average size of merit increases.

TRAINING

Implementation of a successful merit pay program requires managers to make two key sets of decisions:

- Evaluation of performance
- Allocation of increase awards

An accurate, reliable, and credible performance-appraisal program is the foundation of a successful merit pay program, and it is imperative that managers and supervisors be capable of evaluating employee behaviors and results objectively and critically.

The skills required to appraise performance, assess employee contributions, and assign rewards are not intuitive. To ensure adequate interpretation and understanding of program requirements and consistent application of program tenets, training should be provided for all managers who are given the task of implementing the merit pay program. Training should include the following components:

- How to plan performance that links individual efforts and accomplishments to business plans and strategies.
- How to measure and evaluate performance fairly and consistently.
- How to provide feedback through intrinsic (e.g., coaching and praise) and extrinsic (e.g., pay increases and incentive payments) rewards.
- How to use the merit matrix to allocate rewards.
- How to communicate the assessment of performance and the allocation of rewards to employees.

PERCEPTION OF FAIRNESS

Program credibility is key to gaining a favorable response among employees to merit pay. Employees need to feel that increases and the process used to derive the increases are accurate and fair. To help ensure the perception of fairness, the merit pay program should incorporate the following tenets:

- Relevant laws and regulations must be followed (e.g., Title VII of the Civil Rights Act, the Fair Labor Standards Act, and various tax laws).
- Employees should participate in setting performance goals and standards, they should know what performance is expected of them, and they should be able to control the specific aspects of their performance on which their pay will be based.
- Employees should know and understand how the pay program works, and they should be encouraged to raise concerns, ask questions, and seek clarification on their increases.
- An appeals process should be established to provide employees with an opportunity to discuss their performance evaluation and their increase with an authority other than their direct supervisor.

HOW TECHNOLOGY ASSISTS PLAN ADMINISTRATION

The most conceptually and theoretically sound merit pay program is burdensome and inefficient to administer. Consequently, anything that contributes to simplifying planning and administration will help ensure the program's success.

Computer technology can assist in the management of the merit pay plan in a number of ways:

- Budget planning can be facilitated by generating different increase-matrix models, testing various options and deriving forecasts of the economic impact of alternatives.
- Data can be probed to evaluate the effectiveness, impact and equity of the merit pay plan. Increases, performance distribution, and other factors can be analyzed by department, position, organization, or individual.
- Employee records can be stored, monitored, and analyzed over time.
- Data can be managed to formulate cost projections based on salary-structure changes, the impact of inflation, and other financial factors.
- Summary reporting can be streamlined for internal and external purposes, tedious administrative tasks and reporting efforts can be automated, and productivity can be improved by reducing the amount of time, labor, and expense involved in managing the pay program.

EVALUATING A MERIT PAY PLAN

To ensure that a merit pay plan is operating as intended and is effective in meeting an organization's compensation needs, systematic, post-implementation evaluation of the plan should be conducted. This often-overlooked step is critical to the ultimate success and acceptance of the program. Many factors can be analyzed to assess plan effectiveness:

- Employee satisfaction with the pay program.
- Employee job satisfaction.

- Employee perception that pay is based on performance.
- Employee acceptance of and trust in the performance-appraisal process.
- Employee trust in management.
- Employee and organizational performance (e.g., productivity improvements).
- Employee commitment to the organization as demonstrated through reduced turnover and absenteeism rates.
- Correlation between actual performance ratings and actual merit increases.

Measurement of these success factors before and after implementation of a merit pay plan is likely to yield the most meaningful information, and it can be accomplished through various means: controlled empirical studies, employee-attitude surveys, focus-group discussions, and management and employee anecdotal feedback. Employee attitudes and perceptions ideally should be evaluated by collecting survey data from employees before the introduction of a merit pay plan, and again after the program has been introduced, and employees have received their first merit increases.

Some organizations attempt to gauge the success of newly introduced merit pay plans by measuring productivity and/or performance improvements over time and then correlating that information with appraisal ratings and salary increases. Also, turnover and absenteeism rates can be tracked and correlated with performance and salary increases. These data could be used to modify development of the plan, but it should be remembered that many other factors, including industry and economic trends, can also affect these factors. For example, high unemployment rates will tend to drive down turnover rates, regardless of employee satisfaction with corporate pay plans.

Because employee perception of fairness is so important in determining the success of the merit pay program, one analysis that should be performed is to test how accurately, fairly, and consistently the program has been administered throughout the organization. Some common employee questions that need to be addressed to demonstrate the fairness of a merit pay plan are:

- Does where or for whom you work mean more than how well you perform? Do some departments rate employee performance disproportionately high, and are some supervisors unfairly critical while others are unreasonably generous?
- Are all employees afforded a relatively equal opportunity for high performance ratings and commensurate increases? Is the plan free from racial, gender, and age bias?

MERIT PAY ADVANTAGES AND DISADVANTAGES

While merit pay remains a common means of determining pay increases, the potential drawbacks of the approach should be clear before implementation. Once these drawbacks are recognized, an organization can appreciate

FIGURE 4.11 Advantages and disadvantages of merit pay.

MERIT PAY	
ADVANTAGES ➡	⬅ DISADVANTAGES
Helps improve employee satisfaction with work and pay as well as individual performance	Rewards individual performance, not group performance
	Depends highly on a sound performance-appraisal system
Rewards performance rather than seniority or skills	Clashes with organizational emphasis on tenure
Clarifies performance expectations	
Attracts and retains highly motivated employees	De-emphasizes intrinsic work rewards while possibly discouraging "average" and "below average" performers

the advantages of merit pay and how it will improve employee perceptions of work and rewards (see Figure 4.11).

As is true with any reward system, merit pay must be compatible with an organization's culture and philosophy if it is going to be effective. For example, merit pay will not work for an organization that values tenure over performance. Also, merit pay may be inappropriate for organizations that are trying to emphasize group instead of individual performance. By rewarding individuals, merit pay can undermine the cooperation and interdependency that are needed in a team environment. However, it may be possible to preserve the best elements of a team environment while rewarding the highest-performing individuals by integrating group-based incentives with some form of merit pay system.

Merit pay will not work unless an organization has a sound system of measuring individual employee performance that is accepted by the work force. Even if a good performance-appraisal system exists, merit pay may be discouraging to "average" or "below average" employees, who typically will fail to qualify for high pay raises. By tightly linking pay and performance, merit pay also can deemphasize the intrinsic rewards and satisfaction gained simply from doing a job.

By linking a merit pay program with a sound communications strategy, an organization can clarify its performance expectations and create an atmosphere of trust between employees and management. This atmosphere tends to increase overall employee satisfaction with work and pay, and it is likely to lead to improved individual performance.

The main reason an organization chooses a reward system is to enhance its competitiveness, productivity, and bottom-line results. Positive financial results are more likely when an organization places emphasis on employee performance instead of tenure, and highly motivated employees are more likely to be attracted and retained when their efforts are rewarded regularly. A merit pay system can help ensure that an organization's rewards policy fits the performance-based philosophy it needs to survive and prosper.

LINKING RESULTS AND COMPETENCIES TO BUSINESS STRATEGY

A performance management system functions as a management tool to help ensure that employees are focused on organizational priorities and operational factors that are critical to the organization's success.

Organizations should operate from business strategies that include critical, measurable success factors. These include:

- Financial success (e.g., return on investment, return on sales)
- Productivity (e.g., cost per labor hour, units per day)
- Quality standards and customer service (e.g., customer satisfaction scores, waste, and reject indices)
- Work environment (e.g., attitude survey scores, employee grievances)

An organization's critical success factors form the basis for key result areas for the measurement of organizational, department, team, and individual performance. Key result areas define what is to be accomplished (e.g., the job's end results, which in turn reflect the job's primary purpose) and generally are defined as key responsibilities, one-time or periodic projects, or annual objectives. Examples of key result areas are:

- Types and proofreads department correspondence and reports
- Researches leading practices in the area of real estate acquisition
- Develops and implements a new purchasing management system

In addition to key result areas, an organization may include the identification of competencies that focus on *how* results are to be attained.

Competencies generally are defined as the knowledge, skills, and abilities exhibited by individuals as they work to accomplish key result areas. Competencies may be developed universally for the organization, for job families or for individual jobs. Competencies often are selected to reflect an organization's values and may include some or all of the areas listed in Figure 4.12. These factors should be included in the performance management process and used as input when evaluating performance at the end of the assessment period.

While using competencies, it is important to identify specific behaviors associated with them. For example, associated behaviors for teamwork may be communicating openly with others and achieving win–win solutions

FIGURE 4.12 Examples of competencies.

- Teamwork
- Achievement orientation
- Customer service orientation
- Relationship building
- Analytical thinking
- Developing others

while working with peers. Generally, organizations identify 5–10 competencies to focus employees on key organizational priorities.

If an organization has developed comprehensive performance measures that are evaluated and used regularly to manage overall organizational performance, these measures should be included in the system so all employees can focus their priorities and energies on these strategies. For example:

- If an organization has established a company-wide quality or customer service performance measure, it should be incorporated into individual performance plans at all levels.
- If teamwork is a key organizational value, the performance management system should hold each employee accountable for behaviors identified with teamwork.
- If maintaining a positive environment and high employee morale are organizational priorities, managers should be held accountable for the environment and morale in their work units.

DETERMINING THE PERFORMANCE MANAGEMENT CYCLE

Any performance management system is an ongoing cycle. For most organizations, the typical performance period cycle is one year, although this period may vary depending on business cycles and probationary periods for new hires, promotions, and transfers. The cycle also may be determined by the link to organizational measurements of success. For example, if financial measurements are included in the system, the performance cycle may be tied to the fiscal cycle. If an employee is involved in a project team with specific target dates for various stages, the performance management cycle may reflect the project's schedule.

The design team should consider the typical performance management cycle within the organization. This cycle is likely to consist of three phases: planning performance for the upcoming period, coaching performance, and giving feedback throughout the period and evaluating performance for the just completed period.

Phase I: Planning Performance for the Upcoming Period

Planning performance for the period includes defining key results for each position as well as establishing performance standards against which key result areas are measured. The design team should consider the most appropriate approach to conducting the performance planning process, focusing on the roles that will be played by HR, immediate supervisors, and employees.

In many organizations, HR will be responsible for working with line management to devise a framework for developing key result areas and performance standards. HR also typically is responsible for developing training materials to communicate the approach to line management and employees and for training line management and employees in the performance planning process. After training has been completed, HR often works with line management to ensure that performance plans are developed appropriately. This function also may be accomplished by appointed performance planning teams that include employees from all levels of the organization who have been trained to help facilitate the performance planning process.

Because the performance planning process requires detailed knowledge of job responsibilities and performance expectations, line management should play a significant role in the process and be ultimately accountable for the performance plans of their employees.

The advantages of having managers and/or employees define key results and establish performance standards each period include:

- Managers and/or employees can structure each job to the individual's and the department's best advantage, increasing flexibility in what is measured.
- Managers and/or employees are more knowledgeable about their department's day-to-day needs.
- Job responsibilities and standards can be modified to reflect special projects or assignments for the period.

At the same time, HR can play a key role by providing coaching and training, and by ensuring consistency of key results and standards throughout the organization.

Typically, each position should list 5–10 key results that support the organization's business strategy. If more results are listed, they no longer are likely to include only "key" results of the job. If fewer results are listed, the full scope of responsibilities might not be closely defined.

In most cases, all key results do not have equal impact on the job. It is common practice to assign a weight of importance to each key result based on impact, frequency, and relative significance to the overall list of responsibilities as well as to the department and the organization. Weights may be determined informally and discussed when planning performance for the period. Weights also may be assigned to each key result, using:

- Percentage weighting (adding up to 100 percent)
- Numerical weighting (1 = highly significant, 2 = significant, 3 = moderately significant, 4 = insignificant, 5 = highly insignificant)
- Word descriptions (critical, important, etc.)

The design team should decide how weighting will be handled, keeping in mind both the organization's culture and the desired goals of the system. Results that best meet the organization's overall goals generally should be assigned the greatest weight.

Phase II: Coaching Performance and Giving Feedback throughout the Period

An important step for the design team involves the concept of open, honest, positive, two-way communication between supervisors and employees throughout the period. The goal of a performance management system should be to improve employee performance, not to find an easier way to terminate an employee for poor performance. Therefore, a system should emphasize coaching and feedback from the supervisor as well as feedback and input from the employee throughout the performance period.

The design team should plan structured feedback throughout the period, including mid-period, quarterly, or monthly progress reviews. A more structured feedback approach works especially well for poorly performing employees who require more frequent monitoring and coaching. Feedback, which should include constructive criticism, should be offered in a private, formal setting. In addition, the system should encourage supervisors to give informal feedback throughout the period. This is especially true for positive feedback, which may include verbal praise or even a brief suggestion to "Try doing it this way next time." Employees should be encouraged to ask for frequent feedback from their supervisors.

Phase III: Rating Performance for the Just-Completed Period

One of the most challenging aspects of developing an individual performance management system is developing the approach for rating employee performance. When identifying an approach, it is important to focus on the characteristics of the organization and the objectives of the performance management system. For example, a traditional hierarchical organization tends to focus on judging employees' past performance. An organization oriented toward total quality management might focus less on judging past performance and more on strategies to improve future performance.

PERFORMANCE RATING APPROACHES

Deciding on the number of categories in the rating scale is not without controversy. On the one hand, the more levels of performance that are identified, the more accurately performance may be evaluated. For example, rating an employee on a scale with five performance levels (e.g., consistently exceeds expectations, exceeds most expectations, meets expectations, does not meet most expectations, does not meet any expectations) seemingly differentiates performance more accurately than does a three-point scale (e.g., exceeds expectations, meets expectations, does not meet expectations). On the other hand, how does one objectively differentiate performance at each of the five levels? If one is measuring units of production in a factory or words typed per hour, objectively identifying performance at all five levels may be possible. However, in a service-based work environment, it often is not feasible to implement performance standards at five levels. Evaluating performance then becomes the subjective judgment of the supervisor, and it is difficult to communicate so that employees understand the performance expectations at different rating levels.

For example, within a manufacturing operation in which five performance levels may be appropriate, making five units per hour may be considered level-five performance, making four per hour may be considered level-four performance, and so on. When evaluating performance in this environment, there is little or no interpretation as to the performance rating that should be given.

However, in an environment in which it is difficult to compare performance against established standards, such as a service or office environment, the question is whether it is acceptable for supervisors to make subjective judgments among the different levels of performance. Further, although most supervisors believe they can make this differentiation, they find it virtually impossible to communicate these distinctions to employees in a way that employees can understand and accept. For example, if one of an administrative assistant's responsibilities is to make travel arrangements through a travel agency, how will a supervisor identify and communicate the five levels of performance so they will be accepted by the employee?

In addition, it is a common perception among employees that it is unacceptable to be rated more than one level below the top rating. In fact, supervisors often rate employees one level below the top to minimize conflict and avoid spending a significant amount of time attempting to justify the performance rating. For example, in the five-point rating scale, a rating of "meets expectations" has the connotation of "average" and would generally be perceived as unacceptable, even though it is acceptable. Because of these perceptions and an increasing focus on improving future performance, the trend is toward using fewer rating categories when using rating scales – in many cases, as few as three. With the three-point scale, only one level of performance falls above "meets expectations" or acceptable performance.

When determining ratings levels, it is important to focus on definitions that compare performance to performance expectations, such as "consistently meets expectations" or "frequently exceeds expectations." It is equally important to avoid ratings that compare employees, such as "average" and "above average." Many organizations today favor not only fewer performance rating levels but also nonquantified ratings systems. Although it may be tempting to view performance management as an objective and precise process that can be weighted and scored, in most cases it is a subjective process based on supervisors' judgments that are difficult to communicate. Many organizations have concluded, therefore, that performance management systems should include rating levels that are fewer in number and that are qualitative.

Using Summary Ratings

The design of a summary rating should focus on the objective of the system. With that in mind, the design team may consider three options:

1. *Summary point scores.* In a weighted and scored system in which the rating of each key result is assigned a number (consistently exceeds

expectations = 5; exceeds most expectations = 4; meets expectations = 3, etc.), the overall rating is a point score. The issue, then, is to convert the overall point score back into a rating category.

2. *Summary labels.* If the purpose of the system is primarily to judge past performance, and if the method for evaluating performance is fairly objective, then the use of rating categories, or "labels," may be appropriate. These labels may be the same as those used to rate each key result: "consistently exceeds expectations," "exceeds most expectations," "meets expectations," and so on.

3. *Summary statements.* To reduce the subjectivity of performance management systems and increase the focus on continuous improvement, organizations have tended to move away from rating categories or labels toward summary statements that are behavior-oriented and more focused on future improvements. For example, suppose Joe's performance occasionally fails to meet expectations for the job. Joe meets most standards and exceeds one of them, but he needs to increase his sales per month. This overall level of performance is acceptable this year because Joe is a new employee; however, he will be expected to increase his output next year. Assuming most employees generally meet performance expectations, it is much easier for the supervisor to focus on strategies for improving future performance when there are no summary labels. With this approach, the challenge for supervisors is to communicate the performance evaluation clearly to employees so there are no misunderstandings when employees are – or are not – considered for promotions or transfers, or when they are terminated for poor performance.

Employee Responsibility

The role of the employee is an important aspect of the evaluation process. As organizations flatten and the scope of supervision expands, it becomes increasingly difficult for supervisors to interact with employees to judge performance. Looking at this situation along with organizational initiatives to empower employees, the design team should consider the extent to which employees may be involved in the evaluation process. This involvement may include these steps:

- Evaluate their own performance.
- Complete a self-evaluation that includes identifying development plans and career objectives.
- Gather performance-related information.
- Schedule evaluation sessions.

Employee involvement in performance evaluations can facilitate the evaluation process. If used as part of a multirater assessment process, employee involvement can allow supervisors to function more as coaches and less as judges of performance.

MULTIRATER ASSESSMENT

One question for the design team to consider is who will rate performance. In an organization focused more on developing future performance, that development includes a high degree of involvement by those other than the supervisor, including the employees themselves. Under these circumstances, a technique known as multirater assessment, or 360-degree feedback, might be used. With multirater assessment, employee performance evaluations are compiled by several – usually five to nine – people who come in regular, direct contact with the employee, including peers, internal and external customers, supervisors, and subordinates. Most important, employees are able to evaluate their own performance.

The advantage of the technique is that the larger number of sources of evaluative input is likely to provide a more complete, well-rounded picture of the employee's performance, and employees often view this picture as more credible than single-source assessments conducted only by the supervisor (see Figure 4.13).

The disadvantage is that the process involves greater administration to collect, compile and distribute feedback while ensuring the anonymity of evaluators and the confidentiality of results. Because one rater who deviates from the others can significantly affect an employee's evaluation, many organizations opt to discard the highest and lowest ratings before compiling results. Further, it can be helpful to provide feedback to raters who deviate significantly from others so they may modify their techniques and provide more consistent evaluations in the future. With a multirater system in place, supervisors can assume greater roles as performance coaches rather than acting simply as performance judges.

Although research has indicated that it is possible to obtain more objective performance feedback from multiple sources, the design and implementation of a multirater feedback system often depends on the level of

FIGURE 4.13 Advantages of using multirater assessments.

Some Users Perceive Multirater Assessment as More:
- Fair: less rating inflation, less adverse impact on diversity, and more process and technology safeguards
- Accurate: less bias and more balance
- Credible: more believable because of respect for the opinions of multiple work associates
- Valuable: more specific feedback and greater distinctions among performance criteria
- Motivational: more encouragement for constructive behavior change because of peer pressure and the desire to be recognized by the team

FIGURE 4.14 Sample multirater evaluation questions.

Rater #3				
Rater #2				
Rater #1				
		EVALUATION		
		Not Satisfactory	Satisfactory	Highly Satisfactory
COMMUNICATION SKILLS				
Keeps other informed of specific issues affecting them		1	2	3
Listens attentively to others		1	2	3
Participates effectively in meetings		1	2	3
DEVELOPING SUBORDINATES				
Provides subordinates with detailed performance feedback on a regular basis		1	2	3
Empowers subordinates by delegating responsibility and authority whenever possible		1	2	3
Provides subordinates with the resources needed to get the job done		1	2	3
LEADERSHIP				
Leads by example		1	2	3
Considers customer/client satisfaction to be a top priority		1	2	3
Challenges people to extend themselves to the fullest		1	2	3
PROBLEM SOLVING AND DECISION-MAKING				
Is open to new and creative suggestions when solving problems		1	2	3
Analyzes situations to get to the root cause of problems		1	2	3
Develops step-by-step solutions to problems		1	2	3
KNOWLEDGE AND TECHNICAL COMPETENCE				
Keeps up to date with developments in his/her field		1	2	3
Is knowledgable about a number of fields related to his/her specialty		1	2	3
Is expert at performing the specific tasks and technical skills required of his/her job		1	2	3

employee trust that the feedback will be handled confidentially and that it will be used appropriately. Many organizations begin by providing performance feedback only to the individual employee. During this time, the system is focused on improving performance rather than rating performance. Once an appropriate level of employee trust has been established, the multirater system can evolve so both supervisors and employees receive the information. Both can use it for evaluating performance and providing feedback for individual development (see Figure 4.14).

LINKING PERFORMANCE MANAGEMENT AND PAY DELIVERY

Effective performance management should include both formal and informal aspects. Formal aspects include appraisals and links to incentive plans, such as merit pay. Informal aspects include coaching, feedback, and links to employee development. When designing a performance management system, the design team should consider whether and how the system will be linked to employee compensation or to the determination of pay increases. Traditionally, an overall rating – either numerical or a rating summary – has been developed that determines a pay increase from merit guidelines. Although this approach directly links performance and pay, it may cause budget overruns unless the guidelines are based on an analysis of past performance rating distributions. Supervisors may overrate employees' performance to justify larger merit increases for them.

When there is a direct link between the performance evaluation and merit pay increases, especially when the two are done at the same time, the performance evaluation system is likely to be perceived as part of the pay system. The evaluation often is focused on the "judgment" of past performance, instead of on a positive discussion of an employee's strengths and weaknesses and on how performance should be developed in the future. Further, management may lower performance ratings in some cases to ensure that merit increases do not exceed budget, which obviously causes negative reactions from employees.

One solution may be to separate performance appraisal ratings and pay increases by deemphasizing the "judgment" aspect of point scores or overall rating labels and shifting to a narrative statement that summarizes overall performance. The performance appraisal may be further separated from the pay increase by changing the timing of the two activities or by changing the appraisal and pay cycles. For example, the performance evaluation may be given on each employee's anniversary date and pay increases may be given on a common date, perhaps based on the fiscal period. Another solution may be to provide a merit budget to department heads and require them to allocate pay increases to their employees on the basis of relative performance. Department heads then have to determine who their top performers are in order to allocate merit money without exceeding budget.

Organizations need to consider carefully whether or not pay will be linked to a performance rating, and if so, the impact this linkage will have on the operation of the overall performance management system. If the primary objective of the system is to determine ratings for pay increases, the system should be designed to differentiate performance levels. Organizations that are more interested in using performance management as a tool to develop their employees may want to separate the performance management and pay delivery systems to prevent either system from having a negative impact on the other.

Although performance may be an important factor in determining pay increases, there may be other contributing factors such as the rate at which salaries are increasing in the marketplace, internal equity factors or an employee's position within the salary range. When the two systems are directly linked, employees may assume there is a one-to-one relationship between performance and pay, and not recognize the impact of these other factors, which may be difficult to communicate. A pay system may be designed to target an employee's pay at a certain position within the salary range that is consistent with the employee's contribution to the organization. For example, employees who consistently meet expectations may have their pay targeted toward the middle of the salary range, while employees who consistently exceed standards may have their pay targeted toward the top. Once employees reach the middle of the range or the market value, future increases may be limited, or they may be delivered as variable pay in lump sums.

In general, the design of the performance management system should be compatible with the pay delivery system philosophy and should support that philosophy. At the same time, how performance management is linked, or not linked, to pay will send a strong message to the workforce about organizational priorities and values. The decision as to how performance management and compensation will be related should not be made lightly.

5 Executive Pay Disclosures, Trends, and Challenges

Executive pay disclosure goes hand in hand with other legislative and regulatory attempts to achieve accountability and transparency in all matters relating to corporate governance. The SEC's expanded disclosure rules adopted in 2006 and 2009 and the 2010 Dodd–Frank legislation (including SEC rules adopted thereunder) have considerably altered the disclosure landscape. Companies must now provide more detailed tabular information, additional narrative in the Compensation Discussion and Analysis (CD&A), information on the qualifications of directors and their fees, the degree of risk-taking inherent in pay programs, and the rationale behind the company's leadership structure.

The disclosure of so much information in numerous public documents, each with a distinct reporting schedule and format, makes the work of the compensation committee increasingly more difficult and time-consuming. This is especially true when it comes to disclosing equity compensation, comprised as it often is of several different vehicles and overlapping grants over multiyear periods. The actual total value of equity pay granted and realized over time may be quite different from the snapshot that appears each year in the proxy.

In addition, the need to communicate with shareholders effectively regarding *say on pay,* coupled with expanded SEC and stock exchange disclosure requirements, has undoubtedly resulted in longer proxy statements. This trend will likely continue, as the remaining disclosure rules required by Dodd–Frank ultimately are implemented (as of this printing). Consequently, compensation committees need to collect and analyze data in a way that allows for a more complete understanding and communication of reported values.

This chapter:

- Reviews the purpose of the CD&A, its connection with the new compensation committee report, and issues and actions to make the CD&A a more meaningful document.
- Discusses the key issues of the SEC's 2009 final rules expanding proxy disclosure in public companies, including the requirement to discuss the extent that pay programs might encourage harmful risk-taking, equity awards to directors, and the company's leadership structure.
- Provides a three-part mechanism for measuring executive pay to better understand how pay programs interact over time and facilitate the communication of executive pay programs to shareholders.
- Reviews say on pay, say on parachutes, clawback policies, and other provisions of Dodd–Frank related to executive compensation.
- Discusses the reasons that companies should plan for continued scrutiny by major stakeholders, their advisers and regulators, and ways in which companies and their compensation committees may better prepare for each proxy season.

CHALLENGES OF THE COMPENSATION DISCUSSION AND ANALYSIS

In 2006, the SEC adopted substantially expanded executive compensation disclosure rules that were described as a wake-up call by the director of the SEC's Division of Corporation Finance. Of particular importance is the CD&A section that was added as a required component of annual proxy statements. Companies have been forced to focus not just on the "what" but also the "why" in executive pay disclosure.

Objectives of the CD&A

In its commentary on the CD&A, the SEC envisioned the section as an "overview providing narrative disclosure that puts into context the compensation disclosure provided elsewhere" for a company's NEOs. The expressed objective was to explain material elements of these executives' compensation. Critical to this process are seven questions that should be addressed:

1. What are the objectives of the company's compensation programs?
2. What is the compensation program designed to reward?
3. What is each element of compensation?
4. Why does the company choose to pay each element?
5. How does the company determine the amount (and, where applicable, the formula) for each element?
6. How does each element and the company's decisions regarding that element fit into the company's overall compensation objectives and affect decisions regarding other elements?

7. Did the company consider the results of the most recent shareholder advisory vote on executive compensation (say on pay) in determining compensation policies and decisions? If so, how?

At the time of the 2006 rulemaking, executive pay disclosure at many companies had become standardized – even largely boilerplate – and often furnished little meaningful guidance on how executive pay actually is determined. In requiring a CD&A, key SEC goals were to encourage much more thoughtful analysis by compensation committees in determining executive pay and to have these pay considerations thoroughly disclosed. Many statements in the CD&A require significant elaboration; it is not sufficient to state that "pay is based on performance" or that "compensation is targeted at the median of comparable (or peer) organizations." Rather, how these standards are applied needs to be described, along with relevant policies, factors, and regulatory impact.

In addition, the latest trends in shareholder engagement call for companies to begin preparing for the proxy season sooner and with greater deliberation regarding their compensation plans and programs. The proxy should tell a company's compensation story, but the decisions behind the story need to balance any shareholder concerns about its compensation programs with how these arrangements support the company's business strategy and objectives. We believe that the best way to demonstrate this balance is to show due consideration of shareholder issues coupled with effective shareholder engagement; the CD&A section of the proxy should clearly explain the compensation committee's final decisions and why they were made.

Relation of CD&A to the Compensation Committee Report

Although the CD&A discusses compensation policies and decisions, it does not address the compensation committee's deliberations because it is not a report of the compensation committee; rather, the CD&A is the company's responsibility. However, the 2006 SEC rules also mandated a new form of compensation committee report that requires the committee to state whether:

- It has reviewed and discussed the CD&A with management, and
- The committee recommended to the board of directors that the CD&A be included in the company's annual report and proxy (based on the aforementioned review and discussions).

Potential Liability under the CD&A

While the compensation committee report is considered "furnished" to the SEC, the CD&A is a filed document. This technical distinction means that the CD&A is considered to be part of the proxy statement and the disclosures are covered by the Sarbanes–Oxley Act of 2002 certifications required of principal executive officers and principal financial officers. The potential liability was designed to increase attention to the statements made.

Issues to Address in the CD&A

The CD&A is principles-based (rather than rules-based), and the SEC intends that it furnish perspective on the numbers and other executive pay information contained in required tables and elsewhere. A significant challenge presented by the CD&A has been articulating the rationale underlying the components of the executive compensation package for each NEO. The SEC's rulemaking provided nonexclusive examples of potentially appropriate issues that might reasonably be addressed in the CD&A; each should be considered in light of the organization's particular facts and circumstances. The CD&A must be comprehensive in scope; a company should describe any compensation policies it applies, even if not covered in the SEC's examples. The discussion also should address post-employment arrangements relating to compensation.

Besides the breadth of its requirements, the CD&A calls for greater depth than had been customary in compensation committee reports. While a CD&A generally should avoid repetition of the exhaustive information presented in tables and other portions of the proxy, it should identify material differences in compensation policies and decisions applicable to individual NEOs. Considerable thought and effort can be required to determine what should be discussed and then to prepare the appropriate explanation – which is supposed to be written in plain English (a standard not often met).

Areas That May Require Particular Attention

The examples provided by the SEC include some items that previously received scant attention in most proxy statements. In expanding the scope of executive pay disclosure, the SEC implicitly furnished its views on items that should be considered in executive compensation design.

- The SEC identified the familiar concept of benchmarking as a particular subject for disclosure. Information is needed on the benchmark for any material element of an executive's compensation, including the component companies (peer group) used for the benchmark. This requirement has increased the focus on having an appropriate peer group and choosing reasonable benchmarks. In comment letters from the SEC during the first few years of proxy filings under these rules, benchmarking was one of the main sources of SEC inquiries.
- One example from the SEC suggested discussing how gains from prior option awards are considered in setting other elements of compensation. By identifying the topic, the SEC implied that compensation committees should look at this issue.

- The well-publicized concerns some years ago at dozens of companies regarding the timing (a concept broader than backdating) and pricing of stock options caused the SEC to specifically provide for extensive disclosure regarding the timing and pricing of option grants. Various elements and questions were identified by the SEC for disclosure; these should be considered in determining the appropriate use and design of stock options in a company's executive pay program.

- Another example refers to a company's equity ownership guidelines and mentions any policies regarding hedging an executive's economic risk of such ownership. Many organizations have since developed hedging policies rather than state that they do not have any such policy. As mentioned later in this chapter, hedging policies were addressed in Dodd–Frank and extended to all employees and directors.

- Because the impact of the accounting and tax treatment of a particular form of compensation is one issue that the SEC views as potentially appropriate for discussion, an organization might consider the role played by various regulatory provisions. For example, companies routinely address the $1 million deduction cap for certain executives under IRC section 162(m).

Recommended Actions

The following actions should be useful for most companies:

- Start the process early each year. Based on anticipated changes, future proxy seasons likely will involve more input from a wider group of stakeholders than ever before (e.g., legal/corporate secretaries, HR/ compensation professionals, communication, marketing, investor relations, shareholder advisory firms, and board members). Every party with responsibility regarding a CD&A needs to appreciate the significant effort that can be required to satisfy the disclosure standards – a narrative approach that considers a lengthy list of issues. A critical factor in managing this compliance process involves having sufficient time to fully vet all compensation issues that might need to be discussed.

- Develop an overall understanding of the objectives and requirements for the CD&A, working with advisers as needed.

- Internal personnel and external advisers (ideally including attorneys, accountants, and compensation consultants) should work together and undertake the preparation of a "mock" CD&A. Generally, it is helpful to take the company's most recent CD&A as a starting point, but then view everything with fresh eyes to assess its applicability for the relevant year. New information is added, irrelevant material is deleted, and the whole reconsidered in light of the particulars of the company and its industry as well as relevant legislation and rules, economic considerations and a host of other factors. A key focus is on clarity, organization, and presentation. When the parties actually commence this process, they realize how much is involved in crafting a focused discussion of the appropriate issues for the CD&A.

- Many companies now dedicate a section of their annual proxy statements to addressing expressed and potential concerns of shareholders. This type of disclosure is typical when the company fared poorly on the previous year's say-on-pay vote. Consequently, some companies include discussions of how a compensation committee or board engaged with shareholders and made subsequent changes to the compensation program.
- Inevitable scrutiny follows certain policies (e.g., parachute tax gross-ups or special one-time awards to executives). A company needs to provide a strong rationale for any important programs or provisions that are likely to be controversial.
- The compensation committee should be involved. While a company has responsibility for the preparation and filing of a proxy statement and the CD&A, it is the handiwork of the compensation committee that is being explained in the CD&A. The SEC clearly expects that compensation committee decisions will be affected by the knowledge that they will be subject to disclosure.
- Once an organization understands the scope of the tasks involved in crafting the CD&A, it should identify any issues that need to be addressed and information to be included. As instructed by the SEC, each company needs to focus on its particular facts and circumstances. Minutes of compensation committee meetings, reports of internal staff and consultants, and various plan documents and summaries may be helpful to examine as part of this process.
- A draft CD&A should be circulated among the working group for comment. During an iterative review process, all parties should keep in mind the ultimate goals of a clear yet comprehensive overview of the company's executive pay determinations.

Enhanced Disclosure of Executive Pay

The regulation of executive compensation accelerated in 2009 as Congress, the Obama Administration and various regulatory agencies all added their voices to the debate surrounding sound executive pay practices. Near the close of 2009, the SEC adopted final rules further expanding proxy disclosure of executive compensation for public companies. Following is an overview of these SEC rules and some of the key compliance issues.

Relationship of the Company's Compensation Policies and Practices to Risk

Under the 2009 rules, public companies must discuss compensation policies and practices for all employees – not just NEOs – to the extent that risks arising from them are "reasonably likely to have a material adverse effect" on the company. Companies need to identify and then review all compensation arrangements to determine whether there are potential risks that might trigger disclosure. Any problems discovered in the review process then can be fixed or appropriately mitigated.

The SEC furnished examples of situations that could potentially trigger discussion and analysis:

- A business unit of the company carries a significant portion of the company's risk profile.
- A business unit has a significantly different compensation structure than other units.
- A business unit is significantly more profitable than others within the company.
- Compensation expense at a business unit represents a significant percentage of the unit's revenues.
- Compensation policies and practices vary significantly from the overall risk and reward structure of the company.

In assessing the degree of risk, companies can consider any compensation policies and practices designed to alleviate risk or balance incentives (e.g., clawbacks and recoupment policies, bonus banking, stock ownership requirements). The type of disclosure is determined on a case-by-case basis, but may include:

- The general design philosophy of compensation policies for employees whose behavior would be most influenced by the incentive programs.
- The company's risk assessment or considerations in structuring its incentive compensation policies.
- The ways in which the company's compensation policies relate to the realization of risks resulting from the actions of employees (e.g., through the use of clawbacks, holding periods).
- The company's policies regarding adjustments to its compensation practices to address changes in its risk profile.
- Material adjustments the registrant has made to its compensation policies or practices as a result of changes in its risk profile.
- The extent to which the registrant monitors its compensation policies to determine whether risk management objectives are being met.

As a topic that relates to all employees and not just NEOs, risk-related disclosure should have its own section in the proxy statement and generally not be included in the CD&A. Importantly, the SEC does "not require a company to make an affirmative statement that it has determined that the risks arising from its compensation policies and practices are not likely to have a material adverse effect on the company." In view of this limitation on the disclosure that is required, companies have been split on whether they should take the next step to voluntarily make such an affirmative statement that they maintain no such unreasonably risky compensation programs.

Disclosure Regarding Fees Affecting Independence of Compensation Consultants

The disclosure rules require a company to disclose the fees paid to a compensation consultant if the consultant furnished consulting services related to executive or director compensation as well as other services to the company. However, fee disclosure is not required if the fees paid to the consultant for additional services did not exceed $120,000 during the company's fiscal year. When disclosure is required, it must include:

- Aggregate fees paid for executive and director compensation consulting services
- Aggregate fees paid for other services
- Whether the decision to engage the consultant for other services was made or recommended by management and whether the committee or board approved the other services, if the consultant was engaged by the compensation committee.

Disclosure on the Qualifications of Directors and Nominees

Under the disclosure requirements, a company must discuss the particular experience, qualifications, attributes, or skills that qualify an individual to serve as a director for the company, based on the company's business and structure at the time the disclosure is being made. However, the rules do not require disclosure regarding the specifics that qualify the individual to serve as a committee member. Disclosure is required for all directors, even if they are not standing for re-election in the applicable year, and should include:

- Any business experience during the past 5 years, including the principal occupation and employment.
- Any directorships at public companies held by each director at any time during the past 5 years (instead of only disclosing currently held directorships).
- Certain legal proceedings involving any director or executive officer during the past 10 years (instead of 5 years).
- Whether and how diversity is considered when identifying director candidates.

The SEC has not defined diversity; rather, each company is allowed to define it as it determines to be appropriate for its particular circumstances (e.g., experience, skills, education, race, gender). If a policy on diversity exists, the company must disclose how the policy is implemented and how its effectiveness is assessed.

Discussion of Company Leadership Structure

A company is required to disclose whether and why it has chosen to combine or separate the CEO and board chair positions, along with the reasons why the company believes that this board leadership structure is the most appropriate for it at the time of the filing. If the same person serves as CEO and chair, the company needs to disclose whether and why the company has a lead independent director and the role of the lead independent director in the leadership of the board. As discussed later in this chapter, Dodd–Frank confirmed this requirement through a statutory mandate.

In addition, the rules require companies to describe the board's role in the oversight of risk (which may include credit risk, liquidity risk, and operational risk). For example, a company may describe whether the entire board reviews risk or if there is a separate committee. Further, a company may find it helpful to discuss how risk information is communicated to the board or relevant committee members.

The Continuing Challenge of Appropriate Disclosure

The 2009 rules:

- Responded to some criticisms of the 2006 overhaul of the SEC disclosure rules relating to executive compensation;
- Addressed various executive compensation issues that became important after experience with companies' disclosures; and
- Generally expanded the scope of required disclosures.

Companies are faced with the challenge of accurately explaining their programs and policies in a way that is sufficiently detailed yet understandable and meaningful to investors and other interested parties.

MEASURING EXECUTIVE PAY: THE EQUITY COMPENSATION CHALLENGE

The 2009 changes in proxy disclosure rules caused a shift in the method and outcome of future years' executive compensation reporting. The reported numbers that tend to be the focus of media, pay critics and analysts do not always capture the true story of executive pay.

Understanding Reported Values of Executive Pay

The complex structure of executive compensation, dominated by various forms of equity and cash-based LTIs, can lead to significantly different interpretations of pay. These differences result from the interaction of varying approaches to data collection, analysis, and reporting. Ensuring that all relevant data are collected for incorporation in the analysis, applying meaningful analytical tools to construct pay models, and reporting the information in a way that recognizes the complexity of pay practices all are essential for board-level decision support. Increased disclosure requirements, governance pressures, and continued media attention make it imperative that pay values are understood and clearly communicated – internally and externally.

Effect of Prior Year's Compensation Actions

Special circumstances underlying a previous year's equity awards can be misinterpreted the next year. As an illustration, in 2009 many companies acted to address the results of a depressed stock market, increased market volatility, poor business results, and the effects of those conditions on executive pay. These special, often one-time actions held potential for misinterpretation – either because they might be deemed part of annual pay or, conversely, because they might be excluded from pay calculations altogether. Such decisions made during the data-collection process can lead to a flawed analysis as true pay levels resulting from these items are not represented properly. A particular executive's compensation often can only be interpreted properly by understanding pay actions on a before-and-after basis.

In the 2009 example, companies that implemented stock option exchange programs canceled many years of stock options and re-granted some or all of those at a more favorable price. Merely reporting the Black–Scholes value of the re-grant as an element of 2009 pay oversimplified the total compensation implications. Some of those companies excluded officers from their programs yet took other action – such as skipping or deferring the normal annual grant – that also needed to be considered. A company whose compensation peer group consists of several companies that made these types of pay decisions may have raised its executives' pay levels without recognizing these dynamics.

These complexities highlight the need for heightened attention to a three-faceted approach to executive equity compensation interpretation – collection, analysis and reporting.

Data Collection

Discussions of executive compensation focus primarily on single-year values, forming the root of many misunderstandings. But executive equity awards often are developed as part of a multiyear plan. SEC proxy disclosure rules recognize this through the required three-year reporting format for the Summary Compensation Table and the multiyear aggregations in other tables. A common example is when an executive receives a large new-hire equity grant, often two to four times the size of a typical annual grant, and then receives no equity award the following year(s). The single-year approach often leads to the conclusion that there has been a pay cut or an elimination of LTI awards when pay in year two is compared to that of year one. Much of the important detail is contained in footnotes and narrative in the proxy statement, without which the tabular figures may be misinterpreted.

In addition, many pay actions not captured in the tables are nevertheless disclosed in the CD&A section or appear in Form 8-K filings subsequent to the issuance of the proxy statement. Given the dated (look-back) nature of tabular information, these additional sources are critical to understanding the true current market for executive pay. The complexities of executive equity compensation have long required a multiyear, multisource perspective and any economic turmoil can increase the importance of this approach.

Data Analysis

While the valuation of equity instruments receives much attention, the variations in fair value that may result from volatility or expected life assumptions are less significant than the effects on deemed value from a series of decisions that guide the equity compensation calculation. Such analysis often is bypassed and the fair value resulting from the reporting process – typically what appears in SEC filings – is accepted as the pay value without any further consideration. Compensation committees and executives need to understand these dynamics to ensure effective pay decisions.

Volatile equity markets can result in equity grants with an unprecedented variation of values relative to business fundamentals and significant intra-year variations in relative grant values. For example, looking back to 2009, assume two companies whose share prices directly track the NASDAQ index both granted stock options in 2009, the first in early March and the other in early September. The first company reported grant-date fair values approximately 50 percent lower than the second company, but by the end of 2009 provided intrinsic value that was 260 percent greater. Variations of this magnitude were unprecedented in the history of executive pay and teach important lessons. An unusually large number of companies awarded stock options in February through April 2009 near the market low, and in many cases those grants quickly accumulated value far greater than the artificially low Black–Scholes value that was reported in SEC filings. Ironically, many of those companies granted a larger number of shares to offset the lower fair value at the time, exacerbating this effect.

These dynamics require that companies understand not only what was granted (i.e., stock options, time-vested shares, performance-based shares, cash LTI) and how much was granted, but when it was granted. In addition to understanding award type and timing, performance features require attention to the effect of performance contingencies or accelerators, thresholds and targets, absolute versus relative performance measures, and the interaction of time-based and performance-based conditions. Also, as publicly traded companies now typically have stock ownership guidelines and share retention requirements, the risk–reward balance has changed. Thoughtful analysis is required to understand the real effect on executive pay value resulting from the interaction of these features.

Data Reporting

With proper data collection and analysis, pay can be reported in ways that provide a meaningful picture of executive pay practices over the past years. A single snapshot of pay is not adequate for telling the story in this complex environment. Merely viewing pay as a single number may lead a compensation committee to reach flawed conclusions about the company's competitive position in the market. Scenario-based pay projections – incorporated into tally sheet and wealth accumulation analyses – will provide the compensation committee and the executive team with a point of view consistent with other business decision processes.

Pay Granted, Earned, and Realized

A greater scrutiny of pay values introduces a need for the multidimensional view of pay, with at least three possible pay views to be considered. This approach requires taking pay analysis beyond a grant-based focus to a dynamic view of the life cycle of executive pay – when granted, earned, and realized.

Under current SEC rules, equity incentive figures in the Summary Compensation Table can be misleading or difficult to interpret. The fair value of all equity awards made during the reporting year are deemed to have been what was "paid" to the executive for that year rather than what was accrued for accounting purposes. There are lengthy and complex arguments around which of these two methods is preferable, and why, but sound pay analysis does not force an either/or decision. It is important to understand what was granted, the incremental amount earned, and – as media organizations often do – the pay realized over a period of time to obtain a true picture of executive pay. Thus, we have seen the development of supplemental disclosures to show "realized pay" or "realizable pay" (with still some notable variance among users in the meaning of these terms), depending on the organization and what it believes most helpful in understanding the compensation of its executives.

While no single analytical structure will make sense for all companies, compensation committees and executive teams should:

- Think through the three data processes (collection, analysis, and reporting) in the context of three alternative views of pay (granted, earned, and realized), and
- Ask a series of questions to ensure a comprehensive approach. Table 5.1 illustrates the types of questions that may help guide a year's analyses and decisions.

Various tools – tally sheets, wealth accumulation models, "walk away" value calculations, and scenario-based analysis – address some of these issues. A methodical approach can help a company understand the tools being used and the rationale for using a tool to the exclusion of others. It can be

TABLE 5.1 Data Processes of Collection, Analysis, and Reporting

	Granted	Earned	Realized
Collection	Did we capture all of the grants and actions taken last year? Have we properly categorized "annual" pay actions?	Did many of our peers grant during the market lows? How is that affecting reported grant value and fair value?	Were there significant realization events that created compensation not captured in the typical proxy and survey formats? Have we compared vested but unexercised in-the-money option gains?
Analysis	Have we explored the stock price patterns of our peers and reviewed scenario-based pay values?	Have we analyzed competitors' changes in vesting schedules, acceleration provisions, and holding requirements to understand changes in earnings opportunities?	Have we conducted an historical analysis of realized pay to understand how this may be affecting current grant patterns?
Reporting	Have we accounted for new hires, promotions, terminations, founders, and special qualifications of incumbents?	Are we considering risk-adjusted differences in pay values: options vs. time-vested full-value awards vs. thresholds and targets on performance awards?	Do our tally sheet and wealth accumulation tools capture realized value including post-vesting accumulation?

helpful to view these alternatives in this three-by-three analytical framework to capture the issues surrounding the collection, analysis, and reporting of equity compensation data and recognize alternative measurement points of grant, earning, and realization to ensure a clear understanding of market pay levels and practices.

FURTHER EXECUTIVE PAY DISCLOSURE UNDER DODD–FRANK

While broadly targeting the financial services industry, including provisions that address consumer and investor protection, the Dodd–Frank legislation contains important executive compensation and corporate governance provisions that apply to most public companies regardless of industry. To a considerable extent, Dodd–Frank left the specifics of the new requirements to rule-making by the SEC and then inclusion in listing standards by the securities exchanges.

Most of the executive compensation provisions of the Dodd–Frank legislation added new disclosure requirements for public companies.

The effective dates of the various parts of the act varied; certain changes were effective on enactment (July 21, 2010), while other provisions only were designed to take effect either after a transition period or after the regulatory authorities promulgated rules fleshing out the statutory mandates. The SEC devoted its initial focus to the Dodd–Frank provisions with specified effective dates and only began to address the last group of statutory provisions affecting executive pay disclosures in 2015. Dodd–Frank undoubtedly is having a substantial effect on executive pay processes at most public companies.

Understand Investor and Proxy Advisory Policies

Companies should understand the key policies of various parties that now weigh in on executive compensation, especially those that may affect the acceptance of their compensation programs. Accordingly, the regular review of the current policies and past recommendations of proxy advisory firms and major investors should identify programs that risk adverse reaction from these groups, allowing companies to reconsider their programs or explain their effectiveness from the company's viewpoint. Modification or engagement (or a combination of the two) may help avoid the negative consequences that could follow a violation of such policies. See Figure 5.1.

Say on Pay

Resolving a long-running debate on whether and how to obtain the views of shareholders on executive pay, Dodd–Frank requires a public company to provide shareholders with a nonbinding vote to approve the compensation of its NEOs. A say-on-pay vote must be held at least once every three years, which started with the first annual shareholders' meeting occurring after January 21, 2011 (six months after the date of enactment). As of the same effective date, and at least once every six years thereafter, shareholders must be afforded the right to vote on whether a say-on-pay vote occurs once every one, two, or three years.

A company's say-on-pay vote covers the compensation shown in its CD&A and Compensation Tables (including narrative disclosures). Effective communications with shareholders is especially important in connection

FIGURE 5.1 Review of investor and proxy advisory firm policies.

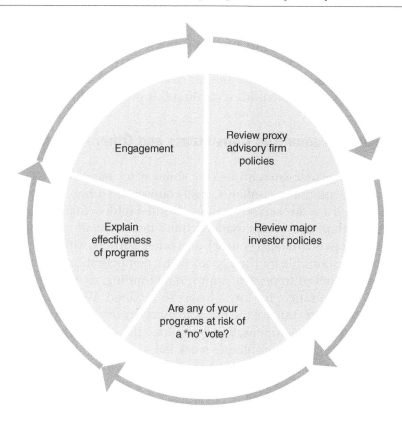

with a say-on-pay vote. Before a vote, a company should make an effort to address potential shareholder concerns with the goal of obtaining strong majority approval. After either a negative vote or one with a narrow approval margin, outreach to large shareholders to obtain their feedback can help the company understand shareholders' concerns so that they can be addressed.

Advisory or not, a failure to respond effectively to a high level of dissatisfaction may result in "withhold" or "against" votes regarding the re-election of compensation committee members.

Say on Parachutes

Executive compensation payments and other benefits triggered by a change in control of the organization (golden parachutes) are common at US companies. However, well-publicized examples of particularly large payments to executives sparked controversy over the authorization of what some perceived to be overly executive-friendly arrangements. The initiatives regarding say on pay ultimately led to the related requirement of disclosure and a nonbinding shareholder vote regarding executive compensation arrangements related to proposed change-in-control transactions – coined "say-on-parachute" votes. The disclosure for a say-on-parachute vote is required in any proxy for a shareholders meeting at which shareholders are asked to approve an acquisition, merger, consolidation, or proposed sale of all (or substantially all) of the company's assets. A say-on-parachute vote is not required if the parachute arrangements already have been subject to such a vote, although the conditions imposed by the regulations regarding this provision limit its utility.

Compensation Committee Consultants and Other Advisers

Two critical and related issues involve the ability of a compensation committee to engage compensation consultants, legal counsel and other advisers, and the independence of any advisers so retained. Dodd–Frank contains separate provisions that authorize a compensation committee to retain a compensation consultant, independent legal counsel, and other advisers, with the committee to "be directly responsible for the appointment, compensation, and oversight." A company is required to provide appropriate funding, as determined by the compensation committee, for any advisers so retained. With respect to compensation consultants (but not the other advisers), proxy disclosure is required regarding whether the compensation committee has retained a compensation consultant, whether that consultant's work led to any conflict of interest, the nature of any conflicts, and how those conflicts are being addressed.

With respect to independence, a compensation committee "may only select a compensation consultant, legal counsel, or other adviser . . . after taking account the factors identified by the [SEC]. . . ." The SEC's rulemaking identified factors that may affect independence, and the securities exchanges subsequently adopted listing standards within the bounds of the SEC rules, including six general factors contained in the SEC's rules. After considering these factors and other considerations that it deems relevant, the compensation committee then is free to select a compensation adviser but must disclose how it has resolved any potential conflicts.

Pay-for-Performance Disclosure

Dodd–Frank mandated that the SEC craft rules requiring a public company to disclose in the proxy statement for its annual shareholder meeting a "clear description" that "shows the relationship between executive compensation actually paid and the financial performance" of the company, taking into account any changes in the value of the company's stock and any dividends and distributions. The disclosure may include a graphic representation of the required information. Although the SEC's rule is still not final (as of the time of the writing of this edition), most experts read the last portion of this statutory language as a requirement to discuss performance in terms of TSR. See Figure 5.2.

While publicly traded companies will ultimately need to comply with this pay-versus-performance disclosure rule, some companies have developed their own

FIGURE 5.2 Approach for additional pay-versus-performance disclosures.

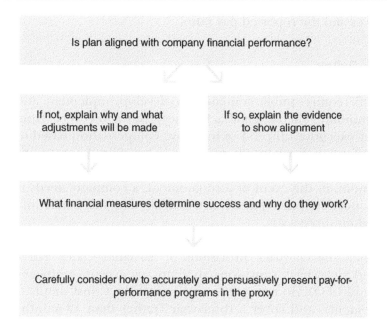

analyses to enhance their proxy disclosures. Some companies may find it useful to present and explain performance using other metrics. These comparisons often involve trends in either reported or realized/realizable compensation versus company performance on an absolute basis (e.g., year-over-year growth) or relative (performance versus peers). In any case, since the relationship of executive pay and performance is of particular interest to investors, a company generally should address the issue in an executive summary of the CD&A.

CEO Pay Ratio Disclosure

In an effort to address the debate about internal pay equity, Dodd–Frank imposed an especially burdensome provision requiring the SEC to mandate a new compensation ratio pay disclosure. The required disclosure (applicable for various SEC filings, not simply a company's annual proxy statement) consists of three items:

- The median of the "annual total compensation" of all of the company's employees except its CEO
- The CEO's total annual compensation
- The ratio of the two numbers.

Much of the SEC's rulemaking was devoted to how a company may determine such median employee and then that individual's compensation. Other than some limited exceptions, all employees (including non-US and part-time employees) need to be considered in determining the median employee. In addition to the required disclosures, companies can include additional information that may provide context regarding the company's pay practices and the reported pay ratio.

Clawback Policy

Dodd–Frank requires public companies to develop, implement, and disclose what is commonly called a "clawback policy" for the recovery (from current and former executive officers) of incentive compensation based on certain financial information where there has been a required accounting restatement due to material noncompliance with a financial reporting requirement. At a minimum, in the event of a restatement, a company needs to recoup any excess incentive-based payments made based on inaccurate information in the previous three years.

In general, the clawback rules under Dodd–Frank are considerably broader than the clawback provisions of Sarbanes–Oxley. For example, Dodd–Frank's clawback provisions apply to any executive officer (not just the CEO and CFO), do not require any misconduct (just simply the requisite restatement), and cover a three-year (rather than 12-month) period. Key features of a clawback policy under Dodd–Frank include who is subject to the policy, the triggers for a recovery, and what elements of compensation are subject to the policy. While clawback policies have become a widespread and best practice, every existing policy will need to be reviewed and updated for compliance with final SEC rulemaking.

Consideration should be given not only to the Dodd–Frank requirements, but also to any additional features or processes that address the organization's particular circumstances or facilitate administration. A company complying with best practices might extend its clawback policy to recoup excess compensation paid as a result of (a) ethical misconduct, or (b) a restatement of financial statements unrelated to changes in accounting rules or interpretations.

Employee and Director Hedging

Under Dodd–Frank, the SEC must require each public company to disclose in its annual proxy statement whether any employee (not just an executive officer) or board member is permitted to purchase financial instruments "designed to hedge or offset any decrease in the market value of equity securities" granted as compensation or otherwise owned by such employee or director. Because equity hedging strategies can enable an employee or director to limit the effect of holding requirements commonly imposed on top executives and directors, the provision aims to shed light on any such actions and indirectly encourages companies to bar or limit such hedging. Even before Dodd–Frank, SEC rules already called for the disclosure of policies regarding hedging; one notable effect of the legislative provision is the extension of such disclosure to all employees as well as directors.

Investors increasingly expect companies to implement and enforce anti-hedging and anti-pledging policies. While prior transactions may be difficult to unwind, companies should adopt prospective policies against hedging and generally pledging. If no policy exists, companies should explain how they mitigate risk associated with these practices.

Perquisites

Perquisites continue to be scrutinized by shareholders. In light of years of reduction or elimination of various perks, the trend is toward limiting perquisites to those that directly relate to legitimate corporate purposes. Companies should be prepared to explain how perks are justifiable; examples have been ones that directly assist the executive in focusing on his/her company responsibilities or enhance the security and health of the executive and his/her family.

Double-Trigger Equity Vesting

Double-triggers have become the favored approach regarding both cash payments and equity vesting in connection with a change in control. Such policies generally prevent payments of cash severance and accelerated vesting of equity (time and performance-based) on a change in control unless the executive is terminated without cause or terminates employment for good reason within a specified time following a change in control. The market increasingly views double-trigger vesting as a "best practice" in compensation. Any company with a single-trigger change-in-control provision should explain in its proxy the rationale for the provision and why it is in the company's interests to maintain such a provision.

Disclosures Regarding Board Chair and CEO Structures

The SEC was directed by Dodd–Frank to issue rules requiring a public company to disclose in its annual proxy the reasons why the company has chosen either the same person to serve both as board chair and CEO or two different people to serve in those positions. Basically, Dodd–Frank provides a legislative mandate for what companies already were required to do under the SEC's proxy disclosure rules.

How to Approach Disclosures

In drafting proxy disclosures, companies should be careful to avoid embellishments that can prompt litigation. Disclose what is material, address what may be unfavorable, and explain why a program, award, or provision works for your company, but be careful of overselling. Tell your story the right way and don't forget to engage shareholders.

MAJOR EXECUTIVE COMPENSATION TRENDS AND CHALLENGES

Say on Pay

Subject to certain exceptions, the 2010 Dodd–Frank Act requires publicly traded companies to seek an advisory vote of shareholders on executive pay at least once every three years. This extremely important development provided shareholders with a distinct voice in pay matters and armed proxy advisers with additional clout in influencing the proxy voting process. Having a true "pay-for-performance" executive compensation program has never been more important.

With this heightened scrutiny, there is a temptation to play it safe and develop pay programs similar to those of their peers. This would be a mistake; compensation strategies that work for both executive and shareholders must consider the unique situation and business strategy of each company.

In addition, a purely legalistic approach to the CD&A section of the annual proxy statement no longer suffices. Companies and compensation committees, out of necessity, must become effective communicators to furnish shareholders and others with clear, user-friendly explanations of the rationales behind their pay decisions. Effective CD&As now tell a company's pay-for-performance "story" while still fulfilling legal requirements.

Institutional Investors and Proxy Advisors

Say on pay has considerably augmented the ability of institutional investors and their proxy advisers to influence executive compensation. Investors have demanded that compensation committees establish a clear link between what management accomplished and the amount of pay delivered. The proxy advisors assist the institutional investors and monitor company pay decisions. The recommendations of proxy advisors carry substantial weight and are a principal factor for weak support on the say on pay vote.

Institutional investors continue to focus on incentive programs and the related payouts, thus complicating the work of compensation committees. They no longer simply look at dilution models and vote yes or no; they now use detailed financial formulas or "black box" approaches to determine pay-for-performance relationships and are active in criticizing companies that do not meet their guidelines.

Long-Term Incentives

Most companies today use a portfolio approach to long-term incentives (LTIs) in order to ensure the adaptability and resiliency of their LTI program. These portfolios typically include a mix of equity vehicles, including stock options as well as time- and performance-based restricted stock.

There is no single approach to equity portfolios. The makeup of equity differs for each company and is influenced by industry, competition for talent, and business strategy. In recent years, however, performance-based restricted stock tends to make up about 50–60 percent of many portfolios, particularly for those of larger companies. Conversely, stock options have slowly lost favor with compensation committees in the past 10 years.

It is not difficult to understand the increased interest in performance-based equity plans. Institutional investors and proxy advisors prefer a substantial portion of the LTI program use performance-based equity. In turn, companies have more heavily relied on these performance awards to earn shareholder approval through the say-on-pay vote. However, these plans can be complicated to design and monitor, and they often increase the workload of committees.

Relative Metrics

Performance-based equity comes with a host of design challenges. For many companies using performance awards, the financial goals used to determine how many shares will ultimately vest are often "absolute" (i.e., the company sets the goals based on their budget or another internal benchmark, typically over a three-year cumulative period). Setting a multiyear financial goal with any level of precision is extremely difficult for most firms, particularly in cyclical industries or times of economic uncertainty.

Given the challenges inherent with absolute financial goals, many companies had moved to relative total shareholder return (TSR) metrics. Relative TSR plans are fairly simple to design (i.e., no need to forecast or set multiyear goals) and they are typically perceived to be defensible to both institutional shareholders and proxy advisors.

However, companies are now recognizing the limitations of a TSR-based program and turning to relative financial metrics, such as revenue growth, earnings growth, or return metrics. One reason for this trend is the growing recognition that while TSR provides strong shareholder alignment, executives often feel that they cannot control the outcome given all the different factors impacting share price. Programs with relative financial metrics provide greater line of sight to executives while still securing proxy advisor and shareholder support.

Environmental, Social, and Governance (ESG) Factors

ESG has emerged as one of the major buzzwords in corporate governance. Large institutional shareholders have now urged boards to consider environmental, social, and governance factors when developing corporate strategy. In turn, companies are slowly incorporating more metrics in the annual or long-term incentive program that touch environmental or socially responsible issues. ESG metrics had been largely limited to heavy goods industries or those in resource extraction. As public interest in these topics grow, however, the use of ESG metrics is extending to many other industries.

Interest in ESG is growing, but related metrics still make up a small portion of incentive programs. In many cases, the ESG factors are not specifically weighted but are part of the qualitative review of an individual's performance. If weighted, the current trend is for companies to base 5–20 percent of the annual or long-term incentive on ESG factors.

Adopting ESG metrics into the incentive programs brings its own set of challenges. Just as the case with financial metrics, picking the right metrics to satisfy investor expectations and propel corporate strategy is a top concern.

Compensation Committees

Dodd–Frank raised the profile and responsibilities of compensation committees – much like Sarbanes–Oxley did for audit committees – which has resulted in increased scrutiny of their processes and decisions. Compensation committees are now more involved in the details of executive compensation planning and implementation, especially regarding long-term incentives.

With the proliferation of performance plans and the need to quantify and justify total pay, compensation committees must focus more on long-term performance drivers.

Committee members need to spend more time ensuring they are choosing the right measures, monitoring the metrics to assure they are driving the right executive behaviors, and adjusting them as appropriate.

Compensation committees are not as close as management to the operations of the business, often leading to concern about how performance is calibrated and not wanting to establish goals that are too easy or too difficult to meet. A frequently asked question is, "How do we know we have set the right targets?"

Internal Pay Equity

Internal pay equity analysis is a growing priority because many compensation committees continue to be frustrated relying solely on external market data. As a result, many companies disclose that they use both external as well as internal pay factors in determining compensation levels. However, the approaches to establishing internal pay equity often suffer from shortcomings in methodology.

Internal pay equity too often focuses solely on comparing pay levels without looking closely at what executives actually do in their jobs. This shortcoming likely will become more apparent as companies supplement the required disclosures under the final rules adopted by the SEC regarding the so-called CEO pay ratio. By going beyond job titles and pay ratios, companies can better judge what is unique about each executive position and determine pay levels that are defensible and fair. Even after this is accomplished, however, there is still the need to reconcile internal pay equity with external benchmarking.

Total Remuneration

Often, in focusing on the technical and motivational aspects of an annual or long-term incentive plan, a committee neglects to put the parts together and look at the total picture. The use of tally sheets was a useful initial step in this process. Other tools and approaches such as realized pay and realizable pay advanced the analytics available to compensation committees.

There is an increased focus on total remuneration, both in terms of total amounts actually or potentially delivered to executives and the role each element plays in achieving organizational goals. This far-reaching exercise needs to encompass extrinsic pay elements (salary, annual and long-term incentives, benefits, and perquisites) as well as intrinsic elements (work culture, job satisfaction, work environment, and development opportunities).

Volatility of Pay Outcomes

The current benchmarking practice is to look at pay levels and mix of pay against peers – what is the total compensation value against peers and what is the value of each pay element. This snapshot approach is useful but only goes so far. It does not capture a true picture of pay value over time compared to peers. Many compensation committees would benefit from undertaking an analysis that projects current grant values into the future under a range of outcomes based on the level of incentive awards and performance scenarios. The resulting volatility score gives an extended and more accurate picture of the competitive landscape by identifying the effects of potential swings in the pay package. It is also a powerful tool in assessing risk in pay programs.

6 Sales Compensation Essentials

The degree of an HR department's involvement with sales compensation plan design and implementation varies from company to company. In some companies, HR's involvement is actively sought by the sales department. In others, HR's involvement is discouraged or prevented. HR professionals frequently ask, "What can I do to play a more meaningful role in plan design and implementation at my company?" This question is not surprising, because having limited or no involvement in the process of shaping and launching a sales compensation plan means that companies miss the opportunity to use the expertise of their HR staff in key people-management areas. These key areas include ensuring that a company's sales compensation plan is designed to attract, retain, and reward talented salespeople who can win and keep customers. It is clear that developing and using a compensation plan that helps a company achieve that goal should draw on the expertise of the HR function. This chapter describes the aspects of sales compensation plan design and implementation in which the HR professional can play a meaningful role. Further, it provides suggestions about actions that an HR professional can take to perform that role effectively.

WORKING WITH THE SALES ORGANIZATION

At many companies, the business partner role defines how HR is expected to work with its assigned organizational client. The assigned client may be either a business unit that includes the sales organization or only the sales organization. When the business partner role is the prevailing model for providing HR services, the HR generalist is faced with a broad range of duties and responsibilities. However, an HR professional's no. 1 priority should be to gain and continually build a thorough understanding of the assigned client's business. When the assigned client is the sales organization, that understanding should include:

- Customer markets served and the product/service offerings provided.
- Sales channels deployed and the jobs operating within those channels.
- Current year's business plan, sales strategies, and sales financial goals.
- Sales leadership's operational style (e.g., centralized versus decentralized management) as it pertains to various sales management programs – territory assignment, quota allocation, sales crediting – that impact compensation.

Some senior HR professionals have said that an up-to-date understanding of the four areas itemized is the entry or "ante into the game." As in many business situations, the key to success is the quality of one's relationships with the individuals in senior leadership positions. Relationships built on trust, confidence, and respect are acquired over time. HR professionals who have successfully developed effective working relationships with senior sales leaders did so through regular, proactive, and meaningful interactions with the sales organization. Figure 6.1 itemizes activities in which an HR/compensation professional should engage to demonstrate a willingness to learn how the sales organization operates. Through these activities, an HR/compensation professional can develop a first-hand understanding of the needs and requirements of the sales organization for compensation support.

Taking the initiative to understand how the sales organization operates assumes that sales leaders are receptive to having HR involved with the sales organization overall, and with the sales compensation plan in particular. Because in some cases this is not a valid assumption, Figure 6.2 indicates some of the more common objections to HR involvement with the sales compensation plan and provides suggestions for overcoming those objections. These suggestions should be helpful to an HR professional in convincing the top sales executive that his or her involvement with the sales compensation plan will be helpful to both the sales organization and the company.

Whether HR is considered an internal consultant or a policy gatekeeper, involvement of the HR professional with the sales compensation plan is important to business success. Meaningful involvement is most likely to take place in situations where the HR professional has developed a thorough understanding of how sales operates and has built an effective working relationship with key sales leaders throughout the sales organization. Additionally, HR/compensation professionals must develop and improve on their knowledge of sales compensation principles, practices, and techniques. Every HR/compensation professional with responsibility for sales compensation should ask, "What am I doing to continually improve my mastery of the tools and techniques required to provide innovative compensation solutions to the sales challenges faced by my company?"

This chapter's overall goal is to provide you with the tools and knowledge required to support the sales organization through compensation solutions.

FIGURE 6.1 HR professional – sales compensation plan involvement.

Who	What (Illustrative Interactions)
• Sales leaders, i.e., top sales executive and regional sales executives (e.g., North America, Europe, Asia/Pacific)	• Regular conversations (monthly, quarterly) about effectiveness of current plans – what's working, what's not; early ideas for change in the future • Participation in sales leadership meetings related to future business planning; implications for sales compensation • Review/discuss with sales leadership teams: quarterly sales results and impact on sales incentive compensation payments, e.g., percent of sales team earning under the plan, percent of sales team achieving target incentive earnings; overachievement earnings; individual sales performance and general staffing concerns
• Field sales managers, e.g., first-level sales managers	• Occasional "work withs" to understand challenges faced by field sales managers in their jobs; role sales compensation plays in motivating and managing their sales team • Regular calls to selected field sales managers to gain feedback on current plans – what's working; what's not • Issues/challenges with current plans – what are the most common questions or problems members of the sales force are experiencing under the plan • Needs relative to managing with the plan, e.g., reports, response to special requests
• Sales staff, e.g., sales operations or administrative executives	• Regular conversations with sales staff supporting the plans to understand their perspectives on what's working, what's not and why; early thoughts about opportunities for plan improvement in subsequent year • Periodic meetings to confirm system capabilities, abilities to meet management information needs
• "Sellers," e.g., sales representatives, account managers, sales specialists	• Occasional "ride withs" to understand sales roles and jobs, i.e., how members of the sales force go about their work, influence they have on customer buying decisions, service work they perform; how sales compensation plan influences their behavior and performance • Periodic sales force surveys to understand what members of the sales force like best/least about current plans

FIGURE 6.2 Overcoming resistance to HR involvement with sales compensations.

Objections – Sales Executives	Suggested Response – HR Professional
• No relevant experience	• Describe experience in sales. • Compensation plan design and design of management-incentive plans. • Explain role in process and key contributions acknowledged by others. • Describe seminars or courses taken in sales compensation.
• No understanding of our sales channels, process, jobs	• Ask for the opportunity to develop that understanding by visiting field locations, doing "work withs" with field managers, going on sales calls with sales reps.
• No time	• Explain that priorities have been adjusted to make time available to work on sales compensation.
• Don't know where it would make sense to involve you	• Suggest a process; offer ideas about specific tasks that HR could undertake and complete; describe outcomes and benefits.

In particular, the goal of this chapter is to describe some of the competencies that require mastery in today's business environment. The following are included in this list of competencies:

- Know how to help sales executives address and resolve sales compensation problems as they arise during the course of a year.
- Know how to assess the effectiveness of the sales compensation plan and therefore how and when to help sales executives make plan changes in order to increase sales effectiveness through compensation.
- Have the ability to lead or participate in a design process that includes advising management on which jobs should be eligible to participate in the sales compensation plan, the appropriate level of pay for those jobs, what type of plan is appropriate, and how the incentive arrangement should be structured.
- Develop a holistic understanding of the company's sales management programs and the role their interdependence plays in the company's achievement of its sales goals.
- Understand how communication strategies and tactics are created and executed in order to ensure that a new or changed plan produces the expected business results.

SIX AREAS OF SALES COMPENSATION PLAN INVOLVEMENT

HR professionals should be proactive in seeking opportunities to become involved with the sales compensation plan. A solid understanding of how the sales organization operates and the respect of sales leadership are important prerequisites for gaining involvement with the sales compensation plan. Once those prerequisites are established, it is equally important to be confident about where and how HR involvement with sales compensation is beneficial to a company and its sales force. HR involvement is most often desired and/or needed in the following six areas.

1. Problem Resolution

Many HR professionals indicate that their first significant involvement with the sales compensation plan was the result of a major problem that sales leaders believed was caused by the plan. This can often occur in companies in which HR's involvement with sales compensation is either a new or emerging responsibility. In such a company, an HR professional might be invited to help address a problem with the plan because there is a new awareness among sales executives that HR can bring an objective perspective and fresh thinking that could help address and resolve the problem. This, of course, means that the HR professional must have the knowledge, skills, and experience to make a meaningful contribution to a solution. HR professionals are too frequently not asked for their involvement because they are seen as not having adequate experience and skills in sales compensation. They are further perceived as not possessing a sufficiently intimate knowledge of the business to be of help to the sales organization. The old adage of "be prepared" is quite relevant here. An HR professional must possess applicable knowledge, skill, and experience in order to make a value-added contribution.

Common examples of plan problems that HR professionals are frequently asked to investigate include: (1) sales employee dissatisfaction with the plan, (2) exceptions to either payout calculations or plan rules, (3) overpayments or underpayments, and (4) turnover either higher or lower than internally expected, industry benchmarks, or both. Seasoned HR professionals should be equipped to help the sales organization address problems such as these.

Most experienced HR professionals understand human motivation and how to tap into the workforce through interviews and surveys in order to determine root causes of job dissatisfaction. Many HR professionals have also acquired analytical skills that can be applied to determining the turnover rate and its relationship to overall industry conditions. The important point is this: Because the problems just mentioned are common sales compensation problems, a thoughtful HR professional should be able to respond with a plan of action when called on for help by the sales organization. This book is one source of information that can help HR professionals develop that action plan.

Generally speaking, the exact cause of the perceived sales compensation problem is less important than how one goes about helping sales leaders address and fix the problem. Two hallmarks of success in resolving such problems, at least from the sales function's perspective, are a willingness on the part of HR to act swiftly and authoritatively to identify the root causes of the problem and the ability to help sales leaders formulate practical alternative solutions that can be implemented quickly. It is worth mentioning, however, that HR should take great care in identifying and isolating the root cause of the problems associated with sales compensation. In a majority of cases in which sales compensation is blamed for shortcomings in its overall effectiveness, the root cause of the problem actually lies elsewhere.

Consider this common situation. When members of the sales force are not earning their incentive compensation opportunity under the plan, field sales managers may report that their people are dissatisfied with the plan. However, the dissatisfaction may have little to do with either the incentive opportunity or the payout formula mechanics. The real problem may well be overly ambitious sales growth targets reflected in sales quotas that may be unachievable by a disproportionately high percentage of the sales force. The important point here is this: It is easy to attach blame to the sales compensation plan, but rarely will a fix to the sales compensation plan solve a performance problem that has its root cause elsewhere.

2. Sales Compensation Guiding Principles

Guiding principles are the main values that best-practice companies follow in order to design effective and successful sales compensation plans. Guiding principles are based on and support the company's philosophy of pay. However, these guiding principles are rarely documented and assembled in one place for ready reference and use. There are two disadvantages to not using a set of documented guiding principles during a plan design process:

1. The absence of guiding principles is analogous to trying to shoot at a target in the dark. How do you know when you have hit the bullseye? The answer, of course, is that you don't know. Thus, guiding principles set forth the standards against which a plan or plans are designed. The principles provide each of the participants in the plan design process with the same understanding of what the design team is shooting for at a conceptual level and in terms of the design results. A statement of sales compensation guiding principles typically includes the following topics: (1) business strategy, (2) competitive compensation positioning, (3) plan types, (4) performance management, and (5) administrative considerations, for example, desire for plan simplicity, management commitment to effective communication.

2. The second disadvantage of not having and using guiding principles is that it is virtually impossible to know the extent to which a new plan has contributed to business success. For example, the statement of guiding principles typically defines the expected performance distribution under the sales compensation plan. Without the benefit of a specific

expectation in this area, it is difficult to determine if the plan paid more or fewer salespeople than expected.

An HR professional involved with a sales compensation plan should encourage the design team to formulate and use a set of guiding principles for the plan design and implementation process. Using guiding principles will provide the design team with a blueprint that both sets forth clear direction and can save time during the process itself.

3. Design and Implementation Process

Companies are increasingly following a documented process for the design and implementation of their sales compensation plans. Most processes include the following four major activities:

1. *Assessment.* How effective is the current sales compensation plan; what evidence is there to suggest that the plan may require modification or may need to be replaced by a completely new plan, for example, change in business strategy; implementation of new or restructured sales channels; jobs; or both; new product launch?
2. *Design and testing.* What changes could be made to incentive pay mechanics – that is, linking performance to pay; will such change redirect sales behavior in the areas management requires for achievement of the coming year's business results; can such changes be supported with sales financial data (i.e., costing and individual performance modeling) that show a proposed change will result in a material improvement in business results?
3. *Implementation.* How will plan changes or a completely new plan be introduced to the sales force so that it will produce maximum motivational mileage and thus contribute to achievement of desired business results?
4. *Monitoring.* What actions are taken to confirm that the sales force has received its plans, that it understands the plans, and that field sales managers are managing effectively with the new plans?

It is easier to lay out these activities than to actually execute them effectively. There are three common flaws in the plan design and implementation process that you should watch out for at your company:

1. The first flaws are those that are present both in the underlying process used to assess the current plan and in the process to either design new plans or modify current plans. There are three common process errors: (1) executing design tasks out of sequence (e.g., modifying the incentive formula without first assessing how well the current plan is working, understanding what the new business objectives may be, or both); (2) limiting design work to a single function such as Sales, when the design process would actually benefit from a multifunctional approach that includes Sales, Finance, HR, and others; and (3) misunderstanding how long the design process takes and thus either spending too little time (the most common mistake) or too much time on it.

It is frequently the HR professional's role to ensure that one or more of these three process errors does not encumber the design process. To do so, HR (or the designated process owner) should pull together representatives from all of the functions that currently have involvement with the plan and agree on the safeguards that will be put into the process – for example, agreeing to a defined project work plan with regular checkpoint meetings – to ensure that none of these flaws will be allowed to creep in to the design process.

2. Design errors are the second most common category of flaws that occur during the process. Common design errors include: salary/incentive ratio that is inappropriate for a particular sales job, leverage (i.e., upside incentive opportunity) that is either too little or too high, performance measures that cannot be influenced or accurately tracked and credited to members of the sales force, and sales quotas (goals) that do not appropriately reflect the sales potential in sales force territories. Here, too, the HR professional should take an active role in confirming with others who are involved with the sales compensation plan that these types of design flaws are common and should be avoided in the process.

3. Ineffective implementation and ineffective monitoring of performance represent the third set of common flaws that occur when changes are made to a sales compensation plan. Examples of ineffective implementation include: no formal process for communicating plan change, no defined/assigned change accountabilities, and lack of a clear leadership message about change (what will change, why change is important now, and how change will benefit customers, salespeople, and the company). Examples of ineffective monitoring of the new plan's impact on the business include: no predefined measures of plan success, no set time period (e.g., after first payout, after first quarter, midyear) for assessing success, and no reports provided to field sales managers so they can see how the sales force is performing under the plan.

HR typically plays an important role in developing materials for communicating the compensation plan to the sales force. Employee communications is a key competency of many HR professionals. This is therefore one area where help is usually welcomed. However, HR generally plays a less active role in monitoring the effectiveness of new sales compensation plans. This should not be the case. Because the sales compensation plan can play an important role in sales force performance management, the HR professional should be proactive in helping sales leaders define how success under the new (or revised) plan will be assessed and measured.

4. Competitive Pay Assessments

In most companies, sales executives look to the compensation plan to help attract and retain the caliber of people they need to successfully sell to and interact with customers. Because attracting and retaining top-notch talent is one of the most persistent challenges faced by sales organizations, HR has an opportunity to make a major contribution to the sales compensation plan through competitive pay assessment. HR's role is to assure sales executives that pay levels are externally competitive and internally equitable (or otherwise consistent with the organization's compensation objectives based on the roles and responsibilities of the jobs).

It is typically HR's job to assemble labor market data that can be used in making decisions about where to set sales pay levels. This means that HR is responsible for identifying and selecting reliable labor market surveys for use in job pricing. A company will usually rely on two to four survey sources for competitive labor market data. It is commonly a company's HR professional who has been given the responsibility to select and purchase the survey data and to assist with or manage the data submission from the company.

HR should help management determine the appropriate competitive position (e.g., median, 75th percentile) in the labor market for use in pricing a company's particular sales jobs. This is an important contribution to the sales compensation plan because the total cash compensation level for each sales job must be large enough to attract, motivate, and retain top-notch talent as well as pay for the performance that drives desired business results.

5. Industry Trends and Practices

Sales executives are vitally interested in how various practices affecting the sales compensation plan compare to others in their industry. The HR professional, through participation in industry networking groups and compensation survey job-matching sessions, can be in an excellent position to gain an understanding of trends and practices that may affect the sales compensation plan. Thus, the HR professional should be a member and active participant in industry and survey groups.

Sales leaders are also typically interested in knowing about changes taking place in sales channels and sales coverage in the markets in which they compete for customers. Job-matching sessions in industry survey groups are often one place to learn about how others in the industry are covering the market. For example, if new jobs that your company does not have are surfacing in either the surveys or the job-matching sessions, that may be an indication of a trend in sales coverage that should be brought to the attention of sales leadership.

A third area of interest to sales leaders is how the operation of the sales compensation plan is affected by administrative practices. For example, draws, sales crediting, and splits (duplicate crediting) are all topics of great importance to sales leaders as they consider the effectiveness of a current plan. An HR professional involved with sales compensation should consistently make every effort to learn about industry trends and practices that are likely to impact both the thinking about and the planning for sales compensation and share those findings with sales leaders. Doing so increases the value that the HR professional provides to the sales organization.

6. Plan Effectiveness Assessment

At most companies, sales compensation return on investment (ROI) is an important topic. In fact, a recent WorldatWork survey reports that 86 percent of the respondents indicated that how to determine sales compensation plan ROI is a top priority at their company. The reason for this interest is that companies have begun to think of sales compensation as an investment in improving overall sales effectiveness instead of thinking about it as an expense to be minimized. Thus, they have shifted their outlook and view sales compensation as a means of achieving increased volume and quality of sales. This shift in thinking provides an opportunity for the HR professional to help sales leaders also rethink their approach to plan assessment.

One of the reasons for the difficulty of assessing plan effectiveness is the existence of unclear expectations for sales compensation. The best time to gain an understanding of what sales leaders expect to accomplish through the compensation plan is at the time the plan is being formulated. The key question is: What are the outcomes that sales executives (and, in turn, top management) anticipate from a new compensation plan? These outcomes are the quantifiable results that management wishes to derive from its investment in cash compensation for the sales force.

The selection of assessment metrics, including ROI, is determined by the goals of the business and the priorities set for the sales organization by top management. Thus, the actual metrics used are situational; that is, they should be tailored to a company's particular situation and should be set at the beginning of the new sales compensation plan year. The optimal environment is one in which the HR professional is a very active participant in the assessment of a current sales compensation plan's effectiveness. Sidebar 6.1 notes that the issue of sales compensation is complicated by COVID-19.

Sidebar 6.1 Key Findings from 2020 "Sales Compensation in a COVID-19 World" Survey

COVID-19 put sales organizations in fast response mode, looking at compensation and beyond for answers. WorldatWork, in partnership with SalesGlobe, conducted a rapid response survey about sales compensation in a COVID-19 world. The final sample included 372 respondents, collected in April 2020.

More than half of organizations defined to the sales team how to engage with customers – and most organizations shifted from selling to helping and refocusing on less impacted segments.

The top sales compensation considerations and actions for organizations at the height of the pandemic were quota adjustments, performance measure changes, and thresholds.

LEARNING A NEW LANGUAGE

Learning about sales compensation can be like learning a new language, a language that has its own unique key concepts and terms. One of the most difficult challenges of working on sales compensation within your organization is ensuring that everyone is using the same language. Your knowledge of the fundamental concepts of the language of sales compensation will add to your ability to effectively participate in your organization's sales compensation plan design and implementation.

COMPENSATION TIED TO TOTAL REWARDS

It is important to first understand the charter and scope of sales compensation. The amount of pay called *sales compensation* typically cannot fulfill all of the attraction, motivation, and retention requirements of a total rewards strategy by itself. In fact, most companies suffer from using sales results and sales compensation earnings as the only indicators of a sales professional's performance. Many companies fall into the trap of overemphasizing the pay results to the point that sellers say, "If it's not in the sales compensation plan, then I'm not paid for it." While no one can argue that these factors do not matter, other results are also important and may not be built into the sales compensation plan or performance management evaluation. This fact becomes even more important when your company asks talented sales professionals to tackle more challenging sales assignments or when your sales organization is integrated into a merged or restructured organization. An important responsibility of the HR professional is to help the company learn to accept and communicate that "total compensation," including all of the aspects of the rewards of work, is used to reward "total performance."

Total rewards, as illustrated in Chapter 1, defines an organization's strategy to attract, motivate, retain, and engage employees. It's the tool kit from which an organization chooses to offer and align a value proposition that results in satisfied, engaged, and productive employees who, in turn, create desired business performance and results. (See the five types of rewards shown in Figure 6.3.) As you work with the sales organization, it is important to have a common understanding of what is included in all the reward types as they pertain to a sales force. This common understanding will help ensure that all components of the total rewards system are appropriately aligned with the company's expectations for sales jobs.

Direct and Indirect Financials (Total Pay)

In some companies, a significant amount of time and energy is devoted to determining the total pay plan for the sales force. Elements of total pay include:

- Base salary
- Incentive compensation – bonus, commission

FIGURE 6.3 Types of rewards.

- Special performance incentive for the field force (SPIFF)s, including sales contests
- Recognition/Overachievers Club
- Benefits
- Perquisites

While total pay is very important in attracting, motivating, rewarding, and retaining a highly effective sales force, putting too much attention on it could create a culture that is counter to business success. Sales leaders in high-performing sales organizations increasingly seek to strike the right balance between total pay and the other types of rewards.

Affiliation

It is critical for most employees to belong to an admirable organization. All employees are interested in the company's vision and strategy. For the sales force, however, such interest is particularly strong because its members "face" company customers regularly. Thus, the following elements of "affiliation" are particularly important:

- Business vision and aspirations.
- Company image and reputation; for example, how customers feel about the company.

- Top management's support and recognition of the sales force.
- Consistent sales performance management activities.
- Support and mutual respect of peers.
- Openness of communication.
- Ethics – commitment to doing business honestly.

Affiliation can have a significant impact for sales organizations in which many sellers are remote or home-based employees. Extra efforts may be required to ensure they remain advocates of the company rather than solely advocates of customers to whom they are closest.

Career

Most sales employees welcome the opportunity to grow in their career, although many find a role as an individual contributor highly satisfying. For the sales force, key elements of individual and career growth include:

- Performance management and coaching style
- Opportunities for career advancement within Sales and other areas of the company (e.g., sales operations or product development and marketing)
- Opportunities for individual development and growth

Work Content

Finally, the quality and content of the job is now more important than ever. With that in mind, sales employees at all levels have heightened interest in the quality of the job and the workplace. Key elements of that building block include:

- Meaningful involvement of first-line sales management
- Working relationships (trust and commitment) with colleagues in other functions
- Effectiveness and efficiency of the selling process
- Effective sales support tools (e.g., customer relationship management [CRM], mobile computing, quote/configuration automation), and resources
- Innovation and commitment to new products
- Investment in training – market, products, and selling skills

You probably hear most often that the sales compensation plan is the "most important tool" the company possesses for the purpose of attracting, retaining, and motivating its sales force. However, work content and other intangibles are often more influential than pay, especially for those in complex selling roles. Understanding how the sales compensation plan fits into total rewards at your company is a key element in working to develop a philosophy and guidelines for the program. While all five areas of the total rewards model are important, most companies fail to excel in all. In advising your company, you should evaluate which areas provide the best competitive differentiation for your current and prospective talent pool and place strong emphasis in those areas.

VARIABLE PAY PLAN CATEGORIES

Before addressing the details of plan design elements, it is important to understand that there are three basic variable pay or rewards plan categories in which customer-facing employees might participate: individual, team, and corporate. These plan categories might be short-term or long-term, and can use cash or noncash as the reward. The right type of incentives must be aligned with each role to ensure an effective total rewards strategy. Appropriate incentives balance the degree of salesperson impact and the company's ability to measure that impact so that the program or plan is fair, equitable, and manageable.

Individual incentives create payouts based on the results of an individual relative to their assignment. While there might be team members (on the account team, for example) sharing in those results, the individual's pay is based solely or primarily on how their accounts or territories achieve. Companies typically use this kind of plan for individual contributors (sales reps, account managers, product specialists) as well as sales management.

Team incentives are based on how a group of similarly functioned or similarly tasked people performs collectively. The plan combines all results, and the members of the team receive payment on the total result. Although on occasion there is some modification at the individual level, the team results drive the payouts. This kind of plan best fits pooled resources assigned to support a range of sellers, in which individuals do not always have direct control over the specific assignments or opportunities to which they are assigned and may work across multiple opportunities.

Corporate incentives represent broader plans based on total company or division performance. This typically occurs through some funding process that may or may not allow for differentiation at the individual level. Companies typically implement this kind of plan for a variety of roles in the company beyond customer-facing jobs. This may include sales support functions that have minimal customer contact, support a wide range of sales professionals, or have many other duties outside of sales support.

Sales compensation generally describes individual or team incentives, or a combination of both. Rewards are shorter-term (the measurement period is typically one year or less) and the reward currency is cash.

SALES COMPENSATION PHILOSOPHY

To develop an effective sales compensation program, the design should be consistent with your company's compensation philosophy. This philosophy is frequently both undocumented and informal. It is therefore very helpful to confirm and document the company's compensation philosophy in order to support alignment across all related programs. Elements of the framework for a sales compensation philosophy are:

1. *Objectives.* Confirmation of the strategic foundation of the programs.

   a. Legal and regulatory requirements.
   b. Business and financial alignment.
   c. Personnel objectives.
2. *Labor market comparison.* Appropriate companies and jobs.
3. *Competitive positioning.* Percentile positioning and relationship to other jobs in the company based on the skills, competencies, and focus required to successfully perform in each role.
4. *Salary/variable pay ratio factors.* Based on the company's philosophy of risk versus reward.
5. *Base salary determination.* Elements/programs that will be used.
6. *Short-term and long-term incentives.* Eligibility/type.

GUIDING PRINCIPLES

Once the sales compensation philosophy is defined and documented, various guiding principles related to plan design can be determined. These principles are based on key elements of the philosophy. They can be used throughout the organization to test decisions as sales compensation plans are developed or revised in order to ensure that the plans are consistent with the company's philosophy. Examples of guiding principles are provided in Figure 6.4.

FIGURE 6.4 Examples of guiding principles.

- Plans are aligned with the company's business strategy and primary goals – sales growth, profitability, new product sales, and other strategic initiatives (as highlighted in the business plan).
- Plans are designed to the specific accountabilities of each job. Plans differentiate various levels of performance.
- The absolute number of performance measures is limited (i.e., up to three) within a specific plan, and the capability to track and report results is confirmed prior to plan finalization.
- The goals of the sales force are based on optimal performance distribution. This means that threshold and excellence performance levels are realistically achievable; that is, they will be set so that at least 90 percent of the sales force achieves threshold, 60–70 percent achieves/exceeds quota, and 10–15 percent achieves/exceeds excellence.
- The company is committed to using plans that are simple, flexible, and self-calculating by plan participants. Approved plans are ones that can be administered in a timely and cost-efficient manner with minimal requirements for manual intervention.
- Management at all levels of the organization is committed to clearly communicating the plans and to providing the support required to enable the sales force to succeed under the compensation plan.

Once the conceptual groundwork has been established, it's important to understand the criteria for determining who should participate in the sales compensation plan and the key components of any sales compensation plan framework: target earnings, the mix of fixed and variable pay, upside earnings potential, performance measures, and performance standards.

ELIGIBILITY FOR SALES COMPENSATION

When your company is going through a change initiative, and the result is new jobs, new products, or new processes, it is critical to validate the eligibility of relevant jobs for participation in the sales compensation plan. Whether the job is direct-to-consumer (like a retail clerk) or business-to-business, the key criterion is the role each job plays in the sales process, particularly the degree to which the job is involved in persuading a customer to buy the company's products or services. To validate the eligibility of relevant jobs for participation in the sales compensation plan, the team must understand the sales process (whether it has been formally documented or can be defined specifically based on case example) from developing and qualifying leads to persuading the customer to buy and then fulfilling the order.

In recent years, there has been an increasing tendency to make more service- and fulfillment-related jobs eligible for sales incentive pay. However, one key differential between sales incentive pay and other variable pay is the degree to which target incentive pay is included in the calculation for market-rate competitive pay. For many jobs, the base wage, or base salary, is considered 100 percent of the target pay for that job, and incentive earnings are added on. As the HR expert on the team, your job may include the need to challenge eligibility assumptions in order to ensure that jobs are treated equitably, consistent with market/industry practice and generally accepted principles of compensation plan design. There are three primary criteria for eligibility to be on either individual or team sales plans:

1. The primary responsibility of employees in designated sales jobs is customer contact and persuading the customer to do business with the company.
2. Employees can affect sales results and may have assigned sales goals.
3. Sales results can be tracked and accurately measured at the employee level.

Target Earnings

Three key compensation terms used in sales compensation are defined in Figure 6.5. The target cash compensation (TCC) for a job includes the base pay that is available for "expected" or "acceptable" performance (either a fixed base salary for the job or the midpoint of the salary range for the job) plus the at-risk pay available for achieving expected results (e.g., the quota).

FIGURE 6.5 Key sales compensation terms and definitions.

- Target cash compensation (TCC): The total cash compensation (including base salary and incentive compensation) available for achieving expected results
- Salary/Incentive Mix: The relationship between the base salary and the planned (or target) incentive amounts in the total cash compensation package at planned or expected performance. The two portions of the mix, expressed as percentages, always equal 100 percent. For example, an 80/20 mix means that 80 percent of the TCC is base salary and 20 percent is incentive pay at target performance.
- Leverage: The amount of increased or upside incentive opportunity – in addition to target incentive pay – that management expects outstanding performers to earn. Leverage may be expressed as a ratio of upside to target (e.g., 2:1), as a multiple of the target incentive (e.g., two times target), or as a total of the target incentive opportunity plus the multiple of target at upside (e.g., triple leverage).

As you work with the sales organization, it is important to remember that TCC is a broadly accepted term, but specific industries may use different terms to describe it. Other names used for TCC include the high-technology term on-target earnings (OTE), and total target compensation (TTC), which is frequently used in the services industry.

Possibly the single most critical factor to use in determining the appropriate TCC for a job is confirmation of that job's role, not simply the title given to that job in your company. Titles vary significantly from company to company, but the job role (e.g., telesales, counter sales, geographic sales, technical specialist) is the designator used to match your company's job to externally available data about how companies pay jobs having the same role.

The process of confirming the TCC for a sales job is essentially the same process used to benchmark other jobs in your company: Once the job has been confirmed, both external market data and internal structure and equity are used to establish the parameters of the job value. See Figure 6.6 for a brief summary of several factors you, or the person on your team charged with market pay determination, should consider.

The results of the competitive/market analysis will need to be balanced against your own internal compensation structure and programs as well as equity requirements across similar job levels in different functions. This can be done on either a "base pay plus" or "total cash compensation" basis, but is generally required to ensure internal equity and consistency with legal requirements. It is also a tool that is helpful during the dreaded "FLSA audit" that you or someone in HR is typically responsible for periodically completing. It is sometimes quite a challenge to confirm (or determine) the appropriate FLSA status for sales jobs, both inside and outside; however, this should always be done in light of the actual requirements of the job rather than a perceived lack of internal standing if job status changes.

FIGURE 6.6 Using survey results.

- Have at least two survey sources for key jobs.
- Ensure the competition is represented (in the participant list).
- Verify job matches with the published descriptions (work with sales management to ensure matches are accurate).
- Based on the company's pay philosophy, decide on the statistics to be extracted (e.g., 50th or 75th percentile, median, weighted average).
- Extract data for each compensation level and productivity analysis (base salary, incentive pay, target cash compensation, quota).
- Use discrete data points instead of using averages or blending different data sources for sales compensation surveys – participants and job matches differ, as does quality of data.
- Synchronize the survey data with economic data (events in the marketplace and the economy).

Salary/Incentive Ratio and Target Upside

Sellers are willing to accept putting a degree of their pay at risk if there is significant upside pay available for achieving or exceeding expectations or average productivity. Several behavioral theories underlie the concept of risk and reward:

- *Achievement need.* D. C. McClelland defines achievement need as the desire to perform in terms of a standard of excellence or as a desire to be successful in competitive situations.
- *Reinforcement theory.* As demonstrated through many studies, most notably those of B. F. Skinner, the frequency of a behavior is likely to be increased when a valuable reward is directly linked to that behavior.
- *Expectancy theory.* This theory of employee motivation suggests that the sales force makes decisions based on the degree of perceived attractiveness of the outcome.

These theories come into play for two important aspects of sales compensation plan design: incentive mix and upside opportunity (leverage). Setting them correctly is important to a successful process.

Salary/Incentive Ratio (Mix)

While the target cash compensation (TCC) for a job is, of course, very important to the job incumbents, salary/incentive mix has at least equal importance because it directly affects take-home pay and cash flow. Incentive mix is typically expressed as a ratio (e.g., 50/50 or 70/30) in which the first number represents the percentage of target pay in base salary and the second number represents the percentage of target pay at risk for achieving expectations or target performance. Some companies describe mix by stating variable incentive as a percentage of base. While this is a fairly simple mathematical calculation, it does not visibly express the concept of at-risk pay as an element of the total cash opportunity.

Because mix indicates the proportion of pay at risk, a job with an aggressive mix (50 percent or more of the TCC is incentive pay) has less predictable cash flow, while a job with less aggressive mix (e.g., with 25 percent or less of the TCC as incentive) has a much more predictable cash flow associated with it. Many of the same factors that were used to help you determine the most appropriate TCC for each job also apply as you consider the right mix of base pay and at-risk or incentive pay as well as the amount of upside (or over-target incentive pay) that should be available. Figure 6.7 provides an illustration of mix.

FIGURE 6.7 Target cash compensation and mix.

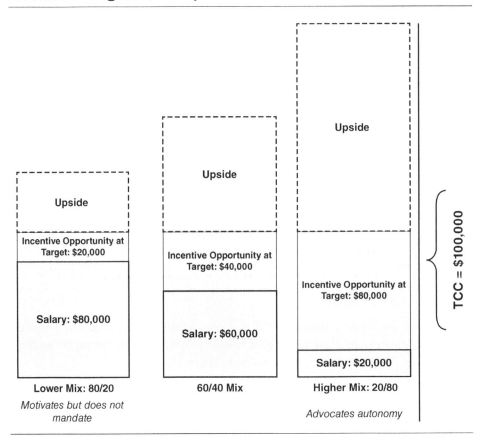

Note: Lower mixes mean less variable incentive. Lower variable incentive results in reduced overall opportunity, although a higher portion of pay (base) is guaranteed.

FIGURE 6.8 Factors that impact salary/incentive mix.

Sales Process
- Transactional (more pay at risk)
- Consultative (less pay at risk)
- Product-focused (more pay at risk)
- Relationship-focused (less pay at risk)
- Many, frequent sales (more pay at risk)
- Few, large sales (less pay at risk)
- Long sales cycle (less pay at risk)

Role in the Process
- Team member (less pay at risk)
- Key impact on decision to buy (more pay at risk)
- Provides leads/access or fulfillment only (less pay at risk)
- Provides key expertise in product, customers, or segments (less pay at risk)
- Limited expertise required for sales success (more pay at risk)

Type of Product or Service
- Commodity (more pay at risk)
- Specialty or custom (less pay at risk)
- Sold on price (more pay at risk)
- Sold on value (less pay at risk)

Several job- and sales process-related factors, in addition to market practice data, should be used to determine the proportion of pay that is base and the proportion that is incentive pay, as shown Figure 6.8.

The most critical element is the role of the seller. The incentive mix should reflect the degree of influence the sales professional has over the purchase decision and the value of that transaction. The more important and influential the seller, the higher the mix (higher percentage put into variable compensation).

Industry surveys indicate that the overall market average mix for sales positions is 70/30. Therefore, a job with a 50/50 mix or less implies that the role places significantly more emphasis on the selling skills and influence of the seller as factors that cause the customer to buy. A 90/10 mix would imply that the salesperson is only one of many factors affecting the customer's buying decision or the absolute volume purchased.

Based on the factors shown in Figure 6.8, establishing or confirming the mix applied to the TCC for each job requires an accurate and current definition of the job. While input from Sales and other functions is useful to confirm roles and processes, as the HR professional on the team, this task is likely to be your responsibility as well.

One final consideration for mix is how it is expressed and the effect of that on merit pay increase. While mix is the proportion of base versus

FIGURE 6.9 Implementing mix.

| Method | Description of Components | | Illustration ($100,000 and 50/50 mix) |
	Salary	Incentive	
Uniform Base/Uniform Incentive: Mix is actual and uniform for all job incumbents.	Uniform salary for all incumbents in the same job.	Uniform incentive opportunity *is a discrete dollar* amount for all incumbents in the same job.	$50,000 base + $50,000 incentive
Base Range/Uniform Incentive: Mix varies by individual; less aggressive (less pay at risk as a percent of the total) for those higher in the range.	Salary range is implemented consistent with practice in other functions; salary midpoint used to determine mix.	Uniform incentive opportunity *is a discrete dollar* amount for all incumbents in the same job.	$40,000–$60,000 base range, $50,0000 midpoint + $50,000 incentive
Salary Plus Percentage of Salary: Mix is actual and uniform for all job incumbents.	Salary range is implemented consistent with practice in other functions.	Incentive opportunity *is the same percent of the individual's salary* for each incumbent in the same job.	$50,0000 base + 100% of base incentive

variable pay as proportions of 100, there are several ways to implement the concept (see Figure 6.9).

How mix is expressed for your sales organization has direct effects on the way merit increase is handled. As discussed previously, merit pay is a useful financial tool for rewarding total performance; however, merit pay increases may also have unforeseen consequences. If merit increases are used with your sales organization, it is important to add dollars to salary while ensuring that this change does not dilute the importance of the variable component of the sales compensation plan. As such, increased dollars should be spread across both base and incentive at the desired ratio to ensure the intensity of focus on the sales results desired.

Target Upside (Leverage)

Once the value of the incentive opportunity has been established or verified, that is, the TCC and the mix have been confirmed, the leverage (the amount of upside pay earned at some defined level of performance above 100 percent) needs to be determined. Mix and leverage are strongly linked in the minds of most sales compensation plan participants; the reason is fairly simple – the more pay there is at risk, the greater the upside opportunity. An important note: Definition of the "leverage" does necessarily mean that a plan is "capped" (i.e., that earnings are limited). However, determination of the additional pay available at levels of performance above expected performance will help immensely when it comes time to design the formulas in the plan.

While upside affects all individuals who overachieve target expectations, the upside/leverage ratio reflects the opportunity available for your sales organization's top performers (typically the top 5–10 percent of your sales force on a job-by-job basis). The amount of upside available is based on the role of the sales job, the ability to overachieve, and financial affordability. For example, sales teams, account managers with very large quotas, and senior sales managers have little opportunity to significantly overachieve their target numbers. In these situations, the upside ratios tend to be lower, which puts more pressure on setting more aggressive target compensation levels for meeting expectations. Figure 6.10 provides an overview of the relationships of role to upside/leverage ratio across industries.

There are several ways to express leverage: as a ratio of upside to target (e.g., 2:1), as a multiple of target (e.g., two times target), or as a total of the target incentive opportunity plus the multiple of target at upside (e.g., triple leverage). The term you should use is the one that has been used in your company in the past – the one that your team finds easiest to use and to explain to others. Figure 6.11 illustrates leverage and how each term could be used to describe the same upside opportunity.

FIGURE 6.10 Typical relationship of upside to role/sales job.

- Direct seller territory—Highest
- Account manager—Many accounts—Highest
- Account manager—Single/few accounts—High
- Outbound telesales—High
- Inbound telesales—Medium to low based on job focus
- Channel account manager—Medium
- Overlay sales specialists—Medium
- First-line sales management—Medium
- Second-line and above sales management—Low

FIGURE 6.11 Leverage illustration.

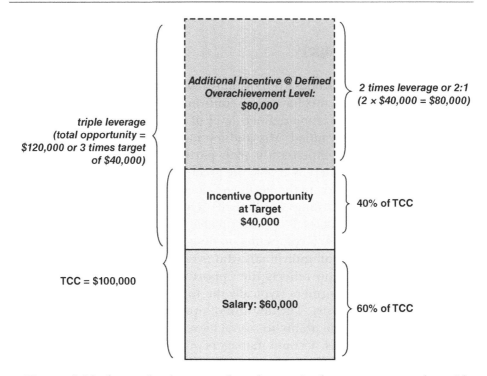

Figure 6.12 shows the impact of a change in leverage on total upside opportunity.

Plan Measures and Performance Standards

Once the percentage or amount of variable compensation and upside are determined, your company must then select the most financially and strategically important measures for which to pay these dollars as well as the range of performance used in calculating payout.

Performance Measures

The following factors are used when deciding on the most appropriate performance measures:

- *Job.* Measures should reflect job accountabilities, and the salesperson must be able to influence the outcomes.
- *Business drivers.* Measures should be consistent with the financial drivers associated with successful achievement of the business plan.
- *Focus.* To ensure focus and meaningful payout opportunity for each measure, it is best to use no more than three performance measures in a sales compensation plan.
- *System capabilities.* If it cannot be tracked and measured today, it does not belong in the sales compensation plan. Inaccurate or late payouts and reports greatly diminish the motivational power of sales incentive compensation.

FIGURE 6.12 Impact of upside on earnings opportunity.

double leverage or 1:1 (1 × $40,000 = $40,000)	triple leverage or 2:1 (2 × $40,000 = $80,000)
Incentive Opportunity at Target: $40,000	Incentive Opportunity at Target $40,000
Salary: $60,000	Salary: $60,000
For every one dollar of incentive at target, there is one dollar of upside	For every dollar of incentive at target, there are two dollars of upside

Performance measures selected for use in calculating payouts fall into two broad categories: financial and nonfinancial.

1. *Financial.* Because sales jobs are focused on top-line growth, and, in some cases, on profitable growth, one measure of success in these jobs must be financial. Financial measures are generally one of two types: volume and profitability.

   They may be measured against expected productivity or quota. Your rule of thumb should be that between 60 and 100 percent of the sales compensation opportunity is based on a sales volume or productivity component. Using this rule ensures that the focus on the sellers is on meeting the company's fiscal plan.

   Examples of financial performance measures include:

   - Sales revenue: overall, by segment or channel, for specific products
   - Growth: overall, by customer, account, channel, segment
   - Absolute volume: that is, number of units or transactions
   - Gross profit: percent, dollars

Any dollars taken away from financial success reduce the impact of the sales compensation plan on achievement of quantifiable results and thus must be justified as secondary or strategic measures that are critical to the "quality" or nature of financial achievement.

2. Nonfinancial: Nonfinancial measures may be either quantitative or qualitative. Quantitative measures such as market share or share of account are relative rather than absolute and are used in situations where growth is achieved by "taking business" from competitors. Activity measures such as number of calls are quantitative in theory, but qualitative in practice, because only effective activities lead to achievement of financial objectives.

Management by objectives (MBO), also known as key sales objectives or key performance objectives, are examples of nonfinancial, potentially qualitative objectives. This type of a component is usually point-based and relies on a manager to develop or select from a menu of possible objectives for the seller to achieve over a defined period of time (typically a quarter or half-year). As a rule, these objectives create an averaging of pay for all participants and thus they fail to differentiate superior performance. The larger the population for which they are utilized, the less effective and more administratively burdensome they become. They can then be short-lived inside a well-designed sales compensation plan for a large sales force.

While there are several drawbacks to MBO-like measures, they can be more effective with smaller teams in which the manager is well trained in objective setting and evaluation. Further, they force a conversation between the seller and the sales manager about what strategic activities need to occur. They are best used to reward for activities or results that have a high probability of creating a booking or billing in a future period but for which the seller will get no sales credit in the current period (e.g., design wins in an original equipment manufacturer [OEM] sales model).

Number of Measures

As stated earlier in this section, a rule of thumb is that no sales compensation plan should have more than three components. Using more than three measures/components detracts from the value of each measure and the true driving impact of the plan on total sales results. As an adviser to your company, you must always reflect on whether the dollars are significant enough to support more than three measures (especially when those dollars are divided by pay frequency and taxes are subtracted). Too many measurements in a plan often indicate either that a company is trying to design one plan for multiple distinctive roles or that management lacks agreement on the objectives of the particular sales job.

Performance Standards

Another consideration for performance measures used in the sales compensation plan is performance standards. One important task in designing plans is confirming expected performance and establishing two other reference points: one below "expected performance," and one significantly above "expected performance." These three achievement levels are:

- *Threshold*: The minimum level of performance that must be achieved before an incentive can be paid.
- *Target*: Expected level of sales results or individual performance. (This is the point at which the target incentive opportunity is earned.)
- *Excellence*: Individual sales performance that is in the 90th percentile (top 10 percent) of all performance measured. (This is the point at which the defined "leverage" or upside is earned.)

Once these three levels are established in a quota-based plan (either bonus or commission), it is then possible to complete the plan payout formula as well as various analyses such as aggregate plan cost and expected return on investment. *Remember:* Many people new to sales compensation assume that a defined "excellence" point means that a plan is capped. This is not the case! It simply means that the value of each percent achievement above 100 percent can have a defined value; it does not mean that there is an achievement level above which people cannot earn more sales compensation dollars. When you are working with a design team or with sales management, it sometimes helps the discussion to refer to the "excellence" point as a "design reference point" that is used for the purpose of developing a payout line and value.

Sales Crediting

One requirement for successful use of any volume measure in the sales compensation plan is well-articulated and well-understood crediting rules. To establish these rules, the sales management team must first have a relatively clear understanding of what customer segments and which products are required to meet the financial plan. Using crediting rules ensures that results that are affected by the salesperson and that support the achievement of your company's business objectives are being tracked and measured. Second, management must take a look at the nature of sales transactions by seller type and consciously determine if all aspects of the transaction provide sales credit toward the volume achievement objective as well as whether they should all be treated equally. In today's complex selling world, all transactions are not alike, and transactions may or may not include all products or services. Furthermore, some transactions are one-time deals instead of ongoing business, which can be paid all at once or over time. Companies thus must know what they need to accomplish and must examine the range of deals that exist in order to determine how to implement crediting toward sales achievement in the core volume component of their plans. Figure 6.13 provides definitions and typical applications of the three kinds of sales credit.

TIMING CONSIDERATIONS

Two timing considerations need to be confirmed for the sales compensation plan. The first is the plan performance period, the period of time for which

FIGURE 6.13 Sales crediting.

Type	Definition	Application
Single	One sales resource receives full credit: 100% credit to one person.	One salesperson completes the entire sales process.
Multiple	Full credit provided to two or more sales resources; more than 100% is credited.	A team is required to complete the sale; it is not possible to distinguish the unique contribution of a single resource; the financial impact can be predicted and managed.
Split	The credit is divided in some way among two or more sales resources; 100% credit in total is provided.	Multiple resources or channels may be required to close a sale, but it is relatively easy to distinguish each resource's contribution; additional financial liability is not acceptable.
Partial	A portion of the full credit is allocated to one or more sales resources; less than 100% credit is given in total.	Resources involved in the sale did not contribute as required and full credit is an unacceptable financial liability.

the company assigns objectives and measures performance for the purpose of earnings. A plan performance period might be annual (with annual objectives), semiannual, quarterly, monthly, or weekly. In general, the more complex the selling activities and sales cycle, the longer the plan period.

There are two alternative approaches to measurement: cumulative and discrete. A performance measurement is cumulative when the performance of the incumbent is measured over subsequent performance periods. As an example: "While payouts are made each month, performance is cumulative because it is measured from the start of quarter to date." Performance measurement is discrete when the performance of the incumbent is limited to a defined performance period without any connection to past or future performance periods. As an example: "Each month is discrete, because performance is measured for that month and payout is made for that month independent of past or future performance."

The second timing consideration is payout frequency, how often a payout is made. Alternatives range from weekly (generally for those jobs that are paid 100 percent commission) to less frequent payouts (quarterly, for example). The decision to pay more or less frequently should be made after a review of such factors as length of sales cycle, motivational value, and the ability of systems to handle payout calculations.

ALTERNATIVE MECHANICS

The math or formulas used to calculate the payout under the sales compensation plan can be as simple or as complex as the designers wish. Of course, "simpler is better" is a cardinal rule. However, there are many alternatives to consider as the formula is developed. These include both the type of plan that is suitable for the job and the formula modifiers that can be used to ensure that the plan is motivational and financially viable.

Plan Types

The formula by which payout is delivered can be based on two types of plan: commission or bonus. One or both types of plan may be used in the incentive formula, based on the message that management wants to deliver about performance requirements, competitive practice, and key business objectives. A commission generally focuses on volume, while a bonus focuses efforts on achievement of one or more specific goals.

Commission is compensation paid as a percentage of sales measured in either dollars or units. A quota can be used with a commission structure but is not required. The following approaches can be used when designing a commission plan:

- *Single or flat-rate commission.* This is the simplest commission to develop and explain. A fixed rate is applied to all relevant sales in order to calculate the commission payout; for example, 4 percent of sales or $100 per unit. This type of commission is most often used in new companies, companies with very small sales organizations, companies with "open" territories (territories that have no geographic boundaries), or for a new product for which there is no sales history. The theme is, "The more you sell, the more you make."
- *Individual commission rate (ICR).* This approach results in a unique commission rate for each seller. This approach has two key characteristics in common with a bonus type plan: It has the effect of "evening out" territories in terms of pay, and it is always used with a quota. The theme is, "Every salesperson has the same opportunity to earn his or her target incentive, no matter how large or small the territory."
- *Tiered (or ramped) commission structure.* A single rate is determined for "target" achievement and different rates are provided for sales below target or above
- *Target.* "Target" may be a specified sales volume, or a percent of quota achievement. If a tiered commission rate is used, the plan can be cumulative or each range can be discrete. If the plan is cumulative, incentive paid versus incentive earned is recalculated at defined intervals. If the plan is discrete, then the new rate is applied only to dollars associated with the new range of achievement. The theme is, "Sales below target are less valuable than sales at and above target."

FIGURE 6.14 Types of commissions.

Type	Examples	
Flat commission: Rate volume	3% ($s) $100/Unit	
Individual commission rate (ICR): Individual's incentive target divided by individual's quota	**Rep 1**: $100,000 incentive target/$1,000,000 quota = 10% rate applied to sales volume **Rep 2**: $100,000 incentive target/$1,500,000 quota = 6.7% rate applied to sales volume	
Ramped: Rate adjusted based on achievement of sales volume or quota	0%–100% of quota achieved >100% of quota achieved	5% rate 7.5% rate
Adjusted: Rate varies based on characteristic other than volume or quota	Product A Products B and C	5% Base Rate 7.5% Rate (Base Rate × 1.5)

- *Adjusted (or variable) commission rate.* This approach to commission is used if several types of products, or types of transactions, will be prioritized in the commission structure. The rate applied to each transaction is adjusted based on the priority or importance of the product or transaction. The theme is, "Some sales are more important than others."

Illustrations of each type of commission plan are provided in Figure 6.14. A bonus is a percent of base pay, or a fixed dollar amount, for accomplishing objectives. A quota or some other kind of goal is generally associated with this type of plan. The three basic approaches to a bonus are:

- *Single or fixed-rate bonus plan.* One incentive opportunity is available for achieving the specified objective.
- *Interpolated bonus plan.* A formula to calculate a defined dollar value for each percent achievement is used.
- *Step-rate bonus.* A tiered bonus structure, with no interpolation between tiers, is used; each tier is discrete.

Examples of each type of bonus plan are provided in Figure 6.15.

Modifiers

In addition to selecting the type of plan or plans that will be used in the incentive formula, other tools can be used to adjust how payout is calculated. These include how measures relate to each other for the purposes of payout and how payout is modified (up or down).

FIGURE 6.15 Types of bonus plans.

Type	Example	
Fixed	$25,000 for 100% achievement of quota	
Interpolated	0–100% of quota achieved	$250 per percent achieved
	>100% of quota achieved	$275 per percent achieved
Step	50–99% of quota achieved	$5,000 (no matter where achievement falls in the range)
	99.1–102% of quota achieved	$20,000

Linkage is the factor that relates one measure to another. Measures are linked if payout for one measure depends on attaining another objective. Unlinked plans (i.e., plans in which payout for each measure is discrete and has no relationship to achievement in other areas) may indicate to the salespeople that they should base their own selling priorities on their own earnings expectations. Plan designers should consider linking performance measures in the incentive formula if it is desirable for the sales force to focus on more than one key area and if they use metrics that compete (like market share vs. profitability, etc.). Three mechanisms, as shown in Figure 6.16, can do this:

1. A hurdle (also known as a gate) requires some defined level of achievement in one performance measure before payout is made for another measure.
2. A multiplier adjusts payout on one performance measure based on some level of achievement of another measure. Positive adjustment is generally preferred, although adjustment up or down can be used to ensure financial viability of the plan.
3. A matrix is the most stringent mechanism, because performance in two areas is used; achievement of one measure is mathematically related to achievement of another to determine payout.

Modifiers include both payout accelerators and payout limiters. While a plan formula could deliver payout on a linear scale, or with a single rate, most plan designers use both payout limitation and payout acceleration tools to modify the incentive formula.

Payout limitation tools are used to manage cost relative to productivity and are frequently used when a company is new to using sales compensation, setting business goals, or allocating quota. The two approaches to payout limitation are: accelerating payout rate (the rate for achievement above some defined level decreases) cap (there is a defined maximum payout

FIGURE 6.16 Linkages.

"Hurdle"

Measures	Sales vs. Quota Bonus Margin Gate	
Total Sales vs. Quota Bonus	120% of Quota	$40,000
Strategic Product Hurdle	100% of Quota	$30,000
	80% of Quota	

Margin Gate: 100% of Strategic Product Quota Must Be Achieved Before Total Sales Bonus Over Target Will Be Paid.

"Multiplier"

Measures	Sales vs. Quota Bonus			Strategic Product Multiplier	
Total Sales vs. Quota Bonus	120% of Quota	$40,000	×	>100% of Quota	$40,000
Strategic Product Hurdle	100% of Quota	$30,000		100% of Quota	$30,000
	80% of Quota			<100% of Quota	

"Matrix"

Measures

	Total Sales			
Total Sales vs. Quota	120%	$20,000	$35,000	$40,000
Strategic Product vs. Quota	100%	$10,000	$30,000	$35,000
	80%	0	$10,000	$20,000

available). If a cap is used, it can be applied either to each transaction or to the total payout.

Payout acceleration tools are used to enhance payout above a linear rate for defined levels of overachievement. Acceleration is generally accomplished using specific multipliers against the target incentive opportunity, including adjusted commission rates. In practice, acceleration is the mathematical application of leverage or upside.

Some modifiers may act as either a decelerator or accelerator depending on achievement levels. For example, a multiplier may adjust payout up or down, based on achievement of the related performance measure. In some cases, additional acceleration is available only if quota is achieved on another measure; payout otherwise remains flat, or has less attractive acceleration. One typical example of this approach is a plan with a financial measure related to quota achievement and another milestone objective such as Design Wins. The qualitative measure would have little or no upside associated with it; however, if it is achieved, the acceleration on over-quota payout is greater.

UNDERSTANDING HOW SALES COMPENSATION FITS

Understanding how sales compensation fits into the total rewards philosophy of your company is a very effective starting point in your involvement in design or redesign efforts. The key concepts begin with a well-documented and clearly communicated philosophy and guiding principles. The amount of pay available, performance measures, plan formulas, and timing of payout are all elements that you will hear about and use in each design process. Figure 6.17 gives you a series of questions that provide a framework for structuring your understanding of how the sales compensation plans at your company now work.

FIGURE 6.17 Questions to ask about your company's sales compensations.

- Is everyone on the same sales compensation plan regardless of sales job?
- Do people in similar sales jobs have the same amount of target pay or different amounts? If different, which parts differ – salary, target incentive, or target total compensation?
- Of the target compensation, how much is delivered through base salary versus target incentive?
- How many different components or performance measures are used in the sales compensation plan? What are they? What is the relative importance of each plan component in each plan?
- What percentage of the sales compensation plan is based on sales volume? Is the sales volume component based on quota achievement or absolute dollars?
- For other components, is payout based on quota achievement?
- Is there a minimum or maximum achievement level at which pay begins or is capped? For which component or components?
- What type of plan (commission or bonus) is used to calculate payout for each component?
- Are any of the plan components or measures linked? If so, how?
- How frequently is each component of the sales compensation plan paid?

7　The Changing Face of Employee Well-Being

Well-being is an integral part of total rewards. Without it, too much emphasis is placed on just compensation or benefits. Well-being is not a benefit that people get. It is a state of being that people achieve because of the way work is done, how relationships are established, expectations people have of each other, and how comfortable it is to work in the environment. It is a culture that is created in the workplace.

Workplace well-being components include societal, organizational, family, personal, and employee wellness. When all components are achieved, a superior workforce experience will be fulfilled resulting in a high level of productivity and organizational performance.

Not everyone has the same definition of what constitutes well-being. Focusing on different aspects of well-being can help organizations address different needs.

WELL-BEING VS. WELLNESS

There is a clear distinction between well-being and wellness. Well-being is bigger than wellness and it takes a bigger commitment from the company. Well-being encompasses making employees happy, healthy, and fulfilled for talent attainment and business continuity (see Sidebar 7.1).

Wellness gets firmly associated with health and prevention, while well-being is more associated with happiness. Wellness is about keeping employees healthy (body, mind, spirit, emotions) with all sorts of prevention programs, in order to diminish health care costs.

Sidebar 7.1 Well-Being and Wellness

What Is Well-Being?

The state of being productive, comfortable, healthy and/or happy, taking into account physical, emotional/mental, financial and environmental factors.

What Is Wellness?

The state of being in good health that extends beyond the traditional definition of health. This includes physical vitality, mental enthusiasm, social satisfaction, a sense of accomplishment, and personal fulfillment.

What Is Financial Well-Being?

A state of security and control to meet financial needs, where an individual can maintain a manageable level of stress due to finances; an ability to meet their financial goals; a strong financial foundation to absorb emergencies; and the freedom to make choices for an enjoyable life.

According to statistics from the Global Wellness Institute, around 76 percent of the 3.4 billion working adults globally report they are struggling with their well-being across a broad spectrum of mental, physical, social, and financial elements. Around 52 percent are overweight; roughly 1 billion suffer from anxiety, and one in four experience a mental disorder. The global workforce is aging and becoming increasingly multigenerational – 18 percent will be over 55 by 2030. On top of that, 74 percent live with serious economic insecurity, according to "The Future of Wellness at Work" 2016 study (Global Wellness Institute 2016).

Most of the workers affected by these challenges are based in developing nations. Yet, for the 306 million living in developed nations that work for an employer that offers some sort of support, physical and mental stress is acknowledged as a key factor affecting personal health and performance.

This is important because the statistics show that at any one moment, a significant number of people in any organization around the globe are experiencing at least one issue with their well-being. In the short term, this can mean reduced productivity and over time, this can potentially lead to long-term absences, with some considering leaving the employer altogether.

FIGURE 7.1 **Workplace well-being.**

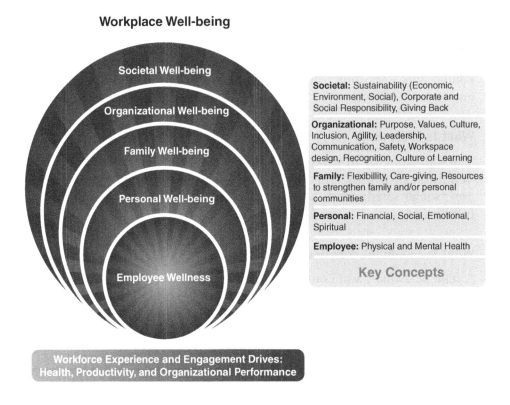

THE DOMINO EFFECT OF WELL-BEING: WHEN ONE
IS COMPROMISED, ALL ARE AT RISK

Employers often don't have insight into their employees' well-being, or
worse, any idea how wellness factors affect job performance and productivity
or workplace happiness and engagement. What is the impact of depression?
Financial strains? Family stress? Since total well-being consists of four
pillars – physical, mental, social, and financial – it makes sense that each rely
heavily on the other for support. The most common mental health issues
among employees are generalized anxiety or depression. The average duration of clinical depression, if left entirely untreated, can last an extended
period of time. What started as a mental health issue can have repercussions
on a person's social, physical, and financial well-being as that person with-
draws from social interaction, perhaps exercises less and seeks solace in
spending or gambling, or another potentially addictive behavior. In another
example, relationship counselors at LifeWorks by Morneau Shepell note
that a divorce currently takes around 7 to 12 months to complete and can
wipe out up to 70 percent of a partner's net wealth, having a substantial
effect on other aspects of their well-being.

The same is true of any stressful situation, which when left unchecked can
transform into a well-being affliction that lasts for an extended period. As

reported by the Global Wellness Institute, the cost of unwell workers worldwide represents 10 percent to 15 percent of global economic output on an annual basis. In the US alone, this amounts to $2.2 trillion a year. In countries where public and national health services are available, such as the United Kingdom and Canada, news reports will typically claim that these services are under severe strain and not properly equipped or capable of supporting the entire spectrum of health, especially mental welfare. In countries where health insurance is required, such as the US, an unhealthy workforce can drive costs up significantly for both the employer and the employee. This is further compounded by lower productivity and higher operating expenses – replacing a highly skilled worker costs up to 213 percent of their annual salary after considering the time it takes to offboard one, onboard another and get them to a place of effectiveness, according to a Center for American Progress "cost of turnover" report.

EMPLOYERS SEEK SOLUTIONS

Through this lens, the benefits of investing in employee well-being are clear. According to the Human Capital Management Institute, companies that invested just $1 per person in well-being initiatives outperformed their peers and experienced a 11.7 percent productivity gain.

That sounds like a strong return on investment. But it matters greatly how that $1 is spent. For many of these employees, typical support solutions at one end of the spectrum include biometric screenings, classes, and counselling to help them cope with stress and its health impacts. At the other end, initiatives might include stimulating healthy habits by offering fresh fruit in the workplace or flexible working practices. Collectively, these initiatives are encouraging and a step in the right direction, but for the most part, they do little to address the modern workplace culture that very often is a key contributor to workers' stress. According to the Global Wellness Institute, when wellness is not a strategic focus, support initiatives are conducted in isolation from the day-to-day operating environment of work and become merely a band-aid solution.

Bestselling author and workplace culture expert Chester Elton has been studying business culture and employee engagement for over 20 years, and has found that in the highest performing workplace cultures, leaders not only create higher levels of employee engagement but they also create environments that support productivity and performance in which employees feel enabled.

"Furthermore, they help employees feel a greater sense of well-being, making people feel more energized," he said.

In 2018, when Morneau Shepell carried out its annual HR Trends survey, more than two thirds of the human resources leaders that responded (67 percent) said that improving employee engagement was a top priority for 2019. Meanwhile, improving the mental health of employees was a priority for 48 percent, which is not surprising given the increase in awareness of the relationship between employee mental health and business objectives.

The World Health Organization defines health as "the state of complete physical, mental, and social well-being and not merely the absence of diseases or infirmity." As such, the attributes that make up a person's total well-being cannot be assessed in isolation because of their interdependency.

To this point, while many organizations will claim to have a well-being strategy, it is often one that has evolved piecemeal, with benefits sourced from multiple providers, internal communications, and an employee assistance program (EAP) existing in separate silos. Not only does this make participation challenging for the employees, it makes it very difficult for HR directors to assess the impact of the strategy. The HR professional tasked with qualifying such initiatives would have to follow the trail of information breadcrumbs from multiple sources to try and take the measure of the organization's health.

Many HR professionals are challenged by working with inconvenient or outdated tools and systems when working to improve and maintain employee well-being. With a workforce spread across geographically disparate locations, multiple shifts or time zones, and an environment that makes sharing and collaboration between employees difficult, this challenge can be amplified.

Consistent participation is a key part of the recipe for a successful employee engagement and total well-being strategy. But it's difficult to see results if people don't sign up, participate in the initiative, and keep up with that involvement. It's here that technology, when used correctly, can be a boon rather than a threat.

Turn on the Tech

We live and work in an era that is increasingly fast-paced. The on-demand economy has been welcomed with open arms into both our personal and professional spaces as we strive to get more done in the now. But it has brought with it a plethora of distractions and new challenges in terms of our social wellness. Amazon, Spotify, Netflix, Uber, GrubHub – all darling brands of the tech sector – are focused on connecting consumers with suppliers, wherever and whenever. As consumers seek out convenience, this same phenomenon is changing the way we approach work, driven further by information intensity and the desire to share and collaborate.

Many of these tech-driven services learn from our interactions and deliver a more relevant and appropriate experience as a result, and this is something we're coming to expect. According to Accenture, 75 percent of business buyers expect companies to be able to anticipate their needs and make relevant suggestions by 2020.

In the developed world, the drive toward wellness is being adopted at scale, in the foods we eat through healthier options; in the devices we rely on through the likes of Apple, Google, and Fitbit; and in the authorities that govern us, through guidance to be more proactive and aware of our well-being.

EAPs have been around for decades and are proven to be very effective at reducing absenteeism and reversing low productivity. Yet EAP providers, like Morneau Shepell, know these services only engage 5 percent to 10 percent of the workforce at any one time. Stigma around mental health may be fading, but it is still prevalent, and people still struggle with the concept of reaching out for support. It remains a challenge for people struggling with depression to take action. As a result, people typically engage with an EAP when they are already at crisis point and have been suffering for some time, which isn't optimal for either the employee or the employer.

With the mass adoption of the internet and mobile devices however, driving social engagement with health and well-being initiatives through technology addresses the main challenge faced by more traditional well-being initiatives that deliver support reactively.

A 2018 study carried out by LifeWorks across 750 workers in the UK, US, and Canada found that the majority of those surveyed would prefer mobile-first access to their company-sponsored well-being support services in order to be proactive about their wellness on their own terms. According to the study, around 65 percent of all respondents had accessibility issues with their current employee well-being services. Less than 5 percent of those surveyed accessed their employee well-being services through a smartphone app and less than half accessed it through a web-based service. Yet more than 75 percent of respondents expressed a desire to access these services from any place at any time.

Meeting employees, wherever they are on their well-being journey through mobile applications, means they can connect in their own time and receive education at their own pace. The anonymity afforded by a screen also means the interaction is less intimidating. In a 2018 survey, 63 percent of new users that connected with LifeWorks by Morneau Shepell through a newly introduced 24/7 instant chat service would not have reached out to a clinical counsellor through traditional methods.

Clearly, the demand is there for a more accessible experience to fit in with our increasingly technology-driven lives. Preventative maintenance of well-being makes financial sense too. The Centers for Disease Control and Prevention (CDC) estimate that more than 75 percent of health-care costs are due to chronic conditions that are largely preventable, just by reducing behavior-based risk factors. The same authority also states that in the US, 25 percent to 50 percent of a typical employers' annual medical care costs could be avoided by addressing such things as physical activity, weight management, smoking cessation, and preventive health care.

With mobile first applications that store access to the EAP, short and long form educational content and 60-second, question-based health risk assessments in one place, it's possible to drive small, incremental changes to people's behaviors. LifeWorks records engagement rates of up to 65 percent with its mobile application, and as people swap negative habits for more positive ones, they are simultaneously kept further away from a well-being crisis and better able to bounce back should one occur.

By putting access and control over well-being in the palm of employees' hands, wellness and work can and should become mutually enhancing in a virtuous circle. Research by Gallup found that people who are engaged at work report better health and lower rates of chronic disease than disengaged workers. They also eat healthier and exercise more, making them more engaged and productive – and so the cycle continues.

"Health and safety" is a well-acknowledged effort in employee well-being, but it's an outdated and physical-led approach. Employers have a duty of care, not just to their people, but also to their shareholders and national economies to invest in their employees' *total* well-being. It's not enough to support employees only physically or in times of crisis alone. It's time for organizations to invest in their culture, their people, and their business.

THE FUTURE OF EMPLOYEE ENGAGEMENT

Successfully threading the needle of a workforce well-being program requires factoring in the inherent value of an engaged workforce – and considering how a culture steeped in well-being serves a company's inclusivity, recruitment, and retention goals.

Today's workforce is comprised of five generations: colleagues born up to a half century apart, seasoned traditionalists collaborating with the greenest of digital natives, and everyone in between. To say the employee landscape is diverse is beside the point; it's filled with opportunities to hear each voice, meet each need, and rise to each expectation. It challenges employers with this question: What does it take to engage such a multifaceted workforce, to help them all feel happy, healthy, and more productive?

Employers need to think differently about their approach to attract and retain the best and brightest – and to support the well-being and livelihood of every employee. In their role as "corporate caregiver," employers need to stay on top of benefits trends and evolve the employee experience in the way modern employees demand. Employers need to recognize that not only are they serving a more dynamic workforce with numerous health and wellness goals, but that employees are getting more technologically sophisticated each day.

There's a new set of requirements for reaching and connecting with employees to support well-being, to enable them to address the myriad dimensions of their physical and emotional life that lead them to feel their best. It's at this juncture of well-being and technology where employee engagement can take shape and start driving results. Offering limited "wellness" programs that focus narrowly on the single dimension of physical health as a routine part of comp and benefits has proven ineffective at inspiring lasting behavior change and boosting productivity. By taking a closer look at today's talent marketplace and its impact on employee benefits programs, employers can learn more about their most valuable assets – employees – and what it takes to engage them for the long-haul.

SURVEYING THE BATTLEGROUND FOR TOP TALENT

As of this writing, there are currently more than 7 million job openings in the United States and not enough workers to fill them (Bureau of Labor Statistics 2020). The labor shortage, which runs the gamut of skill levels, is expected to extend into the coming decades due to the combination of an aging population, falling birth rate, and rising consumer demand for goods and services fueling the economy.

As competition for top talent heats up, the pressure is on employers: They need to re-tool their recruitment and benefits strategies to become employers of choice. In fact, a 2018 survey from Gallagher found that attracting and retaining a competitive workforce is now the top operational priority for 60 percent of employers – and with good reason (Gallagher 2020). They know that as the balance of power continues to shift in favor of the job candidate, they're left with no choice but to "let the most progressive employer win."

It's essential, of course, for employers to understand exactly whom they're trying to attract and retain before they recalibrate their benefits spend. While today's workforce is multigenerational, it's becoming increasingly millennial-centric, a fact that can no longer be ignored. A Pew Research Center analysis of US Census Bureau data reveals that today, more than one-in-three (35 percent) American workers are millennials (born from 1981 to 2000), making them the largest generation in the US labor force – and growing (Fry 2018). But they're also the least engaged, according to Gallup, which estimates that millennial turnover costs the US economy $30.5 billion per year (Adkins 2016). This means employers need to increasingly deliver on their expectations, which are, in broad strokes, different from their baby boomer predecessors.

The "Deloitte Global Millennial Survey 2019" provides some context (Deloitte 2020). Millennials and their Gen Z (2001 and later) counterparts, also examined in the study, demonstrate a relative uneasiness and pessimism regarding their careers and financial situations. Entering the labor market during or in the wake of the last economic recession, they have fewer assets and lower real incomes than baby boomers (1946–1964) and Gen Xers (1965–1980) at comparable ages, not to mention more debt. And, if given a choice, millennials are more likely to quit their current job in the next two years.

The resulting aspirations of this "Generation Disrupted," to use Deloitte's millennial moniker, have evolved beyond the adulthood success markers of buying homes and having children. While they generally value and plan to reach these lifetime milestones – and want to earn high salaries and achieve wealth in good measure – they're prioritizing traveling and making a positive impact on the world over the more traditional goals.

These findings dovetail with those of Pew Research Center, showing that members of Gen Z place a high value on corporate citizenship and meaningful work (Parker et al. 2019). They're seeking purpose, belonging, and balance. Companies that want to earn their loyalty must find a way to fold these cultural elements into their business strategies.

The recruiting and retention conversation must also include the central role consumer technology plays in people's everyday lives. Millennials and Gen Z employees grew up in a digital world – and their older colleagues shed their analog roots long ago. Technology is central to the work experience for all employees today, and as Accenture asserts, "Employees want their organization to provide a workplace experience that matches what they've come to expect as customers and in other areas of their life: meaningful, personalized, user-friendly and digital" (PWC 2017).

The Fourth Industrial Revolution is here. Employees are connected and embracing work styles that, like the revolution itself, are blurring the boundaries of the physical and digital, of work and home. With nearly half of US professionals working remotely at least some of the time and being offered some sort of flexible work arrangement by their employer, top talent doesn't have to settle for a daily commute to a job that keeps them tethered to their desk (Mann and Adkins 2017). They're demanding more flexibility – and want employers to make their day-to-day lives easier and more conducive to a healthy, balanced lifestyle.

GAINING COMPETITIVE ADVANTAGE WITH A NEW BENEFITS APPROACH

This new dynamic in the employee marketplace has given employers a tremendous opportunity to start focusing on the softer side of business – with a digital edge. They can invest in creating a friendlier employer value proposition by building well-being-infused, employee-centric cultures and supporting work–life balance with more flexible benefits programs, initiatives that resonate with millennial and Gen Z workers who want to know that their company's values coincide with theirs – especially when it comes to nurturing a healthier life, both in and out of the workplace.

And since people aren't necessarily working 9-to-5 at their company's home office, on-site benefits are serving fewer and fewer employees. Digital benefits delivery is becoming the modus operandi. If employers don't change the way they answer their employees' call for useful well-being resources, they risk far more than workforce attrition. Remember what happened to Kodak starting in the late 1990s? It turned a blind eye to consumers' preference for digital photography, ultimately filing for bankruptcy protection and back-pedaling into the digital space with minimal applause.

Akin to consumer demand for digital tools, employees are asking for help to feel less stressed and more connected with people, to eat healthier, sleep better, and move more. And they're letting employers know by voting with their feet: US uncovered that 94 percent of employees want benefits that affect their quality of life – and 55 percent have left jobs in the past because they found better benefits elsewhere.

Where traditional employee wellness programs were initiated to connect the dots between physical health and productivity, personalized workforce well-being programs have emerged as the more practical alternative – and more popular, at least from the employee's point of view. That's because in the workplace, the concept of wellness has been associated primarily with physical health and biometrics – a health status, disaggregated from the whole person. On the other hand, well-being is holistic and contextual, highly individualistic and accounting for physical health, mental/emotional health and social connectedness.

The problem with the narrow definition of wellness is that it doesn't reflect what engages people and makes them feel happy and healthy. Today's employees want to be seen as whole people comprised of various, interconnected components that need to be nurtured and balanced. It's widely known that millennials in particular crave authenticity – and employers can't expect them to play into the fallacy or fantasy that they're not struggling on some level to feel their best.

The Centers for Disease Control (CDC 2020) reports that 6 in 10 adults in the US have a chronic disease – and 4 in 10 have two or more such diseases. Employees with serious conditions such as diabetes, high blood pressure, and depression can't bring 100 percent of themselves to work. Employees grappling with back pain, severe stress, and sleeplessness are calling in sick or showing up at work tired and distracted, not as productive as they want to be.

This is exactly where many employers are failing in their efforts to engage their workforce with "wellness," something they're trying to address with biometric screenings and their requisite participation incentives. Biometrics, while useful, are just tiny benchmarks – numbers that do nothing to help what's ailing the employee in the first place.

Data alone doesn't motivate the healthy lifestyle changes required for employees to feel their best – and employers are paying the price. Employee disengagement costs US employers $530 billion each year, $280 billion of which is attributed to productivity losses, according to the Integrated Benefits Institute (2018). This breaks down to $1,958 per employee, or a whopping $19.58 million for an employer with 10,000 employees.

Focusing on Well-Being for Competitive Advantage

If lifestyle-related productivity losses aren't enough to ruffle feathers, the 2018 Gallagher survey found that 56 percent of organizations don't have a strategy to increase employee engagement that supports better productivity and improves workforce well-being, which factors into the ability to secure the right talent (Gallagher 2020). But by giving employees the right set of health engagement tools, employees can take the small steps that lead to significant – and sustainable – lifestyle change that makes a direct impact on their engagement and productivity.

Today's top employers give their employees permission to take care of their whole selves, recognizing that well-being and engagement are two sides of the same coin. In order to derive real value from a well-being benefits program – measured by both employee productivity and the ability to attract and retain top talent – employers need to give employees what they're asking for: benefits they love that are also easy to use, thereby allowing them to bring out their best.

While the road to well-being is highly individualized, all employees need specific tools for the journey. An engagement-driving well-being solution provides:

- *Personalization.* A customized experience for each employee's interests, goals, and abilities.
- *Video.* A comprehensive digital library that engages a global workforce.
- *Community.* Support, camaraderie, and encouragement from peers and experts.
- *Expert guidance.* Trusted well-being professionals that guide lasting behavior change.
- *Motivation.* Incentives, gamification, and fun for ongoing success.

The key here is not simply adding "new layers" to an existing – and perhaps underperforming – wellness program. Employers need to replace what's not working – what's not rising to the demands of employees and prospective employees – with a more effective, app-based solution that people can access and enjoy on-demand when and where they want to, in a way that fits into their daily lives, with content that spans the areas of nutrition, mindfulness, sleep, fitness, and more.

Employee expectations are changing, and employers' approach to workforce health engagement needs to keep up with their demand for help feeling their best across all areas of their lives. By giving employees benefits that help them take care of themselves, they can focus on what supports engagement and productivity: their health and happiness.

CAPTURING THE DATA OF WELL-BEING

In the business world, it's all about data. Data drives almost every decision made in an organization, even down to selecting which size paper clips to buy.

So what happens when data is more subjective than objective?

When it comes to implementing or continuing well-being programs, companies find themselves in this predicament. While companies can look to certain data points, a fair portion of the data is anecdotal.

At that point, the question becomes: How do we prove that this program has value?

Why Well-Being?

In recent years, more companies have started including well-being programs as part of their benefits packages. This could include things such as employee assistance programs (EAPs), elder-care programs, financial planning workshops, or yoga and meditation classes. The list of well-being options seems to grow every day, which can create some headache for the ones deciding on the programs that would work best for their employees.

Headache or not, companies are realizing they have no choice but to start looking into how to help employees "be well."

"Millennials have truly revolutionized work," said Ali Payne, global well-being and engagement practice leader at Gallagher, a global insurance brokerage, risk management, and consulting services business based in Rolling Meadows, Illinois. "It's not just about compensation and benefits anymore. They need all the gadgets."

As such, "Benefits professionals in general are thinking much more comprehensively about what they are offering."

Aside from typical insurance benefits and other more "traditional" offerings, benefits professionals are considering programs that "you would have never talked about 10 to 15 years ago," Payne said.

"The upcoming generations entering the workforce are expecting this," said Daniel Harding, CCP, GRP, SPHR, senior leader of total rewards and employee relations at MVP Health Care Inc. "To them, they think it shouldn't be that hard (to implement a well-being program)."

And to some extent, maybe the newer generations have a point. In this day and age of "I've got an app for that," why should it be so difficult for an employer to, say, launch a sustainability program?

The answer lies somewhere in the data.

Defining Success

In order to get to the data, the HR team needs to first define what success looks like.

"A lot of employers are so focused on the problem and implementing a solution that it becomes sort of the tail wagging the dog when it comes to defining success," said Kristin Parker, a partner, Total Health Management Specialty Practice leader at Mercer.

From Payne's point of view, there are "three buckets where employers are thinking about success." They are employee engagement, rewards and recognition, and testimonies.

Employee engagement is one of the easier data points to focus on. Through surveys or event head counts, it is simple to see if a program is being used. And that data does more than just indicate if a program is well received – it can also help program leaders see if they are offering the right programs to engage their employees.

There are potential downsides, however, to solely focusing on employee engagement; for example, if a company offers a subsidy for a gym membership. "Sometimes employees don't participate," Payne said. "But they still like that they have the option."

In terms of rewards and recognition, this may take a little more legwork. Payne uses the example of "Best Places to Work" lists, which typically lay out all the perks a "best" company uses. This can help other companies answer the question, "Do we have the right resources in place to drive employees to come to work every day?" Payne said.

Testimonies – that is, direct feedback from employees or anecdotal feedback from managers – are where the data starts to get more subjective. But that information is no less valuable, Payne asserts.

"There are certain things that employees stay for and things they don't stay for," she said.

Getting that feedback could be tricky. But Payne suggests using survey comments or even exit interviews as a means to retrieve that information.

MVP began rolling out various well-being programs four or five years ago. The health-care company wanted to "walk the walk," Harding said. At that point, MVP opted to use a scorecard that would help measure a program's success. That scorecard also offered information to help the company tweak programs, as well as decide what programs to keep, add or eliminate.

Furthermore, it gave the company a snapshot into what was next, giving guidance on the question, "What's the next stressor?"

Mercer's Parker urges companies to "make sure success is defined early on." She suggests focusing on the "Triple Aim" approach: improving the patient (in this case, the employee) experience, improving outcomes, and reducing costs – both for the company and the employee.

Once success has been defined, then is the time to figure out the methodology on how to obtain that information (see Sidebar 7.2).

Sidebar 7.2 Four Methodologies to Measure Well-Being Program Success

Once a company has defined what success looks like as it pertains to a well-being program, the next question is, "How are we going to measure that?" Mercer's Kristin Parker lays out four methods that can be used, including the pros and cons of each technique.

Descriptive analysis: Did the metrics change over time?

According to Parker, this method is the "simplest way [to measure program success], but there are significant limitations." Specifically, she said the method does not take into account outside factors that may be influencing the data.

Financial modeling: Are there cost savings?

This methodology also looks into whether certain metrics have changed over time, though it specifically focuses on changes in health risks. But by looking at insurance claims costs, for example, one can "extrapolate the cost savings based on rigorous assumption numbers," Parker said.

Actuarial methodology: How did one group's metrics change over time when compared to another group?

The actuarial method incorporates some descriptive analysis data, Parker notes, though it then applies actuarial tables to calculate for the factors that a straight analysis doesn't. Still, it relies on making assumptions about demographics.

"There are a lot of assumptions going into that as far as what is the right trend to use," she said.

Match case control analysis: A rigorous undertaking

Parker notes that using this statistical approach to measuring a program's success takes the most work and therefore, the most investment.

"The more rigorous the methodology, the higher the cost," she said.

Still, this method can help remove assumptions from the equation, making it easier to adjust for population factors. She acknowledges, however, that it can only adjust for variables in the data set.

"Culture, for instance, can be difficult to measure and adjust for," she said.

Whatever methodology – or methodologies – a company uses, Parker stresses the importance of regularly checking the data.

"We encourage employers to not wait for these outcomes analyses, but (to also be sure that) throughout the year, you are measuring the data," she said. By doing so, a company can "course correct as needed."

Getting Buy-In: Data Is Currency

In addition to measuring the success of a well-being program, data can also come in handy in one very important way: getting buy-in from leadership.

Traditionally, leadership has focused on health-care metrics, such as health-risk assessments, behavioral-health claims and pharmacy claims, Parker noted. But as more types of well-being programs pop up and the usual data is less concrete, there are other things to consider (see Sidebar 7.3).

Take, for instance, a meditation program. Given that distraction is the leading cause of injuries at work, teaching an employee mindfulness "could significantly decrease the number of injuries on the job," she said. That could, in turn, increase productivity and could "ultimately be a bottom-line revenue generator, or increase the creativity and innovation that can lead to revenue generation."

Understanding what services vendors might provide – and if those services are already included in your contract – is crucial to getting leadership on board, Payne said.

"The worst thing you could do is go to your executives and say, 'I want to spend more money,' but you haven't done your homework."

For example, perhaps your insurance provider offers other resources, such as financial planning. Finding out that you are already paying for that benefit but didn't realize it is a good way to get the OK.

"You do want to make sure you are using all the services your vendor has," Harding said.

Harding stresses that it's also important to make leadership understand that it's not just about return on investment that counts when it comes to well-being: It's also value on investment.

"You hope that your retention rate goes up, turnover goes down and attraction goes up," he said. "But ultimately, there is a return," financially and otherwise.

In some cases, "It's tough to sell," he said. Still, "if I can save 1 percent, even 0.5 percent, on my medical spend year after year (through the reduction of various health claims), that's quite a change."

"The money is going to get spent somewhere," he said. So why not on well-being?

Sidebar 7.3 NPS: The New Kid in Town

There is a new metric that is being considered when it comes to making decisions on health and well-being programs: the Net Promoter Score (NPS).

What is NPS?

According to the Net Promoter website, NPS "measures customer experience and predicts business growth." Though it was originally intended to measure brand loyalty, its scope is expanding.

To find your score, you must first ask a question, such as "on a scale of 0 to 10, how likely are you to recommend X product or service?" Respondents that answer 0 to 6 are considered "detractors," or those who could have a negative impact on your brand or program. Answers in the 7 to 8 range are deemed "passive," or those who are perhaps satisfied, but have little to no enthusiasm. "Loyal enthusiasts" are those who answer 9 or 10. People in that group are likely to refer a friend or provide some otherwise positive impact on your program/brand.

Once the data has come in, subtract the percentage of detractors from the percentage of promoters. That number – which can range from –100 to 100 – is your NPS.

NPS and well-being

"Historically, a customer satisfaction survey was used (to measure a well-being program's effectiveness)," Mercer's Parker said. But those scores tended to come in pretty high – 90 percent to 100 percent, on average, she said. Meaning that perhaps such surveys were "not good indicators" of a program's success.

Now that NPS has entered the scene, companies are using it to study the impact of their health and well-being benefits. It has "added to the ethos" of the metrics, Parker said.

The bonus of using NPS is that it has "more sensitivity" to certain factors that other methodologies can't quite get to. As it is structured as one simple question, it is easier to standardize and cross-compare, she said.

"Using NPS for this is an interesting application and it could help organizations determine if their health and well-being programs are good or if their programs are actually something that differentiates them from the competition – something that their employees brag to their friends about," said Alicia Jenkins, program manager of survey research at WorldatWork. "If they see many scores below a 7, it would indicate that the program is likely not performing as predicted."

CHANGING THE DYNAMIC OF OPEN ENROLLMENT

Traditionally, employers have viewed open enrollment as an annual opportunity for employees to make positive impact on their total well-being – not just in terms of improving their financial standing, but also to protect themselves from unforeseen events. Yet, few workers actually take full advantage of the occasion and end up fundamentally cheating themselves out of wellness benefits, while employers waste valuable dollars that could potentially strengthen their workforce individually and their organizations as a whole.

Research from employee benefits provider Unum, revealed that nearly half of US workers (49 percent) spend, at most, just 30 minutes reviewing their benefits package prior to enrollment (Unum 2018). Additional research by financial insurance provider Aflac (2018), found that 93 percent of respondents in its study choose the same benefits year after year, regardless of changes in their own circumstances or other influential factors.

The same study identified a clear disconnect in the perception of employers, which for the most part (83 percent) believe that their workers have a thorough understanding of the benefits they offer. But, 76 percent of employees instead revealed that there were at least some parts of the available benefits offering they did not understand.

Going back to the Unum study and we can see the repercussions of this disconnect, with respondents reporting feeling stressed (21 percent), confused (22 percent), and anxious (20 percent) when enrolling in their benefits. The unfortunate upshot is that the same benefits intended to help improve employee well-being have the potential to become a source of stress. Furthermore, sweeping changes to health care, such as those introduced following the Affordable Care Act (ACA) in 2010, can leave employees and employers alike confused and bewildered by the impact of new legislation.

"There's lots of research out there that shows that around 70 percent of employees don't understand the benefits offered by their employer," says Daniel LaBroad, president and CEO of Ovation Health and Life Services, a benefits broker based out of Dallas, Texas.

Just 10–15 years ago, the approach from visiting benefits consultants was quite different. They could go into an organization and directly engage with the employee on a one-on-one basis and walk them through the benefits, answer any questions, and help them make decisions.

"This really made education a hand-holding opportunity, where you could explain the benefits to employees in greater detail and help them understand how to best leverage them for their individual situations." LaBroad says.

But times have changed, and while a one-on-one approach remains the most effective solution to the education challenge, it's no longer always a viable one. A lot of employees are not in the office every day, or they consistently work remotely from other cities or states. Some industries, like manufacturing, retail, and hospitality, have shift workers that work hours outside of the typical 9–5 workday, making communication difficult. Overall, workers are not getting as much face-to-face interaction as they used to, and the reasons aren't always office dynamics. If we look at the broad impact of social media and mobile technology, it's easy to argue that both employers and employees alike are moving away from face-to-face interaction on a cultural level, too.

"Being able to offer 24/7 support to the workforce is crucial when you have lots of shift workers and rostered staff," says Robert Sinclair, CEO of London City Airport in the UK. "In that environment it's not always easy for people to be able to communicate with each other."

So, from a business perspective, organizations in every sector are benefiting from, and seeking to take advantage of, new technologies that were developed in the consumer space and this is changing the way we work. Like in so many areas of our lives, the smartphone is the real agent of change here, even across generations, with 92 percent of millennials and 85 percent of Generation X almost glued to the device (Vogels 2019).

The perceived digital dexterity enabled by the smartphone is driven by information intensity and the desire of humans to share and collaborate, as well as the convenience. We're all used to an on-demand experience in our personal lives – order a movie on Netflix, it plays immediately; order a taxi on Uber, it arrives within minutes; order an item on Amazon, it arrives within the hour. Furthermore, these are *our* experiences, with many of these services learning from its users to deliver a more relevant and appropriate interaction, and this is something we're coming to expect from every technology. According to Salesforce, by 2020, 51 percent of consumers and 75 percent of business buyers expect companies to be able to anticipate their needs and make relevant suggestions (Salesforce 2017).

When it comes to benefits, employees will turn to their employers as the owner of the employee experience and employers will turn to their specialist suppliers for guidance. Erin Barnhart, Benefits & Reward Manager at MSA Safety, based in Cranberry Township, Pennsylvania, said her employer has a robust well-being and benefits program that is outsourced and supported by someone onsite to drive better health for the people and the company.

"We have sales people who are out on location. We have a wide range of ages in the company with lots of long timers – people been here nearly 40 years," Barnhart says. "We really try to be inclusive so everyone can participate in the initiatives one way or another."

As HR leaders know well, humans are unique and have very individual needs, pressures and motivations, even though there are some demographic consistencies. The same is true of the well-being needs of a person as a complex combination of multiple factors. Physical well-being benefits may be of little interest to a fitness enthusiast, but that may change if they are rewarded for maintaining their physical wellness. A parent may not be motivated by discounts and savings on luxury goods but may appreciate benefits that help them make their money go further on everyday items.

Yet despite the different motivations and regardless of whether you subscribe to Maslow's hierarchy of needs or Carol Ryff's dimensions of psychological well-being, there is a common theme in well-being of self-acceptance, personal growth, the ability to cope when things inevitably don't go our way, our connection with work and home, and our sense of mission and purpose.

The World Health Organization defines "health" as more than just the absence of disease and infirmity, but as "a state of complete physical, mental, and social well-being." More recently, Deloitte has taken this definition a step further to encompass the financial concerns affecting an individual's mental and physical health. The well-being of the human has more holistic requirements, and this is why we need a human-centered approach.

It may sound contradictory, but technology has a purpose here. If we draw a parallel with the Employee Assistance space over the years, clinical experts have developed a range of tools to support people using a multitude of modalities. These are tried-and-tested programs that are proven to help the 10 percent of the employees that seek them out when they reach a time of crisis.

But the question for business leaders now is how that support can be moved upstream to reach the entire workforce proactively and preventatively? To scale to meet the needs of 100 percent of an organization's people, technology must play a role. Smartphones help us be more productive, in terms of how we learn, how we communicate, how we do our banking, and how we shop. These consumer-grade mobile-first user experiences create an environment that is free of friction and meets our every need as quickly and easily as possible.

It's well understood that the younger generation looks for interaction when they need it and where they need it, while the older generation still wants that more traditional face-to-face experience. Yet as a status quo this is changing.

"We live in a pretty computer literate society," says Alastair Macdonald, senior vice president of HR at Nestle Canada. "People are pretty adaptable and see the power that technology can have. If you see a shift change at our manufacturing facilities, people are walking to their cars or public transport staring at their phones."

But when it comes to the well-being experience for employees, the story is often different. The HR industry is saturated with point solutions that only focus on a small part of an individual's well-being. Human resources is one sector that has fallen behind in terms of adoption of consumer grade technology. HR professionals are often working with outdated tools and data that lack context, as well as being tasked with "keeping the boat steady," rather than driving change. But if the human is connected by the different pillars of well-being, then why aren't we looking at tackling this is a more unified way – perhaps with a user experience that people love to use and keeps them returning?

As employee experience moves away from face-to-face, technology is allowing businesses to reach further when it comes to delivering benefits, while still hand-holding when necessary. The result is a user experience that empowers people and benefits businesses.

As a specialist that sells workplace benefits, Daniel LaBroad, has some insight: "Lots of benefits portals are not intuitive, and anyway, getting information into the most used employee content platforms is key to getting the message out there," he says. "With a platform like LifeWorks that has a News Feed and is something that employees are using on a daily basis, you have the perfect opportunity to communicate with people.

The key is to look at which interface employees are logging into most frequently – is it the benefits portal or something like LifeWorks? If it's the latter, it makes sense to use that as your entry point to push out engagement and education to employees.

Furthermore, the research suggests that engaged and educated employees are good for business. Deloitte's Josh Bersin, one of the foremost experts on HR technology and employee well-being noted in the 2019 Global Human Capital Trends survey, that as the definition of well-being expands, organizations now see well-being not just as an employee benefit or responsibility, but as a business performance strategy (Deloitte 2019).

Tellingly, 43 percent of Deloitte survey respondents believed that well-being reinforces their organization's mission and vision, 60 percent reported that it improves employee retention, and 61 percent said that it improves employee productivity and bottom-line business results.

Indeed, author and workplace culture expert, Chester Elton, notes that 20 years of research has shown that the financial performance of organizations with high employee engagement is 44 percent higher than those with low engagement. The reason? People who are engaged at work are more likely to be happy in their personal lives and healthier, happier employees are more productive.

"It's the people that make a culture and those people need to be engaged, enabled and energized, because ultimately, the better the culture, the better the customer service. The happier the customers, the more successful the business," says Elton.

If culture is a key ingredient for a successful business, then communication is a fundamental part of culture. By using the most popular employee communication channels to distribute benefits information, you can successfully engage employees year-round, and not just at open enrollment. The discussion about benefits and well-being then becomes part of daily life, and people naturally become more engaged. The result? A more educated workforce that feels more valued, loved, and respected.

EMPLOYERS BOOSTING INVESTMENT IN WELL-BEING PROGRAMS

As the global pandemic and resulting financial crisis continue to affect how and where employees work, 95 percent of employers around the globe now include emotional and mental health programs in their corporate well-being platforms (see Sidebar 7.4 on Ocean Spray).

This is according to the "Health and Well-Being Survey" of 152 large and mid-sized US-based employers by Fidelity Investments and Business Group on Health, which revealed that teletherapy (69 percent), stress management (50 percent), and resiliency programs (49 percent) are the most commonly offered mental/emotional health programs organizations are providing.

> *Editor's Note*: *This survey was fielded in the fall of 2019 before the COVID-19 pandemic, and some employers may be adjusting their well-being strategies going forward. However, many of the results are applicable to the current workplace environment.*

The survey's findings suggest that emotional and mental health programs can be particularly valuable to employees who may be adjusting to working from home or may have had changes to their workspace due to health safety.

Employers are also increasing their emphasis on helping employees improve their work/life balance, with 78 percent of employers including these types of benefits in their well-being platforms. Popular work/life balance benefits included caregiver support (46 percent), programs and tools for new parents (36 percent) and child-care support (35 percent).

Multinational employers are also focused on well-being strategies, with 67 percent offering programs to their global workforces and 51 percent tailoring their well-being program to the needs of their regional workforce. Similar to well-being strategies in the US, almost a third (32 percent) of multinational employers include emotional and mental health programs in their well-being programs in other countries.

Well-Being Budget Increase

As well-being platforms evolve and expand, the average well-being budget continues to increase, along with the number of employees dedicated to managing these programs. The average budget for well-being programs increased to $4.9 million in 2020, up 36 percent over 2019. Among large employers (20,000-plus employees), the average budget earmarked for well-being programs jumps to $10.4 million. Furthermore, 31 percent of employers indicated they will have two or more full-time staff members dedicated to the company's well-being program, while 13 percent will have more than five full-time employees dedicated to managing these programs.

Financial incentives continue to play an important role in encouraging employees to partake in well-being offerings. While the percentage of employers offering a financial incentive dipped slightly to 78 percent from 82 percent, 13 percent of employers surveyed indicated that they plan to increase the maximum incentive amount in 2020. The average maximum amount that can be earned per employee stayed fairly steady, dropping to $757 in 2020 from $762 in 2019.

Most incentives are tied to physical health initiatives, but 15 percent of incentives are tied to initiatives designed to address nonphysical issues such as mental, financial, and emotional health. And while only 12 percent of multinational employers currently offer financial incentives to employees outside of the US, 17 percent indicated they will consider offering in 2021.

Increased Support for Teleworkers

According to the survey, employers are planning to increase their on-site well-being programs and services in 2020, which will benefit employees who may soon move back to a more traditional work environment. However, since the survey was conducted prior to the pandemic, many employers may have evolved their workforce management strategies and will continue to have a significant percentage of their employees in a work from home environment, Fidelity and Business Group on Health concluded.

As a result, employers are likely to consider allocating additional resources and well-being support for the increasing number of employees who continue to work from home on a regular basis.

Sidebar 7.4 Case Study: Ocean Spray Takes on Mental Health

At Ocean Spray, the Plymouth County, Md.-based agricultural cooperative best known for its cranberries, there are four pillars holding up the organization's benefits and wellness program: physical, financial, emotional, and work–life.

Susan French, senior manager of benefits, wellness, and mobility, began taking a deeper look at how the organization addressed each pillar. As she started to research the emotional pillar, she noticed that mental health and issues related to it – such as suicide and addiction – "started showing up more."

French realized that while mental health is technically placed under the emotional umbrella, it had a broader impact on the other pillars – and the other pillars could have just as much impact on mental health.

"We decided to do an overarching campaign [addressing the issue]," French said. The goal was to explain what mental health means and why it's important, address the stigma that is often attached to mental illness and provide statistics that underscored the importance of the issue. This came via a three-pronged approach:

1. Reduce the stigma.
2. Provide resources and remove barriers to treatment.
3. Invest in programs.

Addressing the Stigma

Ocean Spray's company motto is "Act Tiny, Be Mighty," giving a nod to the powerful properties of the small cranberry. For its mental health program, that motto was turned into "Tiny Acts Make a Mighty Impact."

The purpose of this new slogan, French said, was to not only start the conversation about mental health, but also to "provide tiny steps to reduce stress in each pillar." Instead of looking at all areas of your life, or even one area, as a daunting, uncontrollable mess, think of small ways you can start to address an issue. For instance, if your financial state is causing you undue stress, run a credit report or make some sort of savings plan – a small step toward a larger goal.

French said the thought was to encourage employees to "piece it out" to make the problems they face seem smaller.

Seeing a Need and Filling It

When it came to the second part of the mental health program, Ocean Spray recognized – accurately – that getting the right care at the right time is essential to addressing mental health needs.

"Chances are the need is immediate," French said.

As such, the organization did away with co-pays for mental health care. It also implemented a telemedicine program that included a behavioral health component. French noted that a good thing about the telemedicine counseling benefit was that those who used it could speak to the same counselor.

Additionally, the organization started connecting disability claims to its EAP, which provided a level of convenience for employees.

And speaking of the EAP, Ocean Spray also launched a new EAP, changing the name to "Fit for Life Cares" – a play on the broader "Fit for Life" slogan of the benefits and wellness program – as a way to "get around the clinical stigma."

Worth the Spend

In order to really make a difference for its employees, Ocean Spray acknowledged that it would need to invest in programs that could help, whether that was via partnerships or internally led initiatives.

For example, Ocean Spray partnered with Maven Clinic Co., a health-care company focused on providing access to women and families. Maven offers assistance covering all aspects of maternity, including fertility issues, postpartum depression, and returning to work after parental leave.

French said there was also an informal partnership with Make It OK, an organization that aims to end the stigma of mental illness. At meetings, leadership handed out "OK" stickers to employees as a way to encourage them to speak up about their issues.

The point of Make It OK and the "OK" stickers, French said, was to let everyone know "it's OK to feel how you feel and it's OK to ask for help."

Soon, the stickers were popping up all over the office, French said.

"That says to me that it's resonating with people," she said – including senior leadership.

Inside the company, there were other actions taken in an effort to lighten the load of the employees. French noted that Ocean Spray's corporate office is open concept, so "It's hard to get a private moment." To address this, the organization built a "Zen Den" in the office, a space that could be privately booked for 10–15 minutes, allowing an employee to get a recharge.

Ocean Spray also wanted to make sure that the work–life aspect was considered. Therefore, things like flexible schedules and onsite perks, such as an eye doctor, a "floss bar," and a dry cleaner, were added.

Ultimately, Ocean Spray's goal has been to help address the mental health conundrum by encouraging people to speak out about their issues and being responsive to them.

"We wanted to focus on helping people bring their best selves to work," French said.

EMPLOYEE WELL-BEING IS AN ORGANIZATIONAL IMPERATIVE

The importance of employer-sponsored well-being programs has come into focus. A survey by Alight Solutions developed with Business Group on Health and Kantar found that employees are placing a higher premium on employer well-being programs that affect their personal and professional lives.

The "Employee Wellbeing Mindset Study" of 2,500 employees found that 44 percent feel optimistic about their well-being, which is up from 38 percent in 2019. Since 2019, employees' perceived value of well-being benefits and programs, decision tools and information sources all increased by at least 10 points. "While employers have been increasingly focused on the diverse needs of their workforce, the global pandemic has and will continue to advance employer strategies that integrate well-being into employees' lives and create great experiences," said Ray Baumruk, vice president of employee experience research and insights at Alight. "Many employers are taking this opportunity to enhance well-being support that ensures their people and their families are cared for during these tough times."

The researchers predicted the pandemic will have a significant impact across the five dimensions of well-being – physical, mental/emotional, financial, social, and career – and many well-being trends will accelerate. The survey also revealed there are potential opportunities for employers to improve their well-being strategies:

- *Promote health-care consumerism.* Employees who make savvier health care decisions and take cost-related actions jumped to 90 percent (73 percent in 2019). Also, 65 percent of employees value personalized support for navigating the health system and affiliated costs, which will likely be further complicated in the wake of the pandemic. Proactive, better decision-making can be supported by employers that offer tailored health-care tools and resources.
- *Prioritize mental health.* Efforts to reduce mental health stigmas have coincided with a sizable increase to 41 percent of employees (25 percent in 2018) who have sought counseling or other related services. Due to the massive, sudden shift to working-from-home arrangements, as well as pandemic impacts on lifestyle, employers should continue to prioritize mental health for employees who may be dealing with social isolation, higher stress, greater anxiety, and emotional exhaustion.
- *Support financial security.* Financial well-being is the lowest-rated dimension, with only 40 percent of employees giving themselves positive ratings. Employee sentiment around overall control over their financial futures (debt burdens, retirement readiness) will likely worsen due to COVID-19's economic consequences, so employers should consider enhanced benefits like extended paid leave and make sure support is more easily accessible.
- *Help build resilience.* Over two-fifths (43 percent) of employees are feeling overworked and desire more efficiency in their work experience.

The growing segment of virtual workers checks in even higher at 50 percent, as they are more likely to feel lonely and burned out and believe their work gets in the way of their social lives. If they haven't already, employers can help curb feelings of burnout by offering flexible work hours and stipends for work-related technology, among other supportive actions.

"Employees are currently in very different places along the well-being spectrum, and rightfully so, during these challenging times," said Ellen Kelsay, president and CEO, Business Group on Health. "At the same time, employers have been boosting their efforts to support employees' emotional and financial wellbeing through a variety of initiatives, including expanding paid leave, providing temporary pay for furloughed employees and enhancing employee communications on well-being."

Video Technology Enhancing Telework Productivity

The COVID-19 pandemic has made working remotely much more commonplace at companies across the globe. And while productivity was a concern for many businesses deploying this teleworking model out of necessity, video technology may have alleviated those concerns.

This is according to the report "How Video Is Changing the World" from Limelight Networks, Inc., which surveyed 5,000 consumers across the globe to find how online video supports daily activities during and after the pandemic.

One-third (33 percent) of global consumers are working from home for the first time and say online video helps them stay connected to colleagues (24 percent) and work more efficiently (36 percent). More than half (58 percent) have or plan to use online video for professional development or to learn a new skill. Most people (83 percent) believe video-based learning will continue in the post-COVID world. Americans said live-streaming job fairs (17 percent) and virtual networking events (16 percent) are good opportunities for online video to improve the job search.

While the benefits of virtual communications tools are clear, Americans may be slower to adopt them, compared to the rest of the world. 37 percent of Americans said they never use video conferencing compared to 31 percent of global respondents. Additionally, just 12 percent of Americans use video conferencing three-plus times each day, compared to 21 percent of global respondents.

The pandemic has sparked a rapid increase in telehealth across the globe. More than one-fifth (22 percent) of people have recently met with their doctor virtually. This trend is expected to last beyond the pandemic with another quarter (27 percent) of global respondents planning to hold telehealth appointments in the next six months. Telehealth usage is highest for India, where 81 percent of consumers said they have met or plan to meet with their doctor virtually.

"The pandemic has pushed the bounds of online video," said Mike Milligan, senior director of product and solution marketing at Limelight Networks. "Applications such as remote collaboration, e-learning, and tele-health, have been widely available for some time now; but today, they're essential to continuing life in quarantine. Many people turned to online video to connect with others and maintain daily activities during the pandemic, but it won't stop once quarantine is over. Our report emphasizes that online video will remain an important part of our lives in the new normal."

8 Benefits Basics

Benefits are a core element of the WorldatWork total rewards model. (See Figure 1.3 in Chapter 1.) Benefits include health and welfare plans and retirement plans designed to help protect and ensure employees' financial security, as well as programs providing pay for time not worked. Over a period of time, employee benefits have evolved from basic "fringe benefits" of insurance coverage and a few perquisites to a comprehensive range of benefits that strike a balance between employees' personal and professional lives.

The ever-growing package of offerings has evolved, along with some compensation programs, into a separate element of the total rewards model, well-being. Can some programs of well-being be considered benefits? Yes, many organizations still consider them benefits. The total rewards model takes into account the fluidity of the relationship between compensation, benefits, and well-being. It will be up to each individual organization to define precisely where the various programs will be categorized.

HISTORICAL PERSPECTIVE OF BENEFITS

The world of employee benefits is drastically different than just five years ago, let alone 15 to 20 years ago. What is not new is that employees need benefits and companies need employees. However, due to the escalation of benefit costs, employers have started to re-examine the employees' role in the selection, payment, and management of benefits.

Historically, employers handled all aspects of benefits. This was the era of providing "cradle to grave" benefits. Employers selected and paid for benefits. Employees had minimal to no input in any benefit-related decision. Benefits were considered "fringe" and employees viewed benefits as "entitlements." (See Figure 8.1.)

FIGURE 8.1 Historical influences – the benefits timeline.

Late Nineteenth Century
- US economy changed from agricultural to industrial
- First pension plan established in 1875 by the American Express Company

1900s: World War I
- New workers entering United States
- Social safety nets; no financial safety nets
- Department of Labor (DOL) formed by Congress in 1913
- Homogeneous workforce (male, sole wage earner)

1920s: Riding High until Stock Market Crash
- Few disability benefits available to workers retired, injured, or killed on the job
- First Blue Cross plan established at Baylor University Hospital
- Kaiser Health Maintenance Organization (HMO) established
- Revenue Acts of 1921, 1926, and 1928 encouraged private, employer-sponsored retirement plans

1930s: Depression
- Public safety net began to develop
  - Workers' Compensation
  - Unemployment insurance
  - Social Security (1935)
- National Labor Relations Act (NLRA)
  - Collective bargaining for pay and benefits

1940s: World War II
- National Labor Relations Board (NLRB) formed in 1948
- Huge growth in unions – unions demanded more for employees
- Women entered the workforce – "Rosie the Riveter"
- Family care issues emerged
- Private pension plans grew significantly

1950s: Post–World War II
- Fringe benefits emerging
- Employers began competing with benefits to address the wage freeze
- Simple benefits packages met the needs of the traditional family: major medical, life, disability, pension plan
- Low costs

FIGURE 8.1 *(Continued)*

1960s: Decade of Assassinations; Vietnam
- Changing demographics
  - Divorce became more common; break-up of families
  - Working mothers (sole income) unsupported with benefits
  - More transient workforce
- Medicare and Medicaid established
- Title VII of the Civil Rights Act of 1964

1970s: Watergate; Oil Crisis
- Economic downturn – high inflation, slow economic growth
- More than 20 major pieces of legislation affecting benefits plans – specifically the Employee Retirement Income Security Act of 1974 (ERISA), IRC Section 125, 401(k), HMO Act
- Initial corporate response to changing workforce
  - Working mother issues began to take force
  - Single fathers became an issue

1980s: Computer Commonplace; Space Shuttle Challenger Explosion
- Benefit costs skyrocketed
- Gradual development of flexible benefits
- Announcement: Social Security is broke
- Cost shift to employees
- Consumer education
- Employers moving to "self-insurance" of health plans
- Beginnings of managed care (utilization management)

1990s: Information Technology; Internet
- Focus on benefit value and personal responsibility – optimizing the value for each dollar spent
- Performance orientation of benefits plans consistent with corporate goals
- Flexible benefits expanded, addressing the needs of a diverse workforce
- Employer accountability to expand choices for employees
  - Segmented benefits for different demographics
- Greater employee accountability for decision-making
- Emerging shift in definition of dependent
  - Domestic partner, aging parents, elder care, adoption
- Consolidation of health-care industry

FIGURE 8.1 *(Continued)*

2000s and 2010s: Focus on corporate accounting/governance; health-care coverage debates; Social Security solvency
- Movement away from "entitlement" (paternalism) to partnership and shared accountability between employers and employees
- Consumer-driven health plans expand; consumerism opportunity provided by technology
- Wellness initiatives and well-being programs expand
- Funding for Social Security coverage debated
- Triple whammy: child-care, elder-care, and retirement planning at the same time
- Uninsured and underinsured increases; issue of universal health-care coverage debated
- The Patient Protection and Affordable Care Act

Today, initiatives from the US government (involving Medicare) and employers are placing more responsibility and accountability on employees for benefit decision-making and cost responsibilities. Businesses and government still have important roles, but the trend is for employers and government to share the platform with benefit recipients. Some call this shared accountability.

ELEMENTS OF BENEFITS

Benefits programs may be categorized into the following two elements: (1) income protection programs; and (2) pay for time not worked programs. (See Figure 8.2.)

FIGURE 8.2 Benefits programs at a glance.

Income Protection Plans (Mandatory)	• State and Federal Unemployment Insurance • Workers' Compensation • Social Security • State Temporary Disability Insurance (New Jersey, New York, Hawaii, Rhode Island, California)
Income Protection Plans (Mandatory)	• State and Federal Unemployment Insurance • Workers' Compensation • Social Security • State Temporary Disability Insurance (New Jersey, New York, Hawaii, Rhode Island, California)

FIGURE 8.2 *(Continued)*

Income Protection Programs (Non-Mandatory)	**Health-Care Benefits** • Medical Plans (Indemnity Plans and Managed Care Plans, such as HMOs, PPOs, and POS) • Prescription Drug Coverage • Dental Plans • Vision Plans • Hearing Plans **Welfare Benefits** • Employee Term Life Insurance • Dependent Term Life Insurance • Accidental Death and Dismemberment • Sick Pay (Salary Continuation) • Short-Term Disability • Long-Term Disability • Long-Term Care Insurance **Flexible Benefits** • Premium Conversion • Flexible Spending Accounts (Health Care and Dependent Care) • Full Flexible Benefits Plans **Retirement and Investment Plans** • Defined Benefit Plans • Defined Contribution Plans (Savings/Thrift Plans, Profit-Sharing Plans, SIMPLE Plans, Money Purchase Plans, Employee Stock Ownership Plans) • Hybrid Plans (Cash Balance Plans, Pension Equity Plans) **Executive Benefits** • Supplemental Executive Retirement Plans • Supplemental Health Plans • Supplemental Life Insurance Plans • Supplemental Disability Plans
Pay for Time Not Worked (Non-mandatory)	**At Work** • Rest Periods • Lunch Periods • Wash-Up Time • Clothes Change Time **Not at Work** • Vacations • Holidays • Personal Leave • Jury Duty • Military Duty

Income Protection Programs

Income protection programs are designed to protect the standard of living of the employee and his or her family. The programs include mandatory and nonmandatory or voluntary coverage.

Mandatory plans are required by federal or state law to cover employees for:

- Social Security
- Workers' compensation
- Unemployment
- Nonoccupational disability (five states only)

Nonmandatory or voluntary plans are provided at the discretion of the employer and include:

- Medical
- Prescription drug
- Mental/behavioral health
- Dental
- Vision
- Disability income
- Survivor benefits
- Flexible spending accounts
- Retirement plans

Pay for Time Not Worked Programs

Pay for time not worked programs are designed to protect the employee's income flow during certain periods, both at work and not at work, when the employee is not working.

For example, common paid time-off benefits would include vacation, holidays, sick-pay, and leaves of absence including time off for jury duty, voting, military duty, and medical or bereavement leaves.

BENEFITS PLAN OBJECTIVES

Employers and employees value benefits differently. They will rarely agree on the level of benefits that plans should provide. Employers seek to balance the employees' needs and the cost to the organization. Employees wish to maximize the value of benefits received and minimize out-of-pocket expenses.

Employer Objectives

The employer objectives for benefits plans are influenced by:

- Meeting corporate, business, and compensation objectives
- Actual dollar cost and percentage of payroll

- Administration complexity and cost
- Tax and accounting issues
- The role benefits play in the total rewards objectives of the organization

Employee Objectives

Employee objectives for benefits plans include income protection for:

- *Cash flow.* Ensure cash flow is not compromised due to large medical and/or dental claims.
- *Income replacement.* Replace income if employee becomes disabled.
- *Income for surviving dependents.* Provide income for surviving dependents in the event of death.
- *Adequate retirement income.* Provide adequate income upon retirement.

In order to design a benefits program, an organization should define its program objectives. Additionally, program objectives need to be aligned with the organization's and HR's philosophy and strategy. Because company philosophies and strategies differ, no two companies will share the same objectives for employee benefits plans.

Review the objectives listed in Figure 8.3 and rank the three to five objectives that are most important to your company regarding employee benefits.

FIGURE 8.3 Employee benefits plan objectives.

Please prioritize the top three to five objectives for employee benefits in your organization.

Objectives	Rank
Increase employee morale	_____
Motivate action	_____
Attract good employees	_____
Reduce turnover	_____
Keep unions out	_____
Better use compensation dollars	_____
Enhance employee security	_____
Maintain favorable competitive position	_____
Enhance organization's image among employees	_____
Increase employee productivity	_____

GOVERNMENT REGULATION OF BENEFITS PLANS

Management of employee benefits includes compliance with numerous federal and state laws and regulations. Sanctions and penalties for noncompliance can be severe, including plan "disqualification" under the Internal Revenue Code. Disqualification can cause employees to lose tax exemption or tax deferral of benefits values, and employers to lose the advantage of tax deductibility of plan expenditures.

Figure 8.4 highlights major laws affecting benefits plans and identifies principal agencies that issue regulations and monitor compliance. At least one new law each year affects some aspect of employee benefits. It is important to know that benefits continue to change due to legislation.

Federal regulations with the most significant influences include:

- *Internal Revenue Code (IRC)*
  - Refers to tax laws passed by Congress and administered by the IRS.
  - Early statute governing private pension plans.
- *Title VII of the Civil Rights Act of 1964*
  - Employers can never legally base benefits decisions on race, color, religion, sex, or national origin.
- *Age Discrimination in Employment Act of 1967 (ADEA)*
  - If an employer provides benefits to its employees, it generally must do so without regard to an employee's age. ADEA does permit employers to provide different benefits to older employees only under certain circumstances.
- *The Employee Retirement Income Security Act of 1974 (ERISA).*
  - ERISA introduced federal government involvement in the employee benefits arena.
  - ERISA establishes minimum standards to provide protection for participants and beneficiaries in employee benefits plans (participant rights). Among other things, ERISA standards cover access to plan information and fiduciary responsibility.
  - ERISA covers most private sector health and pension plans but does not apply to public-sector benefits.
  - Those individuals who manage plans (and other fiduciaries) must meet certain standards of conduct under the fiduciary responsibilities specified by law.

- *The Economic Growth and Tax Relief Reconciliation Act of 2001 (EGTRRA)*
  EGTRRA was a massive piece of federal tax legislation that:
  - Enacted substantial changes in the income and estate tax rate structures
  - Made major changes in the alternative minimum tax rules
  - Established qualified tuition programs and college savings accounts

- Created a new tax credit for low-income savers
- Liberalized estate and gift tax rules
- Adopted a broad range of enhancements affecting tax-qualified retirement plans

The changes affecting qualified retirement plans represent a major retirement-policy turning point. Prior to EGTRRA, the trend in tax and benefits policy was to progressively limit the amounts that could be contributed to, and benefits that could accrue, under tax-qualified retirement plans. While it is true that the deferral limits for 401(k) plans were rising modestly over time with increases in the cost of living, the overall contributions limits under Code §415, among others, had been cut substantially. EGTRRA represents an abrupt departure from this trend, and it opens up significant new planning opportunities, especially for small, closely held businesses. With the passage of EGTRAA (as supplemented by certain technical corrections made in the Jobs Creation and Worker Assistance Act of 2002 [JCWAA]), Congress liberalized and rationalized the rules that govern the design, adoption, and operation of qualified plans.

FIGURE 8.4 Regulations of employee benefits.

Laws/Regulations	Scope/Provisions	Enforcing Agency
Family and Medical Leave Act of 1993 (FMLA)	Consolidated Omnibus Budget Reconciliation Act of 1985 (COBRA)	Group health plans – requirement to continue regular coverage during periods of qualifying leaves (as many as 12 weeks per year)
Civil Rights Act of 1964	Health Insurance Portability and Accountability Act of 1996 (HIPAA)	All benefits plans – regulations prohibiting discrimination against women and other protected classes in benefits plan "terms and conditions"
Group health plans – requirements for continuation of coverage following termination of employment and other "qualifying events."	US Department of Labor (DOL) Equal Employment Opportunity Commission (EEOC)	

(*continued*)

FIGURE 8.4 *(Continued)*

Laws/Regulations	Scope/Provisions	Enforcing Agency
Group health plans – requires employers to provide terminated employees with a certificate of group health plan coverage, when requested.	US Department of Labor (DOL) Internal Revenue Service (IRS) US Public Health Service (for state and local employee plans) US Department of Labor (DOL)	
Securities and Exchange Commission (SEC) Regulations	Plans that provide employer stock to participants – information requirements	Securities and Exchange Commission (SEC)
State insurance regulation	Insured benefits plans – standards for coverage, conversion and coordination of benefits	State insurance commissioners
Health Savings Accounts (Part of Medicare Prescription Drug Improvement and Modernization Act of 2003)	Provide tax incentives to lower health-care costs. Includes high deductibles; must be under age 65 to participate	Department of the Treasury
The Patient Protection and Affordable Care Act of 2010	Transformed the regulation of health-care financing in the United States	Department of Health and Human Services

Family and Medical Leave Act of 1993

The Family and Medical Leave Act (FMLA) entitles employees to take as many as 12 weeks of unpaid, job-protected leave each year for specified family, medical, and exigent military service reasons, and as many as 26 weeks of unpaid, job-protected leave each year to care for a family member who is a covered service member. The FMLA is intended to allow employees to balance their work and family lives by taking reasonable unpaid leave under limited circumstances.

Employer Coverage, Employee Eligibility, and Leave Entitlement

The FMLA applies to public agencies, including state, local, and federal employers and local education agencies (schools), and it applies to private sector employers with at least 50 employees. Spouses employed by the same employer are jointly entitled to a combined total of 12 workweeks of family leave for the birth of a child or for placement of a child for adoption or foster care, and to care for a parent (but not a parent "in-law") who has a serious health condition. Leave for birth or adoption (including foster care placement) must conclude within 12 months of the birth or placement.

Intermittent Leave

Under certain circumstances, employees may take FMLA leave intermittently. This means that an employee may take leave in blocks of time or by reducing his/her normal weekly or daily work schedule.

If FMLA leave is to care for a child following the birth of the child or the placement of a child with the employee for adoption or foster care, use of intermittent leave is subject to the employer's approval.

FMLA leave may be taken intermittently when medically necessary for planned and/or unanticipated medical treatment or a related serious health condition by or under the supervision of a health-care provider or for recovery from treatment or recovery from a serious health condition. It also may be taken to provide care or psychological comfort to an immediate family member with a serious health condition.

FMLA Eligibility

To be eligible for FMLA benefits, an employee must meet the following conditions:

- Work for a covered employer
- Have worked for the employer for at least a total of 12 months
- Have worked at least 1,250 hours during the past 12 months
- Work at a location where the employer within a 75-mile radius employs at least 50 employees

Note: An employee also is eligible if he/she has worked at least 12 months for a covered employer that has failed to keep records regarding service time.

A covered employer must grant an eligible employee as many as 12 workweeks of unpaid leave during any 12-month period for one or more of the following reasons:

- Birth of a child and to care for the newborn child or for placement of a child for adoption or foster care
- To care for an immediate family member (spouse, child, or parent) with a "serious health condition"

- To take medical leave when the employee is unable to work because of a "serious health condition."
- For "any qualifying exigency" arising when a military family member is on active duty with the National Guard or Reserves or called to active duty status in support of a contingency operation

A covered employer must also grant an eligible employee as many as 26 workweeks of unpaid leave during any 12-month period to care for a covered service member with a serious illness or injury incurred in the line of duty on active duty.

Designation

The employer is responsible for designating leave as FMLA-qualifying. An employee giving notice of the need for FMLA leave must explain the reasons for the leave so as to allow the employer to determine whether the leave is FMLA-qualifying. If the employer does not have sufficient information about the reason for an employee's use of leave, the employer should request more information from the employee to determine whether leave is potentially FMLA-qualifying. An employer may deny leave if the employee fails to explain the reasons for the leave.

Once the employer has acquired knowledge that the leave is being taken for an FMLA-qualifying reason, the employer must notify the employee within five business days that the leave is designated and will be counted as FMLA leave. An employer may, however, retroactively designate leave as FMLA leave with appropriate notice to the employee provided that the employer's failure to timely designate leave does not cause harm or injury to the employee. In all cases where leave would qualify for FMLA protections, an employer and an employee can mutually agree that leave be retroactively designated as FMLA leave.

Military Leave Policies

In 2009, the Department of Labor issued final regulations updating the FMLA to include two types of military leave:

"Qualifying exigency" leave provides up to 12 weeks of leave to eligible employees with a covered military member serving in the National Guard or Reserves for "any qualifying exigency" arising out of the fact that a covered military member is on active duty or called to active duty status in support of a contingency operation. A qualifying exigency includes one or more of the following:

- Short-notice deployment
- Military events and related activities
- Childcare and school activities
- Financial and legal arrangements
- Counseling
- Rest and recuperation

- Post-deployment activities
- Additional activities not encompassed in the other categories, but agreed to by the employer and employee

"Military caregiver" leave provides up to 26 weeks of leave to eligible employees who are family members of a covered service member will be able to take leave to care for a covered service member with a serious illness or injury incurred in the line of duty on active duty. Military family leave is available to "next of kin," defined as the nearest blood relative, other than the covered service member's spouse, parent, son, or daughter, in the following order of priority: (1) blood relatives who have been granted legal custody of the service member by court decree or statutory provisions, (2) brothers and sisters, (3) grandparents, (4) aunts and uncles, and (5) first cousins.

Substitution of Paid Leave

In most cases, FMLA leave is unpaid. However, under certain circumstances, an eligible employee may use paid leave provided by the employer concurrently with unpaid FMLA leave, which is referred to as substitution of paid leave for purposes of the FMLA. If an employee does not choose to substitute accrued paid leave, the employer may require the employee to substitute accrued paid leave for FMLA leave.

An employee must qualify for paid leave under the terms and conditions of the employer's normal leave policy in order to substitute paid leave. If an employee does not meet the additional requirements in an employer's paid leave policy, the employee is not entitled to substitute accrued paid leave, but remains entitled to take unpaid FMLA leave. Thus, for purposes of substituting paid leave, an employer may require that an employee take a minimum period of leave time, such as one full day, or provide a minimum number of days of notice, if those conditions are required under the employer's paid leave program.

Serious Health Condition

"Serious health condition" means an illness, injury, impairment, or physical or mental condition that involves one of the following:

- Inpatient care (i.e., overnight stay) in a hospital, hospice, or residential medical care facility, including any period of incapacity (i.e., inability to work, attend school, or perform other regular daily activities due to the serious health condition, treatment therefore, or recovery there from), or any subsequent treatment concerning such inpatient care. The first (or only) in-person treatment visit must take place within seven days of the first day of incapacity.

- Continuing treatment by a health-care provider. A serious health condition involving continuing treatment by a health-care provider includes any one or more of the following:

  A period of incapacity of more than three consecutive calendar days and any subsequent treatment or period of incapacity relating to the same condition, which also involves:

  - Treatment two or more times, within 30 days of the first day of incapacity, by a health-care provider, by a nurse or physician's assistant under direct supervision of a health-care provider, or by a provider of health-care services (e.g., physical therapist) under orders or on referral by a health-care provider

- Treatment by a health-care provider on at least one occasion that results in a regimen of continuing treatment under the supervision of the health-care provider

  - A period of incapacity due to pregnancy or for prenatal care.
  - A period of incapacity or treatment due to a chronic serious health condition that continues over an extended period, requires periodic visits to a health-care provider, and may involve occasional episodes of incapacity (e.g., asthma, diabetes).
  - A period of incapacity that is permanent or long-term due to a condition for which treatment may not be effective (e.g., Alzheimer's, a severe stroke, terminal cancer).
  - Any absences to receive multiple treatments for restorative surgery or for a condition that would likely result in a period of incapacity of more than three days if not treated (e.g., chemotherapy or radiation treatments for cancer).

Note: According to the DOL regulations, an employee is unable to perform the functions of the position if the health-care provider finds that the employee is unable to work at all or is unable to perform of any one of the essential functions of the employee's position within the meaning of the Americans with Disabilities Act (ADA).

An employee who is injured on the job will likely qualify for workers' compensation and thus will not use accrued paid leave. When workers' compensation only replaces a percentage of an employee's salary, though, an employer and employee may voluntarily agree, subject to state law, to use paid leave to supplement the workers' compensation benefits. The workers' compensation absence will count against the employee's FMLA entitlement if the employer properly designates the leave as FMLA leave (as described above).

Maintenance of Health Benefits

A covered employer is required to maintain group health insurance coverage for an employee on FMLA leave whenever such insurance was provided before the leave was taken and on the same terms as if the employee had continued to work.

Where appropriate, arrangements will need to be made for employees taking unpaid FMLA leave to pay their share of health insurance premiums while on leave. For example, if the group health plan involves co-payments by the employer and the employee, an employee on FMLA leave must continue making his/her portion of the insurance premium payments to maintain insurance coverage, as must the employer. The employer must provide the employee with advance written notice of the terms and conditions under which these payments must be made.

The employer is responsible for designating whether paid leave used by an employee counts as FMLA leave, based on information provided by the employee (as described above). Continued health insurance coverage during FMLA leave must be at the same co-payment rates as for active employees. Higher COBRA premiums may be required only after FMLA leave ends.

An employer's obligation to maintain health benefits under FMLA ends if an employee informs the employer that he/she does not intend to return to work at the end of the leave period, or if the employee fails to return to work when the FMLA entitlement is completed. In certain instances, the employer may recover premiums it paid to maintain health insurance coverage for an employee who fails to return to work from FMLA leave. However, an employer cannot recover premiums paid to maintain group health coverage if the employee does not return to work due to (i) the continuation, recurrence, or onset of a serious health condition of the employee, the employee's family member, or a covered service member, or (ii) circumstances beyond the control of the employee.

In addition, an employer's obligation to maintain health insurance coverage generally ceases under FMLA if an employee's premium payment is more than 30 days late. To stop coverage for an employee whose premium payment is late, the employer must provide written notice to the employee that payment has not been received. Such notice must be mailed to the employee at least 15 days before coverage is to cease, advising that coverage will stop on a specified date unless payment has been received by that date.

The Health Insurance Portability and Accountability Act of 1996

Title I: Group Health Plan Portability

Title I of the HIPAA amended Title I of ERISA, the IRC, and the Public Health Service Act (PHSA) to impose new requirements on employer-sponsored group health plans, insurance companies and health maintenance organizations (HMOs). These rules include provisions that limit exclusions for pre-existing conditions, prohibit discrimination against employees and dependents based on their health status, and guarantee renewability and availability of health coverage to certain employers and individuals.

While these protections are often referred to as the "health-care portability" rules, they do not provide for true portability in that a person transferring from one plan to another is provided with and entitled to only the benefits under the new plan. Coverage under the new plan could be less or greater. Moreover, employers and insurance companies may continue to establish waiting periods before enrollees become eligible for benefits under the plan, and HMOs may have "affiliation periods" during which an enrollee does not receive benefits and is not charged premiums. Affiliation periods may not last for more than two months, however, and they only are allowed for HMOs that do not use preexisting condition exclusions. Even after HIPAA, the provision of health coverage by an employer is still voluntary.

Preexisting Condition Limitations

HIPAA limits the extent to which group health plans can limit coverage of preexisting medical conditions by requiring plans to cover an individual's preexisting condition after 12 months (or 18 months in the case of a late enrollee). Moreover, for purposes of determining the preexisting exclusion period, employees must be given credit for previous coverage that occurred without a "break in coverage" of 63 days or more. This is referred to as "creditable coverage." Any coverage occurring prior to a break in coverage of 63 days or more would not be credited against an exclusion period. Significantly, COBRA coverage counts as creditable coverage.

Preexisting Conditions

Under HIPAA, a preexisting condition is a condition for which medical advice, diagnosis, care, or treatment was recommended or received within the six-month period ending on the enrollment date in any new health plan. Thus, if an employee had a medical condition in the past, but he/she received no medical advice, diagnosis, care, or treatment within the six months prior to enrolling in the plan, the old condition is not a preexisting condition for which the exclusion can be applied.

Certificates of Creditable Coverage

HIPAA requires insurers and group health plans to provide documentation (referred to as "certificates of creditable coverage") to individuals attesting to their creditable coverage. Insurers and group health plans that fail or refuse to provide certificates of creditable coverage in a timely manner are subject to penalties. HIPAA also requires that a process be established that will allow individuals to show they are entitled to creditable coverage in situations where they cannot obtain a certification from an insurer or group health plan.

Nondiscrimination

Group health plans and issuers may not establish eligibility for enrollment based on an employee's health status, medical condition (physical or mental), claims experience, receipt of health care, medical history, genetic information, evidence of insurability, or disability. For example, an employee cannot be excluded or dropped from coverage just because he/she has a particular illness. Employers may establish limits or restrictions on benefits or coverage for similarly situated individuals under a plan, but they may not require an individual to pay a premium or contribution that is greater than that for a similarly situated individual based on health status. HIPAA does not require specific benefits, nor does it prohibit a plan from restricting the amount or nature of benefits for similarly situated individuals.

The Patient Protection and Affordable Care Act of 2010

The Patient Protection and Affordable Care Act of 2010, as amended by the Health and Education Reconciliation Act of 2010 – referred to collectively in this chapter as the "Affordable Care Act" or, simply, the "Act") – together transformed the regulation of health-care financing in the United States. The Act's provisions include:

- An expansion of Medicaid eligibility, extending funding for the Children's Health Insurance Program (CHIP), and subsidizing private insurance premiums and cost-sharing for certain lower-income individuals.
- A series of measures aimed at enhancing the delivery and quality of patient care.
- Pilot, demonstration, and grant programs to test integrated models of care. This includes accountable care organizations (ACOs), medical homes that provide coordinated care for high-need individuals, and bundling payments for acute-care episodes (including hospitalization and follow-up care).
- A new agency to test payment and service delivery models, primarily for Medicare and Medicaid beneficiaries. It mandates pay-for-reporting and pay-for-performance programs within Medicare that will pay providers based on the reporting of, or performance on, selected quality measures.
- Incentives for promoting primary care and prevention, for example, by increasing primary care payment rates under Medicare and Medicaid; covering some preventive services without cost-sharing; and funding community-based prevention programs, among other things.

Each of these programs, while important in the larger context of health-care reform, are beyond the scope of this work, the focus of which is employee benefits and programs.

Titles I and X of the Act, which include insurance market reforms, individual and employer mandates, state-based insurance exchanges, low-income premium support, and cost-sharing subsidies, and tax financing, are of particular concern to employers and employer-sponsored group health plans. It is these provisions that – directly or indirectly – required significant design and operational changes to all employer-sponsored group health plans, whether fully insured or self-funded. The market for individual health insurance coverage has been similarly affected. Most of these "employer" provisions of the Act took effect in 2014, but certain insurance market reforms affecting group health plans took effect on or shortly after enactment.

The Affordable Care Act represents the culmination of decades of efforts to reign in health-care costs, improve the quality of medical outcomes, and expand coverage. The law implemented a series of market-based reforms that built on existing structures, i.e., the commercial insurance market and employer-provided group health insurance to reach its goals. This approach stands in marked contrast to other approaches, such as single-payer, which are politically far less palatable. To say that the law is politically divisive is an understatement. While outright repeal is unlikely, it is likely to undergo significant changes.

As of August 2020, the individual mandate (health insurance coverage) is no longer mandatory at the federal level. Some states, however, still require individuals to have health insurance coverage to avoid a tax penalty.

In addition, as of this writing (August 2020), while cost-sharing subsidies are still available for eligible marketplace enrollees, the federal government will no longer be reimbursing insurers for these subsidies. Insurers, however, are required by law to provide reduced cost-sharing for lower-income enrollees.

For many years, the federal government has encouraged the development of employee benefits plans because of their social value. One way this has occurred is through changes in the tax code. In recent years, however, increasing controls and regulations have offset some tax advantages. These include:

- Federal tax advantages for both employers and employees.
- "Qualified plans" that meet IRS requirements and receive allowable offsets for statutory coverage.
- Pension plan changes (see Sidebar 8.1).

Sidebar 8.1 The Pension Protection Act's Impact on Total Rewards Professionals

The Pension Protection Act (PPA) of 2006 ushered in perhaps the most significant changes to impact retirement security in 20 years. Most of the provisions did not take effect until 2008, but the bill had immediate and long-lasting effects on how employers provide retirement security to their employees.

Highlights of the Act include:

- The PPA requires plans to be 100 percent funded and tightens the actuarial assumptions that apply when employers calculate the accrued liability and the return on plan assets.
- The PPA amended section 409A of the Internal Revenue Code to provide a 20 percent excise tax penalty to certain executives if funds are set aside to pay nonqualified deferred compensation if the employer or a member of its controlled group is bankrupt, has an at-risk plan, or a plan that has terminated with insufficient assets to cover all liabilities. In addition, the PPA blocks the

employer from taking a deduction for tax gross-up payments intended to cover the penalties triggered by funding nonqualified deferred compensation.

- The PPA restricts payments from plans that are less than 60 percent funded and prohibits benefit increases for plans that are less than 80 percent funded, using a special liability measure, and limits lump-sum payments.
- The PPA permits employees who reach age 62 to continue working and to receive pension payments without being penalized under tax law or the Employee Retirement Income Security Act (ERISA).
- The PPA sets a single age discrimination standard for all defined benefit (DB) plans under ERISA. It clarifies that hybrid plans such as cash balance or pension equity plans do not violate the age discrimination provisions in ERISA, the Code or the Age Discrimination in Employment Act (ADEA) if the individual's accrued benefit would be equal to or greater than any similarly situated younger individual who could be a participant.
- The PPA places restrictions on conversions from traditional DB to hybrid plans. It requires employers to start benefit accruals under the new plan immediately after a conversion takes effect.
- The PPA makes it easier for employers to encourage employee participation in 401(k) plans by creating a safe harbor from fiduciary liability and state garnishment laws for automatic enrollment programs.
- The PPA provides for the purchase of long-term care from annuity and life insurance products, making these products more flexible.
- The PPA allows employees to diversify at any time out of employer stock purchased with employee contributions. It requires employers to allow diversification out of employer contributions after the employee has been in the plan for three years and may be phased in over three years.
- The PPA requires all employer contributions, whether matching or nonelective, to vest entirely after three years or phased in 20 percent per year starting in the second year the employee participates in a plan.

The role of government in addressing the social needs of the nation underwent a dramatic and controversial change in the 1980s and 1990s. Federal budget deficits forced Congress to:

- View with caution any proposals for new programs that would require increased federal spending.
- Look for additional methods of increasing revenues by taxing items that had not been taxed before.

Federal governing agencies that influence employee benefits plans include the following categories.

Equal Employment Opportunity Commission (EEOC)

Established by Title VII of the Civil Rights Act of 1964, the EEOC began operating on July 2, 1965. It enforces the following federal statutes:

- Title VII of the Civil Rights Act of 1964
- The Age Discrimination in Employment Act of 1967 (ADEA)
- The Equal Pay Act of 1963 (EPA)
- Title I and Title V of the Americans with Disabilities Act of 1990 (ADA)

Department of Labor (DOL)

The Employee Benefits Security Administration (EBSA), formerly known as the Pension and Welfare Benefits Administration (PWBA), of the US Department of Labor (DOL) is responsible for administering and enforcing provisions of ERISA.

Securities and Exchange Commission (SEC)

The SEC is responsible for ensuring that employees as investors receive financial and other significant information concerning securities being offered for public sale (e.g., company stock, 401(k), and employee stock ownership plans).

Pension Benefit Guaranty Corporation (PBGC)

The PBGC, an agency under the EBSA, guarantees vested defined benefit pensions up to a maximum amount established annually. Employers offering covered pension plans pay insurance premiums.

STATUTORY BENEFITS

Federal and state laws require all companies to offer the following "core" benefits:

- Social Security (federal)
- Workers' compensation (state)
- Unemployment compensation (state) and
- Nonoccupational disability (five states)

Social Security

Since its creation in the 1930s, Social Security has been at the center of national public policy debates. In 1945, there were 20 workers for every retiree and few sources of retirement income security outside the extended family. Today, there are only three active workers to support each retiree, and extended families provide minimal support.

The Social Security system has four distinct types of benefits:

- OA – retirement income in "old age"
- S – survivor income
- D – disability income
- HI – health insurance benefits (Medicare)

The federal Old Age, Survivors, Disability, and Health Insurance Program (OASDHI) emerged as a result of the Social Security Act of 1935. The federal budget now includes almost $500 billion in spending toward Social Security; less than half of that amount goes toward retirement.

Old Age (OA): Retirement Benefits

Presently, the earliest age at which one can start receiving Social Security retirement benefits is 62. Those born prior to 1938 are eligible to receive full benefits beginning at age 65. Those born after 1959 cannot receive full benefits until age 67. Those born between 1938 and 1959 are on a graduated scale. An individual who wishes to retire early may do so but is subject to a reduction in benefits as follows:

- 5/9 of 1 percent for each month (up to 36 months) that the benefit is paid prior to full retirement age (FRA), plus 5/12 of 1 percent for each month that the benefit is paid earlier than 36 months prior to full retirement age.

Individuals also are eligible for increased benefits beyond full retirement age (between 5 percent and 8 percent per year depending on the year of birth).

Floor of Protection

Monthly Social Security benefits provide a minimal standard of living. Compensation is taxed and benefits are calculated based on the employee's covered compensation up to each year's taxable wage base. Social Security, however, was never intended to be a sole source of retirement income.

Previously, some retirement benefits were withheld from workers ages 65 through 69 when they reached a certain earnings level. In 2000, the "Freedom to Work Act" was passed, allowing older workers who reached full retirement age to work and receive their full Social Security retirement benefits. There continues to be an earnings limitation for Social Security retirees under the age of full retirement whose employment earnings exceed a certain level.

Survivor Benefits

Sidebar 8.2 addresses the features of survivor benefits.

Sidebar 8.2 Social Security Survivor (S) Benefits Key Characteristics

- $255 lump sum death benefit payment.
- Benefit has not been indexed.
- Was originally intended to cover funeral costs.
- Widows and widowers.
- Survivors age 60 and older.
- Survivors ages 50 to 59 if disabled.
- Any survivor age if caring for dependent children (under age 16).
- Dependent children to age 18 (19 if a full-time student).
- Dependent parents (age 62 and older) who had been receiving at least half of their support from the beneficiary at the time of death.

Social Security Health Insurance (HI)

Medicare is the most expensive component of Social Security. It covers persons aged 65 and over and persons who are disabled and have been receiving disability benefits from Social Security for two years.

Covered individuals pay the deductible for each confinement. The deductible is the amount that covered individuals pay for hospital charges, as determined each year by the government, prior to Medicare paying. Medicare pays the full cost of remaining charges for the first 60 days per occurrence of illness. Many people choose to add Medicare Part B, a supplemental insurance program (see Sidebar 8.3).

Other limited hospital insurance benefits include skilled nursing facilities, home health services, and hospice care. Custodial care is not covered.

Social Security FICA Tax

Federal Insurance Contributions Act (FICA) taxes are the taxes for Social Security. Employers and employees equally share the tax, which was separated into two components in 1991. As coverage has become more comprehensive and more people have become eligible, the tax rate and wage base (indexed each year) have increased steadily. For the health insurance component, 1994 was the first year that no maximum tax applied.

Sidebar 8.3 Medicare Part B: Supplementary Medical Insurance Key Characteristics

- Cost

  - Individuals who choose to participate in Part B: Supplementary Medical Insurance are required to pay a premium that is adjusted annually by the government. If a person does not enroll upon initial eligibility, he or she remains eligible to enroll during a future enrollment period but will pay a higher premium.
- Annual deductible

  - After deductible, covered individuals pay 20 percent and Medicare pays 80 percent.
- Basic list of covered services

  - Physicians' services

  - Physical and occupational therapists

  - Diagnostic X-ray, laboratory, and other tests

- Prescriptions

  - In December 2003, President George W. Bush signed into law the Medicare Prescription Drug, Improvement, and Modernization Act (H.R. 1). This act created a prescription drug benefit for the first time in Medicare history (see Sidebar 8.4).

Sidebar 8.4 The Impact of Medicare Reform

H.R. 1, the Medicare Prescription Drug, Improvement, and Modernization Act of 2003, had – and will continue to have – a major impact on employer-provided benefits. A good start to understanding the Act's implications would be to examine the key provisions that affect employers in this era of consumer-driven health care.

H.R. 1, commonly referred to as the Medicare Modernization Act (MMA), ushered in some important changes by creating health savings accounts (HSAs), which greatly alter the landscape of employer-provided health-care arrangements.

An HSA is a trust created for an individual that is established to pay the qualified medical expenses of the individual (or the individual's dependents). The trustee typically is a bank, an insurance company, or a third-party administrator. HSAs are not taxed on any earnings accrued while the assets are held in trust.

HSAs, which took effect at the beginning of 2004, are portable (meaning rollovers are permitted from other HSAs) and may be funded on a pretax basis and through a cafeteria plan. Additionally, an individual's HSA can be transferred tax-free upon divorce or separation to another individual or to the individual's spouse upon death. If the HSA is transferred to someone other than the individual's spouse upon death, the account ceases to be an HSA and the HSA assets become taxable income at the fair market value to the individual or the individual's estate.

The Tax Relief and Health Care Act of 2006 includes important changes for HSAs. The law, according to the Employee Benefits Institute of America Inc., affects HSA eligibility for certain individuals who are covered by health flexible spending arrangements (health FSAs) during a grace period, changes the limits for allowable HSA contributions, and allows a rollover from an IRA, health reimbursement arrangement (HRA), or health FSA to an HSA under certain conditions.

Medicare Part D

Under MMA, Medicare Part D provides a limited, voluntary benefit for outpatient prescription drugs. Although the number of employers offering post-retirement health benefits has declined significantly in recent years, Medicare's new drug benefit has revitalized discussions about whether and how to provide retiree health care.

The Medicare prescription drug benefit (Part D) is delivered to beneficiaries either through a private prescription drug plan (PDP) or Medicare Advantage plans (either Medicare HMOs or PPOs).

Medicare prescription drug plans must, at a minimum, provide a standard level of coverage. There are various plans available, much like private coverage. Those who qualify for extra help because of limited income and assets receive help that pays for all or part of the monthly premiums, deductible, and fills in the coverage gap and lowers the prescription copayments.

If a beneficiary's employer continues to offer prescription drug coverage, he or she can decide whether to keep the existing coverage or switch to another plan. Note: Those who drop their employer-sponsored drug coverage may not be able to re-enroll.

As of this writing, employer-sponsored plans that provide an "actuarially equivalent" prescription drug benefit to Medicare beneficiaries are eligible to receive a financial subsidy to help offset their costs. For up-to-date information, go online and visit www.medicare.gov.

Workers' Compensation

Workers' compensation is employer-paid and offered by all states. The employee receives income and the employer pays for medical and rehabilitation costs associated with a work-related incident resulting in an injury or illness.

Unemployment

Like workers' compensation, unemployment compensation is employer-paid and offered by all states. Unemployment compensation provides income (for a period of time) to an employee who loses employment and is willing and able to work.

Nonoccupational Disability

Five states (New York, New Jersey, Rhode Island, California, and Hawaii) offer a nonoccupational disability benefit. The benefit provides temporary or short-term income due to a nonoccupational incident resulting in a disability.

HEALTH AND WELFARE PLANS

Health and welfare plans are critical components of the employee benefits package. These plans have been affected by significant changes over the years, including the introduction of managed care in the 1990s. However, escalating health costs, particularly for prescription drugs, have placed increasing pressure on benefits professionals attempting to continue to offer competitive benefits while maintaining fiscal responsibility for their employers' benefits budgets. As a result of these challenges and changes in the tax code, programs such as consumer-driven health plans have emerged, offering employees greater benefits choices with certain tax incentives.

Health and Welfare: A Brief History

When Social Security first surfaced in the 1930s, it excluded health insurance, causing the private sector to take the lead in sponsoring health insurance coverage. Blue Cross/Blue Shield developed private plans, soon to be followed by commercial insurers.

The wage freezes of the post–WWII era prompted companies to offer noncash rewards in the form of health care. This is where the entitlement mentality began, with employees feeling entitled to health-care insurance. Soon after, the Taft–Hartley Act mandated the inclusion of benefits in collective bargaining. This era also saw the first major medical benefits introduced, supplementing the hospital and surgical coverage previously offered.

Over time, more companies began offering health insurance and other options, such as dental. However, health-care costs began rising faster than the consumer price index. US workers began to retire as they reached age 65 and they found no viable health-care insurance available. The federal government responded by instituting programs such as Medicare and Medicaid.

The lack of cost-cutting initiatives soon led to rising health-care costs and the emergence of health maintenance organizations (HMOs) to curb these costs. Congress then enacted ERISA to protect qualified benefits plans, and the introduction of diagnostic related groups of service (DRGs) helped curb Medicare costs.

Soon, unions began to reduce bargained benefits due to most companies' inability/unwillingness to sustain current levels of coverage. Larger numbers of employers self-insured, finding they had more control over benefits offered and associated costs.

Although HMOs did help to control costs, quality of care and choice of providers became a prevailing issue with employees. Enter the era of preferred provider organizations (PPOs) with negotiated-fee contracts and a larger choice of providers.

Now, as health-care costs again rise, many employers are opting to embrace a strategic approach to consumerism.

Health and Welfare Plan Elements

Health and welfare plans are primarily categorized as follows:

- Health care
  - Medical
  - Prescription drug
  - Behavioral health
  - Dental
  - Vision
  - Long-term care
- Disability income
  - Sick leave
  - Short-term disability and/or salary continuation
  - Long-term disability
- Survivor benefits
  - Term life
  - Accidental death and dismemberment
  - Dependent life
  - Business travel accident

HEALTH CARE

Health-care programs, specifically medical care, are generally the most popular and most expensive component of a company's employee benefits program. Managed care plans, the most prevalent medical care programs, attempt to control cost and ensure quality of care by encouraging the utilization of network providers who have agreed to accept discounted fee payments. These models include health maintenance organizations (HMO), preferred provider organizations (PPO), point of service (POS), and other hybrid arrangements. Indemnity plans, now rare, are traditional plans that provide specific cash reimbursement for covered services.

Health Maintenance Organization (HMO)

An HMO provides a network of physicians and hospitals for employees and their dependents to receive comprehensive care, including preventive care. The traditional HMO model requires receiving a referral from the primary physician or "gatekeeper" to receive care from a specialist. Otherwise, the employee could be liable to pay the total cost to see the specialist (see Sidebar 8.5).

Sidebar 8.5 Health Maintenance Organization (HMO) Key Characteristics

HMOs are managed care plans that attempt to control the cost and ensure quality of care by encouraging preventive care. They provide both the financing and delivery of comprehensive medical coverage. Key features include:

- Primary care physician (PCP)
  - Employee-selected physician that provides all routine medical care.
  - Serves as gatekeeper by controlling specialist referral, therefore curbing unnecessary medical expenses.
- Preventive/routine care typically includes:
  - Well-woman, well-man, well-baby care
  - Routine physicals
  - Immunizations
- Copayments eliminate deductibles and coinsurance.
- Provider pay is sometimes on a capitation or discounted fee-for-service basis; physicians are sometimes salaried.
- HMO models
  - Independent Practice Association (IPA)
  - Group Practice Association (GPA)
  - Staff
  - Combinations

Preferred Provider Organization (PPO)

Unlike HMOs, the PPO model does not include a primary physician or gate-keeper. PPOs include two levels: *in-network* providers (physicians and hospitals) and *out-of-network* providers. By using the in-network providers, employees receive a higher level of reimbursement for care. The PPO provider should not bill the employee for any differences between the discounted contracted rate and the provider's normal fee. In contrast, out-of-network providers could charge more for services rendered (see Sidebar 8.6).

Sidebar 8.6 Preferred Provider Organization (PPO) Key Characteristics

PPOs are arrangements where providers agree to discount their normal fees. They continue to have the highest enrollment on a national basis. Key features include:

- Discounted fee for service
  - To achieve greater volume
  - No capitation
  - Fees subject to a schedule
- Broader choice of providers
  - Choice of provider is usually made at time medical care is needed.
- Incentives to use preferred providers
  - Lower or reduced deductibles and coinsurance
  - Increased coverage, such as preventive care
- In-network/out-of-network
  - Patient may access in-network specialty care without primary care physician gatekeeper coordination.
  - If patient chooses out-of-network care, financial incentives do not apply.
- Utilization reviews
  - Assessment of medical necessity
  - Curbs unnecessary procedures and monitors hospital stays

- Choice of providers
  - Selected at time of treatment.
  - Primary care physician gatekeeper coordinates in-network specialty care in network/out-of-network benefits.
  - Out-of-network provider, deductibles, and copayments tend to be higher. Meaningful coinsurance differential provides incentives to use in-network.
  - Patient retains some coverage for services even if not authorized by primary care physician.
- Models
  - Open-ended
  - Gatekeeper

Point of Service (POS)

A typical POS is a combination of HMO and PPO. The employee would need a referral to see an in-network specialist (similar to an HMO). However, the cost for seeing an out-of-network specialist would be higher than an in-network provider (similar to a PPO).

Point of service (POS) evolved as a response to a market force. It addressed the concerns employees had about being locked into the narrow network of an HMO plan. POS combines discounted fee agreements for cost savings with employee choice. Key features include:

- A hybrid between traditional indemnity, HMOs, and PPOs
- A coordinated delivery system aimed at managing utilization and cost by means of:
  - Eliminating excessive utilization
  - Reducing costs through negotiated discount payments and capitation
  - Aligning the interests of all payers

Indemnity Plans

Traditional indemnity medical plans (offered by Blue Cross/Blue Shield) are still available, but at a rapidly decreasing rate. The first health insurance plan in existence, an indemnity plan is designed where the employee pays a deductible after base benefits are exhausted. Indemnity plans offer greater "freedom of choice" in selecting providers because referrals are not needed, and the employee is free to visit any provider. However, the indemnity is now rare since it is the most expensive medical model.

Prescription Drug Coverage

Prescription/drug programs are growing in popularity and costs. These programs can be part of the medical program or carved out and managed by a Pharmacy Benefit Manager (PBM). Companies are now offering three or four tiers of coverage. Employee copayments also increase by tier. Examples include:

Tier 1: Generic drugs	$10–$15 copayment
Tier 2: Brand drugs	$20–$25 copayment
Tier 3: Lifestyle drugs	$30–$50 copayment
Tier 4: Mail order	Three-month supply for "maintenance" drugs. Copayment can be equal to one or two months' copayments.

Copayments can be a percentage of costs instead of a dollar amount.

Behavioral Health

Coverage includes mental health and chemical dependency services. Services can be provided on an inpatient or outpatient basis and are often integrated with an employee assistance program (EAP).

Dental Plans

Most dental plans have four components:

1. Preventive and diagnostic
2. Basic services
3. Major services
4. Orthodontia

Dental plans often provide 100 percent reimbursement for preventive and diagnostic services; charges for these services usually are not subject to a deductible. The rationale is to encourage employees to have periodic dental visits because these exams can help prevent future dental services more costly to both the employer and employee.

Deductibles can apply to all other services. Because of costs, orthodontia (installation and adjustment of braces) is not included in all dental plans or only applies to dependent children. In addition, orthodontia services are usually subject to a per-person lifetime maximum ($1,000–$1,500).

The traditional dental model is the indemnity approach (similar to medical indemnity model). To control costs and expand services, companies provide managed care models called DMO (dental management organization – similar to medical HMO) or a DPPO (dental preferred provider organization – similar to medical PPO).

Vision Care Plans

Vision care plans often provide a flat-dollar rate of reimbursement or a specific percentage reimbursement for an annual eye examination and a new pair of lenses per year. New frames are usually limited to one pair every two years.

Concern for eyewear and strain is growing due to increased computer use.

Long-Term Care

Long-term care is growing in importance as people live longer. Coverage commences when a person is unable to perform at least two of the five daily living activities – bathing, dressing, eating, walking, and using the bathroom.

DISABILITY INCOME

Disability income benefits are income replacement programs provided by employers or public agencies during the time an employee is unable to work due to a qualified disability.

Sick Leave

Key features:

- Specified number of days
- Based on service
- Continuation of full pay
- May be carried from one year to the next

Short-Term Disability (STD)

The STD benefit provides income when an employee is unable to work due to a short-term nonoccupational illness or injury. There is usually a seven-day calendar waiting period to qualify for benefit coverage that commences after the seventh day from the incident. Benefits can extend for up to six months. Payment is a percentage of pay, often 50 percent up to a weekly maximum.

Long-Term Disability (LTD)

The LTD benefit provides income due to a nonwork illness or injury; payments can be up to age 65. The waiting period to qualify for coverage ranges from three to six months from the date of incident. Payments range from 50 percent to 67 percent of wages up to a maximum monthly amount.

While an employee collects LTD, most employers will continue to accrue pension benefits for the employee at the pre-disability rate of pay.

If the employee pays the full cost of LTD coverage with post-tax dollars, then any benefits paid are nontaxable. If the employer pays the full cost of LTD coverage or the employee pays the premium with pretax dollars, then any benefits paid are subject to tax.

LTD plans typically have a split definition of disability eligibility. To be eligible, an employee must be unable to perform current job duties for the first two years when benefits are payable; and thereafter, unable to perform job duties of any occupation. This transition period is designed to help an employee prepare to change careers without a loss of income.

SURVIVOR BENEFITS

Term Life Insurance

The most typical form of survivor benefits is term life insurance. The insurance is paid to the employee's designated beneficiary (who can be anyone) in a lump sum. In contrast, under statutory programs such as Social Security and workers' compensation, payment of survivor benefits depends on whether the employee has a spouse or eligible dependents as outlined by applicable law.

The practice for lump sum payments for exempt (salaried) staff is usually multiples of annual salary. The norm for nonexempt (hourly) workers is a flat dollar amount (independent of annual wages) but in some companies is multiples of annual wages. Term life insurance ends upon termination of employment. Employees have the right to convert within 30 days of termination to a whole life or universal life insurance policy. Rates per $1,000 of coverage are based on age. The benefit to employees is the waiving of passing a physical.

The Internal Revenue Code permits an employer to provide up to $50,000 of noncontributory group life insurance to an employee without any tax consequences, provided the plan does not discriminate in favor of higher-paid employees. Employees who receive more than $50,000 of employer-paid group life insurance are subject to additional taxes depending on an employee's age and amount of coverage in excess of $50,000. This additional tax is called *imputed income tax*.

Accidental Death and Dismemberment (AD&D)

AD&D provides a benefit to the employee in the event of dismemberment or the beneficiary in the event of accidental death. It often duplicates the term life amount and has two components: company-paid portion and supplemental (employee-paid) portion.

Supplemental Life Insurance

It's common for employers to provide employees with opportunities to purchase additional term life insurance. Rates vary by employees' ages. Older workers pay more per $1,000 of coverage than younger workers.

Dependent Life Insurance

Employees can purchase life insurance for a spouse and dependent children. This benefit is often called *burial insurance*. The monthly premium is usually very low, and the benefit is a set dollar amount.

FLEXIBLE BENEFITS

Flexible benefits provide employees with choices that allow them to select between cash and one or more qualified (nontaxable) benefits (e.g., health, life, disability insurance). Made possible by Section 125 of the Internal Revenue Code (IRC), flexible benefits plans are also referred to as *cafeteria plans.*

Employees have a chance to change elections to their flexible benefits plan during an annual open enrollment period held by the employer. Changes during a plan year are only allowed in the event of a "qualified status change" as defined by the IRS. Qualified status changes include the birth or adoption of a child, the death of a dependent, open enrollment at a spouse's place of employment, marriage, or divorce.

Flexible benefits allow employers to:

- Manage rising costs
- Maximize employee perceptions of benefits
- Facilitate program design
- Readily adapt to change in laws, benefits, and business conditions
- Reap advantage of tax savings
- Support a total rewards focus
- Meet competitive pressures
- Maintain progressive company image

RETIREMENT PLANS

Under the Employee Retirement Income Security Act of 1974 (ERISA), and the Internal Revenue Code (IRC), employer-provided pension plans are classified as either:

- Defined benefit (DB) plans, or
- Defined contribution (DC) plans.

Key differences between these two types of plans are highlighted in Figure 8.5.

Defined Benefit (DB) Plans

A defined benefit plan promises an employee a specific future benefit if certain age, tenure, and income projections are achieved. The actual plan formula and the definition of earnings in the formula have a significant impact on the level of benefits an employee will receive. Many DB plans use the average of an employee's highest five consecutive calendar years of earnings during the employee's last 10 years of service to calculate benefits. This "high" five of past "10" method frequently is referred to as FAP, or final average pay.

FIGURE 8.5 Primary differences between defined benefit and defined contribution plans.

Defined Benefit Plans	Defined Contribution Plans
Benefit is known.	Benefit is unknown.
Cost is unknown.	Cost is known.
Employer bears financial risk.	Employee bears financial risk.
Generally provides higher benefits for long-service employees.	Can provide substantial benefits to short-service employees.
Separate account for each employee is not required.	Separate account for each employee is required.
Requires sign-off by an enrolled actuary.	Actuary not required. However, record keeper is required.
Subject to PBGC premiums.	Not subject to PBGC premiums.

FIGURE 8.6 Sample defined benefit plan.

Eligibility
Date of employment
Formula
1.75 percent final average pay X years of service
Final Average Pay
An employee's highest five consecutive calendar years of earning during his
or her last 10 years of service
Normal Retirement
Age 65
Early Retirement
At least age 55 and 10 or more years of service
Vested Benefit
100 percent vested after five years of credited service
Payment Option
Lump sum or 50 percent joint and survivor annuity or 100 percent joint and
survivor annuity

An example of a DB plan is found in Figure 8.6.

Cash-balance plans, also categorized under hybrid pension plans, are DB plans. Companies have switched from traditional pension plans to cash-balance plans since they are less costly to the employer and provide a guaranteed pension to workers. An employee's vested balance is portable on termination.

In DB pension plans, employers typically fund the plan 100 percent. Employees make no contributions and become vested (entitled to pension) upon being vested. However, even after becoming vested, an employee may have to wait to receive the pension. Normal retirement is age 65 with early retirement at age 55. Plans can have lower age limits.

Most companies use either "cliff" or "graded" vested schedules. Cliff means the employee becomes fully vested after five years of qualified service. With graded, an employee becomes partially vested after two years and increases a percentage of vesting for each year after two, but must be fully vested after seven years. These vesting schedules are used for "qualified plans" as defined by ERISA. Qualified plans mean both the employer and employee receive favorable tax treatments on pension monies.

Most DB pension plans provide a variety of payout options. A key consideration is whether anyone is financially dependent on the employee. Generally, a single life annuity option will provide the largest monthly premium. Following are the most prevalent:

- *Single life annuity.* Benefits are payable only to the employee. There is no survivor benefit. When the employee dies, all payment ceases. This is the default option for single employees. This means if the single employee dies before selecting an option, the plan automatically selects single life annuity.

- *Joint and survivor option.* The employee is the "joint" and the spouse is the "survivor." This is the default option for a married employee who dies before electing an option. If a married employee wishes an option other than joint and survivor, then the employee's spouse must sign a form agreeing to permit the employee to do so. Otherwise, the employee must use the joint and survivor option.

    If the employee (joint) dies first, then the spouse (survivor), depending on the percentage for this option, will receive 100 percent, 75 percent, or 50 percent of the employee's monthly pension. Payment will stop once the survivor dies. If the survivor dies before the employee, then payments will stop once the employee dies.

- *Lump sum.* The employer provides the employee with a lump sum amount that is calculated by determining the present value of the future annuity payments the employee could have received. Most plans give employees a lump-sum payout if total payment is less than $5,000.

- *Period certain.* The employee receives a monthly amount for either three years (36 months) or 10 years (120 months). If the employee dies before receiving total months eligible, then the employee's beneficiary will receive the remaining number of monthly payments based on option selected.

Defined Contribution (DC) Plans

DC plans are increasing in popularity since companies can control costs by adjusting employer contributions, and many employees like the possibility of managing their own pension monies. DC plans are also easier for employees to understand and, in many cases, provide short-service employees with higher benefits than DB plans. With DB plans, the company makes all decisions, including selection of investment vehicles. In contrast, with DC plans, employees have greater say on investment options and amounts to invest.

The most prevalent DC plan is a "savings/thrift" plan, with a 401(k) feature. Sometimes these 401(k) plans are called "capital accumulation" plans. An attractive feature is that employee contributions are tax deferred. Many plans have "matching" employer contributions that can be viewed by employees as "free money." The match amount varies by company. While in the plan, all monies compound tax-free. This means that an employee pays federal and state withholding tax on redeeming funds, preferably on retirement when the individual tax rate is usually lower than while working. An example of a 401(k) plan is found in Figure 8.7.

FIGURE 8.7 Sample 401(k) plan.

Eligibility
First of the month coinciding with or next following date of employment
Employee Contributions
2 percent to 15 percent of an employee's earnings
- Pretax basis or
- After-tax basis or
- A combination of pretax and after-tax
Company Contributions
50 percent match on first 6 percent contributed by employee
Vesting of Company Contributions (Cliff)
100 percent vested after three years of credited service
Investment Choices
Employee contributions
- Common stock fund
- Company stock
- Bond fund
- Fixed-rate-of-return vehicle
Company contribution – company stock
Withdrawal Provisions
Age 59 ½ or older
Death or disability
Retirement or termination of employment
Loan Provision
Up to 50 percent of value of vested account balance or $50,000, whichever is less
Payment Options
Cash
Company stock

Employees can make withdrawals for specific reasons, but the withdrawals are generally subject to taxation. Therefore, many plans contain a loan provision that enables employees to borrow rather than withdraw funds when necessary. IRS regulations limit the size of a loan to 50 percent of the employee's vested account balance or $50,000, whichever is less.

Distribution options are available when an employee terminates employment. These include a lump-sum payment, an annuity arrangement, installment payments, and a direct rollover to an IRA or another employer's qualified plan. By directly rolling over a lump-sum distribution to an IRA or another qualified plan, an employee is able to avoid the 20 percent withholding tax required by government regulations.

Vesting for employer contributions in 401(k) plans are:

1. 100 percent vested after three years if "cliff option" is selected.
2. 100 percent vested after six years if "graded" option is selected.

An employee is 100 percent vested immediately for all monies the employee invests.

Other types of DC plans include:

- *Money-purchase pension plans* whereby the company contributes a specified percent of each employee's salary to purchase annuities.
- *Employee stock-ownership plans* whereby the employee receives an annual allocation of employer stock.
- *Deferred profit-sharing plans* whereby the company contributes an amount of profits each year, and each participant is credited with a share.

PAY FOR TIME NOT WORKED BENEFITS

Pay for time not worked benefits are generally not regulated by the government. Typically, they are covered by company policy. The most frequently provided time-off benefits are:

1. Vacation
2. Sick leave
3. Legal holidays
4. Bereavement leave
5. Military leave
6. Jury duty
7. Personal holidays
8. PTO (paid time off) banks

Vacation

Vacation allowances are often based on service and position. Exempt staff usually receives more generous vacation time than nonexempt, especially during the earlier years of employment. Increases based on service can be as follows:

Years of Service Annual Vacation Allowance

3 months to 1 year	5 days
1 to 5 years	10 days
5 to 15 years	15 days
15 to 20 years	20 days
20 or more years	25 days

Sick Leave

Companies provide a set number of days per year for salary continuation in the event an employee is unable to work due to a personal illness.

Legal Holidays

Most companies provide employees with payment for not working on legal holidays. Holidays typically include:

- New Year's Day
- Martin Luther King's Birthday
- Memorial Day
- July 4th
- Labor Day
- Thanksgiving Day
- Christmas Day

Companies often pay nonexempt employees "premium" time if they work on a legal holiday and grant another day off with pay as the legal holiday.

Bereavement Leave

Companies often grant time off to attend the funeral of an immediate family member. Typical number of days off with pay is three.

Military Leave

According to the Uniformed Services Employment and Reemployment Rights Act, employees who serve in the armed forces are entitled to the continuation of their position, seniority, status, and pay rate as if there had not been a break in employment.

Jury Duty

Companies are required to grant employees time off for jury duty. The employee receives nominal payment for serving from the court. Additional compensation is based on company policy.

Personal Holidays

Companies frequently provide two to three paid personal days per year for an employee to use for any purpose. Some companies view these days as "emergency days."

Paid Time Off (PTO) Banks

Unscheduled absences are costly and can negatively affect a company's ability to meet customer demands. In response, companies are implementing paid time off (PTO) programs to control costs associated with unscheduled absences and give employees time off with pay to balance work and nonwork pressures.

With PTO programs, an employee receives a bank of time to use for time off activities regardless of reason. PTO replaces traditional separate accounts for vacation, personal time, sick time, and in some cases legal holidays. When designed properly, PTO can save a company money and still provide a safety net of time off with pay for workers to meet nonwork pressures.

OTHER BENEFITS

Many "other benefits" are self-explanatory. However, it is important to note that a specific written company policy should be prepared and available for employees to use. Written policies help to ensure equity among all employees and resolve disputes if an employee questions the appropriateness of any procedures. Examples of "other benefits" include:

Adoption benefit. Some companies decided that because medical plans provide maternity coverage, it is appropriate to also provide some reimbursement to employees who elect to adopt a child. Reimbursements can range from $1,500 to $3,000 per adoption.

Commuting assistance. This benefit includes vans or vouchers used for public transportation.

Credit unions. These employee-run endeavors provide loans for employees and give interest on account balances.

Dependent care and health-care reimbursement accounts (flexible spending accounts). Both accounts use pretax dollars to reimburse for eligible services and have a "use it or lose it" provision. This means any money left in the plan at the end of the plan year's grace period is forfeited back to the plan.

With a dependent care account, an employee uses the money to reimburse caregivers who provide covered services to an employee's dependent child or children. With the health-care reimbursement account, an employee pays for services not covered by the company's health-care plans. Also included are deductibles, copayments, and co-insurances.

Educational assistance plans. These plans are sometimes called *tuition reimbursement* plans. The plan provides for full or partial reimbursement of eligible educational expenses per year that are incurred by employees.

Employee assistance program (EAP). This program often features a toll-free telephone number employees can call to seek help to resolve personal matters (i.e., financial, marital, or substance abuse problems).

Employee health services. This benefit usually provides on-site medical care in the event an employee becomes ill at work or is injured on the job.

Financial counseling. This benefit provides financial advice to workers, especially for those enrolled in 401(k) plans.

Flextime. This policy allows employees to choose convenient starting and quitting times and under some plans, extended lunchtime, while still requiring the standard number of hours worked each day or week.

Product/service discounts. Employees use many companies' services and products. Therefore, it's common for companies to make their services or products available to workers at a reduced cost.

Relocation allowances. Companies often ask exempt staff to relocate to a different company facility. To assist with the move, companies underwrite the costs to help cushion any upset associated with relocation. Allowances are sometimes provided to new hires, but generally are less generous than for current employees.

Subsidized food service. Employers typically subsidize the cost of food served in employee cafeterias.

Job share. This is where two part-time workers end up doing the work of a full-time employee. The two employees share the workload. This arrangement is often effective when employees do not want to work full-time and can complement each other.

THE IMPORTANCE OF EFFECTIVE COMMUNICATION

Effective communication (both written and oral) is essential for employees to understand and appreciate the value of your company's total rewards program. Compared with wages and salaries, which are relatively easier to understand and highly visible, benefits tend to be complex, diverse, and, to some extent, hidden. You only use benefits when you need them. Therefore, unused benefits tend to be invisible.

To be effective, a benefits communication program should:

- Meet legal requirements (ERISA) for reporting and disclosing critical information to employees and regulators.
- Have means for employees to express interests and concerns and include a feedback mechanism to respond to workers' comments.
- Enable employees to clearly understand the provisions of their benefit package.
- Gain employee confidence that the information about their benefits is easily accessible and accurate, and that the benefit plans will deliver what they promise.
- Highlight value of benefits.
- Have employees realize the dollar investment made by employers for providing employees with benefits.

Legal Requirements

ERISA (Employee Retirement Income Security Act) requires plan sponsors (employers) to give participants (employees) various documents. Two basic ones are:

1. A summary plan description (SPD) is the benefits "handbook." This document should explain the benefit in a way an average worker would understand. The SPD must be given to each plan participant within 90 days of participation.
2. A summary annual report (SAR) includes key financial information about the benefit plan. The SAR must be given to participants within nine months following the end of each plan year.

In addition to satisfying ERISA reporting and disclosure provisions, benefits administrators need to comply with other federal and state requirements for distributing and posting various information affecting employees.

Cobraize Employees

Employees become eligible for COBRA (Consolidated Omnibus Budget Reconciliation Act of 1985) on losing welfare benefits due to various qualifying events (e.g., loss of job). COBRA allows an eligible employee to continue receiving some benefits for themselves and their eligible dependents and spouse for up to 18–36 months by paying the full monthly premium, plus a 2 percent administrative fee.

Most workers are shocked with the high cost of medical coverage. The information causes many employees to appreciate what the company had done for them; unfortunately, this awareness occurs when most workers leave the company.

What is recommended is to "Cobraize" employees the first day of employment (in addition to meeting traditional COBRA requirements). This means informing employees what the employer is paying for benefits (in particular, medical) in addition to what workers pay. Numbers convey value, and perhaps the disclosure will cause employees to have a greater appreciation of what companies are doing for them.

Creating and Building Awareness of Benefits

In some instances, employees and their dependents become aware of benefits coverage only when needs become acute. For example, when someone becomes ill or disabled, when the day of retirement nears, or when a death occurs, there will be a search for and inquiries about necessary application forms. However, workers may fail to use other company-provided benefits unless they receive periodic reminders. Examples, as described earlier, include educational assistance, employee assistance programs, long-term care, and adoption benefits.

Ways to inform employees about benefits include:

- Articles in company newsletters and company intranet site
- Notices posted on bulletin boards
- Information mailed to employees' homes
- Payroll inserts
- Benefits fairs
- Special programs (e.g., a representative from the Social Security Administration makes a presentation and answers questions)

Permit employees to invite nonworkers to attend benefits information meetings held by the company. Often, benefit decision makers are not the workers. Allowing employees to bring a family member or friend will help foster better understanding and decision making.

Enhancing Confidence and Trust

Credibility is enhanced when employees have confidence in the accuracy of plan information and believe they can obtain information about benefits on a timely basis. Responding quickly and accurately is the key to building credibility. The delivery of benefits information to workers can be facilitated by the use of:

- Interactive voice response via touch-tone telephones
- Touch-screen kiosks
- Intranet
- Email

Involve Employees in Benefit Changes

Many companies find success by actively involving employees when changing benefits programs. This includes use of "employee task forces" or "focus groups" to review ideas and express opinions of planned changes. Other task forces are asked to review proposed communication pieces to ensure employee understandings. These interactions are similar to companies asking a group of paying customers to critique a new product or service before being marketed.

Marketing executives have learned the value of customer feedback to ensure new products or services meet customers' needs. The best way is to ask for comments rather than wait until after the product or service goes live. The same logic applies to asking employees for comments prior to finalizing a new benefits program or communication piece.

9 How to Reskill Your Workforce through Continuous Development

In today's global business environment, markets are rapidly changing, competition is growing, employee engagement is low, and employee retention is a challenge. In addition, with the advent of the cognitive age, the line between employees and technology is blurred. Organizations are in a constant state of change and evolution. Workers have more opportunities than ever to leave companies for a better fit.

There is a new awakening. Organizations are realizing that the old management style of command and control has become obsolete. There is a shift in focus from governance and administration to delivering a human employee experience, resulting in stronger employee and company performance.

To improve performance and agility and effectively compete, employees need to grow and evolve as the organization changes. The traditional method of driving employee growth has been the yearly performance management process. However, there is growing research that this process is ineffective and does not improve performance or employee skill growth. According to data gathered by leading human capital research organizations, 86 percent of companies are unhappy with the lack of results (Rock, Davis and Jones, *People & Strategy*, Volume 36, Issue 2, 2013).

EIGHT PILLARS TO ACHIEVE CONTINUOUS PERFORMANCE DEVELOPMENT

Forward-thinking organizations understand that to grow profitably, they need to figure out how to grow employee performance. What follows are eight pillars that organizations should embrace to achieve continuous performance development.

1. Build a Culture of Appreciation Through Recognition

Today, organizations need to win the hearts and minds of employees and provide positive experiences in which employees feel inspired to do their best work. A positive employee experience is best defined as an impactful and powerful – and ultimately human – experience in which employees become motivated and feel they can bring their whole selves to work. It allows business leaders to make significant progress regarding top of mind issues like retention, culture and employee happiness – all while improving the bottom line.

> *There is a shift in focus from governance and administration to delivering a human employee experience.*

Employees are no longer motivated strictly by money. They want to work for organizations where they feel appreciated and recognized and understand how they are making a difference. Harvard Business School published a study on the connection between praise and productivity. Participants visited the Harvard Decision Science Laboratory and were asked to solve a problem. According to Jooa Julia Lee, PhD, from the University of Michigan, "Approximately half of the participants were told to ask friends and family members to send them an email just prior to their participation that described a time when the participant was at his or her best."

The result: More than half of those who received positive emails solved the problem, versus only 19 percent who didn't receive emails. The study also noted that participants who received praise found themselves significantly less stressed.

This is just one study. There are several additional industry studies and statistics demonstrating the proven links between social recognition and quantifiable business metrics. According to the WorkHuman Analytics and Research Institute at Globoforce, recognition programs make 92 percent of employees feel appreciated.

In cultures where employees feel appreciated, you can feel it when you speak to them. They are engaged. They are passionate. They are connected to the organization. When an employee feels appreciated, he or she works harder, has higher trust and is happier at work. All of this leads to higher productivity, reduced turnover, and increased agility to evolve and change.

This is the first pillar of the new thinking around performance development. Start with a culture of recognition to build trust and enable employees to bring their best self to work, driving productivity, growth, and retention. Build a culture in which people are recognized for doing not only outstanding work but for celebrating small wins as well. As individuals start to get on board with culture changes, recognize those change ambassadors.

2. Create a Safe Environment for Candid and Frequent Communication

A psychologically safe climate means that teams and individuals listen to one another, learn from their mistakes and have a high level of engagement in an atmosphere of constructive conflict management. This culture can be created through recognition and appreciation by creating a human environment with high levels of trust, connection and authenticity. When individuals feel safe, they are more comfortable growing, learning, and making mistakes to improve performance on an ongoing basis.

In safe environments, leaders also set an example by talking to their employees and teams about their mistakes and subsequent lessons learned. Employees are comfortable giving their honest feedback to both their peers and their leadership in environments in which leaders model feedback and learning. For example, if a product is failing in the market, then the chief product officer takes full ownership of the issue, discusses why this has happened with his team, and asks for input on improvements that can be made.

According to a leading academic in the field, Amy Edmondson of Harvard, "Organizational research has identified psychological safety as a critical factor in understanding phenomena such as voice, teamwork, team learning, and organizational learning."

Creating a safe environment of trust can be fostered with these steps:

- Ensure that managers and employees are communicating with each other on a frequent basis, at least every two weeks.
- Have leaders acknowledge mistakes and the learnings from mistakes to the organization in forums such as town halls.
- Give employees a line of sight as to how the work they are doing ties to corporate goals.
- Encourage peer-to-peer recognition, which then creates connections and positivity throughout the organization.

3. Facilitate a Continuous Dialogue Through Crowdsourced Feedback

When employees can bring their authentic selves to work and are comfortable growing and developing, learning through feedback becomes something to embrace. In general, constructive feedback is something that thwarts productivity and increases disengagement. Biologically, our brains go into fight, flee, or freeze mode when feedback is given. When this happens, absolutely no learning occurs.

However, in a safe environment where employees feel appreciated and have strong emotional connections with their peers, feedback is no longer threatening but rather an opportunity for learning and growth. Frequent check-ins through crowdsourced feedback help employees feel more valued within an organization, driving their motivation and productivity levels. Crowdsourced feedback also facilitates a continuous dialogue, which reduces the risk of misunderstanding or delayed communication between employees and managers. Strong emotional connections enable people to ask others for feedback that will help them grow without worrying that they look weak.

Coaching from the crowd can be facilitated in this way:

- Lead by example and request feedback from people above and below them. This sets an example that it is safe to gather feedback.
- Empower direct reports to give feedback on how their check-ins could be improved.
- Reflect on how teams could do things more effectively as a group during major project milestones, fostering team-based feedback.

4. Unleash the Power of Community and Teams

We've all heard the phrase, "I am here to work, not to make friends." The reality is, social connection at work is critical for employees to grow and learn; it's an essential piece of our shared humanity. Relationships at work can positively or negatively impact stress, productivity, and happiness.

Abraham Maslow, PhD, a pioneering social psychologist, ranks belonging as third in his hierarchy of needs for human satisfaction and fulfillment. This need for belonging exists in all aspects of one's life, including work. When a person does not feel like they belong at work, they are disengaged, unhappy, and do not bring their best self to work. To grow, improve, and connect within the organization, employees need to feel this tribalism and emotional connection. Employees need to know they can have authentic discussions, even disagreements, and not be kicked out of the tribe.

The process of connection and trust is built through appreciation and recognition. Once this connection of trust is established, then feedback across the spectrum, including constructive feedback, becomes a comfortable process. The interchange of feedback and appreciation builds this sense of community, strong relationships and connections in the organization. Ongoing performance development can only occur when there is a sense of community and connectedness.

Connectedness throughout the organization can be encouraged by:

- Celebrating not only work-related events but life events as well. For example, weddings, or the birth of a baby. This helps others in the organization see not only the work side of their peers but also the personal side as well.
- Supporting community events where people can get to know each other outside of the work environment.

- Investing in team-based recognition and feedback. When the team accomplishes a milestone, celebrate the team. This also is a good time for reflection and feedback. Building team-based communities creates connections, builds trust, and enhances productivity.

5. Be a Coach, Not a Task Delegator

To improve the development of employees on a continuous basis, the role of the manager must change. It needs to move beyond command and control to one of collaborator and coach. In fact, according to recent research, the single-most important managerial competency that separates highly effective managers from average ones is the ability to coach employees versus manage employees.

The relationship between the employee and the manager also is critical for building a sense of connection to the organization's broader goals.

When employees are coached, they can grow, build their skills, and have an emotional connection to the organization. Coaching consists of the following elements:

- Understand the values important to each employee and be able to connect that person's work to the organizational mission objectives and values.
- Provide feedback to enable employees to grow on an ongoing basis.
- Allow employees to fail and learn from those mistakes.
- Give employees a voice in their development and the work they do.
- Move the nature of check-ins beyond status to an environment of learning, growth, and collaboration. The manager must ask probing questions to not only motivate the employee but also leverage his or her skills and provide growth input.

The relationship between the employee and the manager also is critical for building a sense of connection to the organization's broader goals. Organizations looking to continually grow employees must ensure that managers are not only meeting with employees regularly, but also making sure employees understand how their work ties to the broader goals.

When the nature of the relationship between a manager and employee changes to one of coach (mentor) and player (protégé), communication is focused on learning and growth, and ongoing performance development becomes automatic.

The key to creating cultures in which managers are more coaches than task delegators includes these steps:

- Train (and demonstrate to) managers how open-ended questions help facilitate collaboration. Provide managers with a few key open-ended questions to ask during check-ins.

- Build mentor programs for managers where they can learn how to lead from other managers.
- Show employees how they can drive communication with their manager. Provide employees with key questions they can ask their managers to enable managers to coach versus direct.

6. Embrace a Personal Growth Mindset

How can we enable employees to do their best work and grow? What behavior changes are needed from employees and managers to support this development? Which coaching questions should managers ask during check-ins with their team?

Each organization needs to evaluate its culture, employees, and human capital strategy to determine the right philosophy that will drive continuous performance development. One example of a driving philosophy is Carol Dweck's growth mindset paradigm, which she covers in her book *Mindset: The New Psychology of Success.*

Once a philosophy is chosen, it needs to permeate many aspects of the organization, including leadership development, organizational values, employee development, and goals.

7. Learn and Develop Through Ongoing Reflection

There is growing research that the ability to learn from feedback and experience is more effective when coupled with reflection. In fact, this makes individuals more productive and builds on their confidence to achieve a goal (i.e., self-efficacy). Reflection allows the employee to move beyond fight-or-flight mode into a more rational mode to learn and truly understand the feedback they received.

> *It is critical to decide what to change first, measure, gather feedback, and adjust as needed.*

Here are some good reflection questions that can be used as part of check-ins to drive employee growth:

- What do I know for sure?
- What possibilities for action are available?
- Who can help with this?
- How does this situation look from the other person's perspective?

8. Let Employees Drive Their Development

Remember the days when learning meant going to a weeklong training? Then you would get back to your routine and only apply a sliver of the learning. This is the old paradigm of learning and growth. Today, employees want in-the-moment learning. Employees at all levels expect dynamic, self-directed, continuous learning opportunities from their employers, according to Deloitte. Millennials and other young employees have grown up in this self-directed learning environment, and they expect it as part of their working lives and careers – and they will move elsewhere if employers fail to provide it.

The key for ongoing performance development is to enable this learning in the moment, as the need arises. This can take the form of learning and guidance embedded in the products employees use. It also can take the form of in-the-moment feedback, requested by the employee to the people with whom they actually work. When an employee requests feedback on a specific project, behavior, or activity, he or she is in the driver's seat of their learning and ongoing performance development.

MANAGING CHANGE

The key to each of these best practices is to embed them in the culture. This requires change management to facilitate this culture growth. For example:

- Ongoing communication from leadership about the changes. Support from the top is critical.
- Leaders must lead by example up and down the organization.
- Celebrate small wins as the culture starts to evolve.
- Build change ambassadors in each organization to support the changes.
- Support training, micro-learning, and leadership development.
- Form focus groups to gather input from employees before and during the change.
- Leverage data to understand which groups are embracing the changes, and which tools are effective or need to evolve.

Changing culture takes time. It does not happen overnight. It is critical to decide what to change first, measure, gather feedback, and adjust as needed.

Igniting Passion and Purpose

There is a new awakening in how we grow employees and our organizations. For employees to grow, they need to feel safe, empowered, and coached by their leaders. They need a culture in which their passions and purpose are ignited – where they wake up every day excited to come to work and are connected to both the organization and its mission, as well as their peers and leaders. Those organizations that embrace this human culture will have the competitive edge in employee retention, engagement, and organizational agility.

Reskilling Revolution

There has been plenty in the way of research that suggests work as we know it today will be drastically different in 10 years.

To wit, the World Economic Forum estimates that artificial intelligence (AI) will displace 75 million jobs across the world by 2022 – and that pace will continue to increase. A PwC report predicts that 38 percent of jobs in the United States could be gone by 2030. The figures were 30 percent for the United Kingdom, 35 percent in Germany, and 21 percent in Japan.

Thus, the onus lies on organizations to prepare their workforce for the coming tide by upskilling and reskilling them. This very topic was discussed at the World Economic Forum Annual Meeting in Davos, Switzerland, in 2020. The "Reskilling Revolution" was launched as a global priority and its objectives were outlined.

As noted by Gallup, laying off unqualified workers and hiring new ones produces an ever-accelerating cycle of recruiting and firing, which is expensive, builds inefficiencies into the system and drains organizational knowledge. Gallup added that "a chronic labor shortage from layoffs puts a business behind its competition and it also weakens its position in the labor market, given the toll that mass firings have on an employer's brand."

There are other ancillary benefits that reskilling and upskilling have on an organization as well.

"At a baseline, it just offers more engagement to employees," said Ashley Jordan, senior customer success manager at Docebo, a provider of AI-powered learning technology. "It signals to the employee that their employer cares about their development and wants them to not only succeed in their current position by giving them the tools necessary to do so, but they're also offering them the opportunity for movement within that company. So, you'll see greater engagement within that job role, but also more productivity overall."

Jordan noted that most organizations are trying to assess and determine what the return on investment (ROI) is for each business process. When it comes to reskilling your workforce, the roadmap to the ROI is fairly easy to track, she said.

"If you offer more training opportunities, they're probably more likely to stay in your organization," Jordan said. "You'll notice less turnover, less attrition, and more ROI in the long-term by developing existing talent rather than going to market and finding new talent."

The first step of this process is employers identifying the areas where they need to reskill their workforce to be more equipped for the future. The second part, Jordan said, is establishing what outcomes the business is trying to achieve and determining whether they have the tools to achieve these desired outcomes.

"Do you have the tools necessary to achieve this engagement? If not, then you probably need to go to market to evaluate what you need," Jordan said. "The process of implementing a new platform can be lengthy, but if you have the right stakeholders and the right buy-in with incentive for employees, then you can get that done pretty efficiently."

As noted by Gallup, another variable is that leaders need to know the practical difference between talent and skills. That understanding, it said, can have a major impact on profitability and the capacity to compete in an evolving business environment.

Aside from the obvious business case for organizations to invest in upskilling and reskilling to better secure their future, the younger generations are also forcing their hands, Jordan said.

"Organizations need to provide those opportunities if they want to be successful as business and technology changes," Jordan said. "Technology is changing exponentially, and that's changing the nature of the work that we do every day, so adaptability and agility on the job is going to be everything moving forward."

A FUNDAMENTAL SHIFT IN HOW BUSINESSES OPERATE

Say the word *reskilling* and it conjures up a worker in mid-career, or even one nearing retirement, who needs to learn how to use new technology.

But what the World Economic Forum has dubbed the "reskilling revolution" goes far beyond graying employees. It's a fundamental shift in the way that businesses – and employees – should function to keep on top of rapidly evolving technology.

What's at stake? Not only individual jobs but also the health of the economy as a whole. Traditional retraining efforts, particularly in the public sector, have focused on workers who have already been laid off after their skills became obsolete. That system requires government services, such as unemployment benefits or welfare assistance, to support workers while they gain new skills and education.

Experts suggest that the private sector can take a leading role in disrupting this cycle by planning ahead, and that it makes good business sense to do so.

Ravin Jesuthasan, co-author of the World Economic Forum's 2019 report "Skills as the Currency of the Labor Market," said the old model of "learn, do, retire" suited a job market in which the basic functions of a job changed little over time.

As some old job functions become automated – and technology continues to change – the business world is adopting a new model of continuous learning and relearning.

"The promise going forward is not jobs for life; it's the promise that as a company, I will ensure that you stay relevant," Jesuthasan said. "The talent experience will increasingly emphasize the need for companies to give workers access to acquiring new skills and rewarding them when they do – that the company is going to give you the ability, access, and opportunities to continue to develop yourself."

A New Cost–Benefit Analysis

Standing in the way of widespread adoption are outdated views about everything from how companies perceive costs to how to deliver continuing education.

For example, some traditional accounting practices tend to reward the cost savings of laying off employees with obsolete skills and hiring ones with more updated portfolios, without considering the costs of recruitment or ramp-up time to productivity. In addition, organizations often must pay a significant premium for new employees with high-demand skills, particularly in a tight labor market.

In "Towards a Reskilling Revolution," a report published in January 2019 by the World Economic Forum, the authors caution that a successful job transition takes an average of up to two years in additional education and work experience.

UpSkill America, an employer-led group that promotes training and education, has released a calculator to help employers better pinpoint the costs of turnover, from recruiting a new hire to integrating that new person into the workforce. The calculator was developed in partnership with the Aspen Institute Workforce Strategies Initiative to achieve a new cost–benefit analysis that companies could use to justify spending their money in retraining their employees, rather than replacing them.

Changing the Culture

Chief learning officers also need to redefine their role in providing education opportunities, said George Westerman, the faculty director of workplace learning at MIT's Jameel World Education Lab. Such leaders have a chance to be "transformers" for their employers.

HR is well-situated to work with various departments to identify skills gaps, determine best practices for reskilling, and track what training creates an impact or falls short.

"It's completely changing your mindset to be much more strategic," Westerman said. "Your role is to change the culture, not to deliver courses. It's to be part of the conversation about where the company is going and to help drive that conversation, not just sit back and say, 'What courses do you want?'"

Several reports, such as "Humans Wanted: Robots Need You" by workforce consultant ManpowerGroup, suggest that even as technical skills become more important, the most successful workers will be those who possess "human skills," such as communication and creativity, which robots can't reproduce.

If a company already has employees who demonstrate those soft skills and who fit well in the company culture, then it makes sense to invest money in reskilling rather than replacement, said Marion McGovern, an entrepreneur and the author of *Thriving in the Gig Economy*.

"To the extent that people talk about the need for resilience and critical thinking and adaptability and flexibility, these are not necessarily job skills, these are competencies," McGovern said. "And if that's what you really want in the worker of the future, if you have those competencies, then you can train people for a new job."

There is some evidence to suggest that the tide is turning in favor of reskilling.

In 2018, large corporations announced more than $600 million in new reskilling programs, according to UpSkill America.

A ManpowerGroup survey of 19,000 employers worldwide found that 84 percent of responding companies had planned to invest in upskilling efforts in 2020, quadrupling the percentage of businesses that had such initiatives in 2011.

Future Ready

AT&T is among the early adopters of reskilling efforts. The company launched its "Workforce2020" program in 2013 to create educational opportunities for its employees. The company later renamed the program "Future Ready" to reflect the open-ended nature of learning. It currently invests about $200 million a year in internal training programs for employees and $23 million more on tuition assistance, said Dahna Hull, senior vice president of AT&T University and Talent Acquisition.

AT&T measures its ROI in part by following the number of employees who take part in training, then move into critical roles, Hull said. The company reports that it fills 75 percent of its management roles with internal candidates and that those who have taken part in "Future Ready" are more likely than their colleagues to advance.

Two years ago, AT&T added an online search engine that allows employees to plan and track their learning. In addition, the feature allows employees to search for other jobs in the company based on their current skills, find out what jobs for which they are at least 50 percent qualified, and figure out what training they need to bridge the gap.

"It's really about transparency and empowerment – creating tools and processes that can help empower employees to take control of their own development and their own careers," Hull said. "It's about creating a culture of continuous learning and inspiring employees to continue thinking about learning and development throughout their careers." (See Sidebar 9.1.)

Sidebar 9.1 Talent Pipeline Management Academy

Employers may want to invest in their current employees, but they may not always know how to overcome hurdles such as cost and logistics.

One potential resource is the US Chamber of Commerce Foundation's Center for Education and Workforce (CEW).

The CEW has an upskilling and reskilling component to its Talent Pipeline Management (TPM) Academy, a training program for local and state chambers of commerce and workforce development groups.

The academies train such groups on how to lead local employers through the process of identifying their talent needs and then creating solutions around education, training, and development.

The issue is particularly difficult for small- and mid-sized employers, who struggle with how to upskill or reskill existing employees who already fill necessary functions.

"What we hear firsthand from our practitioners is that employers are interested in different types of solutions because they are unable to find the talent that they need," said Jaimie Francis, the CEW's senior director for programs and policy. "For a lot of them, it's a natural starting point to look at the employees you have and see how you can keep them in your company. They just don't usually have the understanding of how to do that while not sacrificing their current business needs."

HOW TO SPOT TALENT TO DEVELOP STRONG LEADERS

It is well accepted that the senior management team has responsibility for shaping a company's business strategy. But what about leadership strategy and who has the ultimate responsibility for its development? While the business strategy defines what a company plans to do, the leadership strategy governs how a company will do it. Shouldn't a management team, with the support of its board of directors, be equally focused on both? That said, the senior HR team can, and should, play a vital role in bringing a leadership strategy to life.

First, let's assert that leadership strategy is more than the mere identification of a group of current and future executives. It is broader than a succession chart and encompasses the development and stewardship of a company's priorities and values – that is, its culture.

Second, let's acknowledge that recent high-profile examples of flawed culture (e.g., Wells Fargo, Uber) have elevated the issues of leadership and culture to a boardroom concern. Historically, boards have generally limited leadership oversight to the hiring and firing of the CEO and other C-suite executives. A company's talent management and corporate culture have largely been viewed as the purview of senior management, and boards are reluctant to be seen as micromanaging or second-guessing their executive team.

In fact, a 2016–2017 Pearl Meyer study of 1,400 public companies in the United States shows that nearly 20 percent have formally expanded the purview of their board compensation committees to incorporate some aspect of leadership and talent. This finding is consistent with Pearl Meyer's in-boardroom experience, where committee members are increasingly engaging in discussions with management that go beyond the traditional focus on the compensation and benefits packages for a handful of senior executives. There is more emphasis on pinpointing and developing leaders one and two layers down the organization.

With that shift in priorities, there are clear implications for senior management and human resources.

Add Proactive Leadership Development to Succession Planning

While leading boards are now thinking beyond basic CEO succession planning, an effective management team is actively identifying strong potential successors for all key senior positions, including those who are "ready now" and those who could be "ready soon." These assessments are likely to include an overview of each recognized employee's position history, most recent performance reviews and management's view on each individual's strengths and weaknesses. (For ready-now candidates, the overview should also include the succession plan for that person's replacement.)

Human resources has a key role to play in helping the management team create plans to address any individual developmental needs, such as rotational assignments, internal and external coaching and more exposure to the C-suite and board. Likewise, human resources can facilitate a high-level, comprehensive review of the overall team composition and dynamics.

This complex process may be rooted in a skills matrix, which first identifies the combination of experience and expertise necessary to successfully deliver the company's business strategy. Further refinement of the matrix may include some of the following questions:

- Do we have any skills gaps in the current leadership team?
- Have recent or anticipated changes in our business strategy changed the skills/expertise required?
- Is the team appropriately diverse (gender, age, ethnicity, geography, tenure)?
- Is it reflective of the employee population and/or the company's customer base?
- Has there been strategic consideration of which positions are best suited to internal versus external candidates?

The discussion of ready-now candidates also needs to touch on retention risks and mitigation strategies. After all, if your organization believes someone might be ready for a promotion, chances are good that at least one competitor agrees. Some level of transparency around the company's leadership development process may help in this regard, as will a careful alignment between leadership development and total rewards, including annual and long-term incentive compensation.

Know Your Culture at Its Core

In the same way that boards have historically limited their leadership development focus to CEO succession and pay programs for senior executives, their corporate culture concerns have tended to focus on the "tone at the top." And yet, it's with increasing frequency that we see companies dealing with scandals that result from actions taken by employees much lower in the corporate hierarchy. Certainly, a tone at the top can create a corporate culture that allows – or encourages – employees to act in ways that maximize short-term results but are contrary to the long-term health of the company. On the other hand, it is possible that there is a disconnect between the company's tone at the top and the day-to-day culture at the core of the organization. A company's leaders need to identify ways to assess culture from top to bottom.

It's likely through a combination of formal and informal mechanisms that a senior leadership team can gain the clearest view of the organization's culture at all levels. First, senior leaders should be able to articulate their vision for the company – its mission, values, and common goals. Next, they can determine what leadership qualities are present and desired in the team, such as tolerance for risk, flexibility, or attitudes toward mentoring. This may be done through a matrix similar to the skills assessment. Finally, it is critical that senior management walk the talk. Not only do those leaders' personal actions need to align with the espoused culture, but they need to be willing to take action when cultural rules are broken. HR guidance can be invaluable in establishing expectations, and setting policies and procedures to help ensure that transgressions are addressed promptly, fairly and appropriately.

In looking farther down the hierarchy, a leadership team can plan for opportunities to spend time formally and informally with individual teams and make a concerted effort to spend quality time at sites beyond headquarters, providing an opportunity to interact with and observe employees at various levels in the organization. Other activities – for example attending trade shows or user conferences with an eye toward understanding internal culture and external perception of the company – offer management a deeper understanding of employee behaviors, as well as the company's competitive positioning and reputation in the industry. Sources such as Glassdoor and customer chat sites can also provide clues to the real and unscripted views of the workforce.

While it is just one facet of a corporate culture, understanding the role and perception of compensation should not be overlooked. In fact, pay is a powerful tool that boards and senior management can use to reinforce and communicate company priorities, values and culture.

In the current business climate, issues of pay equality and fairness will continue to increase in importance regardless of what happens with regulatory mandates and reporting requirements. Even absent the pending CEO pay ratio disclosure, there will continue to be public scrutiny over the levels of CEO pay and the disparity of CEO pay levels and increases compared to rank-and-file US workers. On the gender equality front, there are several examples of prominent companies in the US, including Amazon, Apple, and Facebook, voluntarily disclosing gender pay ratios. Human resources can help senior management consider the implications of these and other pay issues, including the possible unintended consequences of incentive plans, and devise a communications strategy that helps illustrate how compensation is structured to support the desired culture of the company.

Human resources has a strategic opportunity to take the lead role in helping uncover this deeper core culture. This is where the crucial nature of many HR functions, particularly well-constructed employee engagement surveys, is evident and can help inform valuable assessments of culture.

Actively Promote Your HR Philosophy

The generally stated primary goal of leadership development, compensation and benefits programs is to attract, retain, and motivate both executives and the workforce at large. Companies obviously need programs that are competitive. But shifting from a mindset of "attract and retain" to one of "engage and align" can be one method of proactively focusing on promoting the right corporate culture. A shift in positioning can impact how programs are designed and communicated to employees and the marketplace.

Human resources plays a central role in determining the talent profile that best suits the company's business strategy and its culture, as well as the leadership and skills development opportunities that can help build that talent from within (see Sidebar 9.2). An ongoing and open dialogue, and continual assessment of success, will help align the tone at the top with the culture at the core. Taking this deeper view of the importance of the internal climate in combination with thoughtful talent development enables senior leaders to directly influence a company's differentiation in the marketplace and its ability to deliver on its business strategy.

Sidebar 9.2 How Human Resources Can Take the Lead in Leadership Development

Identify and Retain Leaders

1. Continually assess top talent to identify strong potential successors for senior positions.
2. Identify any gaps among high potentials in experience or expertise.
3. Help management teams create targeted plans for individual growth and development.
4. Conduct a high-level review of the entire team's skills and dynamics as a functional unit.
5. Remember to think about retention risks and strategies to retain top talent.

Discovery Channels

1. Know what leadership qualities are present in the current team and what qualities are desired.
2. Consider whether leaders' actions align with the cultural mission.
3. Have a process in place and take decisive action when cultural boundaries are crossed.
4. Help senior leadership plan for spending quality time – formal and informal – with individual teams.

5. Explore the company's culture from the outside in. Trade shows, conferences, customer feedback, and web postings all offer clues to the *real* culture at the core of an organization

---

MANY EMPLOYERS INVESTED IN RESKILLING EFFORTS AMID COVID-19 OUTBREAK

Employers increased their reskilling and upskilling efforts during the COVID-19 pandemic.

This was a main finding from "The State of Employee Upskilling and Reskilling" survey by TalentLMS, *Workable and Training Journal,* which found that 43 percent of 282 organizations surveyed enhanced efforts to reskill and upskill their employees. The researchers also found that 42 percent of the 400 US employees they surveyed have pursued training on their own after the coronavirus outbreak.

"In this collective time, companies across industries, no matter their size or needs, moved their training online to keep going," said Eleftheria Papatheodorou, customer support and training director at TalentLMS.

"We're entering a period where online training is not another solution but the only way to go."

The survey revealed that 68 percent of companies invest in upskilling/reskilling training to handle changes within the organization and another 65 percent do so to train employees on new technologies. Additionally, 50 percent of employers said they target both hard and soft skills through their training initiatives.

Both employers (91 percent) and employees (81 percent) agreed that upskilling/reskilling training has boosted productivity at work. A disconnect, however, was found between employers and employees, as 62 percent of employees hoped that upskilling and reskilling training would lead to promotions and/or a raise in salary. However, only a third of employers said there's been a significant change in compensation and growth within the company.

The top motivation for most employees (66 percent) to reskilling or upskilling is the joy of learning new things and developing new skills. What's more, 52 percent said the training has boosted their confidence and 74 percent of employees who haven't received skills training said they would prefer to work for a company that offers this career development opportunity.

Other key findings:

- Upskilling or reskilling training has been beneficial to companies' goals (84 percent), reputation (74 percent), and employee retention (69 percent).
- Lack of time (55 percent) and lack of training resources (46 percent) are the two main upskilling and reskilling barriers for companies.
- Communication (57 percent), leadership (54 percent), and proactive thinking (50 percent) are the most important soft skills the employees are lacking, according to employers.
- 66 percent of employees think hard skills training would help them advance more, compared to only 34 percent for soft skills training.
- 74 percent of employees believe their managers need upskilling or reskilling.

10 How to Recognize and Reward Your Top-Performing Employees (with Cash Bonuses and Praise)

An organization can applaud employee performance by awarding a spot, or recognition, award. A spot award is intended to acknowledge and demonstrate immediate and spontaneous appreciation and recognition for the exceptional contribution of individuals or teams. Recognition rewards usually are relatively small and are given at the time of achievement.

In most cases, managers typically can give spot awards based on direct observation and/or feedback from others of exceptional effort or exceptional results. They might come in the form of a cash award, a thank-you note, movie passes, sporting event tickets, dinner vouchers, etc. An outstanding accomplishment by an individual or team may warrant monetary reward and recognition above and beyond a company's regular pay and bonus programs. Larger rewards usually are bestowed at a formal recognition event or ceremony. For all intents and purposes, this chapter will focus on cash spot bonuses.

In high-flying days (e.g., a bull market), companies are eager to award spot bonuses to topnotch employees for fear that they may jump ship. When the job market eases and money is tighter at many companies, organizations still see the importance of rewarding top performers for a job well done to keep them around. Companies that have tightened their salary budget belt find that when pay increases aren't feasible, a spot bonus is an affordable option that makes an employee feel valued and appreciated.

Spot bonuses award employees for a "job well done" and have stayed in vogue because of their direct link of showing employee appreciation. They serve as motivational tools to inspire high-level performance.

At management's discretion, employees are recognized for making material contributions to a project or task that adds value to the organization, for example:

- Meeting or exceeding project goals and expectations ahead of schedule
- Increasing productivity and efficiency
- Cost-saving ideas implemented
- Improvements in the quality of teamwork
- Excellent customer service
- Effectively handling a particularly complex and/or sensitive issue

Employees also can be recognized for:

- Performance
- Productivity
- Safety
- Sales

There are many reasons to offer a spot bonus, but equally important are the business drivers, which may include:

- Using it as a recruiting tool to demonstrate a performance culture to prospective employees
- Rewarding positive contributions to product or service quality
- Recognizing improvements in productivity
- Positively impacting morale and loyalty to the organization
- Retaining qualified employees by providing spot bonus recognition

The most common strategies of recognition programs are:

- Rewarding employees for making exceptional contributions above and beyond their daily job functions
- Strengthening employee morale
- Increasing retention
- Tying performance to the company's mission

SIZE OF SPOT BONUS

Spot bonuses are non-base pay and generally range from $50 to $250. However, some spot bonuses aren't just a few extra bucks in the employee's paycheck – many companies regularly award between $1,000 and $2,500 for a job well done. For executives and upper management, awards greater than $10,000 are not uncommon. The amount awarded should be commensurate with the achievement or contribution. The presentation of the award should be personalized and made as soon as possible following the employee's accomplishment.

SPOT RECOGNITION PROGRAM GUIDELINES

Spot bonuses have elements that fit with both a formal and informal recognition program. A spot cash bonus provides immediate recognition much like an informal program but still has definitive structure like a formal program.

A spot recognition program is relatively easy to implement, and training time is minimal for participants. Simply follow these eight easy steps:

Step 1: Define the program's purpose. This does not have to be a complicated defined purpose but should state simply what the program is trying to accomplish. For example: "The purpose of the informal recognition program is to recognize those actions by employees that can be readily observed and immediately rewarded."

Step 2: Determine who will be eligible. All employees usually are eligible to participate in a spot bonus program. Generally, administrative staff and possibly department directors are excluded. Some organizations also exclude temporary, casual, and contracted employees from the program.

Step 3: Establish monetary and program guidelines. The recognition should be meaningful, but also stay within established program boundaries: For example, recognition should be given only for performance considered over and above established standards (e.g., excellent customer service); cash bonuses will not exceed $1,000 for any recognition event; the program will not duplicate any current total rewards program.

Step 4: Establish program expectations. The expectations should be built around areas where the organization is seeking to make improvements. Examples include customer service, organizational morale, team development, productivity, and personal development. The following expectations are an example and are not as well defined or developed as what is generally seen in a formal recognition program.

- Increase management visibility with employees and provide them with a tool to reward positive work performance.
- Provide a positive work environment that recognizes employees for their contributions.
- Gratify employees who will feel good about their work and contributions.
- Recognize those employees who provide exceptional customer service.
- Encourage similar performance by the employee in the future.
- Recognize those employees who provide meaningful contributions to the organization.

Step 5: Define what behavior and actions are eligible for recognition. The following bullet points are the types of behavior and actions that would warrant recognition. The difference between these behaviors and those listed in the spot recognition policy (see Figure 10.1) is that managers still have some discretion when using an informal approach to recognition:

- Behavior or action resulted in a compliment from an internal or external customer.
- Employee exceeds expectations on a project or work assignment.
- Employee displays an unusual cooperative spirit in working with other team members or with other work areas.
- Employee's actions enhance the organization's image.
- The manager/supervisor observes the employee engaging in actions that will improve morale or enhance the organization's image.
- Employee goes above and beyond the call of duty without being asked to do so.
- Employee makes a work improvement or changes a process that will increase productivity or efficiency.
- At the supervisor's discretion, any action that in her/his estimation adds significant value to the organization should be recognized.

Please note that it is often difficult to define exactly what will be rewarded. Often, it is easier to define what is rewarded, for example, not awarding a spot bonus to an employee who is doing his job as expected.

Step 6: Identify exclusions, if appropriate.

Step 7: Establish who has the ultimate responsibility for administering the program (i.e., human resources department, recognition committee, program coordinator). What approval processes, if any, need to be followed? When approval is granted, the timing of awarding bonuses is critical.

Step 8: Establish the program procedures and guidelines that will be used to recognize an individual. The recognition should reflect what is important to the organization's culture. For example, if the culture is mature and conservative, a more traditional approach, such as certificates of appreciation and cash awards, may be more appropriate. In younger organizations, departmental parties, gift certificates, and other types of public recognition may be needed. What works best for your organization?

Be careful to monitor the culture for the department or work team that may be significantly different than the organization's culture. The supervisor should identify those unique characteristics present in their work area and work with the recognition committee to build an effective recognition program.

HOW TO EFFECTIVELY USE SPOT RECOGNITION

A spot bonus program should effectively align with the organization's business strategy. This only happens when the program is built on trust and credibility. Informal programs can be severely impacted if it becomes an

FIGURE 10.1 Sample spot recognition policy.

Policy Statement: It is a policy of BioKing to provide a spot cash bonus to reward employees immediately for exceptional performance or who provide exceptional customer service. The recognition committee is responsible for coordinating the spot recognition program.

Purpose: The purpose of the spot recognition program is to reward employees immediately. The monetary value of spot recognition awards can be as high as $1,000. Awards of $50 or less do not require approval.

Definition: Employees will be recognized for meaningful contributions that exceed expected levels of performance, which are detailed in the employee's job description and/or the employee's performance evaluation. Spot recognition should be timely and immediate and encourage similar performance or behavior in the future.

Eligibility: All employees, with the exception of department directors and higher-level positions, are eligible for the spot recognition program.

Eligible Actions/Behavior: The following guidelines should be used to determine if the performance or behavior qualifies for spot recognition:

- The employee's performance exceeded normal expectations for the job. The employee's action(s) or behavior(s) enhanced the organization's image. The employee's action(s) or behavior(s) delighted a customer.
- The employee's action(s) or behavior(s) exceeded the supervisor's expectations. The employee's action(s) or behavior(s) exhibited an entrepreneurial/intrapreneurial spirit in resolving a problem or handling a customer concern.

Exclusions (1) If the employee is already being compensated or rewarded for the performance or effort, the employee will not be eligible for spot recognition, for example an employee who agrees to work an alternate work shift and receives additional compensation for working the shift; (2) The employee performs a duty that is expected or that is not beyond normal work expectations, for example directing a customer to the appropriate office for service.

Program Guidelines: (1) Any employee can nominate or recommend another employee for spot recognition. The recommendation can be presented to the employee's supervisor or to a member of the recognition committee. (2) A customer also can recommend an employee for spot recognition. (3) The supervisor/leader will present the recognition to the employee. (4) The recognition should be documented and sent to the Human Resources Department for inclusion in the employee's personnel file. (5) Items that can be used for spot recognition can be obtained from HR.

approach used on a "hit-and-miss" basis. It should be consistently applied and continuously communicated to employees. Informal recognition programs have five basic principles:

- *Acknowledge and recognize employees in a timely manner, using specific and concrete examples of the positive performance.* Employees want to know what they did right. They also want to be able to receive recognition in conjunction with the contribution. This adds value to the employee and to the achievement.
- *Bridge the recognition with organizational goals and business strategy.* If the recognition is not focused on the organization, it will appear disjointed and unimportant to participants. The message to employees should be that the organization values their contributions and wants them to be a partner in meeting goals. For example, excellent customer service is often a focal point for the organization. When employees are recognized for good customer relations skills, it emphasizes that customer service is valued and appreciated by the organization.
- *Center the program on the organization culture and values.* As discussed previously, this means matching recognition with the culture.
- *Develop positive performance skills in employees by recognizing their achievements.* The recognition should reinforce positive work behavior.
- *Enlist support from all program participants.* The recognition should focus on how to keep the program meaningful and still meet the needs of all participants.

These principles provide a foundation from which to administer a successful program. The following obstacles should be avoided if the program is to be taken seriously by employees and other key stakeholders.

POTENTIAL PITFALLS

The following obstacles should be addressed up front to ensure that the program does not stall. The last two bullet points, in particular, should be scrutinized since they often are responsible for the program's long-term failure.

- Inconsistent and infrequent application of the program.
- Failure to match the reward with the achievement.
- Failure to adapt the recognition to the individual's preferences.
- Poor communication by the supervisor/leader with the employee.
- Person doing the recognition has a low level of trust and credibility with employees.
- No clear definition of what actions/behaviors are being recognized.
- Lack of understanding by participants of what the program is trying to accomplish.
- Failure to communicate tax implications of some rewards.

- Inadequate time allotted by the supervisor/leader when recognizing the individual.
- Failure to keep the program fresh and fun.
- Lack of enthusiasm for the program by participants.

CONDUCTING THE RECOGNITION EVENT

According to Ken Blanchard and Spencer Johnson in *The One-Minute Manager,* "You can never over recognize; the more you recognize people, the more productive they'll be." If this is true, why do so many leaders avoid recognizing employees? The problem is that leaders are uncomfortable telling employees that they did a good job. The recognition event is the cornerstone of the recognition process. The leader should be fully prepared when communicating the recognition to the employee. Bear in mind that different employees will prefer different kinds of recognition; make sure they do not experience discomfort instead of the intended pride in their accomplishment.

If at all possible, the recognition should be done face-to-face by the supervisor/leader. In this digital age, some leaders like to use the internet and email to recognize employees. The recognition's impact may be less in those cases unless the leader follows up with a video call to show sincerity and add a personal touch. Some guidelines still apply for virtual recognition. The key is to personalize the recognition and use active verbs to indicate excitement and enthusiasm to the reader. After completing the recognition event, document the specific achievement and the recognition event.

DOCUMENTING RECOGNITION

A well-documented recognition event helps the leader link it with the employee's performance evaluation. The documentation also is important to employees when they are seeking a promotion or job transfer. An employee who has a history of being recognized as an outstanding performer will have an easier chance of moving up in the organization. Documented recognition reinforces and encourages the employee to repeat his/her outstanding performance. It is a template for employees to use for future work behavior.

- Focus on specifics.
- Cite the performance standard or organization goal that was exceeded if appropriate.
- Describe in detail the achievement: Who was involved? List the names and individuals involved. What happened? Describe exactly what the employee achieved that was extraordinary.
- When and when did the achievement occur?

- Why is this event being recognized (e.g., exceeds a departmental goal, an example of exceptional customer service)?
- Comments of appreciation by the individual giving the recognition.
- Provide the date the recognition was given.
- Indicate type of recognition approach used, if appropriate.
- Provide a copy of the documentation to the employee.
- Place a copy of the recognition in the employee's personnel file.

MOTIVATING MILLENNIALS

While the topic of millennials shaking things up in the US workforce has been well covered by mainstream media, not nearly as much has been written about what an incredible asset they can be to companies that know how to keep them motivated.

Before frustrated managers start throwing around words like "entitled," "trophy generation" and "instant gratification," it would behoove them to rethink their approach to millennial employees. After all, millennials, born from 1981 to 2000, make up 38 percent of the US workforce and are a generation equipped with unique talents and perspectives that businesses can benefit from. Making a few adjustments to your employee rewards and recognition programs can be enough to begin transforming your workplace into an environment where millennials thrive.

Effective incentive programs for millennials require:

- *Connected communication and meaningful feedback:* Embracing new media of instant communication and using those channels to provide millennials with interactivity and regular feedback.
- *Personal growth and "higher order values":* Inspiring personal development, incentivizing core values and making sure millennials know what your company stands for.
- *Rewards that enhance lifestyle and offer experience:* Understanding what kind of rewards appeal to millennials and incorporating those rewards into your employee incentive program.

Shifting the Status Quo

Before getting into the more technical aspects of employee rewards and recognition, it's important to be flexible and to make an effort to be empathetic to the sensibilities of a new workplace demographic.

According to "How Millennials Want to Work and Live," a 2016 report by Gallup, millennials are fiercely idealistic and have a strong desire for a purpose-driven life. They want to learn and grow, to develop their skillsets and to feel like their work has meaning. Millennials want to challenge the status quo. Rather than settling for, "That's just the way it is," millennials want to know *why* it's that way and explore ways to make it better.

That said, it's time to get rid of the idea of "the old 9-to-5" or "toeing the company line." Instead of shaping their personalities to conform to institutions, millennials expect institutions to change. So, rather than worrying about beards, tattoos, blue hair or whether jeans are OK at work, we would all be better served by exploring ways we can capitalize on millennials' innovative thoughts, facility with tech, and awareness of new trends.

Incentives for a Connected Generation

Millennials are a connected generation that is highly tuned into the world around them. Digital natives, millennials view technology as an extension of themselves and are adept at utilizing tech to expand their agency and ability to communicate.

In order to create an employee rewards and recognition program that motivates millennials, it's important to place a focus on connectivity. Here are incentive program ideas to maximize employee engagement:

- *Interactive quizzes and trivia.* Interactive quizzes and trivia are a great way to build brand awareness or inspire staff to improve their product knowledge.
- *Leaderboards.* Millennials have spent their whole lives competing against their friends for the high score. Sparking a little bit of fun, in-house competition can go a long way toward increasing engagement among your staff.
- *Social media recognition walls.* Social media–inspired walls where co-workers and managers can give each other shout-outs for exemplary behavior are another form of interactivity millennials can relate to.
- *On-the-spot points certificates.* Modules that incorporate recognitions are another way to make your employee rewards program more engaging by adding an element of unpredictability and spontaneity.
- *Mobile apps.* A successful incentive program makes your brand part of participants' day-to-day lives. For millennials, this means your employee incentive program needs to be mobile-ready.
- *Omni-channel communication.* More modern media like SMS, push notifications, and live chats not only improves engagement with your employee incentive program, it can also improve organizational workflow and facilitate instant collaboration.

Automated incentive technology makes life easier for employers, as well, by eliminating the need for paper trails and Excel spreadsheets or concerns about keeping your program in compliance.

Another perk you might consider incorporating into your employee rewards program is the ability to earn flexible scheduling and remote workdays. These are a powerful incentive for millennial employees, who value their work–life balance. With modern tech, offering your employees the option to occasionally work remotely doesn't have to result in a dip in productivity. In fact, it's found the opposite. Teams often work *harder* on remote days because it's a privilege they value.

Clear Goals and Regular Feedback

One of the advantages of an employee rewards and recognition program, especially when it comes to millennial employees, is that it provides clear goals, measurable progress and frequent opportunities for feedback. While these are all factors that millennials crave from their work environment, they are missing from most workplaces, according to the 2016 Gallup study,

Regular feedback is one of the highest predictors of millennial engagement at work, but only 19 percent of millennials report that they receive routine feedback and even fewer report that this feedback feels meaningful. While an employee rewards and recognition program can't replace in-person meetings, it can provide clear goals and immediate feedback to keep employees engaged.

Millennials will work extremely hard when they feel their work is meaningful and that the organization they work for is invested in their personal development. Employee rewards and recognition help inspire this feeling in a way that's efficient and scalable for management.

Incentivizing an Idealistic, Purpose-Driven Work Life

Millennial employees want to work for organizations that stand for something beyond annual revenue and bottom lines. Incorporating your organization's core values into your employee rewards and recognition program is an effective way to improve organizational culture and show that your core values are more than just words on a piece of human resources collateral.

While millennial employees may not intuitively feel a sense of belonging to a corporation, they do feel a sense of belonging to a group of likeminded people – those who are open to collaboration and whose actions align with the "higher order," inspirational values that millennials appreciate. Basing your employee incentive program on core values should improve other key performance indicators (KPIs) as well, by inspiring collaboration, sales growth, and better customer service.

As you begin to make changes to your organizational culture to appeal to a millennial workforce, it can also be effective to make community outreach and charity part of your focus. Millennials are idealistic and value the opportunity to give back. On that note, offering the ability to redeem reward points toward charitable donations is an important part of an employee incentive program for millennial workers.

Rewards That Motivate Millennial Employees

When it comes to choosing rewards for millennial employee programs, there are two words to keep in mind: *lifestyle* and *experience.* Millennials value rewards that enhance their experience or lifestyle, such as kayaks, bike racks, camping gear, concert tickets, or travel opportunities. Connected electronics are also popular with millennials.

While millennials spend more on travel and leisure activities than past generations, growing up in the recession has also made them mindful of keeping money in their pockets, so it's savvy to provide gift cards and certificates for services they already use as part of your rewards program. Certificates to Uber Eats, Amazon, and various streaming services, which millennials use to facilitate their lifestyle, are popular redemption categories.

Travel, whether it's the ability to redeem points towards plane tickets and hotel rooms or a group incentive travel trip for top performers, is also an effective reward for millennials, who have a strong desire to see the world and experience life. One of the most successful sales promotions we facilitated involved an incentive travel event. For the small price of flying out several hundred of their top-performing in-store reps to a movie premiere, a billion-dollar cellphone company was able to increase its sales nationwide.

Beyond that, rewards that inspire a sense of community among millennial employees are also strong motivators. Rewarding millennials with catered lunches, trips to the bowling alley, or other inclusive activities is a good way to build camaraderie and personalize your relationship with employees.

USING MARKETING TACTICS TO ROLL OUT A SUCCESSFUL EMPLOYEE RECOGNITION PROGRAM

Aon's "2018 Trends in Global Employee Engagement" report identified rewards and recognition as the top worldwide opportunity for increasing engagement, and it's no surprise. As the war for talent and retention heats up, many companies are investing a significant amount of time and effort into crafting enterprise-wide recognition programs designed to give employees a fun and rewarding work culture.

But even the most thoughtfully designed and robust recognition program will struggle if simple things like the program theme, award rules, and enthusiasm are poorly communicated to employees leading up to its launch. Pre- and post-launch marketing campaigns are largely unsung keys to recognition program success. When done well, they can maximize initial program participation, keep people engaged, and be a main channel for communicating goals.

Here are three tips for developing energetic recognition program marketing that sets clear intentions and builds peak awareness:

Tip #1: Develop a Brand

When you think about consumer products, the most successful ones have strong brand awareness and a clear, succinct message. Your employee recognition program can be made more meaningful and memorable with a catchy name, logo, and tagline – just like a consumer brand. How you choose to name your program will depend on factors that include:

- *Organizational culture.* Would your audience respond better to a traditional, descriptive program name, or would an inspirational or aspirational name resonate more?
- *Program objectives.* A name could reflect the behaviors that the program is designed to reward. For example, excellence in customer service or operational outcomes like patient health or increased efficiency.
- *New or relaunched program.* A recognition program that's being revitalized could have a name that reflects its evolution or growth, while a new program wouldn't need that kind of differentiation from its predecessor.

Once you've selected a program name, take the time to clarify a few brief messages about the program and the key points you want the audience to understand. This is often called the *value proposition* and should distill the main benefits and goals into a few short phrases. These phrases will be used in the program's promotional materials and by all parties who talk about the program. Clarity and consistency are the hallmarks of a good message.

A program tagline isn't required, but it further reinforces the name and key messages with a catchy identifier. It's an added dimension that provides an opportunity to engage the audience and motivate them to participate.

Tip #2: Choose Appropriate Communication Channels

Distribution channels for your message go hand-in-hand with the types of communication your audience will receive. You're essentially asking the question "how will our audience learn about the program?" The answers will be as diverse as the audience itself and their working environments:

- *Office-based employees* may spend all day on their computers, where they live and die by email, or get their news from a company intranet.
- *Production floor or warehouse employees* might interact with the organization via kiosk, hard copy newsletters, or announcements and videos in the break room.
- *Remote workers or field reps* who are always on the go might be accessing work-related information in transit, chatting, or sending text messages on their mobile devices.
- *Retail or hospitality associates* may rely on local or regional managers for updates or largely connect at home or via mobile device to a training or benefits portal.

When you have a clear understanding of how employees engage with the organization, you'll be able to match your communications with the best delivery channels.

Tip #3: Create a Strategic Launch Plan

If you've done all this preparation work, don't let the program fizzle through a failure to launch. This is where creating a plan and sticking to it will carry you over the finish line. Good project plans have clear deadlines and achievable milestones that steadily move the project toward completion. They also actively involve needed resources and stakeholders from the earliest phases of the initiative.

Depending on the size, geographic distribution and structure of your organization, you may adopt a phased roll-out approach. For a multinational enterprise, it might make sense to go country-by-country or do one or two languages at a time. For a smaller company, it could be manageable to have a single kick-off launch. Choose the best strategy for your workforce.

Your launch plan is also the vehicle for keeping senior leadership informed. Make sure leadership is fully on board with the introduction of the recognition program and has committed their support. Since managers and supervisors will be on the front line of awarding recognition and answering questions from employees, they need to be familiar with the program before it is introduced so they can serve as advocates.

Think Like a Marketer

Human resources professionals that apply high-level marketing concepts to kickstart a new or revitalize an existing employee recognition program help generate more awareness and enthusiasm for their initiatives. It all starts with knowing your audience. While you've likely given significant thought to the kinds of recognition that your employees value, you may not yet have considered how your employees will receive the program – that's where marketing comes in.

At its most basic principle, marketing is about communicating what an audience needs to hear in exactly the way they want to hear it. While that's certainly a simplification, it's a helpful one for HR professionals charged with companywide initiatives like an employee recognition program. If you take the time to craft your key messages and deliver them across multiple channels, you'll reach everyone effectively. Then, let the recognition and rewards begin.

THE ROLE OF RECOGNITION IN THE EMPLOYEE EXPERIENCE

"Employee engagement," once the paramount focus in human resources, has evolved into the idea of "employee experience," which envelops any and all factors that contribute to an employee's satisfaction, from engagement to wellness to physical environment. The end goal of building positive relationships with employees, however, remains. Employees who have a positive relationship with their employer perform better, contribute more, and positively impact the organization's profitability. In fact, Deloitte Insights found that 80 percent of executives rated employee experience as "important" or "very important," but only 22 percent said they are excellent at building one.

What's the Motivation?

Before employee experience was recognized as a concept, organizations focused on narrower measures of employee satisfaction, such as whether workers liked their benefits and compensation or felt that their boss supported them. These are all important factors on their own, but employee satisfaction is largely a qualitative assessment of how happy or unhappy an employee is at work.

Human capital professionals realized that some areas of satisfaction couldn't necessarily be quantified, so they began to look at measures that would translate how people felt about their jobs into how "engaged" they were. Employee engagement became a key performance indicator, using data analytics to correlate metrics such as absenteeism and turnover with productivity and revenue.

Engagement is largely an indicator of how motivated employees are to do their jobs, and it manifests in their behavior. Gallup defines engagement as employees having basic psychological needs met that are required for performance. Some needs are more straightforward, such as knowing what's expected in the job and having the materials or equipment to do it properly.

Other needs are emotional or social, and not always so straightforward. In his widely referenced TED Talk on motivation, expert Dan Pink examined what keeps people engaged with their jobs and proposed that in the business world, the desire to do more for personal reasons – "intrinsic motivators" – are important drivers. Pink outlined these drivers as autonomy to direct our own lives; mastery and the urge to get better or develop skills; and purpose, the need to do what we do for reasons bigger than ourselves.

In addition to intrinsic motivators, people also thrive on extrinsic motivators, those that originate outside the individual. In a business setting, these take the form of rewards from the organization, such as money, praise, and positive feedback. Formalized employee reward and recognition programs offer extrinsic motivation for people to do a good job. The entire gamut of intrinsic and extrinsic motivators is what adds up to the employee experience.

What Works When

When Gallup examined the difference between engagement and experience, they found an employee's complete experience in the workplace moves through seven stages: attract, hire, onboard, engage, perform, develop and depart. It is also influenced by several other aspects of their workplace, like their manager, role, team, workspace, wellbeing, purpose, brand, and culture.

Employees spend most of their time in three of the seven employee experience stages: engagement, performance and development, where building strength and purpose, driving expectations and career growth present the best opportunities for companies to make a lasting impression on them. Recognition programs at these stages can have a significant impact on the overall employee experience.

- *Recognition that boosts engagement.* Employees value knowing that their work is appreciated and that their contributions have been noticed. Whether it's verbal praise, public recognition, or a premium parking spot, reward programs provide positive reinforcement for a job well done. The Cheesecake Factory recognizes its frontline workforce through an initiative called "Wow Stories," a collection of stories that share associates' outstanding service across the organization. Reinforcing and praising positive behaviors – like putting in extra hours or finding a unique solution to a problem – keeps employees motivated and coming into work with vigor and enthusiasm because it helps them realize that what they are doing matters.
- *Recognition that enhances performance.* One of the best ways to encourage future performance is to offer incentives or rewards for achieving individual, departmental, and organizational objectives. It's important to keep in mind that incentives need to be tied to measurable goals that can be accomplished in a reasonable period of time, such as a month or a quarter. We often think of incentives as associated with meeting sales goals, but organizations are increasingly using cash and noncash incentives to drive particular behaviors and meet other kinds of performance objectives, like reducing safety incidents.
- *Recognition through training and development.* Most people want to learn and are motivated by the chance to enhance their proficiencies or gain new skills. Employer-provided training, attendance at conferences and workshops are all good ways to recognize and retain employees. Supermarket chain Wegmans invested $50 million in employee training in 2017, which included programs to help workers gain specific skills or move into management positions. Professional development opportunities are a clear demonstration that the company values the individual

by investing in their future. Once employees have attained a particular level of professional development, they should be recognized for that accomplishment, too.

Organizations can structure employee recognition programs in many ways, but with the increased focus on the employee experience it is important to evaluate whether the program is providing adequate opportunities for recognition across these three important stages. Viewing a rewards and recognition program through this lens helps maintain organizational focus on a positive, end-to-end employee experience.

11 The Cornerstone of a Global Employee Engagement Strategy

Far from being the latest buzzword, employee experience is turning into the key element of the future-proof workplace. It's time to change the outdated twentieth-century mindset that dismisses employees as dispensable and infinitely replaceable and instead recognize that business *is* all about people.

The employer–employee relationship has changed. While the employer had the power in the last century, that balance is shifting in this century, and potential employees are being choosier about which opportunities they accept.

Just as user experience is driving the digital interface, and as customer satisfaction programs morph into the customer experience, we need to refocus our people strategies to improve the entire employee experience. Forward-thinking organizations are broadening their focus from engagement and culture to a holistic perspective that considers an individual's experience before, during, and after a career within the company.

It's not an isolated phenomenon: The 2017 Global Human Capital Trends report by Deloitte found the attention on employee experience is gaining momentum. While organizational culture, engagement, and employee brand proposition remain top priorities, employee experience ranks as a major trend:

- 80 percent of executives rated employee experience very important (42 percent) or important (38 percent), but only 22 percent reported that their companies excelled at building a differentiated employee experience.
- 59 percent of survey respondents reported that they were not ready or only somewhat ready to address the employee experience challenge.

WHAT IS THE EMPLOYEE EXPERIENCE?

It starts before you even join an organization and continues long after. It's inclusive rather than exclusive, and answers three critical questions for each person:

1. *Future employee:* Why would I come and work for your company?
2. *Current employee:* Why do I choose to stay at this company?
3. *Former employee:* What do I tell others about my time at your company?

The employee experience is the sum of all employee interactions with his or her employer, in and outside of work, and is influenced by many things, including:

- *Relationships:* Quality of the connections and interactions with coworkers, bosses, and customers.
- *Workspace:* The physical environment in which an employee works.
- *Culture:* How an employer demonstrates its commitment to the physical, emotional, and professional success, as well as the health and financial well-being, of its employees.
- *Technology:* The tools and technologies an employer provides to help employees get their work done.

Is Experience the Same as Engagement?

Well, not really. It reminds me of the statement, "All Hoovers are vacuum cleaners, but not all vacuum cleaners are Hoovers." In a similar vein, "All employee experience programs consider engagement, but not all engagement programs consider the employee experience." Clear?

Despite all the care, attention, and resources lavished on employee engagement programs since it first came to prominence nearly 30 years ago, the needle has barely moved. Engagement numbers remain abysmally low. Gallup reports that 87 percent of employees worldwide are actively disengaged and that employee disengagement costs in the United States alone run in the range of $450 billion to $550 billion annually.

The challenge is that engagement scores are a snapshot in time, often completed annually (or less frequently), and many factors influence the results. For example: "Did I get my bonus last week?" "Do I like my boss?" "Are we doing yet another reorganization?" Engagement scores are a lagging indicator of your employee experience efforts. If you aren't investing in the holistic experience, then you'll forever be playing catchup.

It's time for a new approach – one that builds on the foundation of culture and engagement to focus on a more comprehensive employee experience, considering all the contributors to worker satisfaction, engagement, and wellness. This can help create a place where people want (not just need) to go to work each day.

The employee experience is not what you hope employees think about your company – it's what they actually say to their family, friends, and, perhaps more importantly, to the world.

Why Now?

In researching our book, *The Future-Proof Workplace*, Dr. Linda Sharkey and I had the opportunity to interview leaders around the world about their experience of organizational cultures, both good and bad. We heard tales of inspiring workplaces that enabled employees to thrive and of the toxic environments that crushed motivation and left careers in tatters. In our work with business leaders and teams around the world, we find too many companies are missing out – still operating according to twentieth-century mindsets, practices, and technologies.

Heather Scallan, senior vice president of Global Human Resources at NTT Security told me, "It's putting the employee in the driving seat. Successful businesses think deeply about their customer/client experience, and we need to think about our employees in a similar way. The competitive talent marketplace demands that organizations do everything they can to make the employee experience as positive as possible. It's no longer just a differentiator; it is fast becoming a requirement."

Understanding and improving the employee experience is critical for companies operating in a highly competitive global economy. The skills shortage across industries remains an ever-present challenge. As Dan Pink observed, "Talented people need organizations less than organizations need talented people." Providing an engaging employee experience helps companies succeed in attracting and retaining skilled employees, and research shows a strong employee experience also drives a strong customer experience.

Sir Richard Branson has a reputation for building companies around happy and engaged workforces, and as Chris Boyce, CEO of Virgin Pulse wrote, "Your employees are your company's real competitive advantage. They're the ones making the magic happen – so long as their needs are being met."

It's common sense, but with an uncommon discipline.

DO YOU HAVE THE CULTURE YOU WANT OR DESERVE?

A strong employee experience influences more than just your engagement numbers or Glassdoor reviews. These are the lagging indicators of employee experience.

Jacob Morgan, author of The Employee Experience Advantage, shares that organizations that invest in their employee experience were:

- Included 28 times more often among Fast Company's Most Innovative Companies
- Listed 11.5 times as often in Glassdoor's Best Places to Work
- Listed 2.1 times as often on the Forbes list of the World's Most Innovative Companies
- Appeared 4.4 times as often in LinkedIn's list of North America's Most In-Demand Employers
- Twice as often found in the American Customer Satisfaction Index

His research goes on to report that those companies investing in their employee experience "had more than four times the average profit and more than two times the average revenue." It makes a compelling case for action. If you aren't actively focused on creating and nurturing your employee experience, you will end up with the organizational performance and reputation you deserve, not the one you want. In the age of smart phones, we are all aspiring paparazzi – just one click away from having your dirty laundry making headline news. Forget the six degrees of separation: In the twenty-first century, it's closer to two degrees of connection. If good news travels fast, bad news travels even faster.

Who knew, the best companies are people-focused and invest in creating an environment where it's possible (and even expected) that employees love their jobs? Are your employees in love with coming to work? Do you know what people are saying about your organization?

It's Not about the Ping-Pong Table

It's going to take more than bright colors, a ping-pong table, or the latest in standing desks to tackle the employee experience challenge.

Silicon Valley firms have long been held up as the poster-children for the new-age office, offering a myriad of perks and environments for their employees. Whether it's gyms, professional kitchens with all-you-can-eat food, gaming facilities, music equipment and sound stages, bean bag chairs and slides, fancy coffee (with baristas), food trucks, or concierge services, no wonder people work long hours. Why would they want, or need, to be anywhere else?

It's certainly helped to attract the talent those Silicon Valley firms need. However, there is hope for the small and medium-sized enterprise. It turns out that these perks may be distractions from what is really creating the high-powered workplace of the twenty-first century.

The employee experience seeks to create the right environment around the needs of the workforce, rather than trying to fit the workforce around the needs of the work or the building.

Don't Focus on Exit Interviews

In the past, employee engagement or culture initiatives have been the purview of human resources. It's a "people problem," so let the people team handle it. And they did, to the best of their ability, while also juggling learning and development, benefits programs, career mapping, and performance management – often as separate projects, each with their own measures of success.

While short-term gains were made, long-term impact was not achieved. As a result, every few years, each initiative was dusted off, rebranded, and relaunched. Unfortunately, credibility was eroded each time, with employees rolling their eyes at yet another "unifying" drive.

The key to creating a powerful employee experience is to involve employees in the process and move beyond the campfire songs and (de)motivational posters. Instead, engage the very people at the heart of your business, seek out and listen to the feedback from your employees (see Sidebar 11.1).

At SendGrid Inc., the key was to identify the opportunities to improve experiences people were having as they tried to do their daily job. According to Pattie Money, chief people officer, "We identified the bottlenecks and barriers, where were systems breaking down and making the job harder than it needed to be, where were managers not building strong relationships or providing the right level of support. We then developed the training and tools to include in their management toolkit that enabled managers to better understand the experience of their direct reports and make the changes necessary to affect the experience in positive ways."

Don't just focus on exit interviews and why people are leaving. Also analyze the new hire experience. Why did they choose to join your organization? Who turned down offers, and what influenced their decision? What is your onboarding experience like – was a computer and desk ready for your new hire on their first day? Did colleagues welcome them into the team and help them to integrate into the organization or did they eat that first lunch alone?

We have one client who ensures that a "welcome box" of donuts is on each new recruit's desk on their first day, which helps to ensure that team members from far and wide stop by to say hello and start bringing the new hire into the fold. How willing are your employees to refer others to join your organization? Think of it as your internal net promoter score.

LinkedIn Corp. and Accenture plc both host HR hackathons, where employees help break down and rebuild the people and HR functions to reflect the work that they really do (and need to do). An effective employee experience isn't a one-size-fits-all solution. Even though the trend is global, and the focus is organization-wide, successful approaches may vary by geography and region.

Sidebar 11.1 All Aboard the Employee Experience Train

This is all well and good, but where do you start? Dr. Linda Sharkey shared with me her advice for embarking on your employee experience journey:

- **Get the facts.** Don't rely on what you believe the current culture to be or what you hope for. Use a valid and reliable instrument to measure your culture so you know exactly where you stand.
- **Define your desired state.** Ask your current and former employees what the culture needs to be to enhance the employee experience. With this information in hand you can start to design your strategy to close the gaps.

- **Pick one or two gaps and really work on them.** It is likely addressing just one or two will have a ripple effect and close other gaps as well. Make the employee experience approach and discussion part of your regular DNA – just like you would have financial and customer reviews, have regular fact-based culture and employee experience reviews.
- **Become the "undercover boss."** Experience your recruiting and hiring processes. Do they live up to the employee experience culture you aspire to have? Often these are the first experiences a candidate has of your company, and let's be real, most recruiting processes are awful from a candidate perspective. Ghosting (never hearing back), automated systems that suck up resumes like a black hole never to be returned, multiple hoops and interviews (often with the same ill-prepared questions being asked) to "win a role" in the company. Be honest: If you recognize any of these symptoms as part of your recruiting process, if you are thinking "but we can't possibly communicate with all candidates, there are just too many, ghosting is just a fact of life," then you need to stop right here. This is the first place to start to improve your employee experience, and you didn't need an assessment tool to uncover it. If you treated your customers as you treat your potential candidates, I am sure that there would be conversations happening at the highest levels!

GE regularly brought back former employees to take their pulse on how they viewed the company. Don't shy away from the tough questions, regularly ask "How can we continue to build a better employee experience?" and don't be afraid of the answers.

Here is my approach for any leader seeking to improve their employee experience, and if you use these consistently, you will have a thriving employee and customer focused organization:

1. **Ask.** Learn to ask the questions of current, future, and past employees.
2. **Listen.** Really hear what is being said, not what you want to hear.
3. **Think.** Reflect on what is being said.
4. **Respond.** Most importantly, act. This is all fruitless spinning unless you commit to take action.
5. **Repeat.** Make these behaviors part of you daily routine.

WE HAD IT BACKWARD

Twentieth-century HR was largely reactive, but twenty-first-century HR must become more intentional and proactive. The twentieth-century approach to business was to prioritize stakeholders as shareholders first, customers second and employees third. We now realize we had it backwards. If we put employees first, they in turn take care of our customers, and they in turn take care of our shareholders. It's like the safety briefing on an airplane. You must put your oxygen mask on first before you can take care of others.

Today's organizations need leaders who apply as much effort to the people portfolio as they do the rest of the other levers that drive organizational performance. An integrated employee experience is as valuable and can have as much (or more) of an impact as other elements of your corporate strategy.

Understanding the workforce in a more detailed way means we can understand individual aspirations, skill preferences and how these intersect with company values. As a result, we can truly align personal goals with company goals in a very clear way.

The employee experience is far more than an HR initiative: It is a business imperative. One that is influenced and needs to be driven from the top of the organization. Every leader needs to consider themselves a chief people officer. I believe that the employee experience is the next big area of investment for every organization. We may be experiencing a digital revolution, but it's those who embrace the people revolution who will thrive.

I dare you to act. If you can create a future-proof workplace that considers the employee experience, there will be no stopping you.

Recognition: A Key Driver of Engagement

In 2013, "employee engagement" averaged one tweet per minute. In 2020, Google rendered approximately 4.3 billion results for the term. Walk into a room full of human resources leaders and start droning on about all the wonderful benefits of engagement – you will likely be met with a fair amount of glazed-over stares.

We get it. HR practitioners around the globe have long since connected the dots between how engagement impacts employee retention, performance, and all the other metrics that lead to bottom-line success.

Although the "engagement crisis" may be considered cliché within HR circles, there is ample evidence suggesting that the situation will continue to get more dire. Economic conditions in many parts of the world are improving, increasing the volume of unfilled job openings while the talent pool gradually shrinks, the skill gap across many industries widens and average job tenure declines.

The fact that global engagement levels largely remain stagnant year over year – they haven't budged in the last decade – is just one of many indicators that the engagement and retention strategies of the past aren't cutting it today.

The Missing Link for Multinational Corporations

Although it would be a colossal oversimplification to claim that one solution alone is enough to have a sustainable, lasting impact on performance, one fact remains true: Whether you're looking at analyst data, academia, or thought leadership from consulting houses, it's unequivocally indisputable that recognition is one of the top drivers of engagement. Employees simply can't be inspired to do their best work if they feel like the people around them routinely fail to acknowledge their contributions.

However, implementing an effective recognition strategy is more complicated for global organizations and not just because of time zone differences and linguistic barriers.

A tremendous amount of nuance exists internationally when it comes to recognition culture and preferences. For example, in Japanese culture, a notion exists that praise implies there is no room for further enhancement, which violates the spirit of *kaizen* (continuous improvement). In the Netherlands, if an individual gets formally recognized for performing basic job duties, a Dutch phrase exists to describe the sender of the recognition that roughly translates to "you need to be more cool." Historically in Russian society, there's a deeply rooted belief that community should supersede individual needs, so incorporating a touch of humor into moments of praise can be used to mitigate any potential awkwardness in the public recognition of an individual. And in Korea, a term for "recognized" doesn't even exist.

However, as Razor Suleman, founder of I Love Rewards, explains, "Although recognition is vastly different around the world, we all have a deep biological human need to be appreciated." And indeed, the science supports the idea that the need for recognition is universal. Regardless of an individual's country of origin, there's consistency from a neurological perspective when recognition is received: Praise ignites a hit of dopamine in the brain, which is associated with a temporary emotional high and uplift in performance.

USING DATA TO FIND GLOBAL INSIGHTS

Dr. Natalie Baumgartner, chief workforce scientist of Achievers' Workforce Institute (WFI), explains that using global data can help uncover the story it tells about the role of the employee voice and how different types of recognition can play in engagement and retention strategies.

"We're able to analyze how social recognition across an organization, or even a department or location, impacts turnover, engagement scores, customer satisfaction – or really any metric that's reliably being measured," she said.

Although the WFI's Insight Papers and correlation studies have identified trends unique to specific regions and countries around the world, the most fascinating findings they've uncovered have to do with the characteristics successful recognition programs hold in common. Namely, they discovered that high frequency recognition programs were consistently associated with the most significant increases in employee engagement and decreases in turnover.

Recognition Must Be Frequent

Here's the thing; Nothing in life works unless it's consistent: learning a new language, training a puppy, exercise. You'd never show up to the gym three or four times a year and expect bodily transformation. Recognition is no different. *In order to have a sustained, lasting impact on engagement, recognition must be frequent.*

Regardless of the variance in cultural and societal norms surrounding recognition, it is clear that all the benefits of recognition are, unfortunately, extremely short lived – and much shorter than organizations previously assumed.

So, that begs the question: What's the magic number? How often should employees be recognized?

According to Gallup, "Recognition is a short-term need that has to be satisfied on an ongoing basis – weekly, maybe daily." Based on WFI's 19 years of recognition data, organizations that average one unique recognition received per employee per month tend to experience the strongest measurable impacts on engagement scores, regardless of the industry, geographical location or variances in employee demographics.

"One recognition per employee every 30 days seems to be the tipping point associated with the most predictable improvements to retention and other key metrics, such as customer satisfaction or performance scores," Baumgartner said. "Recognition programs that average at least eight recognitions per employee per year can still move the needle on employee performance and engagement, but those programs with 12 recognitions per year – or more – represent the 'sweet spot' where we start to see true organizational transformation."

But How Do We Get There?

The most vital consideration global organizations need to take into account to reach optimal levels of recognition frequency involves decoupling rewards from recognition.

Although program design recommends a blended approach – offering both social recognition and localized rewards – no organization in the world has unlimited budget to award employees every time they exhibit positive behavior. The good news is that studies show nonmonetary recognition can have just as powerful an impact as rewards-based recognition.

Professor Alex Stajkovic from the University of Wisconsin compared the impact of non-monetary and monetary recognition programs on job performance. At baseline, recognition associated with rewards tended to result in slightly higher performance increases than non-monetary recognition – 23 percent vs. 17 percent, respectively. However, when cost-benefit analyses are performed, non-monetary recognition often prove to be more cost effective with maximizing budget.

Social recognition isn't just good for optimizing reward spend. People are wired to crave meaningful praise. One study found that 66 percent of people said their top motivator was appreciation vs. 15 percent who said financial reward. Furthermore, a values-based, peer-to-peer recognition that's specific to why the demonstrated behavior was appreciated and that outlines the overall impact can foster a sense of connection and belonging that breaks down distance between departments, hierarchies and borders.

"When non-monetary recognition is normalized and employees view rewards as being separate from recognition, an organization has effectively fostered a culture of appreciation, which is why our recommendation for global organizations is to strive for at least 50 percent nonmonetary recognition," said Vanessa Brangwyn, chief customer officer at Achievers.

"At the point employees embrace the intrinsic value of the recognition itself and are no longer expectant of rewards, recognition levels will increase and serve to amplify your core values, so they are integrated into the daily workflows of employees," she added.

Rehumanize the Workplace to Gain the Advantage

Creating a thoughtful, people-centric employee experience that has a measurable impact on success metrics outside of HR involves challenging previously held assumptions about employee motivation and embracing the truth that employees want to show up to work for a reason other than a paycheck.

The time has come for HR leaders to acknowledge that the collective mindset, expectations, and values of the workforce have drastically changed over the last decade and relying on top-down, infrequent, traditional recognition programs is not an effective way of aligning and engaging geographically dispersed or siloed teams.

If the end goal is to bolster overall performance and profitability, frequent, peer-led, nonmonetary recognition shouldn't be viewed as just a component to overarching total rewards or engagement strategy – it must be the cornerstone.

Use Positive Psychology to Boost Performance

Positive psychology, when used as part of continuous performance management and a comprehensive talent strategy, has been shown to address many workforce challenges.

Positive psychology focuses on building positive emotions, enabling people to innovate, grow and inspire others. What are the concrete tools an organization can use to leverage this powerful framework within performance development and the employee experience? Here are some examples.

Build Gratitude into Check-ins

According to Martin Seligman of the Positive Psychology Center at the University of Pennsylvania, gratitude is the positive emotion "felt after being the beneficiary of some sort of gift. It is also a social emotion often directed towards the person (the giver of a gift)."

Expressing gratitude during manager/employee check-ins builds positive connections and establishes a strong frame of reference for the rest of the meeting. Here are some tips for building gratitude into check-ins:

- Allocate a few minutes within each check-in to discuss positive outcomes and behaviors. Even simple questions like, "What went well this week?" or "What are we celebrating today?" can set a positive tone.
- Discuss how teams have collaborated to move projects along and encourage employees to give their peers recognition.

Inspire Peer-to-Peer Gratitude to Build Connection

The check-in is not the only place to create gratitude moments. Showing gratitude should be encouraged up and down the organization, whether peer-to-peer or manager-to-employee. It must be sincere and authentic to create a sense of positivity for both the giver and the receiver. Some things to consider when giving gratitude:

- Leverage storytelling to fuel positivity. Instead of saying, "That was a great presentation," you may want to elaborate and say, "When you presented the product strategy today, I was able to fully understand why we are changing direction based on the customer insight you provided. When you were describing the customer, I felt like I was there with the customer experiencing the same issues."
- Avoid lengthy processes for an employee to express their gratitude. Make expressing gratitude simple, easy and inspirational, without unnecessary overhead.

Drive Learning with Feedback

Although positive emotions are less intense, they play an essential role in building resilience and regulating negative emotions. One way to use positive emotions is in the process of giving and receiving constructive feedback. If not provided correctly, constructive feedback can have a detrimental impact on productivity and morale. Positive psychology researchers recommend the number of positive moments to negative moments should be three-to-one to build trust and connection. Here are some ways positive psychology can improve the process:

- Start from a place of positivity and goodwill. Implement a well-funded social recognition program that allows everyone to give and receive recognition for good work in the moment, as it happens.
- Feedback should be actionable, future-focused, and something an employee can immediately put to use. For example, instead of saying, "You did a terrible job connecting with the audience at last week's presentation," try, "Next time you present, try connecting with the audience throughout the presentation. I have several tools I can send you that may help."

Build Connections with Empathy

We've all heard the saying, "Put yourself in their shoes." This is essentially a call for empathy – the ability to relate to the thoughts, emotions, or experience of others. When leaders display empathy, they reinforce a personal interest, reassurance, and acceptance of their employees. Here are some ways people leaders can use empathy in their check-ins:

- Focus on the discussion as well as the emotional response of the employee. 80 percent of communication is non-verbal, so pay attention to tone and body language.
- Before responding to questions and comments, pause to think about the other person's perspective. For example, when an employee says they are frustrated about a particular situation, try to see the challenge from their point of view, instead of immediately perceiving it as a complaint.

Embrace Strengths

Positive psychology research shows when people leverage their strengths they are more engaged and energized by their work. Martin Seligman and other researchers have found "when work demands our engagement, such as using our strengths in new and innovative ways, we experience higher levels of happiness and lower levels of depression." Consider the following tips to help employees leverage their strengths and increase positivity and engagement:

- Give each person a strengths-based assessment and review the results to collaborate on how those strengths can be leveraged to meet business goals.
- Create a safe environment for openly discussing both strengths and weaknesses. In this type of environment, someone could say, "Mike, could I ask for your input on creating some good questions? Curiosity is not one of my strengths."

Ensure Employees Have Focus Time

Flow is a mental state of focused attention so intense that a person nearly loses their sense of time. Being in flow amplifies performance, according to Steven Kotler, benefiting both the employee and the organization. It has also been shown to increase positivity and engagement.

A person is more likely to enter a flow state when they are working on tasks that both challenge them and leverage their skillset. Here are some ways to help employees increase their productivity through flow:

- Give employees focused time each day where they are not interrupted. Research indicates that switching between tasks costs an individual as much as 40 percent of their productivity. Try blocking particular hours of the day as focus timed when meetings cannot be scheduled.
- When creating goals, balance challenge and skill. As people rise to manageable challenges, they gain the confidence to accomplish increasingly more difficult goals.

Embed a Growth Mindset into HR and Talent Processes

Gallup has found that one of the top benefits that employees want from their employer is the opportunity to learn and grow. Here is where growth mindset, a key concept from positive psychology, can help. According to researcher Carol Dwick, growth mindset is when a person believes that their abilities and skills and those of others can be improved with effort. To embed a growth mindset within your organization, consider the following:

- Human resources and talent processes should be evaluated to ensure they focus on learning and growth. For example, in the interview process, ask questions to understand if a candidate has a growth mindset. A former Starbucks executive said she asks candidates about challenging work experiences to help discern whether a candidate is willing to learn from their mistakes.
- Have leaders add "yet" to statements of limitation. For example, "We can't do this – yet." Just adding this one word helps overcome the perception of negativity in the face of challenges.
- Leaders should be encouraged to use inclusive language such as "we" and "us" to create a sense of shared purpose and community when speaking with their teams.

Trigger Resilience and Grit During Goal Setting

Angela Duckworth, noted researcher from the University of Pennsylvania and TEDx speaker, defines grit as the "perseverance and passion for long-term goals." Resilience is the optimism to continue even when you've experienced failure. Both resilience and grit can be used to facilitate organizational and employee growth.

- Goals should be reviewed continuously throughout the year and adjusted as needed. Short-term, achievable goals tied to the longer-term corporate strategy help employees foster grit and motivation. For example, one goal could be to focus on three new marketing campaigns for new customer acquisition, which is tied to a corporate goal of increasing revenue by 10 percent.
- When you experience challenges in meeting a goal, consider bringing the key players together for collaboration, reflection, and an open discussion to dig into what happened and how to keep things moving forward.

AMPLIFYING THE EMPLOYEE EXPERIENCE THROUGH TARGETED ENGAGEMENT EFFORTS

One in three employees in the United States will leave their jobs this year to work for another organization, according to projections from the Work Institute.

As business leaders and human resources professionals are keenly aware, each time an employee chooses to leave their organization, the business must invest in funding recruitment efforts and training of the replacement hires. In addition to these overhead costs, high turnover rates lead to a decrease in overall employee effectiveness and productivity.

As organizations continue their search to uncover the reasons for these increasing turnover rates, new research conducted by market and strategy research firm Chadwick Martin Bailey (CMB) suggests that the role of employees' psychological benefits should not be overlooked.

CMB, a subsidiary of ITA Group, found that a consistent employee experience amplified by targeted engagement efforts during the critical one-to-two-year tenure range will position businesses to effectively retain the talent they need to ensure organizational success.

Up the Engagement Ante

Through their research, CMB explored what organizations must do to connect with and engage employees on a deeper psychological level. Through a survey of 1,466 workers of varied tenure and roles across nine industries, CMB's findings validated the impact of what they call "psychological benefits" on employee engagement.

The survey results show that there are five key psychological benefits that motivate employee advocacy:

- Personal identity
- Social identity
- Cultural identity
- Emotional benefits
- Functional benefits

Out of these five, the three identity benefits – personal, social, and cultural – play an especially vital role in inspiring stronger employee engagement and retention. Personal identity is particularly notable, as it focuses on an individual's self-esteem and pride in working for an organization. Organizations can support this benefit by aligning and reinforcing a sense of shared purpose across employees.

Leadership should begin fostering these important psychological benefits from the time talent is recruited and continue throughout the onboarding process and beyond.

Focus on Improving the Employee Experience

The new research by CMB shows that organizations effectively reinforcing the psychological benefits are approximately three times as likely to have an engaged and loyal workforce. In an effort to bring greater consistency to the employee experience, organizations should consider focusing specific, targeted engagement efforts on employees who have been with the organization at least one year, but less than three years.

Essential steps to improving the employee experience among this segment include:

1. *Meeting them where they are.* Take time to understand the needs and desired support of people with one-to-three years of tenure. Use this feedback to guide your decisions about what type of programs, initiatives and other support your organization will offer.
2. *Capitalizing on known onboarding success.* Often, employees are simply struggling to adjust to the lack of consistent support they may have felt during initial onboarding. Consider expanding the onboarding process through initiatives like extended welcome programs, roundtable conversations specific to employees at different stages of the employee journey or periodic celebrations for smaller achievements.
3. *Reinforcing people-to-people connections.* To support emotional connection and cultural cohesion, create more opportunities for team members to connect with their peers outside of their departments or projects, such as through employee resource groups, interest clubs, organization-sponsored events, mentorships, or volunteer opportunities.
4. *Helping them grow internally before they get the itch to look externally.* Getting ahead of employees' desire to search for other professional opportunities is crucial in the one-to-two-year tenure period. To help them see that you're supportive of their long-term aspirations, consider creating a hierarchy within your hierarchy to enable smaller promotions or investing in building skills for future managers.

Why Onboarding Is Important

When employees first land a new job, they are eager to connect with their organization and peers. CMB's research found that this eagerness also leads to a peak in pride and self-esteem levels during the first year, when employees are most likely to report sentiments such as, "Working at my company makes me feel good about myself," and, "I am proud to tell people that I work for my company."

Organizations that report recent successes in improving engagement often credit their ability to tap into this eagerness, typically by making investments in the onboarding process. This could include developing social network channels specific to new hires or checklists to aid leaders in supporting continued onboarding throughout the first day, week, and month on the job.

An underlying reason that these strategies work is because they are tapping into the identity benefits. When organizations go to greater lengths to build on this inherent excitement, they're nurturing those critical feelings of pride and self-esteem. These positive feelings lead to high levels of engagement but can also lead to an unfortunate consequence if organizations aren't prepared to offer greater support for the long-term.

Avoiding the New-Hire Reality Slump

While it's encouraging to see such positive feelings and strong levels of engagement in new hires, the research also revealed a concerning trend known as the "reality slump."

This term refers to the period in which psychological benefit performance noticeably drops in the one-to-two-year tenure range across all generations and income levels. Oftentimes, employees never fully recover from this dip. Because psychological benefit performance drives employee engagement and retention, this is a critical takeaway for organizations looking to keep their top talent.

During this time, employees are most likely to express interest in exploring roles at other organizations, making them at-risk for turnover. For organizations, these feelings can be costly. According to insights from the Work Institute, the cost of turnover is estimated at 33 percent of a worker's salary, and many sources cite the costs at much larger figures. By understanding and investing in engagement opportunities that more consistently support employees' psychological benefits after the initial onboarding phase, organizations can help mitigate the risk of this occurring among their own new hires.

According to Thomsons, 82 percent of organizations report that their number one global benefits strategic objective is to attract and retain talent. Given this focus, investing in talent personally and professionally to reinforce support for psychological benefits has never been more crucial.

Armed with the knowledge that employees with one or two years of tenure are particularly at-risk to disengage, implementing strategies that positively impact employees' key psychological benefits consistently throughout the employee experience can be the key to avoiding a spike in disengagement and voluntary turnover (see Sidebar 11.2).

Sidebar 11.2 Case Study: Humana's Career Framework

By Stephanie N. Rotondo, WorldatWork

An emphasis on creating personalized consumer experiences that contribute to their members' best health is at the heart of Humana Inc.'s evolution from a traditional insurer to a senior-focused health care company. From just under 10,000 associates in 2003 to over 40,000 associates in 2019, it became apparent that just as their business strategy had evolved, so must their job architecture.

As Humana undertook the process to define their ideal state, one concept was clear to them: the consumer experience cannot exceed that of the employee experience. To deliver meaningful experiences for their consumers, they needed to ensure that the foundation for talent development, performance management, visibility to career opportunities and growth were strengthened for their associates.

At the outset, Humana's job architecture was "showing its age," said Mark Stone, associate vice president of compensation. Because the company no longer fell into a traditional model, its job roles had evolved. "They were not just the typical insurance jobs of a decade-and-a-half ago."

Furthermore, the needs of Humana's customers had changed, as well as the skillsets necessary to address those needs.

But the needs of the company's associates were not being met. According to Stone, associates had limited visibility to the next steps in their careers or the skills they might need to grow their careers.

Instead of tasking human resources, or even just the C-suite, with solving the problem, Humana went right to the source: the associates themselves.

"We wanted to know, from their perspective, what did [the associates] need to create the culture we wanted," said Brian Fisher, director of compensation.

What they discovered was that associates didn't consistently have answers to four fundamental career questions:

- How do I grow my career?
- How do I develop valuable skills?
- How is my contribution reviewed?
- How am I rewarded?

"If an associate can answer those questions, it can improve their experience," Fisher said.

Keeping in mind the perspectives of culture, marketplace and business needs, solutions were discussed, first with leaders within the company and then with associates, where iterations of the solutions unfolded.

"Very few decisions were made in a vacuum," Fisher said.

"This wasn't, from an HR perspective, an off-the-shelf kind of approach," said Michele Phlipot, senior organization effectiveness professional in compensation. "It was co-created [with leadership and associates], something that belonged to everyone."

And thus, Humana's Career Framework was born, a framework that narrowed down job families and skillsets based on consumer-driven and market-based needs. It led to a more consistent and intuitive approach to creating jobs, which were developed around needed skillsets. From there, associates were better able to understand the opportunities that existed.

"From a business perspective, we're defining our jobs based on the needs of our consumer," Fisher said. With the framework in place, "We can more readily recruit and also reward for those skills in a much more effective way."

But Humana also recognized that leadership needed to be prepared for the new conversations they were about to have with employees. As such, they created digital tools to help leaders engage and dynamically explore the new job structure. These tools provided both a vehicle for leaders to map associates from their previous role to a new job, but most importantly, the tools served to introduce leaders to the new structure and educate along the way. On top of that, conversation guides were created to prepare leaders for one-on-one conversations with their associates.

"We really tried to create a consumer-grade experience throughout," Fisher said.

Phlipot noted that there are ongoing efforts to measure and assess the framework to ensure that things are on the right track.

"We know that we are better positioned from a skill perspective," Stone said, adding that "continued measurement is needed."

"We believe our associates are now in a better position to answer those four fundamental questions, thus improving the associate experience," Fisher said.

In turn, Humana aims to improve the experience of the consumer.

PERSONALIZATION OF THE EMPLOYEE EXPERIENCE

Going beyond the fundamental expectations employees have had for many years, there is another workplace revolution underway: personalization of the employee experience.

"Having the ability to personalize work commitments is a priority for many employees, and companies need to start by taking a 'whole person' approach and increasing the flexible work options available to their workforce," said Tim Morrison, HR business partner at Mercer as well as a boundary umpire for the Australian Football League (AFL).

"With intense competition to attract top talent and ensure staff loyalty, it is necessary that companies progress and look towards the future," he said, adding that as an employee and an umpire, he is constantly juggling two careers – and flexible work options enable him to manage both.

And Morrison isn't alone in his need: Mercer's "2017 Global Talent Trends" research found that, as a direct response to the "era of the individual," more than half of employees (56 percent) are looking for more flexible and personalized work arrangements.

"Globalization and technology are making the world smaller and shaping employees' expectations of when and how they want to work and what is of most value to them," said Michele Glover, people and culture leader, Mercer Pacific. "People want their employers to help them invest in themselves and this can mean different things to different people, such as Tim working as an HR business partner and AFL umpire. This type of personalization is what it's all about for people – meeting them where they are in terms of their life stage and interests."

While some employers still expect employees to make work *work* for their individual circumstances, there are some looking to the future of work, taking a whole person approach and increasing the flexible work options they offer. Mercer's research revealed that one in two employees surveyed expressed concern that flex working would negative affect their promotion opportunities.

"Clearly there is more work to be done to create a culture where flexibility is not seen as a benefit, but as an opportunity for workforce optimization and personalization," Glover said. "By embracing flexible working and demonstrating there are career pathways, employers will not only attract and retain talent, they will cultivate a thriving workforce."

A Good Employee Experience Benefits Business

Optimizing employee experience can boost your organization's bottom line. That concept was reinforced by the chief finding in Globoforce's WorkHuman Analytics and Research Institute and IBM Smarter Workforce Institute's study.

The Financial Impact of a Positive Employee Experience developed an "Employee Experience Index" by surveying 22,000 workers in 43 countries. It found that organizations that scored in the top 25 percent in the index report nearly three times the return on assets compared to organizations in the bottom quartile. Further, organizations that score in the top 25 percent report double the return on sales compared to organizations in the bottom quartile.

"We have robust evidence that the employee experience matters from a bottom-line perspective," said Greg Stevens, analytics manager at Globoforce's Human Research Institute.

So, what defines employee experience? Globoforce and IBM, through statistical analyses, identified five components:

- Sense of belonging
- Sense of purpose
- Sense of achievement
- Happiness
- Vigor

"We have 10 items that measure those five components, so two questions per component, and that formed the eventual scale that we validated," Stevens said, "so that it was truly representative of what people said their employee experience was around the globe."

Improving the bottom line is certainly a desirable, direct effect from optimizing the employee experience, but another positive outcome is increased retention, which indirectly contributes to the bottom line. The study found that a positive employee experience leads to a 32 percent increase in performance and a 52 percent decrease in terms of people's likelihood to leave. There is also a 73 percent increase in those people who are likely to go above and beyond their assigned tasks.

Stevens said the study also aimed at finding workplace practices that lead to the bottom-line improvement. The study found six main drivers:

1. *Meaningful work.* The extent to which you see your work connected to the core values of your organization. You feel your organization makes good use of your skills and ability, so there's a degree of fit there that is meaningful.
2. *Empowerment in voice.* The extent to which you feel like you are heard in the organization and you have a chance to participate in decisions that affect your life.
3. *Recognition feedback and growth.* It's less about annual performance reviews than it is about expanding a continuum of performance that centers around continuous conversations, development and opportunities for growth.
4. *Co-worker relationships.* The connection is more and more important in today's human workplaces. Organizations rely less on organizational hierarchies and your work is done more in terms of teams and networks. So those are increasingly important.
5. *Organizational trust.* The expectation that your organization will behave responsibly and that it will act with integrity.
6. *Work–life balance.* Appreciating the fact that who you are doesn't have to change when you walk into the office. You can bring more of yourself to work, but also have more time to nurture connections that you have outside of work.

Employers can instill this workplace environment that fosters the optimal employee experience by combining a variety of different practices, Stevens said. An example is an employee recognition program, which hits on the basic driver of feedback, recognition, and growth.

"That gets you a positive experience above and beyond having no recognition program. But what really supercharges it is when it is tied to core values," Stevens said. "So, you're integrating more of the meaningful work component. Those two combined leads to the most beneficial outcomes to supercharging the employee experience."

From a global standpoint, meaningful work was either first or tied for first across every country as the main driver for a positive employee experience. However, it doesn't just stop at meaningful work. To get the best results, it's important to have multiple drivers.

> *"If work is meaningful, it's good, but if no one sees you experiencing that meaningful work, if you have a lack of connection, if you don't feel like you're appreciated, it can really derail the positive benefits,"* Stevens said. *"So, it's critical to have an integrated approach to thinking about meaningful work."*

12 Corporate Accountability in a Diverse and Inclusive World

In October 2017, actress Alyssa Milano promoted the use of Tarana Burke's "Me Too" Movement on Twitter using the hashtag #MeToo to draw attention to longstanding issues of sexual harassment and workplace intimidation within Hollywood. A few months later, several more actors, producers, executives, and leaders banded together to launch TIME'S UP in response to the growing call for action and activism against this type of misbehavior and abuse. In the wake of these two events, a conversation opened on both the employee and employer sides about misconduct, discrimination, and what diversity and inclusion really mean in contemporary organizations.

Some companies took immediate action, reorganizing their leadership and creating new office policies. Others seem to be taking a systemic approach, weighing out how these behaviors reflect on the organization's overall culture. Both look to increase accountability within the workplace, whether that be through overt or less conspicuous methods. However, making this happen after years of operating the opposite way requires a deeper dive into corporate culture and how accountability fits into the equation.

DEFINING ACCOUNTABILITY

Until recently, culture and accountability weren't necessarily a priority in many workplaces, driven by years of "*that's how we've always done it*" thinking. But in response to #MeToo and TIME'S UP, these two concepts gained additional traction, coming together around a single vision: doing something about issues of harassment and inequality in the workplace.

For this reason, a culture of accountability means that people are responsible for their own behaviors and the impact those behaviors have on their colleagues. For employers, the organization becomes accountable for ensuring that it creates a safe, secure space for their people to come forward if, and when, they feel that they've been wronged, without fear of repercussions. From there, once an employer receives notice of misconduct or wrongdoing, the organization takes steps to investigate and resolve the complaint in accordance with internal policies – or at least, that's how this is supposed to work.

Why We Need It

In November 2018, Google employees organized a large-scale walkout to protest the way the company handled cases of sexual harassment. In New York City alone, more than 3,000 employees assembled in a city park with signs and speeches, calling out Google's "pattern of unethical and thoughtless decision-making." The #GoogleWalkout also took to the sidewalks in and around the company's offices in Dublin and Silicon Valley, leading additional thousands away from their desks and garnering live coverage from the mainstream media and all across social media platforms. However, since then, two of the protest's key organizers report instances of retaliation against them on the part of Google. Demotions, position and title changes, and ultimatums led one protestor, Claire Stapleton, a 12-year veteran of the company, to human resources. That led to heightened issues that required legal action. After months of trying to make the contentious situation amenable to both employee and employer, Stapleton eventually resigned.

This highly visible and well-documented case exemplifies what can happen without accountability, creating a culture where employees experience harassment or discrimination without a viable option for recourse. Over prolonged periods of time, employees become increasingly afraid to speak up, which leaves them to suffering in silence or leaving the organization entirely.

What It Looks Like

Of course, it's not enough to just say that people should be held accountable for their behaviors; organizations need to demonstrate this commitment in daily practice. Employees and employers alike expect this across all parties, and companies need to take active measures to embed this thinking within their cultures.

Accountability is one of the cornerstones of the modern workplace, and it means a zero-tolerance policy against all forms of misconduct, including sexual harassment, bullying, and discrimination, as well as all types of fraud and theft. However, it is imperative that companies take proactive measures to minimize and eradicate these behaviors. Each claim must be investigated confidentially and thoroughly, with every incident of inappropriate behavior addressed. That might mean speaking with a coworker who made a crude joke in a meeting or offered unwelcome advances toward a colleague around the office, up through dismissing someone caught stealing. It is up to leadership to set the tone across the organization, provide the right resources for reporting, and ensure that swift actions take place.

Avoiding the Pitfalls

As evidenced by the situation at Google and referenced sociopolitical movements, failing to address bad behavior can lead to repercussions across an organization and in the public perception. This can directly impact recruiting and hiring, retention, leadership, brand recognition, and profitability, in addition to the risk of legal exposure. The biggest pitfall for a company in 2021 and beyond is not doing anything – especially when employees come forward with information.

Creating and fostering a culture where employees speak up requires that the organization be ready to act once informed of misconduct. The feedback loop should be tight and quick. If a situation surfaces but the employer doesn't respond in a timely manner, employees will stop reporting and a general lack of accountability is likely why, according to research published by the US Equal Employment Opportunity Commission. In fact, the EEOC reports that some 75 percent of incidents go unreported altogether.

The EEOC goes so far as to comment, "The bottom line is that there is a great deal we do not know about the prevalence of harassment that occurs because of an employee's race, ethnicity, religion, age, disability, gender identity, or sexual orientation. This is so, despite the fact that there is no shortage of private sector charges and federal sector complaints that are filed claiming harassment on such grounds." As such, the main risk to today's employees is that this number stays where it is, stunting current progress and keeping employers open to continued risk of litigation.

For companies that want to be at the forefront of great cultures, driving workplace changes for good, the key to implementing change is ensuring engagement at all levels. That means getting leadership support and clearly communicating the organization's belief and policies to all stakeholders. Progressive, forward-thinking organizations also need to invest in building and maintaining a positive and inclusive workplace, one that facilitates the flow of information and leads by example.

The Role of Technology

And while accountability sits with everyone in every organization, technology gives a voice to those who don't necessarily feel comfortable speaking directly. At the same time, this creates a secure record of the incident, whether delivered in first-person or by an observer. Employees can document the date, time, and place, as well as add evidence – be it a screenshot of a WhatsApp message or a copy of an email – to help create a comprehensive report. This is also where they can name the perpetrator(s) and describe who, if anyone, witnessed the event. Technology permits employees to choose to submit it for review or not, knowing that they've captured all the details in one place and empowering them to decide when they feel comfortable proceeding. Some solutions even give employees the ability to team up with others and report jointly. With a solution functioning as a third party, employees may feel more at ease and subject to less scrutiny than they might encounter after talking to a company representative.

Employers eager to develop and improve accountability within the workplace also benefit from safe and reliable tools. With access to a full report, HR, legal, and compliance teams can review the same materials and collectively determine the next steps. These teams deserve infallible case management systems that allow them to focus their efforts on what they do best.

Accountability for All

In tandem with, or in response to, the #MeToo movement and TIME'S UP, several states across the US passed new protections to address workplace harassment: 11 in 2018 alone, with four new laws in just California, including updates to the sexual harassment training requirements for employers and outlawing "secret settlements or nondisclosure agreements in cases involving allegations of sexual assault, harassment or discrimination." But the rise of accountability directly corresponds with the changing workplace of the last two decades and goes far beyond a two-hour training course. Whether voluntarily or by state mandate, it's even more important for companies to know what's going on in the stern of the ship and how they perform culturally to mitigate the risk of legal challenge.

Recognizing a new legal climate – and echoing a shift away from the patriarchal environments of the twentieth century – the world's leading companies gravitate towards a more democratic environment, balancing the relationships between employers and employees. Unlike other eras in history where workers remained subservient, today's employees seek to own their careers, opportunities, and experiences, with their employer helping to orchestrate – rather than dictate – outcomes. In an effort to develop trust and uphold respect between these two parties, organizations get tasked with holding everyone accountable for their actions and providing an environment where this is possible. This dialogue actively reflects the work being done around diversity and inclusion, as well as training and learning, and mirrors this new attitude towards the workplace.

After giving employees the tools needed to report and capture incidents systematically, it is up to employers to exhibit progress in investigating and resolving issues. By minimizing harassment and inequality in a way that both empowers employees and establishes accountability, employers perpetuate better, more desirable behaviors and deliver on the promise of an exceptional workplace culture.

REFLECTING ON DIVERSITY AND INCLUSION IN THE WORKPLACE

If your company is seeking more diversity and inclusion, experts say you need to start at the top.

In large part, that's because homogeneity is built into the system. If leaders look, think, and act in similar ways, they tend to define successful leaders as looking, thinking, and acting just like them. Those expectations can translate into obstacles for people with different backgrounds and viewpoints or encourage people to play down their differences in favor of fitting into the mold.

Sharon Jones, a diversity consultant whose book *Mastering the Game* addresses how unconscious biases and unwritten rules can stymie the careers of women and people of color, said that companies must commit to the work of promoting diversity, particularly among their top executives.

Companies that demonstrate little diversity on their leadership teams send a powerful – if unintended – message to rising employees that there's nowhere for them to go.

"Diverse leaders, by just being there, provide role models for people," Jones said. "That's what makes people think, 'This person is just like me, we share the same personal goals, or their career is the same one I want to have.' And when they don't see those kind of role models, they assume, 'There is no pathway here for people like me.'"

Demographic trends in the United States also favor diversity, said Carol Fulp, author of *Success Through Diversity: Why the Most Inclusive Companies Will Win*. A more global marketplace, coupled with those shifting demographics, will require companies to become more diverse and inclusive over time, Fulp said.

More than 40 percent of millennials, now ages 23 to 38, identify as nonwhite, according to the Pew Research Center. Fulp also cites census projections that there will be more people of color than whites in the US by 2042.

"In order to attract the best talent of all kinds, we want to ensure that we have cultures in our organizations that are conducive to diversity, given this dramatic demographic shift," Fulp said. "You want to be able to have people in your organization who can produce the goods and services for a global marketplace. So it stands to reason that you want to have individuals in your workforce who reflect the global marketplace."

Why Worry about Diversity?

Efforts to create a more diverse and inclusive workplace can provide a host of benefits. Experts in the field cite research showing that companies where the workforce represents a wider range of thought and background produce more innovative ideas, make better decisions and are more profitable over time.

But diversity among the rank and file has less of an impact than diversity among senior leaders, according to several recent studies.

For example, The Boston Consulting Group published a study in 2017, "The Mix That Matters: Innovation Through Diversity," attributing a higher level of innovation to companies with specific types of diversity. The study highlighted several key differentiators of diversity: leaders from countries or industries different than their current employers; leaders who have taken nontraditional career paths; and leadership teams where more than 20 percent of the managers are female.

In addressing gender diversity, the study's authors emphasized that it matters where in the hierarchy women work: "One thing that doesn't seem to have an effect on innovation is the overall percentage of women in a company's workforce. Only when women occupy a significant share of management positions does the innovation premium become evident."

A 2018 report from McKinsey & Co., "Delivering through Diversity," found that of the 1,000 companies it surveyed in 12 countries, companies with the most gender diversity on their executive teams had higher profitability and better value creation.

Ethnic and cultural diversity also contributed significantly to success. Companies with the most diverse leadership teams were 33 percent more likely to lead their industries in profitability.

Conversely, companies in the bottom tier for gender and ethnic or cultural diversity were almost 30 percent less likely to achieve high profitability.

Such news isn't entirely surprising to Mary Dale Walters, senior vice president of Allsup, which provides employment services for people with disabilities who want to return to the workforce. Allsup makes accommodations for nearly all of its clients, Walters said, whether it relates to physical access within the building or accessibility features for the company's phone and web services.

Walters believes that hiring someone who sees the world from a different perspective provides opportunities for better customer service and product development.

"If I have somebody with a disability who comes up with a creative idea because they're thinking about things differently, it can benefit a company's services and products for an entire spectrum of people, not just people with disabilities," Walters said. "More diverse employees who bring that creativity and innovation can be very refreshing for a leader."

Building a Pipeline

Even companies that want to foster diversity and inclusion in the workplace can make several key missteps along the way. They focus on bringing in a diverse workforce at entry-level positions, then expect the effects to naturally flow up to the top. They rely on informal systems of identifying and promoting potential leaders that feeds into unconscious biases, or they set standards for leadership that reinforce the status quo.

Companies that want more diverse leadership teams need to take a purposeful approach to get there, said Anna Beninger, senior director of research for Catalyst, a nonprofit that focuses on opportunities for women in the workplace.

Many companies focus their efforts on recruiting a diverse workforce at the entry level, Beninger said, only to see that diversity fade away as people move up in the organization. She attributes the effect to homogenous leadership teams that tend to define leadership qualities in ways that favor the status quo.

"The senior leaders are, by definition, what success looks like in an organization," Beninger said. "When you have senior leaders who, in the US, tend to be male and white, they value stereotypically masculine behaviors. As a result, human resources translates those expectations into all of the formal talent management programs, so that everyone is being judged against these masculine standards. By definition, anyone who is not a man is disadvantaged."

Informal systems dictating who participates in high-profile projects or who gets career-making assignments that can lead to promotion can also be prone to bias, Beninger said.

"The vast majority of people's development doesn't come from formal programming – it comes from the day-to-day opportunities they have," Beninger said. "If women aren't given the opportunities to show what they are capable of doing, it reinforces the biases and standards, and it slows their advancement."

Altice USA Inc., a telecommunications company that provides cable and internet services nationwide, has used its year-old diversity and inclusion initiative to help identify potential leaders from a variety of "affinity groups," including blacks, Latinos, women, and people with disabilities. (The writer's husband works in Altice's corporate headquarters in New York.)

The main intent of the program was to create a greater sense of community among Altice's 9,000 employees at about 300 locations across the US, said Lee Schroeder, the company's chief diversity officer and executive vice president of government and public affairs.

The company defined the affinity groups based on employee surveys. Each affinity group has its own leadership team, which encourages employees to take charge of activities in the group that interests them. In addition, many of Altice's affinity group leaders belong to similar organizations outside of the company, making them prime recruiters of external talent for senior positions, Schroeder said.

"By creating these leadership teams, we have started to identify people who are taking the initiative to be a leader beyond the scope of their role," Schroeder said. "We are being mindful about saying, 'Who are our emerging leaders, and how do we make sure they get the support to continue to rise, so that throughout the higher ranks of the organization, we improve our diversity?'"

Creating More Diverse Leadership

Diversity needs to become a metric of success alongside such goals as sales or product development, said Fulp, who also serves as president and CEO of The Partnership, a Boston-based organization that helps companies attract and retain multicultural leaders.

Fulp also recommends that HR adopt practices similar to the NFL's Rooney Rule, which ensures that managers must look at a diverse pool of candidates for any given job.

Having diversity among top executives – and goals around diversity in hiring – sets a strong example for middle managers, who ultimately carry out such initiatives, Fulp said.

"You need to make sure that people understand it's a business imperative, that it's part of the company's performance," Fulp said.

Both Beninger and Jones suggest the use of formal sponsorship programs to develop a more diverse pool of potential leaders. Sponsors serve as advocates for high-potential employees trying to break through to the next level of their careers. Creating a formal program removes the element of unconscious bias that could put nontraditional leadership candidates at a disadvantage for being identified and selected.

Jones helped one of her clients develop a sponsorship program to promote more diversity among its senior leaders. On one of her recent visits to the company, Jones spoke in passing to a black executive who had been promoted twice since finding a sponsor – and now felt he understood how to become a partner at his company.

"He said, 'I see the path, it's been explained to me, so it's up to me to choose whether to pursue it,'" Jones said. "You don't usually hear that message from diverse people. You want people to know that they have got someone in their corner if they want to advance, that you'll be right there for them."

Beninger points to Nationwide Mutual Insurance Co. as an example of a company that has committed itself to the development of its female employees with its Touch Point program, which it launched in 2011 to identify and provide sponsorship opportunities for its female employees.

Through last year, the company matched about 250 high-potential employees with sponsors who reflected their backgrounds, career aspirations and personalities, said Kathy Smith, vice president of talent management and development. The program has helped Nationwide boost the percentage of women in executive roles from 29 percent to 34 percent, and has doubled the percentage of women of color in leadership roles.

Nationwide expanded Touch Point beyond the executive level last year to create sponsorship opportunities for its entire workforce of 31,000 people.

Employees can participate in Touch Point more than once, and they are expected to become sponsors themselves as they move up in the organization, Smith said.

"It's engaging to be lifting other people," said Smith, who has participated in the program both as a mentee and as a sponsor. "It sends multiple messages: We are going to help you personally, and we trust you to help the best talent in this organization succeed too. The part that requires commitment is identifying the talent in your organization and actually managing them."

Why You Should Include People with Disabilities in Your D&I Initiatives

An often-overlooked group in these diversity and inclusion initiatives are people with disabilities. Many organizations already have employees with disabilities at their disposal, but don't account for them in their D&I efforts because they are unaware of their disability.

According to the Centers for Disease Control and Prevention, one in four US adults has a disability. But, because of some of the stigmas attached to what a disability could mean for people's careers, or what it could mean for employers' concern around health-care costs, a lot of people don't self-identify.

A way to solve for this is to foster an environment that is accommodating to people with disabilities, which will lead to more transparency during the hiring and onboarding process. This starts with expanding your talent pool during recruiting and identifying during the interview and onboarding process ways that the organization can help someone be successful in a role based on their disability.

Technology is a crucial part of this, as it lends to a more flexible work schedule if it's difficult for a prospective employee to commute to and from work, among other advantages. Tech allows employers to leverage learning and development in more democratic ways. Many types of learning are available to increase skills that level the playing field.

Ultimately, expanding your talent pool to include people with disabilities not only enhances your diversity and inclusion initiatives, it just makes good business sense.

HIRING PEOPLE WITH INTELLECTUAL AND DEVELOPMENTAL DISABILITIES

Imagine a hiring initiative that taps into undiscovered talent, improves company culture and diversity, and helps the community at large.

It's a movement that has spread through businesses as disparate as the service industry, high-tech companies and professional firms. It operates under different auspices, but it has a single message: People with intellectual and developmental disabilities (IDDs) can become thriving members of your company's team.

Businesses that have actively sought out workers with IDDs have found a new source for employees in a tight job market. That's because workers with IDDs often find themselves left behind (see Sidebar 12.1).

More than 80 percent of people with such disabilities are unemployed or underemployed, according to Best Buddies, a nonprofit that creates social and economic opportunities for people with a range of diagnoses, including Down syndrome, cerebral palsy, and traumatic brain injuries.

The statistics are not much better for young adults on the autism spectrum. The advocacy group Autism Speaks estimates that almost half of 25-year-olds with autism have never had a paying job.

The lack of employment opportunities for young adults with IDDs has the potential to become a pressing economic problem. About 15 percent of children from the ages of 3 to 17 have an intellectual or developmental disability, according to the Centers for Disease Control. Autism Speaks predicts that about half a million teens on the autism spectrum will enter adulthood in the coming decade.

"We're going to be left with a lot of unfilled positions as the Baby Boomers retire, and we need to look at untapped talent that has been underutilized in our workforce," said Leslie Long, vice president of adult services for Autism Speaks. "People with autism and other developmental disabilities could fill that gap."

The Benefits of Inclusion

People with IDDs once found themselves with limited job options, such as sheltered workshops that paid participants less than the minimum wage and isolated them from the larger community.

But over the past few decades, advocacy groups have campaigned to incorporate people with IDDs into all facets of life, whether social or economic.

Those efforts at integration have paid off for people with IDDs – but also for the companies that have created more inclusive workplaces.

TheARC@Work, which helps with workforce integration for people with IDDs, surveyed its corporate partners in 2016 to determine how its help had affected their workplaces.

All companies surveyed reported increased productivity after hiring employees with IDDs, said Jonathan Lucus, managing director of TheARC@ Work; 60 percent reported a happier, friendlier corporate culture.

"Companies are saying it's been a great business decision – not a personal decision, not a feel-good decision, but a great business decision," Lucus said. "Companies who are not doing this are missing out on a part of the workforce that can be helpful to their bottom lines."

Attorney Robert Friedman has seen that dynamic play out in the law firm of Holland & Knight. The firm hired its first employees with IDDs more than 20 years ago in its Miami office, where Friedman is a partner. Over the years, Holland & Knight has employed 22 people with IDDs throughout its network of 28 offices, including people at several of its locations abroad.

Friedman believes that the hiring effort signals that the company cares about more than making money.

"You get an employee who loves having a job, who is friendly, outgoing and just totally loyal," Friedman said. "When you introduce employees with IDDs into your workplace, you're saying to everybody who works there that you are committed to a diverse workplace, and to making sure that everybody has a chance to contribute to the community and the economy."

Some companies that have worked to make their workplaces more inclusive of people with IDDs have found an increased sense of purpose among all employees.

SAP, a software and technology business, asks employees to volunteer as "team buddies" for new recruits who have been hired through its Autism at Work program. Hundreds of SAP employees have volunteered for the program in some capacity, said Jose Velasco, SAP's global co-lead of Autism at Work.

That kind of participation has boosted employee engagement and retention, and attracted new talent as well.

"There are a lot of people today – particularly younger folks – who are looking at the impact of the company they're working for," Velasco said. "People see this type of program and say, 'Here's a company that wants to transform the future of work.' And we are able to attract those people who are like-minded."

Breaking Down Barriers

Companies that have already worked to diversify their workforces say the process starts with listening and education.

TheARC@Work often fields questions about how to treat people with disabilities before the hiring process even takes place, Lucus said. The answer? Not much differently than how they treat any other colleague.

As part of the workplace integration process, nonprofits such as Best Buddies offer training for existing employees and managers about interacting with people with IDDs, said Courtney Rogaczewski, the organization's senior director of jobs.

That often means teaching "people-first language" that emphasizes the worth of the individual – for example, referring to a person with a disability, versus labeling someone "disabled," Rogaczewski said.

HR professionals also learn how to eliminate the barriers erected by the traditional application process.

Some standard language in job descriptions eliminates applicants with IDDs before the process even starts, said Susan Webb, vice president of employment services at Ability360, an Arizona nonprofit that promotes independence for people with disabilities.

Webb, an attorney and HR professional with more than 40 years of advocacy experience, shudders when she sees postings that require a valid driver's license or the ability to lift 30 pounds – for jobs in which the duties do not include transportation or moving boxes.

Her advice is to stick to the essential functions of the job in writing a job description.

"You can label 50 people with the same diagnosis, and every single one of them is going to have a different limitation," Webb said. "There is a broad spectrum of what a person with these types of disabilities can do. So, the best thing that an HR professional can do is to focus on the job you need done."

The interview process can also create obstacles for people with autism or other IDDs, who may struggle with making eye contact or offering lengthy answers to open-ended questions.

To shift the emphasis from interviews, HR professionals can create "job shadowing" opportunities or provide a project that allows an applicant with an IDD to show off skills and strengths, experts say.

For example, SAP offers a six-week Enterprise Readiness Academy to employees it recruits through Autism at Work. Participants are assigned a project at the beginning of the academy, and they present their finished product at the end, Velasco said.

Companies may also create internal impediments by expecting a perfect fit every time they hire an employee with an IDD – an expectation that managers would never have for other employees.

Holland & Knight hired its first employees with IDDs with the help of Best Buddies. A person hired for a position in kitchen services didn't work out. The result immediately caused some concern about whether the program was a good fit for the firm, Friedman said.

But the person hired as a replacement has gone on to work for the firm for 25 years, becoming a valued staff member who knows everyone by name, Friedman said.

Lucus, of TheARC@Work, advises that companies start small, hiring a few people with IDDs and building on their successes. Lucus worked with a company that hired five people with IDDs through their inclusion program. A month later, two of the five new hires had left – not because they didn't have the skills, but because the job wasn't a good fit for them.

"If you have a job with high turnover, it didn't stop you from hiring a neurotypical person again – so why should it stop you from hiring somebody who is neurodiverse?" Lucus said. "That's why you start small, do it purposefully, and get that first win under your belt. Then you grow it over time."

Exceeding Expectations

Companies such as Levy, which operates food and beverage services for stadiums and arenas nationwide, have seen their employees with IDDs flourish, expanding beyond the job skills for which they were initially hired.

Five years ago, Levy partnered with TheARC@Work to hire workers with IDDs for its food and beverage operations at Barclays Center in Brooklyn, N.Y.

Greg Costa, who headed the effort for Levy, started new workers with IDDs at a simple but crucial task: keeping the condiment station clean and stocked. The NBA later recognized Barclays Center for providing the best condiment carts among its 29 arenas, Costa said.

Over time, employees with IDDs moved on from the condiment carts to work in concessions or serve as cashiers, said Costa, who now serves as Levy's director of operations at the T-Mobile Arena in Las Vegas. The Las Vegas arena employs about 200 people in concessions; about 10 percent are people with IDDs, Costa said.

In a similar vein, SAP started its Autism at Work program expecting to fill two technical jobs: quality assurance and software development. Since its inception, the program has created full-time job opportunities in two dozen roles for employees on the spectrum, Velasco said.

More than 320 people with autism have participated in some facet of Autism at Work, which has blossomed into a system of high school mentorships, professional internships, and contract work.

Jeff Wang is among that number. Wang, who is on the autism spectrum, had a limited work history when he graduated from college in 2015 and started applying for jobs. After more than a year of fruitless searching, Wang was referred to SAP's Autism at Work program.

Wang, now 27, started as an intern, then became a full-time employee in SAP's HR department in Philadelphia, analyzing employee data and managing projects.

"It's been a continuous learning experience," Wang said. "It's really about people at SAP. There's a strong sense of community. Everyone is knowledgeable in their areas of expertise, and everyone is willing to help one another out."

SAP has taken a sharing approach to the larger business community as well. Companies such as Microsoft, JP Morgan Chase, and EY have joined forces with SAP to form an Autism at Work Roundtable, sharing best practices and expanding the program to more companies. SAP has fielded inquiries from 160 companies interested in implementing a similar initiative in their own workplaces.

Establishing such relationships has been a satisfying, if unexpected, benefit of Autism at Work, Velasco said.

"Look at the companies that have already done this – we are more than willing to share," Velasco said. "This is not about a transaction. We're not selling a product. We're connecting with other companies to grow in the same direction, and to have a purpose and an impact on the community."

Sidebar 12.1 Defining Intellectual and Developmental Disabilities

The term "Intellectual and Developmental Disabilities," or IDD, serves as an umbrella for a number of diagnoses.

An intellectual disability is generally defined as a limitation in intellectual function, such as an IQ below 75, as well as limitations in a person's ability to navigate everyday social and practical skills, such as self-care or money handling.

A developmental disability describes an impairment in learning, language, or behavioral skills, but it does not necessarily include an intellectual disability. Some examples of developmental disabilities include Down syndrome, fetal alcohol syndrome, ADHD, and autism.

"NO LONGER YOUR FATHER'S WORKPLACE": BEING CULTURALLY INTELLIGENT IS SMART BUSINESS

The workplace is becoming a lot less homogeneous. There is no longer one way of looking at working. Every business needs to be a culturally inclusive organization.

Savvy total rewards professionals must continuously develop their cultural intelligence or cultural quotient (CQ). It is an invaluable bottom-line boost to be nimble and work with people from various backgrounds and parts of the world.

Building CQ rests on three actions – valuing, respecting, and hearing – the employees, clients, and other people with which a business interacts. If you deal with people in a way that shows what is important to them matters to you, they are likely to become much more engaged.

Being culturally intelligent is recognizing and addressing unconscious biases and convincing reticent senior leaders of the benefits of diversity and inclusion.

> **Cultural intelligence** *n* having the knowledge, skills, and ability necessary to effectively and appropriately engage people from different cultural backgrounds to deliver better business results.
>
> **Benefits of Cultural Intelligence**
> - Increases employee engagement
> - Increases innovation and flexibility
> - Attracts quality talent
> - Improves sales and reduces costs
> - Reduces multicultural risks.
>
> Source: Multicultural Foodservice & Hospitality Alliance (MHFA)

Gaining Executive Buy-In for Organizational Culture Change

Developing and sustaining a strong organizational culture now has stature as a critical component in a company's success – especially during inevitable periods of change and disruption. However, it can be difficult to gain the necessary C-suite buy-in for creating and sustaining organizational culture change, particularly if executives who are focused on financial figures don't innately view culture as a priority.

How can those outside the executive suite convince decision makers that organizational culture change is worth the time and investment? Follow these five steps to get the green light.

1. Speak Their Language

Executives are focused on the overarching strategy and trajectory of the company, which naturally centers on profitability. With this perspective in mind, begin by emphasizing the bottom line when presenting culture initiatives.

Here are a few fast figures you can cite to illustrate why culture matters to the bottom line:

- Companies with performance-enhancing cultures saw a 901 percent increase in stock price growth over companies without, according to the book *Corporate Culture and Performance* by John P. Kotter.
- Studies indicate that it costs 6–9 months' salary, on average, every time a business replaces a salaried employee, report Emma Seppala and Kim Cameron in the *Harvard Business Review* article, "Proof That Positive Work Cultures Are More Productive."
- Health-care expenditures at high-pressure, culturally deficient companies are nearly 50 percent greater than at other organizations, says Christina Merhar in her Zane Benefits blog.

2. Relate Company Values to Culture

The financial impact of organizational culture is a strong sell for executives, but connecting the culture of a company to its values is also essential for gaining buy-in. Researching how well your culture actually reflects stated company values is an important task to complete up front.

Make a list of the intangible values your company sees as important. These might include integrity, trust, respect, quality, communication, and leadership. Next, clearly outline how your company culture is or isn't sustaining those values – and articulate what can be done to realign employees with core values.

For example, if the value is communication, the perception might be that people don't want to speak up about potential concerns because they are afraid they will be punished or ignored. To realign, put in a specific process to recognize and reward employees who honestly and productively express their concerns.

3. Benchmark Beliefs and Perceptions

If your leaders are not in tune with the honest feedback of the people beneath them, it can be hard to make the case for change. There are several ways to uncover and enunciate feedback, including 360-degree reviews, polls, and surveys.

Here are a few questions you might want to include:

- Is your supervisor open and approachable?
- Does your supervisor provide you with adequate direction and expectations?
- Do you feel that your supervisor values you and your opinion?
- What would you do to change the employee experience at (your company)?

4. Distill Results

Combing through qualitative survey results can be a daunting and time-consuming task. Here's how you can manage open-response questions to distill results and identify the most important elements to incorporate into organizational culture:

- *Do an initial read-through.* Quickly read through results to get an overview of the tone and themes of comments.
- *Quantify word use.* Try a tool such as WordCounter to see which words appear most frequently in your survey results.
- *Categorize.* Using a spreadsheet, determine a spectrum of categories and group the responses together.
- *Highlight.* Are there answers that are overwhelmingly positive or negative? Highlight them in green or red.
- *Quantify.* Which categories have the most responses? Which have the most green or red responses?

5. Articulate Changes

To recap, there are three core tools that can help secure executive buy-in for organizational culture initiatives:

- The demonstrated knowledge that organizational culture benefits the bottom line
- An understanding of how to identify misalignment between company values and existing culture
- Real-life feedback from all reaches of your company about the necessity of growth.

These three key facets – financial impact, organizational alignment, and employee feedback – are imperative to successfully winning executive approval. By articulating the mission, expense, and potential impact of change through proven research techniques, you will be able to gain the crucial executive buy-in for your cultural change initiatives.

UNIFYING CORPORATE CULTURE: FIVE STEPS TO DRIVE ENGAGEMENT AND PERFORMANCE POST-M&A

In his classic song "Changes," the late David Bowie tells of the inevitable changes we all face over time. Just as people face changes, organizations also must deal with transitions during the business life cycle. One of the most dramatic adjustments a company will ever make comes during and after a merger or acquisition. During this tenuous time, the successful assimilation of the two joining cultures is paramount to the organization's ability to thrive. The establishment of a unified corporate culture enables the new entities to bond to advance the company. The speed of change in today's modern business world is alarming. With or without a merger and acquisition (M&A), success in this dynamic environment requires companies to adapt to technological advances, leverage a diverse workforce, compete in a tight labor market and stay nimble in a global economy. The effectiveness of a workforce is determined by the ability to attract and retain quality employees who ultimately define business outcomes and drive success.

According to LinkedIn Learning, 56 percent of organizations struggle to keep high-potential, top-performing employees. That's a daunting statistic for any organization, especially those undergoing significant changes due to a merger or acquisition. Layer in the uncertainty and transformation associated with an M&A transaction, and you have a complex web of business and people requirements, all needing to be managed concurrently and in a tight timeframe. From the long list of priorities, where should business leaders begin to focus their efforts? The need to integrate and optimize the employee base is critical at this stage and demands a strategic plan. Otherwise, the process becomes an overwhelming task doomed to fail.

While seemingly obvious, if business owners want their companies to succeed, they must create a workforce dedicated to that mission, actively contributing time, energy, and talents to achieving specific corporate objectives. Organizations need engaged employees who are committed to advancing the company to the next level. In fact, organizations with highly engaged employees have an average three-year revenue growth 2.3 times greater than companies whose employees are only engaged at an average level, according to research from the University of North Carolina's Kenan-Flager Business School. The level of employee engagement measures the emotional commitment the employee has to the organization and its goals. This emotional commitment means engaged employees actually care about their work and the welfare of their company.

Disengaged employees are costing the United States from $450 billion to $550 billion each year, according to Gallup (2017). The "2017 Gallup State of the American Workplace" report found that better engagement leads to as much as 21 percent better business profitability. In an M&A environment, the need for engaged employees is amplified as new groups are coming together with new or updated combined missions, expectations, people, and processes – and even new management. It is a transitional time that requires stellar change management strategies to keep people focused on outcomes, not on the fear or uncertainty of what their new world looks like. So what is the glue that holds all of this together and drives an effective merger or acquisition? How do leaders optimally engage their employees amid tremendous change? What is sticky enough to pull people together and positively affect customers, sales and profitability?

Corporate Culture as Glue

It starts with corporate culture. According to *Inc.* magazine, "Corporate culture refers to the shared values, attitudes, standards and beliefs that characterize members of an organization and define its nature. Corporate culture is rooted in an organization's goals, strategies, structure and approaches to labor, customers, investors and the greater community." Leaders in the organization must begin the process of post M&A assimilation by studying their corporate culture – dissect the elements and determine what is driving desired behaviors. What makes people work hard and stay committed to the organization?

In an M&A environment, the combining businesses must evaluate the cultures of each distinct organization and determine which characteristics made each company successful (or not). The identified positive behaviors and habits will serve as foundational building blocks that root the many layers of change management required in any successful M&A action. Therefore, from a human capital perspective, the goal in the M&A process is optimizing the new culture in order to drive engagement, and ultimately business success.

Culture is a daunting concept. It is comprised of repeatable processes, consistent behaviors, and an elusive gut feel that people experience in their dealings with the organization. Workers want to feel connected to their workplace, and culture helps drive that connection in spoken and unspoken ways.

So what elements of culture are most effective at driving engagement? What makes a culture so great it pulls people in, ties them to the organization, and elicits a sense of dedication and loyalty?

Certain organizational habits, when implemented and practiced regularly, will lead to a terrific culture in which people want to go to work and achieve results. In an M&A environment, the key becomes quickly identifying and capitalizing on the most impactful elements of a desirable culture, and driving them throughout the new organization.

Workers want to feel connected to their workplace, and culture helps drive that connection.

1. Integrate HR Practices

Your policies and systems should support your culture and values, too. Do your performance review questions align to your values? Do your rewards and recognition systems reinforce the behaviors you expect from your employees? Similar to the marketing of your values, an organization must synthesize and reinforce those values and expected behaviors throughout the organizational ecosystem. For example, every January, Hodges-Mace hosts an all-employee kickoff meeting. In that session, H-M not only highlights and reiterates their values, but also showcases stellar examples of employees demonstrating those values both internally and with customers. From table tents with customer quotes, to posters on the wall, to scrolling examples on the presentation at break, H-M wants to celebrate those who embrace their values. (Hodges-Mace is an Atlanta-based employee technology and communications company.)

H-M now has yearly "Core Value Awards" when managers nominate employees who have demonstrated specific values throughout the year. Then, a committee gathers to determine the winners with the most outstanding illustrations of living our values. Those winners are highlighted and announced at the all-company meeting. H-M celebrates their personal leadership and commitment to their values. Then, to keep the momentum going beyond their companywide events, they recognize department successes for specific team members who go above and beyond their standard expectations. Employees who get praise from clients are featured on the TV screens around the office for all to celebrate.

Change requires a constant reinforcement. What is expected? How do we achieve it? Why is it important? By aligning your systems and processes to the messages you want to deliver, you can see your opportunity to succeed skyrocket. Employees want clarity, and highly defined systems and expectations provide a roadmap that creates comfort, allowing employees to focus on their jobs.

The integration of core values into everyday work reinforces and drives the conversation during performance reviews. A continuous effort to live out these core values sets expectations and creates meaningful dialogue during review season. For example, Hodges-Mace embeds questions in its reviews that focus on an employee's primary core value, asking, "Which value most represents you; and how have you demonstrated it?" By opening the conversation between managers and employees, H-M highlights the importance of its core values and encourages employee performance that reflects them.

In an M&A, it's especially important to make values a big part of the discussion early to set clear expectations. This allows for a smoother transition, consistent messaging and a meaningful first impression. An example Hodges-Mace currently practices is with onboarding new employees. They have integrated core values into the training program with videos, small-group meetings with the CEO and a prescribed discussion plan to focus specifically on their values. As with a new employee, an M&A employee is part of the new team. It's vital to clearly communicate core values from the beginning and explain how they're lived out within the organization.

2. Lead with Values

Successful corporate values are ingrained in an organization's behavioral fabric, playing an important role in driving intentional aspects of culture. According to BusinessDictionary.com, they are the operating philosophies or principles that guide an organization's internal conduct as well as its relationships with customers, partners and shareholders. When organizations come together in an M&A transaction, the leading organization needs to define the combined values early in the transaction process, setting the tone for expected behaviors and attitudes.

Once new corporate values are identified, the leadership team must articulate them clearly to all employees quickly and regularly, both verbally and in writing. There's something quite powerful about the written word. HR departments should actively market the updated values in order to drive understanding and adoption of the associated expected behaviors. Starting with the employee handbook, the values need to be included in any relevant HR policies and materials. Additionally, the values need to be actively reinforced visually throughout the office. Consider publishing the list of values on the wall above your reception desk so employees see this every day they come to work. Provide employees (new and/or current) mousepads or other practical swag, again printed with the values. Make the reinforcement of the values an ongoing campaign, keeping their importance top of mind for all employees.

Another proven way to reinforce values is to publish corporate values on the home page of your website for all to see. Values need to be actively reinforced visually throughout the office.

3. Identify and Leverage Culture Champions

Corporate champions define the combined corporate culture and keep people focused, to stay engaged and drive organizational performance. In the absence of certainty, people generally rely on established patterns of behavior. Having a well-defined and intentional corporate culture helps ensure that people remain focused and engaged, even in times of change. Layer on the fact that engagement leads to performance and you have a winning combination. Here are some characteristics to look for in spotting culture champions:

- *They have natural credibility and leadership skills.* Others follow these individuals. They get results. If they're not in direct leadership roles, they achieve results through others – through collaboration, and simply by getting things done. You are looking for someone who will be a living example of your organization's values. Effective champions are found at all levels in the organization, serving as change agents to all types of employees. Companies should leverage these individuals to share core messages in a less formal, yet highly effective manner.
- *Culture champions are energetic and supportive of change and have the ability to articulate the need for a successful integration.* When they come across someone who is not moving along in that direction, they can explain why it's so important that the person change course. They understand the critical importance of buy-in across the board, always leading by example.
- *They are empathetic and don't expect change overnight.* They understand that for some it's more difficult. If it reaches the stage where a person has to be transitioned because he or she can't adapt to the change, a culture champion will still have empathy and understanding. They know how to make tough decisions about their behavior and are not afraid to communicate to leadership when they see a repeated instance of others not living the values.
- *Sometimes the best way to seek corporate champions is to let them identify themselves.* By doing this, employers allow hidden corporate champions to step up to the plate and take ownership. For example, Hodges-Mace asks employees to handle leadership roles surrounding their social

and community events. Every summer during its "Summer of Service" charity initiative, H-M seeks a self-appointed team leader to handle outreach with each charity. This identifies these hidden leaders, creates group energy, and reinforces the message and intent around their endeavor. Personalizing the process helps drive engagement with the service group within and across departments. Allowing employees to proclaim being a culture champion gives them the authority and engagement they want and allows the employer to see who can be tapped for future leadership opportunities.

4. Focus on People Development

Employees who don't believe they can achieve their career goals with a current employer are 12 times more likely to consider leaving. With new employees, the number skyrockets to about 30 times more likely, according to LinkedIn Learning. These statistics shine a light on the importance of helping employees excel in their careers via training and professional development.

Humans naturally want to learn and grow. By supporting employees' personal and professional growth, managers foster a sense of progression. Managers should help employees align their capabilities with organizational growth. This way, employees feel like they are learning and growing, fostering intrinsic motivation, with employees typically working harder and more efficiently.

It's important to set the expectation for managers that they need to develop their people. But it's equally important to put tools and processes in place that can be utilized for professional development. The integration of that expectation into performance management improves the manager's effectiveness and encourages employee development.

Hodges-Mace, for example, implemented SmartPath, a training and development tool and program that helps employees hone their skills. With managers on board, SmartPath can be integrated into the workforce, pushing employees to their next level of potential.

5. Commit to Transparent Communications

Effective communication is critical for all businesses and especially critical before, during, and after a merger or acquisition. In fact, lack of communication is a key contributor to M&A failures. Large gaps in clarity and communications exist between employees who have experienced a merger or acquisition in the past 12 months and those who haven't. According to the Quantum Workplace "2018 Engagement Trends" report, these gaps exist around compensation, change management, and performance.

Employees at merged organizations need clarity and communication. The Quantum report reveals two themes relating to favorability among merged and non-merged employees: Merged employees don't have a clear understanding of how the new organizational structure works, and they need more visible signs that the organization values their effort.

Honest communication of roles and expectations is critical in a post-M&A environment. Don't assume employees understand the new rules. Employees will naturally be anxious about their new work environment at first. Clear and regular communications from the top down will allay uncertainty and help assure that their employer has their best interests at heart.

The best way to ensure clear communications after an M&A is to create very clear speaking points to help all managers relay consistent corporate messages. A well-orchestrated communications strategy puts the workforce at ease and shows the whole organization is on the same journey.

When Hodges-Mace acquired two companies in 2013, it was very important that managers from each organization knew and embraced the company's new corporate talking points. Clear, transparent, and consistent communications helped enable their employees to more easily accept the changes and move forward as a unified company striving toward the same corporate goals.

Success Begins at the Top

The M&A world is alive and well. In 2017, companies announced more than 50,600 transactions with a total value of more than $3.5 trillion.

As addressed here, the success rate of an organization after an M&A is directly related to the workforce's ability to come together to achieve a shared vision of the newly formed entity. This requires engaged employees who understand and embrace the new corporate culture. This level of commitment begins with a leadership team that communicates these new values and strives to build community and trust.

13 Pay Equity and Rewards Fairness

"Pay equity," as an issue or broad topic, refers to the outcome of a pay comparison between individuals or groups, where pay is either the same or similar for the same or similar work, or where differences in pay are explained by defensible factors such as role, experience, education and performance. When differences in pay are not explained by defensible factors, the result is a "pay inequity" that requires more examination and *may* be the result of unintended bias within the system.

It's important to understand that if unexplained differences in pay do exist, it is often *not* the result of a failed compensation program or unethical choices made by an individual or organization. Rather, it is often the result of legitimate business-driven decisions that can have disparate and unintended negative impact against one or more protected classes. These differences may subject the organization to risks of legal liability, reputational harm and competitive disadvantage.

The root cause of and/or solution to an inequity or bias may relate to a workplace practice that is not solely owned by the compensation function, such as organizational culture, recruiting/hiring/promotional practices, performance review systems, leadership development programs, benefits policy or diversity and inclusion initiatives. A bias or breakdown in any of these systems may lead to pay inequities. Compensation professionals are often in a unique position to identify and monitor these outcomes and are increasingly being relied on to lead the cross-functional and collaborative efforts aimed to identify and improve the root cause contributing factors.

Organizational objectives and approaches to pay equity work can and do vary. A company can leverage best practices and an array of solutions depending on its objectives and rewards philosophy. And while there are a lot of ways to define pay equity as an outcome, the issue is really around the degree of fairness and transparency in pay and rewards programs.

The work associated with pay equity and rewards fairness often leads to a more nuanced conversation around those previously mentioned workplace practices (e.g., workforce representation and recruiting/hiring/promotional practices) that speak to a broader-than-pay ecosystem.

WHAT DOES THIS MEAN FOR COMPENSATION AND REWARDS PROFESSIONALS?

Compensation and rewards professionals are tasked with delivering internal pay systems that are competitive, compliant, and consistently administered. However, it is possible for unconscious bias to creep into systems and practices, which can lead to unintended pay inequities. Compensation and rewards professionals' access to and understanding of rewards data, systems, and processes, along with key partnerships outside of rewards functions, put them in a unique position to help HR and the overall organization achieve and maintain pay equity and rewards fairness.

Pay equity work is both important and complex, and compensation and rewards professionals play a pivotal role in their organizations' journeys.

WHAT DOES THIS MEAN FOR ORGANIZATIONS?

This issue is global in its scope, touches almost all aspects of rewards work and goes well beyond compliance and legal risk mitigation. It has become a societal issue, organization imperative, and source of competitive advantage.

Pressure is mounting in many countries, stemming from calls to action from employees, boards, legislators, investors, and society at large. There is an almost constant flow of legislation around salary history bans, gender pay gap reporting, pay transparency mandates, and more. But employers can do far more to address these issues than legislation alone could ever achieve – and they should.

Organizations run significant legal and reputational risk if they fail to properly address pay equity concerns but have significant advantage if they are on the leading edge of fairness and transparency efforts. The incentive is great too, as taking social responsibility and ensuring fair practices and rewards are critical to an employer's brand and their ability to attract and retain the talent required to support business growth.

WHAT DOES THIS MEAN FOR SOCIETY?

The gender pay gap is a societal and labor-market issue, not just a problem impacting a subset of employers. The consequence of a pay gap and stalled mobility that compounds over a lifetime is real. Women earn hundreds of thousands of dollars less than their male counterparts over the course of their careers, and that gap in earnings limits their options for housing, continued education, saving, and retirement planning. It is a compounding disadvantage for a lifetime, which impacts the strength of our families, communities, and broader economic structures (see Figure 13.1).

FIGURE 13.1 Topics and terms of pay equity.

Topics Associated with Pay Equity	Topics Not Associated with Pay Equity
• Diversity and inclusive practices • Segregation among industries and occupations • Career growth and mentoring • Family issues that may be a barrier to career growth • Environmental, social, and governance issues (ESG) • Corporate social responsibility (CSR) • Salary history ban • Collective bargaining impact on wage outcomes • EEO-1 Reporting • Remediation strategies • Discrimination/stereotypes • Access to college education	• Employee vs. leader pay ratio • Disparity by profession (e.g., teacher vs. pro sports pay) • Disparity explained within employment contracts • Escalating CEO compensation • Minimum wage • Living wage • FLSA • Rising cost of benefits in the US

Key Definitions

Pay equity: Equal pay for work of equal value. Also used to describe pay comparisons where there is no unexplained difference pay, and that is not the result of defensible and legitimate factors.

Pay inequity: Difference in pay that is unexplained, or not the result of defensible and legitimate factors.

Pay parity: Equal pay for equal work.

Pay disparity: Commonly used when referring to the difference in pay between men and women for comparable roles. It may be attributable to an explained (defensible and legitimate) or unexplained factors.

Internal equity: A fairness criterion that directs an employer to establish wage rates that correspond to each job's relative value to the organization.

Gender pay gap (raw): Calculation that simply compares median pay by gender, regardless of job type or worker seniority. (This is the baseline metric that is most-often cited, indicating that that women working full-time are paid, on average, only 80 cents for every dollar paid to a man).

Role-to-role pay gap: Comparing pay of different demographics in the same role (e.g., males vs. females in the same role).

Group-to-group pay gap: Examines influence of environmental factors that may be contributing to a pay gap for a specific demographic. Examples are long-term systemic workforce trends such as the concentration of women in certain lower-paying occupations and industries, and the cumulative effect motherhood can have on careers.

Protected class: The definition of "protected class" – groups of people that share common, legally protected characteristics – will vary by legal jurisdiction and is in a constant state of expansion. In the United States, protected classes are defined under Title VII of the Civil Rights act of 1965 and provided protections from discrimination based on race, color, religion, gender, or national origin.

Disparate impact: A policy or practice that is applied equally but has adverse effect on one protected class of employees more than another.

Disparate treatment: Any practice and/or policy that treats members of a protected class less favorably than other employees due to a legally protected characteristic.

Pay transparency: The extent to which an organization is open and clear about pay and supports workforce freedoms to share. This includes transparency into pay and rewards philosophies, administrative guidelines, salary structures and grades, pay levels, and more.

Diversity and inclusion: Organizational strategies, programs, and practices that cultivate and support a diverse workforce that is leveraged for competitive advantage.

Rewards fairness: A state of equitable rewards delivery that considers the value of comparable work but omits bias and disparate impact on protected classes. The state of rewards fairness is highly dependent on an aligned ecosystem of organizational culture, recruiting/hiring/promotional practices, performance review systems, leadership development programs, benefits policy, diversity, and inclusion initiatives.

THREE TYPES OF PAY EQUITY GAPS AND HOW TO FIX THEM

While pay discrimination does indeed exist, different pay equity terms are used interchangeably that actually are measuring different forms of inequity and therefore what the magnitude of the gap – and how to close it – varies.

As pay equity legislation sweeps across the globe, this is a crucial time to set the record straight about the different forms of pay inequity and therefore why HR professionals must be discerning about which laws apply to which gaps.

What are the terms and what do they mean?

- **The gender pay gap.** The common "women earn 80 cents for every dollar a man makes," headline refers to the *overall* gender pay gap in the United States – comparing average male and average female salaries

across the board within an organization or an entire national workforce. The gender pay gap does not compare the gap between men
and women *in the same job*. And it does not account for seniority, job
function, job level or size, nor specialized skills, which all account for
legitimate differences in pay.

- **Equal pay for work of equal value**. If a man is an executive and a wom-
  an is a supervisor, it is understandable why their pay may be different given these different roles. However, there are many jobs that men
  and women perform that are similar in size, scope, and accountability
  that would be considered of equal value, while not necessarily titled
  the same. A human resources generalist and an accounting specialist
  are often considered similarly sized jobs because they require similar
  work experience and education. The nature of the problems they solve
  are comparable. These two roles should be paid more similarly than
  dissimilarly.
- **Equal pay for equal work**. If Tina and Tom are both accountants, in
  the same job at the same company with similar skill profiles and backgrounds, their pay should be similar.

The results of the calculations of these different types of gender pay audits
can be quite different from one another (Figure 13.2). We know from experience and research that the pay gap data for individual organizations can
be significantly over- or under-indexed compared to external benchmark
compensation data.

What happens when we look at the norms? When we start with the overall
gender pay gap calculation, we see a large difference of 23 percent. But as
we get more granular in the data and compare men and women in

FIGURE 13.2 Breaking down the gender pay gap.

We have job, pay, and gender information for:			
> 1,200,000 employees in the US	**> 800** companies in the US		**59%** of our sample is female
At a "headline" level (comparing average male to average female salary), there is a **23%** pay gap	Comparing average salaries for men and women at the same job level, there is an **8%** pay gap	Comparing average salaries for men and women at the same job level and in the same company, there is a **3%** pay gap	Comparing average salaries for men and women at the same job level, in the same company and the same function, there is a **1%** pay gap

SOURCE: Korn Ferry. 2018a. "The 2018 Essentials: When Women CEOs Speak," July 13. Viewed:
Dec. 11, 2019. https://www.kornferry.com/institute/womenceopodcast. © 2018, Korn Ferry.
Database includes 1.2M employees from more than 800 companies in the US. 59 percent of
the sample is female. Note: these are average figures, around which there is (often considerable) variance.

similar-sized jobs or the same job, the pay gap decreases significantly when they share certain characteristics:

- Down to 8 percent when comparing men and women at the same job level.
- Down to 3 percent when they are also within the same company.
- As low as 1 percent when they, in addition, are in the same function (Korn Ferry 2018b).

The Cause of Most Pay Gaps: Not Enough Women in Leadership

So how can organizations that are effective in ensuring men and women are paid equitability for the same or similar work be so ineffective when it comes to the overall gender pay gap? The answer is that there are some significant differences in how jobs are staffed in organizations and how women may be tracked into less senior roles or kept from promotions longer. Recent Korn Ferry research shows that women CEOs on average are 4+ years older and have held at least one additional senior leadership role than men, at the time of being appointed CEO (Korn Ferry 2018a). This begins at the entry level to management, according to a McKinsey & Co. study, which found that for every 100 men hired or promoted to the manager level, only 72 women were hired or promoted to manager (Huang et al. 2019). When women fall behind early, catching up is difficult resulting in lower prevalence of women in the most senior positions.

Figure 13.3 captures the percentage of women in jobs at specific job levels. As the level of the job increases, moving from left to right on the graph, the percentage of women decreases, starting at 60–70 percent for clerical roles and declining to 10 percent at the highest executive levels. The data confirms that the gender pay gap is largely driven by lack of female representation than by pay inequity between similar roles. These aggregate pay

FIGURE 13.3 Percentage of female employees by job level.

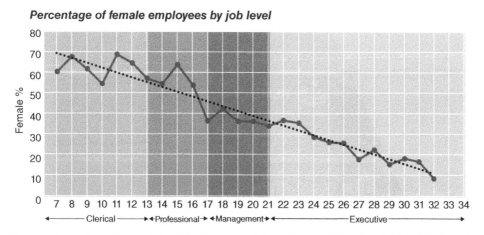

SOURCE: Korn Ferry. 2018a. "The 2018 Essentials: When Women CEOs Speak," July 13. Viewed: Dec. 11, 2019. https://www.kornferry.com/institute/womenceopodcast. © 2018, Korn Ferry.

differences are less about unequal pay and more about unequal representation in management and leadership.

How to Close the Gaps

Legislatively, beyond the baseline reporting requirements of more than one-quarter of the jurisdictions, several cities and states in the United States have recently enacted legislation that precludes employers from inquiring about salary history during recruitment in an effort to ensure more equity in pay across demographic groups.

A growing number of companies are taking matters into their own hands. Research conducted by Korn Ferry and WorldatWork (2019) found that 60 percent of organizations have taken, or are now taking, action on pay equity management in order to respond to or get ahead of legislation.

But what are their motivations? The study revealed that while rewards leaders are largely driven by regulatory compliance concerns (31 percent), only 10 percent of C-suite leaders are. Conversely, C-suite leaders see the primary objective as building or maintaining a culture of organization trust (41 percent), while only 26 percent of rewards leaders do. Secondary for C-suite Leaders is the rationale that it makes good business sense to manage pay equity. Pay inequity does drive away female talent and, according to McKinsey and Co.'s "Delivering Through Diversity," companies with the number of women leaders in the top quartile financially outperform their competitors by 21 percent (Hunt et al. 2018).

Companies addressing pay equity are conducting one or more of the following types of pay equity analyses: foundational, remediation, and drivers (Figure 13.4).

FIGURE 13.4 Types of pay equity analyses.

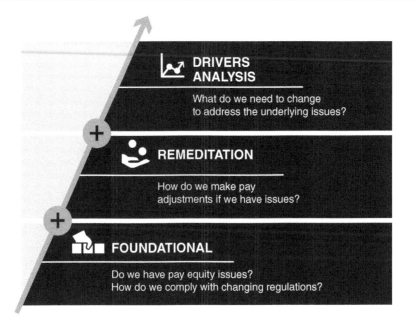

Source: Korn Ferry

The time and energy required from management to address the implications of these analyses increases as they move from a foundational analysis to a drivers analysis, but so does the value-add and ability to have more of an effective and sustainable talent management process that goes well beyond pay.

Foundational Analysis

Helps organizations answer the question of whether they have issues with pay differences between employee groups when isolating on like variables (e.g., job title, job level, function, geography, etc.).

An important part of the foundational analysis – often overlooked by organizations – is the opportunity to validate the system of job classification. Organizations need to examine the process for leveling jobs to ensure that similar jobs are grouped in the same level. Without this audit or validation, the results of the pay equity analysis can be questioned. Put another way, if jobs are classified into levels based on desired pay levels and not based on the content of the job, then the pay equity results will likely show spurious pay equity differences.

Remediation Analysis

Seeks to answer not only the key questions in foundational analysis, but also how the organization wants to fix pay gaps if it has them.

Organizations should take a thoughtful approach to fixing pay inequities. Considerations include defining:

- Who is eligible for remediation? Is it any employee or just those in disadvantaged classes?
- What is the threshold for remediation? Is it a 0.5 percent gap in pay, 3 percent, 10 percent?
- How will it be funded?
- Does the organization fix its issues all at once or over a period of several years?
- How does the organization communicate the reason for the adjustment? Is it explicit about pay equity or does it roll it into the annual merit increase process?

Because of the sensitivity surrounding pay equity analysis, organizations are often unsure how to communicate pay adjustments. Organizations should develop guiding principles around the communication of pay equity by establishing core messages and the level of transparency, in conjunction with leadership, HR, and legal perspectives.

The remediation analysis can move beyond pay adjustments by beginning to address the gaps found by the foundational analysis audit of current job leveling and salary administration processes. Organizations should develop an action plan for closing the gaps that are driving pay inequity.

Drivers Analysis

Identifies the gaps, fixes them, and seeks to understand if there are systems and processes that may be causing or perpetuating pay gaps. A drivers (or root cause) analysis of strategies, design and administrative processes in rewards management, talent acquisition, and talent management areas provide an organization a more holistic picture of what is causing the gaps in the first place.

But while organizations can use remediation processes to ensure work of equal value is paid equitably or to make minor program refinements to other HR policies aimed at supporting women's career progression, organizations will never be able to remediate or tweak their way to fully eliminating the gender pay gap.

To solve the representation issue, organizations must create solutions that address not just the technicalities of pay gaps, but get to one of the key root causes: the leadership pipeline challenges that lead to women still encountering glass ceilings.

This means organizations also have to understand what diversity and inclusion (D&I) actually means and implies and take more structural steps to level the playing field.

Effective Diversity and Inclusion Polices Can Help Close the Pay Gap

First, some quick definitions. Korn Ferry thinks of diversity *being the mix,* and inclusion *making the mix work* – a statement the firm has trademarked. The mix then includes all the differences that make people unique and can be used to differentiate groups and people from one another – physical and cognitive differences.

Making the mix work is about engaging and developing everyone in the organization. It is also about leveraging the wealth of knowledge, insights and perspectives in an open, trusting, and diverse workplace. When organizations make the mix work, it can influence people's levels of contribution, which allows them to unlock the power of having a diverse workforce.

Organizations must get two critical pieces right in order to truly support the mix and create that environment where everyone is contributing.

The first is *behavioral inclusion.* It is necessary to create a culture of belonging where employees in the organization have a more inclusive mindset, make more inclusive decisions and take more inclusive actions. This is the place of addressing conscious and unconscious biases.

The second is *structural inclusion,* where organizations revisit practices and processes that may be holding underrepresented employees back, such as job descriptions, high potential criteria, and performance evaluation checklists. These can be replete with norms, behaviors, and adjectives that inadvertently can be favorably biased toward white men.

Structural inclusion must be in place to successfully address pay equity. This begins with an audit of the policies and core structures of the organization through a holistic and inclusive lens.

Equity across all the talent systems, and not just pay and rewards, acknowledges that some face obstacles that a majority do not. These are headwinds those in the majority often are not even aware of because they don't see or feel them. Equitable practices need to be put in place to level the playing

FIGURE 13.5 Obstacles that women often face in many organizations.

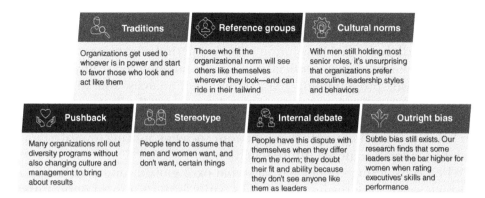

SOURCE: Korn Ferry

field by fixing the systematic obstacles. Figure 13.5 illustrates the headwinds present in many organizations.

Overall, gender pay gaps are a symptom of a broader problem of employment equity and differences in treatment across the entire talent life cycle (i.e., talent acquisition, talent management, and rewards management processes) over the course of an employee's career. Implementing a broad set of initiatives that covers this talent life cycle will achieve greater long-term organizational success and enhance the employee experience.

Organizations that proactively address comprehensive pay and employment equity management, as well as establish more inclusive practices that lead to greater diversity in the highest levels of the organization, will reduce their risk of litigation in a rapidly changing regulatory environment while at the same time enhancing the trust and engagement of their employees.

See Chapter 12, "Corporate Accountability in a Diverse and Inclusive World" for more information on creating a diverse and inclusive workforce.

FIGURE 13.6 Pathway to Workplace Equity.

SOURCE: World at Work, 2020, Workplace Equity Forum. © 2020, WorldatWork.

HOW THE FOURTH INDUSTRIAL REVOLUTION CAN ADDRESS GENDER PAY EQUITY

There is an unprecedented technological transformation taking place today.

The Fourth Industrial Revolution (4IR) is a period of exponential change with technologies, such as artificial intelligence, augmented reality, robotics, neurolinguistic programming (NLP), sentiment analysis, and 3-D printing changing the way that humans create, exchange, and distribute value. Some commentators anticipate this period could present a timely opportunity for a rebalance of the inequity that exists in our societies, moving toward a more inclusive, human-centered future together.

When considering gender pay gaps that exist globally and the slow pace at which we are progressing to earnings parity, is there also an opportunity in this new era to address the way work is structured? Specifically, along the gender boundaries and systemic issues that drive pay inequity?

New Technologies Can Drive Cultural Change

As they are in other areas of business, progressive leaders are looking to harness the converging technologies of 4IR to help drive the cultural change required to eradicate bias. These leaders recognize that a strong record on equality and inclusion converts to increased employee engagement, improved customer orientation, more innovative decision making and ultimately, enhanced business performance. At the same time, a new diversity and inclusion (D&I) technology market is emerging to help address diversity challenges across the employee lifecycle by creating consistent practices, simplifying complex decisions (particularly at scale) and tracking outcomes more effectively.

In fact, analysts are now starting to focus on D&I solutions as a discrete category within the HR tech space. A report from Mercer and Red Thread Research currently estimates the overall market size to be approximately $100 million. In the post #MeToo era, Vantage Point is a prime example of leveraging new technology to address D&I challenges – it provides an anti-sexual harassment training approach for corporations using virtual reality. It solution works on the premise that you don't need to explain what it's like to be the elephant in the room, but rather feel the elephant in the room, and tie that to an action your employees can take at that moment.

But there is a darker side to this innovation, particularly around the risk of bias in AI, which often relies on data collected and algorithms created by humans. So, in today's male-dominated IT sector, where according to a World Economic Forum's report less than a quarter of AI professionals are women, this remains a real risk (Cann 2018). We saw this play out with Amazon's gender-biased recruiting algorithms, which discarded competitive female candidates for roles after learning that the percentage of women in those positions was lower (Dastin 2018).

Similarly, in the book *Invisible Women: Exposing Data Bias in a World Designed for Men*, Caroline Criado Perez (carolinecriadoperez.com) highlights the presence of widespread male bias in science, technology, engineering and math (STEM). Through her work, we learn that most offices are five degrees too cold for women because the 1960s formula to determine temperature used the metabolic resting rate of a 40-year-old, 154-pound man, without accounting for women's slower metabolisms. Likewise, women in Britain are 50 percent more likely to be misdiagnosed following a heart attack because heart failure trials generally use male participants. Even cars are designed around the body of "Reference Man," so although men are more likely to crash, women involved in collisions are nearly 50 percent more likely to be seriously hurt.

So, while technology is associated with innovation, as the people interacting with it, we need to take positive steps to address any inherent bias within. And to fully understand the opportunity and impact 4IR's technology might provide, we need to consider what factors drive the gender pay gap.

Tackling Female Representation in the Workforce

The United Kingdom introduced compulsory gender pay gap reporting in 2017, and the second year of the regulation (UK Government 2017) revealed that in 78 percent of reporting companies, the median hourly pay gap favored men. The most compelling metric of the six statutory calculations required by the Gender Pay Gap Regulations was gender representation by pay quartile; here, 82 percent of employers reported they had more women than men in their lowest 25 percent of earners, while only 17 percent said they had more women than men in their highest 25 percent of earners. This trend is not unique to the UK and plays out across all locales, but UK employers are now actively starting to analyze blockages or leaks in their talent pipeline that may inhibit female progression to senior levels.

In the paper "The Role of AI in Mitigating Bias to Enhance Diversity and Inclusion" (Zhang et al. 2019), IBM's Smarter Workforce Institute states that bias can adversely influence decision-making across the entire employee life cycle, including in talent attraction, hiring, promotion, training, performance appraisal, compensation, and even termination. This is likely why many of the vendors in the D&I market are tackling bias at these critical decision points. At present, 43 percent of this market is focused on talent acquisition solutions helping to source diverse pools of candidates, changing job advertisements and descriptions to reduce bias and provide technology that can standardize the criteria on which people are screened out during background checking.

Leveraging this new bias-free technology to address these issues is a must.

Another more nuanced effect that may favor women's representation in leadership roles is the human vs. robot skills trade-off predicted to take place. Deloitte in its "Tech Trend Predictions" for 2018 predicted, "intelligent automation solutions may be able to augment human performance by automating certain parts of a task, thus freeing individuals to focus on more 'human' aspects that require empathic problem-solving abilities, strong social skills, and emotional intelligence" (Briggs 2017). It is these more human, or softer, skills traditionally attributed as female competencies that may become more valued leadership characteristics: a suitable counter to the current gender stereotypes in leadership that endorse stereotypically masculine attributes like assertiveness, ambition and competition.

Sharing Caring Roles More Equally

All too often, the defense given for why women earn less than men is because of the choices they make in their careers. But to tackle the issue, we need to address as a society why women make those choices.

In many instances, we see caring responsibilities and part-time roles shared unequally, resulting in women pushed into lower-paid, flexible roles or self-employment after childbirth, frequently referred to as the "motherhood penalty."

A quick spin through previous industrial revolutions reveals how the role of the family and gender roles came about, starting with traditional, agricultural societies where families worked together as a unit of production. Women and men could parent together while also playing a role in producing food or goods needed for household income. During the First Industrial Revolution, men, women, and children transferred to working in cities and factories, but with the introduction of heavy machinery, these places became unsafe for children. Men's greater physical strength gave them a productivity advantage over women, resulting in higher wages, and leaving women to take care of the home and family while experiencing a declining economic role.

Today, new technologies are making it easier for employers to accede to requests for flexible working and opening opportunities for remote working. But that alone does not provide the flexibility women (and men) need to balance ambition with caring responsibilities.

Firstly, opportunities to work from home some or all of the time are not enough if expectations of very long total hours of work are maintained. A study by Hilbrecht and Lero (2014), "Self-Employment and Family Life: Constructing Work-Life Balance When You Are Always On," observed that while technology can help facilitate home-based working, to date this has primarily benefitted higher-status, male occupations, while female self-employed teleworkers experience a higher risk of work-life spillover.

Though technology can provide the tools to facilitate flexible working to fit around caring responsibilities, it has also made it easier to work 24/7 and create "always-on employees." Perhaps we need to rethink jobs or working hour norms so they are more human-sized. Changing views of long working hours as a proxy for hard work and commitment might help with the labor productivity and employee engagement issues we are currently experiencing.

This leads some to question whether a growing well-being industry is a band-aid for the real problem of unrealistic expectations of working hours.

If we can shape work that allows for real work-life balance around caring responsibilities, men would also benefit. Some research revealed that many millennial men are looking for equality at home as well – they want to be active fathers as well as at work, to be flexible and to take time out. Embracing this could help to normalize the dual roles of caregivers and earners in households and address gender stereotyping. Thus, creating quality flexible jobs that allow women and men to balance ambition with caring responsibilities must be the aim.

Overcoming Occupational Segregation

Another reason cited for gender pay gaps is occupational segregation, with a historical tendency for women to take on low-paid work sometimes referred to as the 5 Cs: cleaning, catering, cashiering (retail), clerical work, and caring.

The World Economic Forum 2016 report, "The Future of Jobs," highlights that as 4IR takes hold in different industries and job families, it will affect female and male workers in distinct ways. Looking from a sector basis, job families expecting the highest employment growth include architecture, engineering, computer science, and mathematics, which currently have some of the lowest female participation rates. Women may also be considered more vulnerable due to their concentration in lower-skilled or routinized jobs that may be more easily automated. By extrapolating from the current pattern of gender segregation, it's predicted that this will result in a net job loss for women, with 3 million job losses and only 0.55 million gains – more than five jobs lost for every job gained, while men will face nearly 4 million job losses and 1.4 million gains, approximately three jobs lost for every job gained. Clearly, we need to break down those patterns of gender segregation to buck these predicted trends.

Perhaps most fundamentally of all, we can expect the gender pay gap to persist as long as employers' and employees' ideas about gender norms and occupations continue, including stereotypes about men and women's capabilities and skills and the culture associated with different types of work. But as the war for talent rages on, we know people are an increasingly valuable asset. Successful businesses will be those that can reskill their employees in order to deploy the technology of the 4IR. This may well be the antithesis of the First Industrial Revolution, where physical strength became more highly valued. In an economy based less on capital than talent, women are more likely to be treated as equals to foster an environment where there are fewer obstacles to talent acquisition and retention.

Technological disruption in the 4IR will bring many opportunities and benefits at global, national, and organizational levels, but technology alone won't be the cure-all. We need clear, ethical goals to build a society based on cooperation that benefits everyone. Rethinking working time, family time, and personal time, reassessing the gender division of labor and reviewing the rate of female participation and progression across our workforce will all help to build a culture that supports the increasingly diverse and multi-generational workforce that is emerging.

HOW DO SPOT AWARDS PERPETUATE PAY INEQUITY?

One of the key characteristics of most spot award programs is they are largely manager-driven. Many managers have full discretion and autonomy when it comes to spot award decisions with those decisions only subject to HR review and approval if the award is for a large amount (e.g., greater than $1,000). As managers tend to be closest to the impact an employee is having and can therefore reward positive impact quickly and effectively, their role as sole decision maker can be advantageous. The problem is that managers' impressions are not always completely accurate, objective and consistent throughout the organization.

Research suggests that unconscious bias influences what managers notice, how they evaluate performance and how they make other key decisions that affect employees' careers. This unconscious bias can be rooted in a number of factors, but often occurs because of manager expectations around what the ideal person "looks like" in a role or because managers are implicitly drawn toward people who are similar to themselves. Research has shown that similarity between supervisors and subordinates can result in more favorable outcomes including hiring likelihood, performance evaluations and job advancement. For example, a meta-analysis of ratee race effects in performance ratings found that both black and white raters gave significantly higher ratings to members of their own race, and that this bias was particularly likely to occur in settings where black employees composed a small percentage of the workforce. Perceived similarity (i.e., non-demographic similarity) can also contribute to bias. In a case study of professional service companies, more than half of the 120 interviewed evaluators described "fit," most commonly determined by similarity in leisure activities, personal experiences, and self-presentation styles, as being one of the three most important criteria used to assess job candidates.

If the similarity bias or other types of biases such as the escalation of commitment bias influence spot award decisions, this may perpetuate inequity in how those awards are distributed. Companies concerned with pay equity often review information such as salary and total compensation packages, analyzing whether there are significant differences among different genders, racial categories or other demographic fault lines and then adjust pay to ensure equitable distribution. But spot awards and other continuous recognition programs rarely undergo a similar systematic evaluation to ensure equitable distribution. This leaves companies vulnerable to biased reward decisions, and consequently, to demotivating and discouraging their workforce.

What Can Companies Do Differently?

The challenge facing companies is how to leverage spot awards to increase employee motivation and engagement without incurring the risks they pose to pay equity. Fortunately, there are several ways to create an effective spot award program that also alleviate the potential for unconscious bias and unequal distribution. These include:

- *Ensure managers have the resources they need to identify award-worthy behavior.* If managers are trained on how to effectively distribute rewards, they are less likely to base pay decisions on implicit biases and subjective impressions. Providing managers with clear definitions of award-worthy behavior based on the organization's values and goals, and even providing checklists to help managers recognize these behaviors can help ensure that decisions regarding who receives spot awards are based on a consistent set of standards. Managers also should be given guidance in terms of appropriate values for spot awards. Because these awards are often closely tied to managers' budgets, managers may end up determining the value of a spot award based on what remains in their budget rather than on the behavior that was demonstrated. Ensuring that managers have a good understanding of what an appropriate award looks like for specific behaviors can help mitigate the risk of them unintentionally over-awarding or under-awarding employees. Managers should still have discretion over the important aspects of spot awards such as the value of the reward, who receives them, and why. However, they are more likely to base spot award decisions on clearly defined criteria than "gut feel" or a general sense of "I thought he/she deserved this much" with the appropriate resources.
- *Communicate (and celebrate) spot award distribution.* We know that employees actively seek transparency when it comes to pay decisions, and spot awards are no exception. If managers fail to communicate to employees why they are receiving an award (or only communicate this information long after the fact), it makes it difficult for employees to establish a connection that will reinforce the desired behavior. After notifying the chosen employee that he/she is receiving an award and explaining the reason why, managers might also consider sending an email to the rest of their team notifying them of the award and recognizing the receiving employee's great work. While the exact amount of the award does not need to be shared with others, creating transparency around who is receiving spot awards and the types of behaviors that warrant rewarding can be a useful strategy for managers to keep their decision-making consistent and equitable.
- *Conduct a regular review of spot awards.* The informality and relatively small size of spot awards may make it seem like they are "non-essential" to measure. But these awards can add up quickly and their impact on employee engagement and perceptions of fairness over time can be

significant. Compensation professionals should routinely review the awards being provided for potential demographic issues, just as they would review base salary and other components of the comp package. Both the number of awards and the monetary values associated with these awards should be monitored so that potential issues, either with individual managers or across the organization, can be identified and addressed. Note that this does not mean human resources is involved in every single spot award transaction, invariably slowing down what is meant to be an efficient process. But HR is positioned to take a bird's eye view of these rewards over time, noting trends and patterns that may indicate that a manager, team, or business unit is headed toward an unequal distribution of pay.

- *Be aware of signs of manager fatigue.* Biased decision-making is most likely to occur when managers are tired or overwhelmed. When we are drained mentally, we are more likely to use "heuristics," or cognitive shortcuts, when making decisions. The problem is that these shortcuts can hurt the accuracy and fairness of decisions. For example, the familiarity heuristic encourages our choosing familiarity over novelty. This suggests that a manager might be more likely to reward an employee who has received an award in the past than an employee who has never received an award before, potentially further perpetuating inequitable distribution. Indeed, research has shown that raters who previously promoted an employee were significantly more likely to evaluate the employee more favorably, provide larger rewards and make more optimistic projections of future performance for that employee than raters who were not responsible for a previous promotion. It may be wise for human resources to pay special attention to award distribution during particularly busy times for managers, such as the end of the year when managers may be more likely to depend on overly simplified decision-making strategies.

On-the-spot, continuous methods of compensation are becoming increasingly popular means of motivating and rewarding great work. But certain characteristics of spot awards, such as being heavily manager-driven, informal and immediate can be problematic if organizations do not take the appropriate steps to ensure their equitable distribution. Training managers to clearly define award-worthy behaviors, encouraging the transparent communication of awards with other employees and conducting regular and thoughtful reviews of spot award distributions are a few practical tips to help organizations reap the benefits of spot awards without incurring the risks they pose to pay equity. As compensation evolves and organizations continue to adopt new approaches to pay, companies also must adjust how they think about, review, and ensure equal pay for all.

14 Contingent Workers and the New Talent Value Proposition

To what extent gig work has taken part in the marketplace is up for debate, but everyone agrees that it is influencing the work landscape, not just of today, but of tomorrow as well.

It's important to note that many of those workers likely have full-time jobs and are supplementing their income with side gigs, which is to say, it's not replacing traditional work.

"We have to understand these numbers in this context, and there's a big debate about how big the gig economy is today, but there's no question that it has significantly proliferated in the past 5–10 years," said John Bremen, managing director of human capital and benefits at Willis Towers Watson. "The gig economy is thriving, and we have observed that it's here to stay."

So, how are employers responding to this evolving work landscape? Bremen said organizations should approach the gig economy in a few ways. From a talent-acquisition perspective, employers should analyze and identify roles that might be better suited for a freelancer, as it could benefit them from a cost perspective, he said.

Organizations also need to figure out how to then integrate gig economy workers, so they can mitigate risk.

"We've seen boards lately really being concerned about standards for gig workers, because a lot of the corporate scandals over the years have been brought about by contractors or subcontractors, so companies have to have ways to ensure cultural fit as well as quality and process controls as well," Bremen said.

Lastly, organizations should create a talent value proposition (TVP) to supplement their employee value propositions (EVP). By doing this, organizations can align their contingent workforce with the mission, values, and culture without unintentionally exposing the organization to co-employment and misclassification risk, Bremen said.

A key part of the TVP is providing fair pay arrangements and access to retirement and health-care benefits, the latter of which isn't currently possible in the US. This has fueled a national debate around companies such as Lyft and Uber, which are wholly dependent on gig workers yet are unable to provide benefits that adequately support that workforce.

Bremen said he anticipates that part of the equation will change, but how quickly is anyone's guess.

"I am surprised at the slow pace of change on the legislative side in this regard, given the large percentage of workers in the US that are in the gig economy," Bremen said. "I would've thought that some of these rules would evolve, but my sense of it is, the pressure is not going to come from the companies, it's going to come from the voters. So as the percentage of gig workers increases in the US, I think they will be putting pressure on their elected officials to update the laws. But until then, I think it's going to be a little clunky."

Though gig workers lag behind the traditional workforce in those particular categories, they appear to have a leg up in an area that could prove vital in the future, Bremen said.

"Reskilling is playing a significant role in the economy today and we've seen studies that show gig workers reskill at a much faster rate than traditional workers," Bremen said. "I think as we see studies about work being impacted by technology, robotics, and AI, that workers need to reskill. It's fascinating that the gig workers are reskilling at a much faster rate."

THE FUTURE'S SO BRIGHT, GIGSTERS OUGHTA WEAR SHADES

Whether it's more flexibility, interesting work, additional income on the side, or simply because traditional employment is unavailable, people are increasingly looking for work that best suits their evolving needs, lifestyles, and aspirations.

In the United States alone, more than 57 million workers (about 36 percent of the workforce) freelance today, and data found in the Upwork survey, "Freelancing in America: 2017," predicts that most of the US workforce will freelance by 2027. Millennials are leading the way, with nearly half freelancing already.

Supporting the surge, organizations expect to make greater use of freelance talent as they look to both fill skill gaps and consider how best to get work accomplished in consideration of cost, speed to capability, and risk factors. In fact, the Willis Towers Watson "2017–2018 Global Future of Work Survey" projected that employers' use of free-agent workers was set to rise by 50 percent by 2021. The net? Organizations are increasingly engaging with a wider range of talent that has very different needs and expectations of a short-term employment relationship than that of workers in traditional, full- or part-time engagements.

Freelance Fallacies?

Future of work research has dispelled some commonly held myths about contingent workers. Most critically, they are neither disengaged nor uncommitted to an organization's success. Instead, about half of employers said that contingent workers are *just as likely* to put in extra effort as full-time employees. Furthermore, employers believe that freelancers are just as likely as their full-time employee counterparts to recommend an organization to friends as a good place to work, underscoring the importance of leaders and managers in engaging all talent types.

And because nonemployee talent is so critical, committed, and likely to promote the company as a good place to work, nearly half of the employers in Willis Towers Watson (WTW) research reported that they are considering providing some level of rewards to this population. Specifically, organizations are expecting to increase the use of recognition programs and health and wellness programs (e.g., access to the gym) to these alternative worker types.

As the workforce continues to embrace the new gig economy, contingent workers are looking at opportunities through a new lens – and the most highly skilled among them will expect (and even demand) more than just competitive pay. WTW's employee opinions normative database provides some understanding around the preferences of the gig economy. Results from contingent workers in 112 companies were aggregated for analysis, representing more than 100,000 respondents.

So, how does this population feel about the work experience? Contingent workers generally score more favorably on various topics than typical employees in high-performance companies, suggesting a relatively positive work experience. But contingent workers score lower than the usual trend, indicating challenges and opportunities, in three areas:

- Workload and work–life, especially fairness in work distribution
- Goals and objectives, especially understanding how work goals fit with company objectives
- Operating efficiency, especially timeliness of decision-making.

Collectively, the findings suggest that an otherwise positive job experience is marked by (perceived) unfair workload, misalignment with company goals, and poor decision speed (which may instead reflect poor line-of-sight to decision processes). In other words, these workers may feel overly stretched and underappreciated (see Sidebar 14.1).

Contingent Conundrums

The lines between employees and contingent workers are blurring as organizations make greater use of nonemployee talent and as flexible and remote work become more prevalent. From an employer perspective, having a lot of contingent workers is risky. If disengaged, contingent workers can leave a lot faster than employees, taking their knowledge with them and potentially working for competitors the following week. Worse, they might remain working for their current organization, not recommend it as a good place to work, and underperform. Essentially, they could lack *stickiness,* AKA loyalty.

Human resources must shift its thinking to focus on these new talent populations and how their needs may differ from those of a more traditional employee population. How will companies differentiate their organizations from others competing for the same skills and talent groups? How will they create a connection to the organization, its culture, and how work gets done to achieve business objectives and drive high performance? How will they solve for the three challenge areas previously mentioned?

PIVOTING THE PROPOSITION

The employee value proposition defines "the give and the get" by outlining what the organization offers workers and the behaviors expected in return. Articulating an EVP is not new, but the practice of expanding it to include both core and contingent workers is gaining momentum.

The talent value proposition takes the traditional notion of an EVP and focuses on a broader population. It is about creating a competitive advantage by delivering a compelling work experience for all the talent sets connected to the organization. It also is about creating an exceptional working relationship that engages the right people from inside and outside the organization to achieve a shared purpose and goals.

Overall, an EVP may be working well for full-time employees, but the needs and risks of other talent populations likely are different, and the specific programs that can be delivered can differ as well. Pivoting from an EVP to a broader TVP allows organizations to better engage the entire talent network.

Creating the TVP: A 3-D Approach

The first step to developing a TVP is *discovery.* Identify the talent segments that the organization has (and needs) today and tomorrow. Get perspectives from these segments on the elements of the deal that will most drive engagement, referring to the challenge areas revealed by the research.

The second step is *debriefing.* This involves synthesizing a data-driven report on the implications for each talent segment, to include research on the future of work, talent, and drivers of engagement. It also includes identifying risks and assessing opportunities relative to business performance objectives.

The final step is *developing.* This involves exploring the characteristics of the talent population through personal maps and identifying specific talent and rewards solutions that will differentiate the employer. Finally, this concludes with organizing the solutions into the talent value proposition.

Once 3-D design is complete, we recommend creating a personalized total rewards or HR portal to communicate the new TVP (see Sidebar 14.2).

Tailoring Programs for a Broader Talent Network

Many organizations that have started to explicitly articulate their TVP have many part-time, seasonal, contract, or other contingent workers. Some organizations (particularly those where technology is transforming work) recognize the need to engage an audience wider than their direct employees. These companies understand that a strong TVP helps them gain a competitive edge by engaging people with the critical skills they need to get work done.

There are some simple steps to get started and figure out your talent network, how to engage them, and manage the risks:

- Understand the total talent mix: What is it now, and what's likely in the future?
- Figure out what these types of employees want from their relationship with you as the employer.
- Consider the potential risks related to these relationships and how you might mitigate against them.
- Define and execute some quick wins: Decide if you can introduce some tailored programs or activities to help you attract and engage the people who will make a difference for you in the short-term.

TVP: The Link to High Performance

The definition of employees is changing who and what a company relies on for productivity and performance to get work done today can range from full-time employees to part-timers, from seasonal employees to freelancers and volunteers – and let's not forget artificial intelligence.

Never have we had the opportunity to engage a network of talent in so many ways. As a result, how we design the work deal is evolving. Organizations need new value propositions both to engage with this expanded talent network and to mitigate risk. The TVP can develop a true link between the worker, organization, and culture, and subsequently create a highly engaged workforce with the stickiness to help drive performance.

Sidebar 14.1 HR Has a New Gig in the Gig Economy

In the past 30 years, HR has pushed to – and in most cases succeeded in – having a seat at the C-suite table, essentially playing a strategic role in talent attraction, retention, and engagement. This current traditional role of HR covers everything from recruiting to total rewards (design and administration) and employee development. HR today goes far beyond the legacy responsibilities assigned to the outdated term "personnel."

Change, however, is here. A new and critically important role is emerging that will take precedence over everything that has come before. HR needs to address the challenges of the increasingly dynamic work environment with a similarly dynamic workforce. Traditional HR supports traditional employment designed to support legacy approaches to work. New and evolving work, driven by greater speed, artificial intelligence, and automation has created a strengthening workforce of contingent and freelance talent. HR must be at the center of this change and, ultimately, the center of workforce productivity.

As HR continues partnering with the business on total rewards and career opportunities to engage an employee base that is stable (i.e., jobs primarily filled by full-time employees), new workplace realities, including temporary and sometimes unpredictable assignments, create new challenges. Traditional approaches become less important when career paths are evolving into portfolios of broad and nonlinear work experiences. How the work gets done and by whom are the questions HR is increasingly facing.

Just as work found in other occupations is being transformed, so too will the work of HR. Specifically, HR needs to:

- Move from being a business partner to a work and business integrator, focused on productivity.
- Change focus from delivering on the EVP to delivering on the TVP for a broader population.

How will HR accomplish these changes? It must:

- Rethink work and talent management.
- Redefine the talent experience.
- Re-envision HR solutions.
- Match skills and talent to immediate, fast-moving, highly prioritized work.
- Apply data to create meaningful talent insights on a much more frequent basis.

Is HR ready? In most organizations, the HR function needs to be assessed against these new goals and likely modified to accommodate this changing environment. Winning the race for talent is about speed to talent, which includes all talent types: part-time, contingent, freelance, and alliances. Jobs are becoming far more dynamic with shorter assignments and the work being constantly calibrated and iterated to ensure relevance to the current employer circumstances.

HR needs to plan for the shift and make changes. The need is now.

Sidebar 14.2 Co-Employment Considerations and Total Rewards

While the law is still forming around co-employment considerations, some organizations express concerns around the idea of offering a value proposition that might misconstrue the line between employee and nonemployee status. For example, some organizations believe that providing access to health-care or retirement benefits will be viewed as employment. In fact, organizations only run the risk if they provide actual health-care benefits (versus options to purchase health care) or if they provide actual retirement benefits like a defined contribution plan (versus access to financial planning resources).

Furthermore, employers can provide many voluntary benefits to contingent workers, such as learning opportunities or recognition. Within the TVP solution, the challenge is to figure out the optimal combination of rewards for contingent workers and how/why they should be different from those of employees. This is specialized legal ground, so be sure to have your HR and legal teams collaborate on the specifics for your organization.

EMPLOYMENT RIGHTS

The rights of gig workers are playing out in courts around the world. The primary debate is that many who work as contingent workers have limited employment rights. Yet, by law, they actually are a category of self-employed individuals who are entitled to basic rights (e.g., paid holidays, minimum wage, and protection from discrimination).

In the United States, the US Department of Labor's Wage and Hour Division (WHD) offered informal regulatory guidance on gig workers under Barack Obama's presidency. WHD said it would pursue investigations into complaints about worker classification and subsequent pay disputes. However, President Donald Trump's labor secretary, Alex Acosta, removed that guidance. With the lack of clarity from the US government, the courts have been left to define and rule on rights (see Sidebar 14.3).

In the United Kingdom, the Taylor review of modern working practices suggested the problem is confusion in the law, or the inability of the law to keep up, both which can result in workers being inadvertently deprived of rights to which they're entitled. Clearly, those setting the law and businesses using gig workers need to adapt to a structure of working arrangements that better supports the well-being of contingent workers while still retaining the flexibility required by all participants.

Talent Sourcing Challenges

While digital platforms can facilitate direct connections between employers and the vast number of talented individuals in the market, engaging and managing the right talent becomes trickier thanks to such abundance.

Recruiters must be more data focused to find the best talent for the right gig as well as be able to speed up their interview processes to compete for highly mobile talent. Though recruitment can be done online, there may still be a need for screening of skills suitability or even cultural fit.

From an employer's perspective, there also is some work to be done on organizational design to move from the traditional view of work needing to be delivered by employees in jobs to a more diverse view of work that can be completed via outsourcing or by deploying temporary or contract skills. This really requires a shift in approach from "I need to hire a person," to "I need to complete a task." Managing this task-oriented worker is the next challenge.

Sidebar 14.3 What Does the Future Hold for Gig Workers Post-AB5?

California Assembly Bill 5 (AB5), a statewide gig-worker law that could turn thousands of independent contractors into employees with protections and benefits, took effect on January 1, 2020. The legislation represented a watershed moment in labor law and its effects could be felt for years to come across the entire United States.

While much of the focus on the AB5 legislation has been targeted at prominent gig companies like Uber and Lyft, there are ramifications for a wide range of businesses, including those in the trucking, health-care, and media industries. However, various occupations have already won exemptions, such as real estate brokers, commercial fishermen, and hairstylists, while Uber, Lyft, and DoorDash have said they will spend at least $90 million to sponsor a ballot initiative to overturn it. Uber has also said it will go to court to keep its drivers as independent contractors.

So, how should California employers – and employers around the country – prepare for a future landscape that might not allow for independent contractors? Employers' first steps to prepare for this potential shift should be to arrange an attorney–client privilege analysis of their workforce to determine their independent contractors and nonexempt and exempt employees.

Part of determining the cost will involve back-pay liability considerations for existing contractors, as well as future scheduling conflicts and examining existing policies when it comes to providing benefits.

California's various employment laws create further complications with this legislation, including its meal and rest breaks law. The law states that employers must provide a paid rest break for every four hours of work and an unpaid meal break for every five hours. Each rest break must be at least 10 minutes and each meal break must be at least 30 minutes.

This all factors into the flexibility aspect of independent contractors that employers will need to consider in the future if they are required to be employees under the new law.

GENDER PAY GAP IMPLICATIONS

The gig economy has lent itself to more people going the route of freelancer or independent contractor as their main source of income.

The "2020 Freelancer Income Report" by Payoneer, based on a survey of more than 7,000 freelancers from 150 countries, found that the worldwide average hourly rate charged by freelancers is $21, which is significantly higher than the average salaries in many of the countries surveyed.

The popularity of freelancing is attributed to the potential for greater job opportunity, independence, higher incomes, and a promising move in the direction of wage equality. Today's gig economy – powered by social media, global marketplaces, and online payment platforms – equips the global workforce with all the tools needed to chart their own career path, leveraging a freelance work lifestyle to build a full-time career, a "side-hustle," or even just extend their career post-retirement.

"The freelancing economy has grown exponentially over the past decade, and I believe we can now firmly say that the future of work has arrived," said Scott Galit, CEO of Payoneer. "Obstacles that could slow or hinder freelancers' ability to grow, connect, and be successful have been removed. Freelancers from all walks of life and every corner of the world are empowered to acquire work, set their own wages, market their skills, and get paid how and when they want."

The Bright Young Future for Freelancers

The freelance workforce is overall very young, with nearly 70 percent of freelancers surveyed being under the age of 35 and 21 percent under the age of 25. This youth movement is even more pronounced in Asia where 82 percent of respondents are under 35, compared to North America where the number is still high but closer to 47 percent.

Across the board, workers at the beginning and end of their careers are most likely to be exclusively freelancing, whereas the promise of a stable paycheck and the sense of security that comes with it seems to drive workers to seek a company job while raising a family. While more experienced workers command top pay, that gap could close in the future as freelance opportunities provide those with fewer years of experience the ability to sharpen and hone their crafts.

Additionally, education does not necessarily correlate with high earnings for freelancers, as those with bachelor's degrees do not demand higher fees than those without, indicating that the future of work values reviews, references, and a rich portfolio as much as traditional educational achievements.

How Job Satisfaction Is Unlocked with Income Opportunity

While freelancers find value in freedom and the flexibility of being their own boss, happiness is most tightly correlated with income earned. Individuals who work exclusively in freelancing earn a higher hourly rate and are more satisfied with their lifestyle compared to those who split their time working for a company. While freelancers are earning more, businesses are also benefiting by being able to source top talent without concern for location or overhead costs, increasing satisfaction on both sides of the relationship.

Important Steps Toward Wage Equality

One of the more optimistic findings from the report is that women's participation in the freelance workforce has been gaining momentum and the average wage for females is leaps and bounds ahead of the greater workforce. Female freelancers earn on average 84 percent of men's earnings across all fields, and while there is room for improvement, the gap is much smaller than the 64 percent average for all workers reported by the World Economic Forum. However, there are industry-specific nuances, and fields exist where the gender gap remains pronounced, including finance and project management fields. That said, women earn more than men in marketing and web and graphic design.

Other key takeaways:

- Women's share of the workforce is increasing: Female freelancers now represent 39 percent of the workforce, compared to 22 percent in 2015.
  - In some countries, it is much higher, such as the Philippines at 67 percent or US at 47 percent.
- Dedication to freelancing pays off: Those who work exclusively as freelancers earn a higher hourly rate and are more satisfied with their lifestyle than those who freelance part-time and work for a company.

TODAY'S GLOBAL FREELANCE WORKER: YOUNG AND "ALL-IN"

A youth movement of freelancers is leading this worldwide trend, with young workers craving independence and seeking fresh opportunities. Millennials (those born 1981–1996) and Gen Z (those born 1997–2012) represent a vast majority of the global freelance workforce: Close to 70 percent are below the age of 35 and more than a fifth are under the age of 25, according to the 2020 Payoneer report. This wave is led by Asian freelancers, where a whopping 82 percent of freelancers are under 35. By comparison, only 47 percent of North American freelancers are under 35.

But don't count older baby boomer workers out when it comes to freelance success: Experience is a major factor in the hourly rates commanded by freelancers, according to the report. In fact, more experienced freelancers over the age of 55 earn twice as much as their youthful peers aged 18–25.

No matter their age, the majority (69 percent) of freelancers go "all in" – that is, they are committed to the lifestyle and do it exclusively (see Sidebar 14.4). However, this, too, differs by region: For example, in Western Europe, 77 percent of freelancers do so full time. On the other hand, 42 percent of freelancers in Central America and 41 percent of those in the Middle East divide their time between a company job and freelance gigs.

Sidebar 14.4 Gig Workers Fill the Void in a Tight Labor Market

Tenured workers and retirees often capitalize on a tight labor market and skills shortage by turning to gig work.

This was a main finding in the ADP Research Institute's survey, "Illuminating the Shadow Workforce: Insights into the Gig Workforce in Businesses," which also found that one in six enterprise workers are actually gig workers paid as either 1099-MISC (1099-M) workers or short-term W-2 employees working one to six months.

Backed by anonymized payroll data of 18 million workers from 75,000 companies, coupled with 16,800 direct survey responses from traditional employees and gig workers and 21 C-level executive interviews, the research shows that this changing composition of the workforce has significant talent management, budget, and compliance implications for businesses of all sizes.

In addition, the ADP Research Institute identified two worlds of gig workers in organizations. The first is comprised of 1099-M contractors who are independent contractors, often hired for their skillset on a project basis. These skilled, tenured workers tend to be older and highly educated and choose to work on what they enjoy. In fact, 30 percent of 1099-M gig workers are aged 55 or older. For some, their gig work is supplemental income to their retirement savings. The second includes short-term W-2 employees who are younger, less educated, have a lower income, and are typically working on a seasonal or on-call hire basis.

"It is clear that there is a fundamental shift in the workforce as innovation continues to transform work, increasing the demand for skilled workers," said Ahu Yildirmaz, co-head of the ADP Research Institute. "To bridge the talent gap in today's tight labor market, many companies are hiring skilled workers at a premium. Our research shows that companies are turning to tenured, skilled workers and retirees on a gig-basis to meet this growing demand."

Spotlight on the Gig Employment and Key Findings

- **Gig work is growing**: From 2010 to 2019, the share of gig workers in businesses has increased by 15 percent, with both short-term W-2 and 1099-M gig workers contributing equally to this growth. The research indicates gig work will continue to grow, further impacting workforce dynamics and forcing companies to optimize talent management and workforce strategy.
- **Every industry relies on gig workers:** Recreation, construction, and business services are the top three industries utilizing the gig workforce.
- **Contract life is a choice:** More than 70 percent of 1099-M gig workers say they are working independently by their own choice, not because they can't find a "traditional" job. Most seem happy with gig work and place a premium on flexibility as a driving motivation behind their decision, over financial security or benefits. In fact, 60 percent of 1099-M gig workers say they will continue to gig for the next three years.
- **Gig work is not sporadic:** More than half of the 1099-M contractors work for the same company for 12 consecutive months, just like any traditional W-2 employee.
- **Earning potential is similar to a traditional worker:** The average income for employees working for 12 consecutive months is similar, regardless of being a 1099-M worker or a traditional W-2 employee.
- **Millennials and Gen Z gig it their way:** Gig workers under the age of 34 view themselves as traditional employees, perhaps reflecting the shift in the workforce. However, the prospect of health insurance does not appear to change their job behavior. In fact, 74 percent say they would continue to work as a 1099-M worker, even if they lost their current health insurance.

"While the term 'gig worker' has seamlessly integrated into our vernacular and culture, there has been no real data-driven insight into the gig workforce in the enterprise space," Yildirmaz said. "This 'shadow workforce' is comprised of workers with vast skillsets, who work across all industries and in all regions of the US. Additionally, we have found that the majority of these workers are doing gig work out of preference."

WHY YOU SHOULD CREATE A GIG ECONOMY INSIDE YOUR ORGANIZATION

Through education, hobbies, or the pursuit of other interests, people develop a number of abilities that their daily jobs might never uncover. You might find that your employees are participating in activities outside of work to gain more skills and experiences that are not offered in their primary roles (Mosquida 2018).

While many people see the emergence of the "gig economy" as ride-share or delivery drivers making a little money on the side, that is only a partial view.

According to a June 2019 report from the Centre for Research on Self-Employment (Burke 2019), a large portion of people participating in the gig economy – the practice of employees finding employment through short-term freelance work rather than focusing on a more traditional 9-to-5 job – are highly skilled. They know how to program computers, design websites, keep books, and even grow companies – and their expertise is in high demand.

Keep It In-House

If you can recreate the gig economy model internally, you will stand a better chance of retaining the top talent your company needs.

The internal gig economy offers outside-of-your-role activities inside the organization that allows employees to gain new proficiencies and develop new competencies. They can be on a project basis outside of normal duties or doing work across departments.

This might be a new way to look at work, but if done well, it can greatly benefit the organization. You can save on recruitment and employee onboarding costs and you can keep your current workforce motivated and engaged.

Support Development Through Individualized Strategies

By allowing your employees to use a percentage of their time on these internal gigs, organizations will see vast improvements in absenteeism, retention, overall satisfaction, and even healthy internal networks. Here are three ways you can support your workers' development through your internal gig economy.

1. Personalize the Strategy

Customize the plan based on the individual employees. There is not a one-size-fits-all approach, and the employees will respond best if the training actually meets their needs.

Training resources – courses, videos, or, of course, gigs – should dovetail with each employee's objectives and aspirations and connect the work to a sense of purpose within the organization.

2. Offer Guidance

Support your talent with coaching and development. Remember that this is a resource to build skills. Progression opportunities, such as stretch assignments and leadership training courses, help employees grow faster.

With the help of defined roles, employees can understand what skills and level of proficiency each role requires and where they have a gap and need more development.

3. Enable Ownership

According to an Accenture study, a majority of recent college graduates see large corporations as being able to provide everything they seek – things like mentorship and training.

By implementing a career-pathing plan, your organization can be a part of your employees' career progression and give them an understanding of the skills and competencies needed to continue their journeys. As part of that plan, development options are provided with a specific activity related to the required development.

Offering gigs inside of your organization helps employees gain new experiences and develop skills. This benefits the employees who want to take part in different opportunities that help define their career progression (see Sidebar 14.5).

Sidebar 14.5 A Promising Benefits Landscape for Gig Workers?

As the workforce continues to evolve from the standard nine-to-five, full-time employee structure, so do organization's rewards structures.

Today, an estimated 36 percent of employees participate in the gig economy, and it is projected that most of the US workforce will freelance by 2027. However, a key obstacle facing this segment of the workforce – the portion that doesn't have a full-time job as well – is a lack of benefits, as the transaction between gig workers and their organization is usually strictly monetary.

That, however, could be changing.

In 2019 Businessolver, a benefits administration technology and services company, added benefits options to its platform that caters to those employees that are traditionally ineligible for benefits. It allows organizations using Businessolver to direct their freelance or contract workers to the platform to select benefits rather than asking them to purchase their own through the Patient Protection and Affordable Care Act's individual marketplace.

"One of the things that we've done is we've taken benefits that used to only be available in the retail space and we've been able to build

---

those out on our platform," said Sherri Bockhorts, Businessolver's strategy practice leader. "Because of that, we've also been able to attract benefits that normally wouldn't be available to an aggregated group of individuals. These aren't group plans, they're individual plans."

Bockhorts said the benefits offered to gig workers on their platform are coming from the same individual marketplace, but they offer a couple distinct advantages. Because it's being negotiated on a group platform, rates will often be cheaper. And, because the services are all consolidated on one platform, there is an ease-of-use and convenience variable for gig workers who otherwise have to keep track of different premium payments from different providers.

"What we've been able to do is take an employer mentality, but apply it to the retail space," Bockhorts said. "We're taking on the curation of the benefits, the communication, the education, the enrollment, the premium consolidation, so it looks and feels like an employer benefit plan and it's on the same platform as an employer's benefit-eligible population, so it has that same look and feel as the employer-sponsored plans."

Businessolver's expansion of its MyChoice platform is likely the start of a shift in the benefits space going forward. Both government agencies and businesses will need to rethink employee benefits programs so that they adequately compensate the various types of workers participating in the labor force.

The government portion of this equation might have similarly been addressed in late June 2019 when the Trump administration finalized rules that allow companies to reimburse employees who purchase health insurance in the individual market through health reimbursement arrangements (HRAs).

The rules, which went into effect January 1, 2020, loosened Obama-era restrictions on short-term health plans that don't meet the ACA's standards. From a benefits standpoint, a key variable that could be attractive to employers is the portability and convenience factor the HRA rule presents. Employees who purchase health care on the individual market could bring it with them when they switch jobs.

The HRA rule plays into the platform strategy of benefits providers like Businessolver, which could make for an interesting future in the industry.

"I think employers could eventually leverage the individual coverage HRA to support employees, but where I think it could come into play initially is for these alternative workforces like part-time and gig workers that are becoming a bigger part of the workforce," Bockhorts said. "I do think there could be a time in the future where it applies to the benefit eligible population too and it just becomes a new delivery mechanism for employer-sponsored plans."

15 The Present and Future of Work: Digital Disruption, Automation, and Reskilling

Examples abound as to how digital disruption is the present and future of work. The revolution is touching everyday life and traditional industries alike: virtual assistants can now call restaurants and salons to book appointments and navigate complex conversations, while musicians use AI to comb existing tracks and compose a basic score before adding their own original flourishes. Despite the wonder of it all, concerns about job disruption have become all too familiar and the impact on us – on our sense of self, our take-home pay, and future careers – are all too real.

As always, it's more complicated than the attention-grabbing headlines. Yes, organizations must embrace digital transformation to succeed in the global economy, but at the same time their challenge is to engage and empower people to thrive in an age of disruption. Organizations are rethinking their business models, redesigning work to harness the power of technology and adjusting their operating models to a fast-changing world. Yet for all the concern about technological disruption, it's clear they can't succeed without making people a priority.

In the HR world, the potential for digital solutions to contribute to people's performance is increasingly evident. Portable performance management systems, enabled by the hyper-secure networking of blockchain technology, can be leveraged from job to job (or gig to gig). Data and algorithms are nudging managers toward better, more analytically sound talent decisions and helping to enhance managers' interactions with team members. Meanwhile, the evolution of massive open online courses (MOOCs) for employee training and reskilling is opening doors to employee development and employment in ways that weren't so clearly part of the conversation five years ago.

People are the heart of every organization, but it should be just as evident that people are at the heart of technology. With AI infused into today's and tomorrow's work, enterprises need highly – and newly – skilled people to maximize the benefits of digitization. People, not robots or AI software, will continue to brainstorm new ideas, pursue opportunity, inspire each other, and drive organizations to succeed. If anything, we've entered a new Human Age and one where we have to think differently about how we build the skills of the future.

That's a key takeaway from Mercer's "2018 Global Talent Trends" study, which gathered insights from more than 7,600 senior business executives, HR leaders, and employees from around the world. The consensus reveals that global leaders and employees understand that to thrive, organizations need workforces of lifelong learners who grow with the business, embrace continuous change, master new technologies, and build skills for the future that enable them to work with technology and an array of talent partners.

So what do employees need and want if they are to stay the course? Flexibility in how, when, and where they work. Careers that conform to personal lives, not the other way around. A sense of well-being and purpose. And, as they support technology, they want technology to support them back – through state-of-the-art platforms that enable people to connect, collaborate, and innovate together.

While integrating new technologies, leadership must focus on the "human operating system" that powers the organization. The Mercer study specifically identified five workforce trends for 2018 and beyond.

CHANGE@SPEED

How companies prepare for the future of work depends on the degree of disruption anticipated. Those expecting the most disruption are working agility into their model and placing bets on flatter, more networked structures (32 percent are forming more holacratic work teams – based on decentralized authority rather than a management hierarchy – compared to 22 percent last year). More than half (53 percent) of executives predict at least one in five roles in their organization will cease to exist by 2022, so it is no surprise that being prepared for job displacement and reskilling is viewed as critical for survival. The number one reskilling being embarked on this year is building innovation skills, followed by developing digital competence and a global mindset.

In practice, Change@Speed calls for agile organizational design, and 96 percent of C-suite respondents to the survey said they are planning a shake-up, citing new work models such as self-driven teams to make firms more "change agile." Greater efficiency and increased automation are the prime drivers of these changes, while innovation is a greater driver for change in Asia than in other parts of the world.

At the individual level, Change@Speed is about fostering a learning culture that encourages employees to stretch, try new things, and go outside their comfort zones. In the survey, only 50 percent of organizations were viewed as having an ecosystem of shared learning and credentialing to create a portable "skills passport" for employees. MOOC providers such as edX and Coursera are part of the picture, democratizing access to education and "microlearning." And this is upending the traditional "learn and apply" model. For example, in the United States, GE guarantees an interview to all candidates who successfully complete one of edX's MicroMasters programs, and others are following suit, commissioning learnings to fulfill future skills needs.

Technology also is being employed to improve learning outcomes: Fulcrum Labs, an AI-driven education company, has developed an algorithm to determine which individuals won't finish a course and which are at risk of not being able to apply the knowledge learned. In Italy, the business school MIP Politecnico di Milano uses big data and AI to assess learners' skills, benchmark them against job requirements, and make learning recommendations to fill in skill gaps. One result of all these applications is rapid skill development and the outgrowth of a "lab mindset" that drives experimentation and innovation.

WORKING WITH PURPOSE

Three-quarters (75 percent) of thriving employees, those who feel fulfilled personally and professionally, say their company has a strong sense of purpose. To find purpose, employees crave movement, learning, and experimentation. If not received, it is clear that they will look for it elsewhere – 39 percent of employees satisfied in their current job still plan to leave because of a perceived lack of career opportunity. In addition to purpose, the new value proposition that employees are seeking includes a focus on their health and financial well-being.

As AI and automation have the potential to reduce work to a list of tasks, finding meaning in what we do will only grow in criticality. While the "loyalty contract" of yesterday has shifted to today/s "engagement paradigm," what the research shows is that today's forward-thinking organizations are seeking to offer the "thrive contract" to valued employees. This acknowledges the importance not only of pay, benefits, and engagement but also an investment in their future growth, and ensuring that they can find their niche and are inspired by the company's mission. It's tough to do without good talent intelligence. Technology such as Pymetrics' gamified assessments and Fuel50's career apps that assess individual's values and interests in order to "match" them to potential career opportunities are on pulse with this trend.

Permanent Flexibility

Individuals are vocal in their expectations of work arrangements that put them in control of their personal and professional lives. Employees want more flexible work options, with some starting their own enterprises to push the agenda. Australian startup Gemini3 was founded by three women to pair up jobseekers based on skills, personality, and availability so they can apply for jobs together as a job share team. When we are comfortable sharing our homes, cars, and data, why has job sharing been the laggard? And more importantly, what can we do to catch up?

The good news is that organizations are listening – 80 percent of executives view flexible working as a core part of their value proposition (up from 49 percent last year). Yet, only 3 percent of companies consider themselves industry leaders when it comes to enabling flexibility, and 41 percent of employees fear that choosing flexible work arrangements will negatively affect their promotion prospects.

Flexibility is especially important for workers in the financial services and health-care sectors. And of those who say they are thriving at work, 71 percent report that their organizations offer flexible work options (up from 49 percent in 2017). Flexible working also is part of the strategy for many in addressing the widening skills gap by enabling access to a broader talent pool. According to Mercer's When Women Thrive research platform, organizations that make flexibility a core tenet have better representation of women.

Platform for Talent

Given that 89 percent of executives expect an increase in the competition for talent, organizations realize they must expand their talent ecosystem and update their HR models for a digital age. The time is now – two in five companies plan to "borrow" more talent in 2018 and 78 percent of employees would consider working on a freelance basis yet current employment models and legislation struggles to make this operate core and contingent hiring seamlessly.

In the platform model, the organization is no longer a hierarchy of employees. Instead, it's a smart platform that matches skill supply with work demand. Data, especially work feedback, plays a vital role in making this work. Automated feedback mechanisms such as Zugata and work management platforms like WorkMarket – which help businesses source, vet, and manage independent workers – are part of a growing suite of applications that makes this vision possible. And they are finding creative ways to empower managers to scale up and down,

Gaining greater access to talent through a broader ecosystem is, of course, vital in changing times. Companies also need to deploy talent faster and with precision to unlock the potential of their workforce. Many executives report that improving the ability to move jobs to people and people to jobs is the talent investment that would have the most impact on business performance this year. In practice, today's talent platforms require better information on talent supply (by understanding the talent within the company's ecosystem, and the gaps and blockages in talent pipelines), and better insight into upcoming demand (where will value be created in the future, and where will it be hard to source?), AI and Automation can help to streamline the process by predicting needed skills and monitoring individual output, but we are still in our infancy – just 43 percent of the global workforce surveyed proclaims to have a digital interaction with HR. This will change, and when it does, it will free HR to focus on talent strategy, matching execution and other enabling technologies

Digital from the Inside Out

Despite improvement over last year, companies lag on delivering employees a consumer-grade digital experience – only 15 percent consider themselves a digital organization today. And while 65 percent of employees say that state-of-the-art tools are important for their career success, less than half (48 percent) say they have the digital tools today necessary to do their job effectively.

The good news is that most companies are investing in technology to support key HR processes with talent acquisition, performance management, and rewards being the top areas to upgrade. What is of concern is that digital tools that specifically enhance the employee experience often come later in the buying cycle – typically sitting atop a HCM platform. As we embrace the era of the individual, systems that support individuals, not managers or HR, might need to take precedence.

The Mercer Talent Trends study found that implementing an HCM/HRIS system (like Workday or SAP) has a significant impact on being digital from the inside out. In the eyes of employees, it is made-to-order technologies (such as career or HR portals and collaboration technology) that may provide the best return on a company's digital investments. And as we move toward the management of multiple systems to support employees, the user experience becomes even more critical. This has been a huge area of growth this year, with companies like ServiceNow offering chatbots and process management tools to answer employees' routine requests, alleviating frustrations by streamlining and speeding up HR processes.

Significantly, one in three employees report that their roles or responsibilities have already changed due to digital technology, and this percentage will likely double in the next few years. The challenge is to keep the human touch as we embrace a tech-enabled future. Technology that is getting the most positive press is that which helps companies engage with their full talent ecosystems and in ways that support their health, wealth, and careers needs.

To thrive in the new Human Age, organizations must be agile and vigilant – pivoting at the pace of market fluctuations, leveraging the best technologies, and nimbly reforming to take advantage of new opportunities as they emerge. But great strategy and organizational agility is not enough. To sustain growth, companies must bring their people along on the journey. Building the workforce for the future needs leaders with a vision for what that future will be and a workforce inspired by its promise.

THE FORCES THAT ALIGN: HIGH TECH, HIGH TOUCH

HR professionals know that success comes from treating each employee as a person, not a database entry. But there's the rub: while human resources relies on technology to support the entire workforce, there is a fear that the more automated and digital HR operations get, the less personal they'll be – that human insights will be replaced with digital IQ.

As technology changes the nature of work, there's a danger that managers will be held in thrall by it: "Just deploy the tech" will become the mantra to solve our problems. Shiny new technology solutions alone won't tackle real, specific, individual problems. Cutting-edge platforms, mobile technologies, data analytics, and a buffet of digital HR offerings might actually be skewing our ability to see the *people* behind the picture.

The challenge ahead is to determine how to deploy technology, successfully and at scale, without losing the individual, personal touch in the process.

HR and total rewards managers are starting to focus attention on the employee in ways they perhaps haven't considered. Strategically, they want their HR programs to create real options for employees. Those programs need to be designed with employees at the center and delivered efficiently. Finally, program design and execution need to be based on data that may currently be in a mess.

Strategy: Real Options for People

HR has come out of the transactional closet and is now tasked with a far more strategic role. HR managers still will have to figure out the best ways to utilize people within the organization, from determining talent needs, planning effective recruitment and retention programs, discovering effective management tactics, and improving internal processes. Now more than ever, HR professionals need to deploy and motivate talent in line with business objectives.

Companies are now reviewing their people-and-rewards strategies to make sure they create real options and help managers anticipate the unexpected. They're digging deeper into questions about the talent they currently have, how much that costs, whether it is enough to support the business objectives, and what key skills they need to retain and develop. They're asking:

- What will it take to get, develop, and keep the people we need?
- How can we stand out from the competition in this battle for talent?
- What is our internal brand, and does it effectively relate to the new ways people work?
- Is there a connection – and fulfillment – between our values and the personal values of our employees?
- How can we measure and improve our "return on labor" with the right rewards program?

The organization's ability to adapt to, and plan for, the evolution in dynamics in the workplace demands new strategies to truly differentiate the business for potential recruits. That same ability is needed in setting the enterprise's rewards strategy.

Design: Employees at the Center

HR leaders are looking for new ways to align their programs with the needs and values of employees while still boosting the balance sheet. They continue to improve internal processes, create succession ladders, develop professional training, and enhance the corporate culture. In doing so, programs focused on enhancing people's careers, health, and well-being are critical.

But these programs need to be something special for employees, enhancing their work and speaking to how company values and personal satisfaction come together. In doing this, managers are looking at the growing opportunities provided by human-centered design thinking. By putting employees and their needs at the center of the design process, employers are better able to create flexible rewards programs that: align with the varying needs within their employee populations; build awareness of the workplace culture; encourage greater personal responsibility; and enable employees to be more accountable for those actions.

Technology plays its role, of course, but employers are looking at deploying it differently. For example, technology can force employees to enroll online, leaving them to try to get answers to very personal and unique questions, often not to their satisfaction. On the other hand, technology that's designed with people at the center can help anticipate the right mix of plan participation for an individual and then guide that user to the right selections. This can help employees avoid being over- or underinsured, help them meet both short-term and long-term financial goals and remind them of opportunities to best use the programs they selected through the course of the year.

Employers recognize that it's time to take a hard look at their current programs and whether they support the ideal state of the workforce – people's financial, physical, and mental well-being. Businesses need to ask where the best bets are going to be focused as program design and digital technologies intersect.

Service Delivery: Prompt and Personal

HR's administration job is getting even more onerous and includes handling new and changing regulatory compliance tasks and tracking and paying contract workers.

Administrative solutions abound for recruiting, benefits, compensation, wellness, and talent management, but are predominantly best practice, software as a service (SaaS)–based productized solutions. Organizations are forced to fit their HR objectives and processes into often-oversimplified models. Differentiation takes a back seat to efficiency. In an ever-increasingly challenging labor market, employers have been losing their ability to create rewards and development programs that reflect their distinct employee value propositions (EVP).

Alternatives are emerging. Businesses need the ability to share their own story with candidates and employees in ways that resonate with their audiences. Human-centered design comes into play again, with user experiences that make an employer's EVP come to life. Instead of offering each HR program through the distinct lens of the plan, new experiences are available to view them through the lens of the individual. HR professionals are taking a hard look at how they deliver services and information to employees. Are they meeting the changing needs of today's workforce? They already know that workers are ever-more accustomed to streamlined, user-friendly, and extremely prompt responses to their needs delivered through consumer technology. Employees expect their employers to be able to do the same when it comes to decision-making support on the job and in their personal lives – which intersect more and more.

Disparate systems feed data, content, and even transactional services into a single engine so that the entire rewards picture is presented to individuals in their terms. Questions that normally would need to be parsed to myriad applications are addressed through a single interface. Users can turn to the source most convenient for them – the HR portal, their handheld device, Alexa, or even a real person – to get personalized, comprehensive, and empathetic answers to what are often very personal HR questions.

Even with technological advances and the freeing up of HR resources to work with people instead of processes, process is not going away. Employers implementing new solutions, launching new programs, and communicating the corporate vision know they will continue to face change management challenges. The difference today, though, is that those processes don't have to be clunky and dispassionate.

The best use of robotic process automation (RPA) today looks at the multiple systems that make up a process and rethink it from the user's perspective. Onboarding is a great example that often touches HR, IT, finance, procurement, and many other aspects of the business. Too often users have to figure out the path themselves, visiting each system independently and hoping data get passed from one platform to the next. It doesn't have to be that way. RPA offers the ability to simplify data flows and the user experience, handling the dirty work behind the scenes so that administrative tasks are avoided, and valuable learning takes its place.

Administration needs – developing and maintaining platforms, managing vendors, establishing meaningful metrics, staying in compliance with new global regulations – continue to rank high on the list of responsibilities. Taking a human-centered approach, though, can assure these chores are completed while the user gets the best possible experience.

People Analytics: The Personal Dimension

The question HR is expected to answer – How do you know if your programs are successful? – hasn't changed, but the answers can now be analyzed and even predicted in real time.

HR analytics efforts in the recent past have tended to address department-specific questions with basic reporting. Talent objectives such as the effectiveness of recruiting are looked at against attraction and retention data. Health-care challenges such as mitigating medical cost rate increases are addressed through plan participation and population health data. Financial questions such as pension risk are dealt with through actuarial analysis.

The trend, though, is to look across this spectrum of career, health, and wealth data and inject engagement data. Interaction analytics is a hot HR topic because it adds the personal dimension to programs that are ultimately designed to attract and motivate people. With interaction analytics, organizations can measure the impact of any program change, the effectiveness of a communications campaign and even market forces in play outside of the organization. Organizations are now applying this machine learning to help make sense of the treasure trove of data that HR owns.

Relatively new in the HR toolbox is the application of AI to many HR problems. It has the potential to handle routine administration tasks, produce reports, store data, and perform a host of other repetitive tasks, leaving HR more time to focus on its strategic functions of providing talent.

But AI is still in its early stages, and while many organizations are looking into how it might meet their needs, the companies that have tried it for human resources have run across difficult roadblocks. In at least one case, an AI process mistakenly fired an employee and the "fix" was so complex that the employee not only lost pay while off work but eventually left the company with some rancor. In another, a large technology business using AI for recruiting found gender biases that were so entrenched that it's been discontinued.

AI uses mountains of existing HR data. That data will need to be reviewed carefully and the system deployed cautiously. Human resources is finding that automated technology systems without human insights can lead to disastrous results.

As AI advances and machine learning supports it, data across the people-analytics spectrum can be assessed on an ongoing basis, outcomes can be predicted prior to adjusting any levers, and then design can be tweaked as necessary to achieve ultimate objectives. Machine learning in conjunction with AI can assure that people analytics are used to solve the needs of both the organization and the individual, and continually adjust to help each achieve their goals.

DIGITAL INTELLIGENCE AND THE ULTIMATE HR CUSTOMER

At its current pace of advancement, technology will simplify processes, get us answers quickly, and replace many of the administrative burdens we currently face. But unchecked, this increasing digital intelligence can eliminate the personal advocacy and trust we've worked so hard to cultivate in HR.

To get the most benefit out of high-tech solutions, we can't forget the high touch. Technology can be programmed to factor in the human element – and should be to assure that we are meeting the needs of HR's ultimate customer – our people.

More Personal through Tech

As technological advances continue to occur, the role of human resources is evolving. It's clear that the role of HR professionals will be much different 10 years from now, but it's important to point out that different doesn't mean displaced.

"The 2019 Changing Face of HR" report from Sage revealed that 82 percent of the more than 500 HR leaders surveyed believe their role will be "completely unrecognizable" in 10 years. But that should ultimately be a positive, said Paul Burrin, vice president of Sage.

"Inevitably, technology should be used as much as possible to help free up from low-value, mundane tasks," Burrin said. "As that happens, that should enable HR to get out from the back office and get away from the mundane processes and then spend more time working with employees, more so than they do now."

The report highlighted some processes that are already moving toward automation, including recruiting and various people decisions. The survey found that 24 percent of organizations are using artificial intelligence for recruitment, with 56 percent planning to adopt it within the next year. Additionally, 42 percent said that HR/people decisions are data driven, with 51 percent planning to access data in real time within the next year.

Burrin said rather than interpreting this technological overhaul as a threat, it should be viewed with an optimistic lens.

"The way we do things in HR are changing and HR has an immense opportunity to participate in working with their employees to figure out better ways of doing things," Burrin said. "Whether it's around performance management, or whether it's around onboarding or talent development, there's a huge opportunity to design better ways of working. There's also the opportunity of embracing technology in new ways to help free up time to spend more time working with leaders. So, there's a lot to think about, and I think it's a very exciting time to be in the profession."

Perhaps the biggest opportunity is HR's chance to become more personable and hands-on with the employee base. This mentality is supported by Sage's research, as nearly 70 percent of HR leaders said their employees' expectation of HR is changing.

Burrin said the prospect of HR being freed up to engage the workforce more – and help the business thrive as a result – is an exciting possibility. However, it will require a shift in how they operate today.

"Right now, there's way too much focus on transactions and automation, as opposed to really doing what the ultimate goal is, which is how do you find the right people, the right skillset, experience, but also the passion," Burrin said. "If you can get that alignment right, then a lot of things can fall into place, particularly around improving experiences, performance, and learning and development."

Payroll Overhaul

When considering all the possibilities the future of work holds, a process that might go overlooked is how people are paid in the future. Organizations are already in the process of adapting their pay practices to provide employees with more choice.

The ADP Research Institute's "Evolution of Pay" study found that 43 percent of the 2,900 employers surveyed are already offering nontraditional payments such as paycards, mobile wallets, digital platform, and cryptocurrency.

Alight recently identified a few trending topics in the payroll management space that organizations should be aware of moving forward. The first trend is the integration of artificial intelligence (AI) in payroll management. Similar to other tasks across the business, Alight notes that minor transactional tasks can now be automated, replacing manual data entry processing.

"Robotic process automation (RPA) will become the new norm and provide a more efficient and high-quality method for entering high volumes of data," said Wilson Silva, senior vice president, delivery outsourcing at Alight. "For example, RPA will automate reconciliations and help create a consistent process to handle them in the future. To more effectively manage quality assurance, artificial intelligence, through the use of machine learning, will use historic pay information to identify and correct anomalies in the current pay run."

Another trend Alight highlighted involves payment distribution being done in real time. This would fundamentally change the standard payment system of direct deposit on a biweekly basis that is deployed by most companies today. Silva said that providing more choice to employees when it comes to pay, which includes quick access to compensation, will be mutually beneficial.

"Providing workers with quicker access to their compensation is a part of creating an agile work environment that provides employees flexibility in how they work, where they work, when they work, and ultimately, how and when they are paid," Silva said. "Accelerating pay for employees who live check to check will help improve their financial well-being by helping them to avoid high interest pay day loans or expensive late fees on bills due to poor budgeting between pay cycles."

Cryptocurrency is also a potential avenue of future payment, especially as the popularity of digital wallets continues to grow. While it might not ever serve as the main means of compensation, it certainly could prove to be a worthwhile option for employers who are hoping to attract a wide variety of talent.

The final trend that Alight touched on is one that has been creeping into the minds of businesses for several years. The rise of the gig economy and its popularity among the workforce, particularly the younger generations of workers, could force organizations to develop pay structures that align with those of companies like Uber or Rover.

"While the gig economy plays a role in the onset of immediate pay options, we are also seeing the growing popularity of these resources because workers are increasing using their mobile devices to manage their personal finances. As more workers rely on their digital wallet, employers will need to offer distribution options that meet them in their channel of preference," Silva said. "While today gig workers are considered contractors and not employees, employers will have to adapt to the same immediate pay options for their employees in order to attract and retain the best talent."

Silva said that while there will be many tweaks to payroll systems in the future, the fundamentals of the payroll process will not change in the next five years.

"Payroll will continue to consist of checklists in which the same tasks that exist today will exist tomorrow," he said. "However, managing inbound processes and the related reconciliation of control totals will be automated and only involve a payroll analyst when errors cannot be resolved. Post-pay reconciliations, including payroll net pay funding and other outbound processes, will also be automated."

AUTOMATION'S RESOUNDING EFFECT ON WORK AND REWARDS

Automation is the boogeyman buzzword when it comes to discussing the future of work. Yes, it's true that automation will displace workers, as an estimated 32 percent of US jobs are expected to be eliminated by 2030.

However, some economists and futurists have surmised that, if handled properly, new roles will grow from those displaced jobs and that technological advancement is ultimately a good thing.

"Jobs don't go away, they transition, and they transition in different ways," Parminder K. Jassal, PhD of the Institute for the Future (IFTF) said in an interview with WorldatWork. "So, what we do believe is that many more jobs will be affected by automation, but we believe they'll be affected in different ways. We think it affects the entire process and how we do things, not just front-line processes."

When it comes to how those front-line workers will be compensated, however, some economists are reassessing. David Autor of MIT and Anna Salomons of Utrecht University concluded that the use of AI explains the decline in the share of national income going into workers' paychecks over the last three decades.

There's a growing belief that one of the reasons workers have not seen larger wage gains in the past few years is because, despite the significant advances in technology, overall productivity has not improved all that much.

There is some hope, however, that trend could change in the future.

"It takes time for people and processes to adapt to new technology and take full advantage of technological advancements for productivity gains to be realized," said Sue Holloway, CCP, CECP, director of executive compensation strategy at WorldatWork.

Like workers, the professionals compensating them are aware they too will need to adapt. WorldatWork's Compensation Function of the Future survey of 364 members in conjunction with Salary.com demonstrated how the profile of a successful compensation professional is changing. It revealed that while there is an expectation of artificial intelligence (AI), machine learning, and predictive analytics to become increasingly influential in their compensation processes, respondents are anticipating other variables as well.

They expect activities related to creating, analyzing, interpreting and/or presenting analytic results, pay equity and transparency to top the list of their most important responsibilities in two to three years.

"As technology produces more advanced insights, compensation professionals will need to have greater contextual expertise and an ability to articulate powerful stories to aid in rewards decision-making," said Alison Avalos, CCP, CBP, GRP, director of membership and total rewards strategy at WorldatWork.

Tracey Malcolm, global future of work leader at Willis Towers Watson, said that because of automation, organizations will need to consider a myriad of factors to get the right mix of work and value.

"What's coming into play is a need to determine if the job will continue to slope upward in terms of compensation, or do we need to reinvent the job," Malcolm said. "Then there's a need to be proactive about compensation or total rewards decisions in what the optimal equation is for that."

Tip of the Automation Iceberg: Reskilling

In July 2019, Amazon announced that it would spend $700 million over the next six years to help retrain a third of its US workforce.

The impetus behind this large, voluntary investment was to get ahead of forthcoming disruption brought on by automation and new technology. The idea is to help Amazon employees progress into more advanced jobs or perhaps even new positions outside of the company.

Amazon is calling the plan "Upskilling 2025" and with the training, workers will theoretically be able to transfer between positions that they might not have previously been qualified for. An example of this is a warehouse worker in a fulfillment center could be trained to perform technical roles in IT, even if they lack a technical background.

"While many of our employees want to build their careers here, for others it might be a steppingstone to different aspirations," said Beth Galetti,

Amazon's head of human resources, in a press release. "We think it's important to invest in our employees, and to help them gain new skills and create more professional options for themselves."

Amazon's reskilling initiative comes at a time when automation and artificial intelligence are becoming less of a future concept and more of a modern-day reality. Machines are expected to displace about 20 million manufacturing jobs across the world over the next decade, according to a report from Oxford Economics. Additionally, PwC found that 79 percent of CEOs regularly worry about their workforce's existing skills and their ability to meet dynamic workplace needs.

Thus, this is likely the beginning of what the World Economic Forum has dubbed as the "reskilling revolution" and organizations could begin to adopt a new model of continuous learning.

"The promise going forward is not jobs for life; it's the promise that as a company, I will ensure that you stay relevant," said Ravin Jesuthasan, co-author of the World Economic Forum's 2019 report. "The talent experience will increasingly emphasize the need for companies to give workers access to acquiring new skills and rewarding them when they do – that the company is going to give you the ability, access, and opportunities to continue to develop yourself."

This creates an interesting dynamic for total rewards professionals as this kind of movement continues. Whether it's job pricing or reclassifying new roles for existing employees, there will be an adjustment period, said Carole Hathaway, global head of rewards at Willis Towers Watson.

"That's creating quite a lot of challenges for rewards professionals," Hathaway said. "We had been working in this environment where the job was this sort of stable thing and you could go out and evaluate the job and then you could do your market benchmarking and get a market price for the job and that was all very stable. It's much more difficult now. The market is moving very, very fast. These skills are in high demand, such as data scientist and other technology-type jobs, and what we've observed is what's happening is it's not just the pay that is moving rapidly, people are moving rapidly as well."

However, just as the future workforce will need to possess a greater arsenal of digital skills to avoid displacement, rewards leaders, will have to adapt their own processes as well with improved technology.

"As a rewards professional, we know there are more technologies that help people do their jobs better and tools to help manage large amounts of data or various compensation processes," Hathaway said. "We're not seeing a huge amount of that just yet. When will we start to use big data and predictive analytics in rewards to better manage rewards? That's the sort of innovation that's probably not so far in the future."

Blending Automation and an Aging Workforce

When there is a projected 15 to 30 percent increase in the number of employees aged 50 to 64 years old in the workforce by 2030, how should organizations prepare themselves for sustainable growth and development?

How can organizations balance their automation and digitalization ambition with the growing demand to be part of the solution for population aging, especially when large proportions – between 50 percent to 80 percent – of tasks done by older workers are at high risk of being replaced by new technologies, putting them at higher risks of displacement?

Marsh & McLennan's November 2019 report, "The Twin Trends of Aging and Automation: Leveraging a Tech-Empowered Experienced Workforce" proposes a different way of thinking about these questions.

Recasting Older Workers as Experienced Workers

An aging population has commonly been perceived as a threat to organizations and society at large, but this is changing. Projected higher costs of health care paired with a rapidly aging workforce are key reasons why population aging has widely been regarded as a societal challenge – one that corporate leaders need to mitigate. The negative tints in the metaphors used to describe this demographic group, such as "silver tsunami," "silver wave," or the "gray economy," reflect this ageist perspective.

In corporate's quest for higher productivity and efficiency (via automation and digitalization or otherwise), older workers and their valuable experience, are both underappreciated and overlooked. Instead of letting them go, reframing the negative narrative from "older workers" to "experienced workers" and building a comprehensive strategy around this emerging workforce will better prepare organizations for upcoming labor and talent shortages.

When 45 percent of employers globally reported difficulty in filling roles – the highest level in 12 years – experienced workers present a potential talent source that can greatly alleviate the ongoing shortage. Retaining experienced workers does not only prevent a loss of institutional knowledge, it also ensures that companies have an in-depth market understanding and stay relevant in the growing longevity economy – the sum of economic activities driven by those 50 years old and above.

The question, then, is not why we should value and retain experienced workers, but how organizations can build a strategy around the experienced workforce.

A cohesive technological integration process around this workforce, with tailored job and talent redesign embedded in an inclusive organizational culture, will be crucial.

Job Redesign for a Tech-Empowered Experienced Workforce

Integrating technology into an organization will necessitate the process of job redesign. The key questions for executives here are:

- What is the right amount of technology in the new jobs?
- How can these technologies augment the rich industry knowledge that experienced workers are bringing to the company?
- What are the necessary conditions for experienced workers to successfully adapt to these technologically enhanced jobs?

Where a healthy balance between experienced workers and technology is achieved, humans work side-by-side with robots in a complementary manner rather than one being replaced by the other. At a large automotive factory, for example, experienced workers are now working alongside tabletop robots that assist workers in repetitive or physically demanding tasks. The company adopted this combination of robots and humans in response to the increased demand for customization and individualization that require a more sophisticated human touch rather than a fully automated process.

The pace of technological advances compels organizations to keep abreast of the multitude of new technological applications and actively look to deploy them to maintain competitiveness. Such an imperative presents significant workforce challenges, as rapid digitalization means employers will need to quickly upskill or reskill personnel of all generations and at all levels as jobs are redesigned. There are two lenses through which executives can examine experienced workers' roles in this process.

First, experienced workers will need upskilling and reskilling – as will their younger counterparts. Training is most effective when tailored to preferred learning styles. Historically, research has shown that experienced workers tend to prefer hands-on, on-the-job training and mentorship over formal-led training sessions. Mutual mentorship for technological training has also been successfully implemented in several companies and has proven to be a useful tool for technological transformation. But, things are changing. In recent focus groups (Mercer 2019), there appear to be two preferences emerging for the experienced workforce.

Over half are already learning new skills by multiple methods, such as digital higher-level degrees, online specialist courses, or in-person coaching. These employees are ready for their employers to give them new challenges and stretch roles. They feel neglected from a development perspective, and analysis of the allocation of training budgets within organizations shows they are not wrong in this respect. Some employers are offering their rising young professionals' fast track development programs to experienced worker too – with very positive engagement.

The remaining group are ready to "flex down" in order to enjoy a better work-life balance, spend time in voluntary work, or care for a loved one.

Perhaps a more salient point, however, is the recognition that sometimes the upskilling needed is not at all technical. The digitalization of a company is essentially a transformative process, one in which change management skills – from problem solving to effective communication, coaching, and team building – takes precedence over pure technical knowledge. These skills, along with high empathy, are those in which experienced workers tend to excel. Therefore, instead of a one-directional view on compelling the workforce to new technologies, a more effective path forward is to let experienced workers themselves shape this integration process.

The result may be the best of both worlds, as experienced workers – leveraging their rich knowledge – get technologies implemented in the most suitable way for organizations. Technology did, of course, begin in the generation of what we are now calling the experienced worker.

Revamping the Talent Model and the Role of an Age-Inclusive Culture

New and innovative talent models will also need to be explored, not just to optimize efficiency via new technologies, but also to be able to offer a more attractive employee value proposition for experienced workers.

The rise of the gig economy has brought a lot of flexibility and mobility to the workplace and offers a clear win–win for both experienced workers and organizations. As the latter benefits from the fluidity and flexibility that will enable the organization to become more agile, the former can also enjoy the flexibility that gig-style work offers.

However, the attractiveness of gig-style employment arrangements suffers from a number of structural drawbacks, such as the lack of traditional social protection benefits and formal career development, which makes the arrangement suboptimal in the long run.

Addressing these barriers requires organizations to innovate their talent models. Mercer, for example, has worked extensively on what is conceptualized as a Talent Pool Consortium (TPC). A TPC is a talent pool of experienced workers among a group of companies, where a portion of each company's workforce becomes part of a group of "on-demand" talent, to be hired into workstreams and projects by different members of the group. The new employment contract would build in training and protection benefits, and combined with extensive flexibility, offers a unique value proposition for workers of all generations.

The TPC concept offers businesses access to an on-demand talent base and the opportunity for more flexibility in staffing. At the same time, by building in these new levels of development and protections, members of the TPC can overcome the structural problems that have made the gig economy unattractive and unsustainable.

Finally, despite their critical roles in priming for a future-ready experienced workforce, job redesign and talent model redesign alone would not be enough. They need to be embedded in a non-ageist, inclusive organizational culture that does not undermine the values of experienced workers. This will demand a new vocabulary, a clear vision and values, robust stewardship, effective organizational communication and strong accountability from both the leadership and the board, and finally, a strong suite of age-friendly policies implemented across the organization.

Looking Ahead: Experienced Workforce Strategy as an Imperative

Given the dual trends of aging and automation, forward-looking organizations need to go one step further to fundamentally integrate technology into their business models and to empower their experienced workforce. Societal pressure to be a responsible employer to achieve optimal growth means that it is high time corporations refreshed their workforce strategy, with the experienced workforce taking center stage.

Options Galore: The Benefits Wave of the Future

Employers that can successfully deliver a holistic approach to benefits are poised to be ahead of the curve when it comes to attracting and retaining future talent.

Organizations are becoming increasingly aware of this reality, as more than a third (37 percent) said they're making changes to their benefits package or plan to do so in the near future, according to "Aon's Benefits and Trends Survey 2019." While it would certainly make things easier, there's no one-size-fits all approach to creating the benefits package of the future given the extreme multigenerational workforce that's in place.

"You've got to look across your generations and survey your employees," said Jon Shanahan, CEO of Businessolver, a benefits administration technology company. "That's how you get things like different leave programs that employers hadn't considered in the past. There are different leave options around life events, whether it's elder care or different things around family leave outside of what state or federal regulations might have. So, I think you're seeing innovation there."

Part of building the right package, Shanahan said, is making sure to include plenty of voluntary options for employees. One of the most popular voluntary options is pet insurance, which WorldatWork's "2019 Inventory of Total Rewards Programs & Practices" survey found 33 percent of employers offered in 2019. Another popular benefit that has exploded in recent years is student loan debt repayment programs, which went from being offered by 10 percent of employers in 2018 to 26 percent in 2019.

In that same ilk, Shanahan said consumer accounts and emergency savings programs have also become popular. These are employer-contributed accounts that often appeal to millennials.

"It's just the ability to think about the generations of employees that you have and the various needs that they have and reacting to that," Shanahan said. "Are you thinking about someone who is pre-retirement and how they view benefits? And, are you thinking about folks that aren't experiencing life events, so they're maybe not as concerned about the health program, but more so they're worried about time off and other spends in their life that hit them immediately? It's that open view of being in tune with your employees and fine-tuning your benefits program so you can attract and retain talent."

Aside from the voluntary benefits that are expected to continue to be popular moving forward, health-care benefits such as health savings accounts (HSAs) are becoming more standardized and proving to be highly valued by younger generations. According to a Benefitfocus report, employee participation in HSAs grew from 50 percent in 2017 to 81 percent in 2018.

David Vivero, CEO of a digital health company Amino, wrote in *Forbes* that HSAs are the most millennial-friendly benefit.

"It's an excellent way to save money while you're in your young, healthy years," he wrote.

"Your millennial employees will also appreciate the flexibility of an HSA, which can be used to pay for anything from acupuncture to contact lenses to medical supplies."

Some other benefits employers are offering or plan to offer in the future include employee discount programs, long-term care insurance, commuter benefit programs, and tax-advantaged options for commuter benefits.

Having a holistic approach to benefits will set an organization up for future success in attracting and retaining talent, but a key component to successful implementation is having user-friendly technology for employees to access and utilize said benefits, Shanahan noted.

"If you don't have good technology, their first experience is bad," Shanahan said.

"For most benefits programs, the first way they're going to interact with their benefits is through their mobile device or sitting down at their computer either before they start or on their first day.

"If it's difficult to understand and if it's not flexible and the platform doesn't help the employee make a decision about their benefits, then it's going to be a bad experience. But if the user experience is good, then they tend to think more favorably about their employer."

References by Chapter

INTRODUCTION

Block, Lori, and Davidson, Michael. 2019. "*New Perspectives*: How Work, Rewards and Benefits Have Evolved Over the Past Century." *The Journal of Total Rewards* (Fourth Quarter, 28).

Bhuiyan, Faruk, Manir Chowdhury, Mustafa, and Ferdous, Farzana. 2014. "Historical Evolution of Human Resource Information Systems (HRIS): An Interface Between HR and Computer Technology." *Human Resource Management Research* 4 (4): 75–80.

Buck Global. 2018. "Working Well: A Global Survey of Workforce Wellbeing Strategies," December 6. https://content.buck.com/working-well-global-survey-of-workforce-strategies.

Burt, Margaret Allen. 1976. *George B. Buck Consulting Actuaries: The First 45 Years*. Privately published.

Business Roundtable. 2019. "*Business Roundtable Defines the Purpose of a Corporation to Promote 'An Economy That Serves All Americans'*" August 19. Retrieved August 28, 2019. https://www.businessroundtable.org/business-roundtable-redefines-the-purpose-of-a-corporation-to-promote-an-economy-that-serves-all-americans.

Certified B Corporations. 2019. https://bcorporation.net/.

Chartered Institute of Personnel and Development (CIPD). 2014. "HR: Getting Smart About Agile Working." https://www.cipd.co.uk/Images/hr-getting-smart-agile-working_2014_tcm18-14105.pdf.

Coase, R. H. 1937. "The Nature of the Firm." *Economica* 4: 386–405. doi:10.1111/j.1468-0335.1937.tb00002.x.

Deloitte. 2017. "The Robots Are Ready. Are You?" https://www2.deloitte.com/content/dam/Deloitte/tr/Documents/technology/deloitte-robots-are-ready.pdf.

Dent, Fiona, Viki Holton, and Jan Rabbetts. 2010. "Motivation and Employee Engagement in the 21st Century." *EFMD Global Focus* 4 (2).

Economist. 2000. "Solving the Parado: IT Is Making America's Productivity Grow Faster at Last, But for How Long?" September 23. Retrieved August 29, 2019. https://www.economist.com/special-report/2000/09/23/solving-the-paradox.

Fabius, R., R.R. Loeppke, T. Hohn, D. Fabius, B. Eisenberg, D.L, Konicki, and P. Larson. 2016. "Tracking the Market Performance of Companies That Integrate a Culture of Health and Safety: An Assessment of Corporate Health Achievement Award Applicants." *Journal of Environmental and Occupational Medicine* 58 (1): 3–8.

Field, M.J. and H.T. Shapiro, eds. 1993. "Employment and Health Benefits: A Connection at Risk." Institute of Medicine (US) Committee on

Employment-Based Health Benefits. Washington, DC: National Academies Press. https://www.ncbi.nlm.nih.gov/books/NBK235989/.

Fisk, Donald. 2001. "American Labor in the 20th Century." US Bureau of Labor Statistics (BLS). https://www.bls.gov/opub/mlr/cwc/american-labor-in-the-20th-century.pdf.

Fitzgerald, Shawn and Craig Simpson 2018. "Digital Transformation (DX) Understanding the Business Case – Market Spend & Trend Outlook." International Data Corp. (IDC) presentation, June 7. https://www.brighttalk.com/webcast/16645/322677/digital-transformation-market-spend-trend-outlook.

Friedman, Milton. 1970. "The Social Responsibility of Business Is to Increase its Profits," *New York Times,* September 13. http://www.umich.edu/~thecore/doc/Friedman.pdf.

Gelles, David, and David Yaffe-Bellany. 2019. "Shareholder Value Is No Longer Everything, CEOs Say." *New York Times,* August 19. https://www.nytimes.com/2019/08/19/business/business-roundtable-ceos-corporations.html.

Gough, J.W. 1936. *The Social Contract.* Oxford, England: Clarendon Press.

Harter, Jim. 2018. "Employee Engagement on the Rise in the US," *Gallup,* https://news.gallup.com/poll/241649/employee-engagement-rise.aspx.

IBISWorld. 2019. "Corporate Wellness Services Industry in the US – Market Research Report." https://www.ibisworld.com/industry-trends/specialized-market-research-reports/life-sciences/wellness-services/corporate-wellness-services.html.

Kapas, J. 2008. "Industrial Revolutions and the Evolution of the Firm's Organization: An Historical Perspective." *Journal of Innovation Economics* 2 (2): 15–33.

Katz, Lawrence and Alan Krueger. 2016. "The Rise and Nature of Alternative Work Arrangements in the United States, 1995–2015." National Bureau of Economic Research Working Paper No. 22667.

Kiechel, Walter. 2012. "The Management Century," *Harvard Business Review,* November. Retrieved August 26, 2019. https://hbr.org/2012/11/the-management-century.

Mattke, Soeren, Hangsheng Liu, John P. Caloyeras, Christina Y. Huang, Kristin R. Van Busum, Dmitry Khodyakov, and Victoria Shier. 2013. "Workplace Wellness Program Studies." RAND Corp. https://www.rand.org/content/dam/rand/pubs/research_reports/RR200/RR254/RAND_RR254.sum.pdf.

New Vantage Partners LLC. 2018. "Big Data Executive Survey." Retrieved August 28, 2019. http://newvantage.com/wp-content/uploads/2018/01/Big-Data-Executive-Survey-2018-Findings.pdf.

Roethlisberger, P.J. and W.J. Dickson. 1937. "Management and the Worker: Technical vs. Social Organization in an Industrial Plant." https://iiif.lib.harvard.edu/manifests/view/drs:7186827$4i.

Rotich, Kipkemboi Jacob. 2015. "History, Evolution and Development of Human Resource Management: A Contemporary Perspective." *Global Journal of Human Resource Management* 3 (3): 58–73.

Samuelson, Robert. 2006. "The Next Capitalism." *Newsweek*, October 25.

Smith, Adam. 1776. *An Inquiry into the Nature and Causes of the Wealth of Nations.*

US Bureau of Labor Statistics (BLS). 2019. "US Non-Farm Productivity and US Multifactor Productivity Tools." https://www.bls.gov/mfp/.

Whatishumanresource.com. n.d. "History & Origin of Performance Appraisal." Viewed: Aug. 30, 2019. http://www.whatishumanresource.com/history–origin-of-performance-appraisal.

WorldatWork. 2019. "What Is Total Rewards?" https://worldatwork.org/total-rewards-model/.

World Economic Forum (WEF) 2019. "Fourth Industrial Revolution." www.weforum.org/focus/fourth-industrial-revolution.

CHAPTER 1

Brink, Steve. 2020. "Reevaluating Total Rewards Strategies for the Growing Remote Workforce." *Workspan Daily* (July 16).

CHAPTER 2

Evans, Elaine M., *CCP*. 2020. *Compensation Basics for HR Generalists,* WorldatWork Press (revised edition).

WorldatWork Course. 2020. *Regulatory Environments for Compensation Programs* (revised).

CHAPTER 3

WorldatWork Press. 2002. *Market Pricing: Methods to the Madness (updated).*

CHAPTER 4

Seltz, Steven. 2021. *Linking Pay to Performance.* WorldatWork Press (revised edition).

CHAPTER 5

Becker, Irving, and Gerek, William. 2021. *Understanding Executive Compensation & Governance: A Practical Guide, 4th edition,* WorldatWork Press.

CHAPTER 6

Colletti, Jerry, Fiss, Mary, Briggs, Ted, and Sands, Scott. 2013. *Sales Compensation Essentials: A Field Guide for the HR Professional, 2nd edition,* 2nd ed. WorldatWork Press.

CHAPTER 7

Adkins, Amy. 2016. "Millennials: The Job-Hopping Generation." Gallup: *Workplace,* July 12, https://www.gallup.com/workplace/236474/millennials-job-hopping-generation.aspx.

Aflac. 2018. "2018 Aflac WorkForces Report." https://www.aflac.com/business/resources/aflac-workforces-report/default.aspx.

Bureau of Labor Statistics. 2020. "Job Openings and Labor Turnover Survey," September 9, https://www.bls.gov/news.release/jolts.nr0.htm.

CDC. 2020. "Chronic Diseases in America." September 24, https://www.cdc.gov/chronicdisease/resources/infographic/chronic-diseases.htm.

Deloitte. 2019. "2019 Global Human Capital Trends." https://www2.deloitte.com/uk/en/pages/human-capital/articles/introduction-human-capital-trends.html.

Deloitte. 2020. "The Deloitte Millennial Survey 2020." https://www2.deloitte.com/content/dam/Deloitte/global/Documents/About-Deloitte/deloitte-2020-millennial-survey.pdf.

Fry, Richard. 2018. "Millennials Are the Largest Generation in the US Labor Force." Pew Research Center: *FactTank, News in the Numbers,* April 11, https://www.pewresearch.org/fact-tank/2018/04/11/millennials-largest-generation-us-labor-force/.

Gallagher. 2020. "2020 Benefits Strategy and Benchmarking Survey Report." https://www.ajg.com/us/benefits-strategy-benchmarking-survey-report/.

Global Wellness Institute. 2016. "The Future of Wellness at Work." January, https://globalwellnessinstitute.org/industry-research/the-future-of-wellness-at-work/.

Integrated Business Institute. 2018 "Press Release: Poor Health Costs US Employers $530 Billion and 1.4 Billion Work Days of Absence and Impaired Performance According to Integrated Benefits Institute." *November* 15, https://www.ibiweb.org/poor-health-costs-us-employers-530-billion-and-1-4-billion-work-days-of-absence-and-impaired-performance/

Mann, Annamarie, and Amy Adkins. 2017. "America's Coming Workplace: Home Alone." *Business Journal,* March 15, https://www.pwc.com/us/en/library/workforce-of-the-future/employee-experience.html?WT.mc_id=CT13-PL1300-DM2-TR1-LS2-ND30-TTA3-CN_CISWoF-wofblog-citedin-techatwork-web&eq=CT13-PL1300-DM2-CN_CISWoF-wofblog-citedin-techatwork-web.

Parker, Kim, Graf, Nikki, and Igielnik, Ruth. 2019. "Gen Z Looks a Lot like Millennials on Key Social and Political Issues." Pew Research Center, January 17, https://www.pewsocialtrends.org/2019/01/17/generation-z -looks-a-lot-like-millennials-on-key-social-and-political-issues/.

PWC. 2017. *"The Employee Experience: Helping People Get Excited to Do Their Best Work."* PWC, October 5, https://www.pwc.com/us/en/library/ workforce-of-the-future/employee-experience.html?WT.mc_id=CT13- PL1300-DM2-TR1-LS2-ND30-TTA3-CN_CISWoF-wofblog -citedin-techatwork-web&eq=CT13-PL1300-DM2-CN_CISWoF-wofblog- citedin-techatwork-web.

Rotondo, Stephanie. 2019. "Capturing the Data of Well-Being." *Workspan* (June/July). Salesforce. *"The AI Revolution."* https://www.salesforce .com/form/conf/the-ai-revolution/?conf-redirect=true.

True, Jamie. 2019. "Changing the Dynamic of Open Enrollment." *Workspan* (March).

Unum. 2018. "Nearly Half of US Workers Spend 30 Minutes or Less Reviewing Benefits Before Enrollment, Unum Finds." *August* 13, https://www .unum.com/about/newsroom/2018/august/unum-auto-enroll.

Vogels, Emily A. 2019. "Millennials Stand Out for Their Technology Use, but Older Generations Also Embrace Digital Life." Pew Research, *FactTank: News in the Numbers,* September 9, http://www.pewresearch.org/fact- tank/2018/05/02/millennials-stand-out-for-their-technology-use-but -older-generations-also-embrace-digital-life/.

Williams, Patrick, LMFT, CEAP. 2019. "Power to the People: The Changing Face of Employee Well-Being." *Workspan* (September).

CHAPTER 8

WorldatWork Course. 2020. *Regulatory Environments for Benefits Programs* (revised).

CHAPTER 9

Howard, Trisha. 2019. "Reskilling Revolution." *Workspan (August).*

Irvine, Derek. 2018. "How We Grow: Cultivating a Mindset of Continuous Development." *Workspan* (November/December).

Koors, Jannice. 2017. "How to Spot Talent and Develop Strong Leaders." *Workspan* (July).

CHAPTER 10

Gunn, Nichole. 2020. "Motivating Millennials: How to Recognize and Reward Millennial Employees." *Workspan* (January).

Himelstein, Cord. 2019. "Using Market Tactics to Launch a Successful Employee Recognition Program." *Workspan* (September).

Himelstein, Cord. 2019. "The Role of Recognition in the Employee Experience." *Workspan* (April).

CHAPTER 11

Barrett, Mora. 2019. "All Aboard! The Customer-Employee Connection: How Improving the Employee Experience Benefits Customers." *Workspan* (August).

Borenstein, Lorna. 2019. "We Don't Need Roads: The Future of Employee Engagement." *Workspan* (November/December).

Harvey, Brie. 2020. "X Marks the Spot: The Journey to Global Employee Engagement." *Workspan* (May).

Levy, Lynne. 2019. "How Positive Psychology Can Be Used to Boost Performance in the Workplace." *Workspan Daily* (September 11).

Zurek, Christina. 2019. "Using Psychological Benefits Can Improve Employee Engagement." *Workspan Daily* (September 25).

CHAPTER 12

Allen, Pleasure. 2017. "Gaining Executive Buy-In for Organizational Culture Change." *Workspan* (October).

Fickess, Jim. 2019. "Not Your Father's Workplace: Stereotypes, Be Gone." *Workspan* (February).

Gallup. 2017. "State of the American Workplace." https://compass.arizona.edu/file/330.

Howard, Trisha. 2019. "Leaders in the Looking Glass: Reflecting on Diversity in the Workplace." *Workspan* (April).

Hough, Suzanne. 2018. "Unifying Corporate Culture: Five Steps to Drive Engagement & Performance Post M&A," *Workspan* (September).

Howard, Trisha. 2019. "Thriving with Neurodiversity: The Benefits of Hiring People with Intellectual and Developmental Disabilities," *Workspan* (February).

Meidav, Neta. 2019. "Accountability in a #MeToo World." *Workspan* (October).

Quantum Workplace. "2018 Employment Engagement Trends." https://www.quantumworkplace.com/2018-employee-engagement-trends-report.

CHAPTER 13

Belter, Carrie, McMullen, Tom, Riley, Malinda, and Tapia, Andres T. 2020. "Getting It Right: Three Types of Pay Equity Gaps and How to Fix Them." *The Journal of Total Rewards* (First Quarter 29).

Briggs, Bill, ed. 2017. *Tech Trends 2018: The Symphonic Enterprise.* Deloitte Insights. https://www2.deloitte.com/content/dam/insights/us/articles/Tech-Trends-2018/4109_TechTrends-2018_FINAL.pdf.

Burlacu, Gabby, PhD, and Bidwell, Lauren M., PhD. 2018. "Spot Awards in the Spotlight: How Unconscious Bias Sets the Stage for Pay Inequity," *Workspan* (September).

Cann, Oliver. 2018. "*108 Years*: Wait for Gender Equality Gets Longer as Women's Share of Workforce, Politics Drops," World Economic Forum (December 18), https://www.weforum.org/press/2018/12/108-years-wait -for-gender-equality-gets-longer-as-women-s-share-of-workforce-politics -drops/.

Dastin, Jeffrey. 2018. "Amazon Scraps Secret Recruiting Tool that Shows Bias against Women," *Reuters* (October 10). https://www.reuters.com/arti-cle/us-amazon-com-jobs-automation-insight/amazon-scraps-secret-ai -recruiting-tool-that-showed-bias-against-women-idUSKCN1MK08G.

Deloitte, "Tech Trends 2018." https://www2.deloitte.com/us/en/insights/focus/tech-trends/2018.html.

Garr, Stacia Sherman and Jackson, Carole, 2019. "Diversity & Inclusion Technology: The Rise of a Transformative Market." https://www.mercer.com /our-thinking/career/diversity-and-inclusion-technology.html

Hilbrecht, Margo, and Donna S. Lero. 2014. Self-employment and family life: constructing work–life balance when you're 'always on', Community, *Work & Family* 17: 1, 20–42, http://dx.doi.org/10.1080/13668803.2013.862214.

Huang, Jess, Alexis Krivkovich, Irina Starikova, Lareina Yee, and Delia Zanoschi. 2019. "Women in the Workplace." McKinsey & Co., October. https://www.mckinsey.com/featured-insights/gender-equality/women-in-the-workplace-2019.

Hunt, Vivian, Prince, Sara, Dixon-Frye, Sundiatu, and Yee, Lareina. Layton, and Prince. 2018. "Delivering Through Diversity." McKinsey & Company (January). http://www.insurance.ca.gov/diversity/41-ISDGBD/GBDExternal /upload/McKinseyDeliverDiv201801-2.pdf.

Korn, Ferry, and WorldatWork. 2019. "Pay Equity Practices Survey of C-Suite and Reward Leaders: A WorldatWork and Korn Ferry Research Study," *May.* www.worldatwork.org/survey.

Korn Ferry. 2018a. "The 2018 Essentials: When Women CEOs Speak," July 13. https://www.kornferry.com/institute/womenceopodcast.

Korn Ferry. 2018b. US Client Pay Database. (Proprietary).

Thomas, Ruth. 2019. "How the Fourth Industrial Revolution Can Address Gender Pay Equity," *Workspan Daily* (October 1).

UK Government. 2017. "Gender Pay Gap Reporting Overview." https://www.gov.uk/guidance/gender-pay-gap-reporting-overview.

World Economic Forum. 2016. "The Future of Jobs." (January). https://www.weforum.org/reports/the-future-of-jobs.

Zhang, Haiyan, Feinzig, Sheri, Raisbeck, Louise, and McCombe, Iain. 2019. "The Role of AI in Mitigating Bias to Enhance Diversity and Inclusion. IBM Smarter Workforce Institute. https://www.ibm.com/downloads/cas/2DZELQ4O.

CHAPTER 14

Burke, Andrew. 2019. "The Freelance Project and Gig Economies of the 21st Century." Center for Research on Self-Employment (June). http://crse .co.uk/research/freelance-project-and-gig-economies-21st-century.

Christie, Brett. 2019a. "Looking Ahead at the Benefits Landscape for Gig Workers." *Workspan Daily* (July 12).

Christie, Brett. 2019b. "The Gig Economy Is Thriving and Here to Stay," *Workspan Daily* (April 5).

Christie, Brett. 2019c. "What Does the Future Hold for Gig Workers Post-AB5?" *Workspan Daily* (September 20).

Ginac, Linda. 2019. "Why You Should Create a Gig Economy Inside Your Organization," *Workspan Daily* (October 23).

McNicoll, Iain. 2020. "The Wide World of Freelancers: A Growing Choice for Workers Around the Globe," *Workspan* (May).

Mosquida, Fred. 2018. "Top Freelancers Explain Why They Choose to Do Freelance Gig over a Regular 9-to-5 Job." *Thrive Global* (June 29), https:// thriveglobal.com/stories/top-freelancers-explain-why-they-chose-to -freelance-over-a-regular-9-to-5-job/.

Smith, David, LaVelle, Katherine, Lyons, Mary, and Silverstone, Yaarit. 2016. "The Gig Experience: Unleashing the Potential of Your Talent and Your Business." https://www.accenture.com/t20160512T073844__w__/us-en/ _acnmedia/PDF-18/Accenture-Strategy-2016-Grad-Research-Gig-Experience-Unleash-Talent.pdf

Smith, Renee, and Jones, John. 2018. "Seeing the Gig Picture: Contingent Workers Demand a New Talent Value Proposition," *Workspan* (October).

CHAPTER 15

Bravery, Kate. 2018. "FutureWork: Digital Disruption in the New Human Age." *Workspan* (October).

Christie, Brett, 2019a. "Amazon's Reskilling Efforts Are the Tip of the Automation Iceberg," *Workspan* (November/December).

Christie, Brett. 2019b. "Automation's Resounding Effect on Work and Rewards Is Nearing a Fever Pitch," *Workspan Daily* (February 8).

Christie, Brett. 2019c. "Organizations Should Be Primed for Payroll Overhaul." *Workspan Daily* (September 13).

Christie, Brett. 2019d. "Technology Is Allowing HR to Become More Personable." *Workspan Daily* (November 1).

Hedrich, Wolfram, Phan, Viet Hoang, and Chacko, Leslie. 2020. "Future Look: Blending Automation and an Aging Workforce." *Workspan* (May).

Marcotte, Scot, and Block, Lori. 2019. "High Tech, High Touch: Remembering the 'Human' in HR." *Workspan* (February).

Index

Printed and bound by CPI Group (UK) Ltd, Croydon, CR0 4YY

23/04/2025

14660928-0002